A Dictionary of
Ceramic Artists

by Vega Wilkinson

Acknowledgments

The book would not have possible without the research and work done by so many well known ceramic writers, specialists on their pottery, whose work is shown in the bibliography. I have received great support from Miranda Goodby, Ceramic Curator of the of the Potteries Museum & Art Gallery Stoke-on-Trent; Joan Jones, Curator of Royal Doulton Plc.,and Gaye Blake Roberts, Curator, and Lynn Miller, Information Officer, of Wedgwood. John Twitchett's original research into the Derby artists has been invaluable, Wendy Cook, curator of the Royal Worcester Porcelain Museum.

It is not possible to name all who have helped and encouraged this project but my most grateful thanks go to my friends Rodney and Eileen Hampson for their continual help and support and to Olwen Grant who explored the1881 and 1901 census which has provided so many clues to hitherto unsolved queries. Thanks go to Dianne Lloyd, who found many examples of artists' signatures; to Laurence Coombes for original research into the source of designs and patterns; Bill and Marquerite Coles for their editorial help and Margeret Creyke for her research into the relevant historic buildings of Stoke-on-Trent.

Many of the artists' families have provide new biographical details including Peter Goodfellow, Mrs Barker and Mrs Young (Grand-daughter and Great Grand-daughter of Leslie Johnson),and Mrs Slater. Many collectors of fine ceramics have contributed to this book especially Chris and Beverley Marshall.

Christopher Jowitt of Warners Antiques found many new examples. My thanks also go to The Blue Lady who provided Parian photographs and to Martin Greatbatch A.B.I.P.P. who took so many of the fine photographs included in this book.

A Dictionary of
Ceramic Artists

by Vega Wilkinson

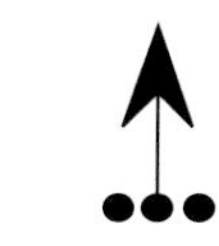

Landmark Publishing

Published by A. F. Wilkinson & Associates, Newcastle, Staffs

Produced for the publishers by Landmark Publishing,
Ashbourne Hall, Cokayne Ave, Ashbourne, Derbyshire, DE6 1EJ England
Tel: (01335) 347349, Fax: (01335) 347303, e-mail: landmark@clara.net

1st Edition

13 ISBN: 978-1-84306-361-2

10 ISBN: 1-84306-361-1

British Library Cataloguing in Publication Data: a catalogue record for this book is available from the British Library.

Print: Gutenberg Press, Malta

Design by: Landmark Publishing

Cover designed by: Sarah Labuhn

Front Cover images (from top left to bottom right):

Frog service Wedgwood plate; Copeland plaque commissioned by Thomas Goode of London. Rose border painted and signed by Wencelas Mussill, centre painting of Osbourne House, attributed to Edouard Rischgitz c. 1890; Royal Crown Derby desert plate painted by Edwin Wood c. 1900; Copeland desert plate painted by William Yale c. 1890; Royal Worcester desert plate painted by George Evans c. 1931; Crown Derby desert plate painted by Count Holzendorf c. 1884; Royal Worcester Desert plate painted by Harry Davis; Dr Wall Factory Tea Bowl engraved by Robert Hancock c. 1758; Minton cabinet plate painted by Albert Gregory

Back cover:

Wedgwood Glacier from the Frog service with three 'windows' grouped to form the finial 1773-1774

Photo, page 3:

Rare inlaid and enameled Vase by Thomas Mellor, signed 'T. Mellor' in script c 1880s

The name Stoke-upon-Trent has been used to denote the parish of that name, where it can be clearly identified. All other references to Stoke have been styled Stoke-on-Trent, although this name was only adopted when the six towns merged to become the current city. This includes the parish of Stoke-upon-Trent where it is not clear where a particular street was situated (several street names were not confined to the one town, e.g. John Street).

Contents

INTRODUCTION

The ceramic industry was born when red clay, dug from the ground, was made into cooking pots and sold at markets and fairs throughout Britain. But when the Honourable East India Company started to trade with China in the late-seventeenth century and brought back examples of fine translucent porcelain, a new era in the history of British ceramics began. The Company held auctions at the trading ports of Bristol, Liverpool and London, and as a result of this trade British potters slowly learnt the secret of making porcelain, and then bone china. The names of Bow, Chelsea, Derby, Worcester, Wedgwood, Minton and Spode became well known. These potteries sold many different types of ware – cooking utensils, garden ornaments, dinner, tea and coffee services and ornamental vases. They catered for the needs of royalty and the aristocracy at home and abroad and for the new market of the expanding middle class, which demanded exciting shapes and designs. Armorial crests, landscapes, floral studies and birds reflected the changing tastes of all strata of the buying public. Modellers designed the new shapes and painters, paintresses and gilders hand decorated the ware.

The industry has always sustained its liveliness and its markets by the quality of the decoration of the wares. From the eighteenth century to the present day, the source of excellent ceramic design was often the works of well-known artists and book illustrators. Ceramic artists copied their work faithfully or used it to create their own designs. Collectors have always been interested in the highly skilled men and women who painted on ceramic ware, some of whom signed their work and others who are only recognisable by their particular artistic characteristics. I hope that the names and details of the ceramic artists listed, some already identified and some recorded here for the first time, will enable collectors to trace the history of the design of pieces in their collections. I hope that the book will also become a basis for on-going research in this field. As more becomes known about ceramic art, myths will disappear and new facts emerge about the lives of the artists. Excellent specialist books have been written about both famous and less well-known potteries, and these works have provided some of the source material for this book, together with new research. The result is a reference book of artists, painters, paintresses, gilders and modellers; of the major fine artists, illustrators and sculptors who inspired their work; and of the external decorating establishments and retailers who contributed to this design field.

The alphabetically arranged biographies of ceramic artists in the first part contain references to recognised roles and titles in the pottery industry. Art Superintendents ran the decorating departments of potteries, and were responsible for predicting future design needs and influencing their ceramic artists accordingly. The term 'artist painter' is given here to those who signed their names on their work and who are recorded in potteries' costing and pattern books. They often specialised in designing and painting one subject – for instance, flowers or birds. Painters and paintresses are skilled craftsmen and women who were often responsible for running painting departments but are sometimes only referred to in the factory books with the words 'painted by men', or 'painted by women'. Gilders have been classified as 'artist gilders', that is, painters who not only painted with gold but also designed patterns and created the jewelled decoration so popular in the second half of the nineteenth century. Gilders whose work in gold enhanced decorated ware are also recorded here.

Factory pattern and costing books are a primary source of information. When they refer to an artist or painter as 'Mr', usually this craftsman is in charge of one of the decorating shops and a person of importance in the pottery. There are entries from the early-nineteenth century that show an artist's or painter's name followed by 'and Co.'. This is interpreted as a person managing a small staff of painters or paintresses, sometimes members of the same family, who were often responsible for painting large tea and coffee services. The practice of naming artists and painters in the books provided an accurate account of whose work was on the ware, from which the foreman could calculate wages. By the 1860s, when master potters had learnt the market value of a signature, more artists were allowed to sign their work and these entries cease. Modellers were equally important as they created both figures and new shapes for all types of ware, but it was not until the end of the nineteenth century that their artistic importance was appreciated.

Popular paintings by Royal Academicians and by artists who exhibited at societies and in galleries throughout Britain were copied onto the ceramic surface. Artists such as Landseer, Watteau and Boucher are well known, but here it is the details of their lives and works relevant to ceramic design that are explored. This will make it possible to identify not only the subject matter but also the style of painting that ceramic artists imitated so faithfully and with such accuracy in their designs. As Parian pieces are often inscribed with both the maker's and the sculptor's names, the identities of sculptors who allowed their fine work to be reproduced are accurately recorded.

Finally, as early as the mid-1700s outside decorating establishments bought undecorated ware, or white ware, from potteries and employed their own painters. And some china warehouses or retail houses ordered goods from potteries decorated with special designs, and their own backstamps can be found on the ware.

In order to identify some unsigned, hand-painted ceramic work of the early 1800s and appreciate the skill of the artists, it is important to understand the techniques the artists employed. In 1878 John Haslem, a talented flower painter at Derby, published *The Old Derby China Factory*, which describes in great detail the work of the artists and gilders he knew. His book is referenced throughout the text here, and his comments on the artists at Derby apply equally to those working elsewhere in the ceramic industry. His descriptions and terminology, of the specialisms, skills and inspirations of ceramic artists, are also generic.

Ceramic floral designs of the late seventeenth and early eighteenth centuries, featuring both wild flowers and those cultivated in the glasshouses and orangeries of the wealthy, were taken from botanical books of the period. The skill of the ceramic artist was not only to reproduce the blooms with accuracy and great detail but also to create an overall design that would appeal to the buying public. The artists of this period appear to have had knowledge of painting in both watercolour and oils, but the use and mixing of ceramic colours was a specific and separate art that they had to learn. To achieve a realistic and appealing pattern, flowers had to be coloured using a sophisticated combination of light and shade, the rose being the most difficult flower to paint. Artists achieved this effect by using strong colour but with a watercolour technique, the highlights painted in with great care. The effect often took a great deal of paint, which could chip and flake after firing, and it had a hardness that is clearly definable from the work of later ceramic artists.

New methods then achieved a much more subtle and delicate look for flowers yet were still accurate. Now the whole flower was washed over with ceramic colour and the highlights achieved by removing colour rather than adding more. Using the handle of his brush or a pencil with great dexterity, the painter removed colour to simulate the natural highlights of the blooms. An effect of light and shade was also achieved by 'hatching', the application of many tiny lines close together in decreasing strength of colour; sometimes lines were 'cross-hatched' in the other direction for greater detail. Stippling describes the use of tiny dots, again very close together and decreasing in colour, to achieve light and shade, a technique used through into the twentieth century. Painters and paintresses were extremely skilled in such techniques. The phrases 'a quick workman' and 'softly painted' were also current. Quick workmen were rare artists and painters with the ability to draw freely and accurately over the ceramic surface to produce a finished effect that needed no correction to either line or colour. 'Softly painted' denotes the use of harmonious colours and tones subtly blended together. These terms apply to pottery designs and decoration throughout the industry and were often noted in pattern books.

In the early 1800s books full of wonderful landscapes, flowers or birds were published. The landscapes were often the work of artists who travelled to far countries, such as India, to see and paint other cultures and geography. They returned with portfolios of sketches, which were then printed and used as source material by ceramic artists. A country gentleman with vast acres of land might ask a known artist or even a local pottery artist to paint the scenes around his estate to be reproduced upon, perhaps, a dessert service for his table. However good the artist, though, the finished piece was rarely complete until gilded, a complicated art form.

Gilding on china was first achieved by using gold leaf ground up in honey with a little flux added so that it would adhere to the surface. By the early 1800s another method had evolved: 'brown gold' was prepared by melting pure gold then pouring it into cold water, making it friable, and mixing in five parts of mercury. This mixture was then put onto a glass slab and ground with turpentine and a little flux to produce a consistency that could be painted onto the ceramic surface. During firing, the mercury burns off in the kiln and leaves the gold outline, which can then be burnished or polished to bring back the true lustre of the gold. John Hancock was probably the first to use not only gold but also silver and steel lustres prepared in this way when employed by Henry Daniel in his factory on the Spode site at Stoke, Staffordshire.

By the end of the nineteenth century, ceramic fashions and techniques had dramatically altered. Hand-painting was becoming very expensive and the effect achieved by hand-colouring transfer prints instead reached a high standard. Potteries employed fewer artists and painters but more and more artist gilders and gilders. Money was now being spent on creating superb gilded patterns on borders, especially of dessert plates. Very few artist gilders and gilders are named in factory records but careful examination of their work makes it possible to hazard some attributions.

Every day new names on all makes of ware appear on new finds. Evidence is slowly gathered and the stories of previously unknown artists and painters are told. This book hopes to extend this fascinating area of ceramic history. The artists may have worked in house, freelance or even as amateurs, but many of them produced fine quality work, as the illustrations here demonstrate. Their lives, places of work and home, occupations, skills and status are recorded here. But this book is only the beginning. As yet more surviving pieces are found, other researchers will continue the story of these talented men and women of the potteries.

Part One

CERAMIC ARTISTS, PAINTERS, GILDERS AND MODELLERS

Ablott, Richard, 1815–1895

Landscape painter, born in Manitoba, Canada, the son of a soldier serving with the Hudson Bay trading company at Fort Garry, Manitoba. He trained at the Derby factory and is shown on the 1832 list of workpeople. By 1840 he and his family had moved to the Potteries and in 1842 were living at Upper Bank Street, Stoke-upon-Trent, near to the Copeland and Garrett manufactory. By 1852 they had moved to Burton-upon-Trent. Ablott was employed by W.T. Copeland c. 1860 as a landscape painter. The Copeland Special Order books of 15 June 1860 record his landscape painting on D pattern numbers, mainly on Cambridge and Osborne shapes and the last entry is for March 1865, when he painted landscapes on a jardinière with a rose du Barry ground.

It is thought Ablott became a freelance artist, as in the Derby exhibition of 1870 included a Coalport dessert service with landscapes, painted for a Mr Carter of Derby; and a signed Davenport dessert service was shown on the TV 'Antiques Road Show' in January 1995. His signed painting has been found on a Powell and Bishop tray c. 1876, and a large signed china plaque in a private collection is painted with *The Harbour at Whitby, North Yorks*, taken from the engraving by E. Finden after the original painting by C. Balmer. In 1881 Ablott, his wife and four unmarried daughters were living in Newcastle Street, Burslem. He died in September 1895, then described as a retired potter's artist living at 5 Newport Street, Burslem.

Abraham, Francis Xavier (Frank), 1858–1932

Artist who specialised in painting figure subjects. He was born in Broseley, Shropshire the son of Robert Frederick Abraham (q.v.) and trained at the Stoke School of Art and the Central School of Practical Art in South Kensington, London. In 1885 he won a travelling scholarship and studied in Belgium. In 1887 he exhibited two landscape paintings in the Royal Academy. Returning to Stoke-on-Trent, he joined his father at the Copeland manufactory and in 1891 was living with his parents at Oak House, Regent Street, Stoke-on-Trent, described in the census returns as Assistant Art Director, China Factory. His daughter Mary remembered her father with great affection, saying he was paid £500 a year. The family moved in 1901 from Sheppard Street, Stoke-on-Trent to Quarry St, Stoke-on-Trent, a far superior residence amongst Doctors rather than Potters! Mary spoke of the day when, attired in his frock coat and top hat, her father went to London by train from Stoke Station to see the Mayfair retailers Thomas Goodes, and the excitement in the house when he came back with important orders. In 1912 he left Copeland after a disagreement with management and was employed at the Cauldon pottery until 1925, when he became Art Director at S. Hancock's and Sons. Here he was allowed more freedom to design. Under his direction Hancock's introduced *Morris Ware*, named after William Morris, shown at the British Industries Fair of 1918. This freely designed highly coloured ware (some designed by George Cartlidge, q.v.) proved very popular. Abraham died in 1932.

Copeland bone china plate painted by Francis Xavier (Frank) Abraham. Left Initials on plate

Abraham, Frederick Bernard, born 1864

Artist, born in Hanley, the son of Robert Frederick Abraham (q.v.), probably trained at the Stoke School of Art where he became a pupil teacher. He lived with his parents at Regent St, Stoke-on-Trent until 1889, when he had moved to London.

Jewitt describes him as 'F. B. Abraham, a figure painter of much promise'.

Abraham, Robert Frederick, 1826–1895

Artist, painter of figure subjects and art director who, born in London, studied art in London, Paris and Antwerp. From 1846–53 he exhibited eleven historical scenes and portraits at the Royal Academy and six at the British Institution, including in 1846 *A head of the Magdalene*. In 1848 *A portrait of a gentleman, a study from the streets of London from the Lay of the last minstrel* was submitted from an address in Brunton Street, London.

Possibly family commitments forced him to leave London and enter the ceramics industry. The 1851 Copeland Special Order books record Abraham as head of the ornamenting department; they also show Abraham junior, both as figure painters. There seemed little opportunity for promotion at Copeland and the Abraham family moved to Shropshire. By 1862 he had become one of the principal artists at the Coalport manufactory, known for painting Boucher (q.v.) subjects in the Sèvres style. His painting was delicate, after the style of William Etty (q.v.) and included cupids and classical figures. A Coalport vase, painted in the Sèvres style, was exhibited at their 1862 exhibition. His copy on Coalport porcelain of Paul Potter's *Cattle* was highly acclaimed (Paul Potter was a fashionable artist of the 1850s, well known for his landscapes and paintings depicting nature in all its forms). Sometime in the 1860s Abraham returned to the Potteries to become Art Director of the Hill Pottery, late S. Alcock and Co, Burslem, Staffordshire.

Detail of the Art Union Tazza designed by Robert F. Abraham

In 1865 Abraham succeeded George Eyre (q.v.), as Art Director at Copeland. He became respected in the artistic world of ceramic painting, a fine painter and designer with a breadth of vision for ceramic design that was ahead of his contemporaries. Jewitt says: 'The softness of touch, purity and delicacy of feeling, the sunny mellowness of tone, chasteness of design, and correctness of drawing produced on the best pieces of his productions, prove him a thorough artist, and render him peculiarly fitted for the post to which he has been called.'

In 1874 The Art Union of London held a competition to design a china tazza, offering a prize of £35. Although this was intended to encourage students, Abraham won. The tazza was large and difficult to produce; only twenty were made that year. It was designed on a musical theme with Saint Cecilia, the Patron Saint of music, in the centre. The Abraham family lived very near to the Spode works in Regent Street, Stoke-on-Trent and he stayed with Copeland until his death on 23 September 1895. He was buried in Stoke cemetery.

Abraham, Robert John, 1852–1925

Artist of figure subjects, son of Robert Frederick (q. v.). He trained at the Stoke School of Art and was awarded a National Scholarship to the London School of Art where in 1872 he won the gold medal for painting from nature. Robert joined his father at Copeland, painting tiles depicting portraits.

In 1874, John Macfarlane of 22 Park Circus, Glasgow commissioned Copeland to design tiles for the billiard room of his new house. The three-foot high frieze of narrative series of large monochrome tiles was designed by Robert Frederick, depicted Sporting Ages, Health, Strength, Courage and Fortitude. The tiles were painted by Robert John and Lucien Besche (q.v.) By the 1880s Robert John became a freelance artist and worked for a firm of independent ceramic decorators in Stoke-on-Trent.

In 1881 he and his brother Francis Xavier (q.v.) were living at 3 Park Terrace, Stoke-on-Trent, lodging with architect and surveyor William Poulson and his wife. Robert was listed in the 1881 census as 'Artist practicing the Art of Painting'. For 1877–92 he is shown in Algernon Graves' *Dictionary of Artists* as exhibiting ten rustic-style paintings at the Royal Academy, four at the New Watercolour Society, one at the New Gallery and three at other exhibitions. One of his Royal Academy exhibits, an oil painting entitled *The Burgundy Peasant or The Spinning Wheel*, dated 1876, was exhibited in The Centenary Art Exhibition in the Potteries in 1953.

Adams, Frederick W., born 1844

Floral painter, born in Hanley, Staffordshire and trained at the Hanley School of Art, where he won many prizes. In 1881 he and his family were living at 13 John Street, Shelton, Stoke-on-Trent. Prior to 1895, little is known of the life of this fine artist, but it is possible he became Copeland's premier painter when Charles Ferdinand Hurten (q.v.) left in 1895. However, from 1895 to 1910 he was certainly employed at Copeland. A floral artist of great skill, he painted flowers in strong distinctive colours with botanical accuracy.

Arthur Perry (q.v.), in an interview with Leonard Whiter (author of *Spode*), said that 'when Abraham [the Art Director] introduced a new rose colour, a pure rose pink without the usual bluish tint, used on two rose blooms and a sprig painting, these became Adams' specialty, the design being used on all shapes and types of ware, which kept Adams busy for years…'.

Adams, Harry William, 1868–1947

Landscape painter, born in Claines, Worcester, the son of a glover's warehouseman. He studied in Paris and made several visits to Switzerland. He specialised in landscapes, especially snow scenes, and was probably apprenticed at Worcester. He is described in the census returns in 1891 as a Student landscape artist, still living in Claines, and by 1901 just as 'Artist visiting a friend' at Frog Hall, Upton, Snodbury, Worcestershire. His work is in the collection of Tate Britain, London.

Alcock, Samuel, 1845–1914

Painter of figure subjects, born in Bucknall, Staffordshire, the son of Samuel Alcock, a farmer. He trained in the Royal Academy Schools and his membership card to the Royal Academy and to the print room in the British Museum are in the family archives. It is thought he went to France; certainly his paintings of Watteau subjects are in the French style. Whilst still an art student, Samuel married Mary Alicia Abraham, the daughter of Robert Frederick Abraham (q.v.) The family did not approve of the proposed marriage and the couple eloped, but they were quickly accepted back into the family fold and given a Copeland dinner service as a wedding present. The 1881 census shows that Mary and four young children were staying with her father at Regent Street, Stoke-on-Trent, whilst Samuel was lodging in Richmond Terrace, the home of a railway agent. Samuel is remembered by Mary Abraham (Francis Xavier Abraham's daughter) who said 'he painted people, but was so superior and self-important that he would not work at the factory (although he was offered a studio) so the work was taken to him'. The family remember that he had a studio at home, and that his children played in the garden so he could work in peace. Samuel made his daughters and wife pose for him, which they hated. Although he earned a large salary, he always seemed to have financial problems. The family believe that he invested in a slate or tin mine in Cornwall that became water logged and failed. He is first shown in the Copeland Special Order books in 1882, painting ladies of fashion, Gainsborough-inspired heads, heroines from Watteau subjects and Shakespearean characters.

He also created designs inspired by songs, for example, 'Down Yonder Green Valley, a Welsh air by Alarms' known now as 'The Ash Grove'. A dessert set of twelve Richelieu-shaped jewelled dessert plates are known. Each plate, named *Old Songs*, illustrates a well-known song of the period and has the title of the song and the author written on the reverse. His work was highly sort after, sold well and was commissioned by Tiffany's of New York.

Wolliscroft Rhead wrote: 'For the past twenty years they have had the advantage in the services of Mr S. Alcock, a figure painter whose work is extremely decorative, soundly drawn, pure and subtle in colour, and daintily executed' and he was described by Jewitt as 'a figure painter of great power and excellence'. Samuel was extremely temperamental; he and Richard Pirie Copeland, then owner of the pottery, were in continual correspondence and dispute. He demanded paper and paints and refused to sign pieces that he thought were not up to standard, constantly complaining that he had not been paid enough. His work, jewelled and gilded by the finest gilders, was in such demand that compromises were reached. At the Exposition Universelle, Paris of 1889, Copeland exhibited the Midsummer Night's Dream service painted by Samuel, which was highly praised. The comports and side pieces were modelled by Owen Hale (q.v.) and illustrated the fairy characters of the play. The last entry in the Copeland Special Order books is dated July 1895, the year his father-in-law died and one wonders if Richard Pirie Copeland decided at this point that he would no longer put up with his temperamental behaviour.

The next nineteen years of his life remain a mystery, but there is little doubt he had become a freelance artist as an example of his work, dated c. 1910, has been found on Foley China.

Allen, Harry, 1899–1950

Painter, son of Robert (q.v.) who trained at the Burslem Art School. His artistic talent was recognised by his father and his close friend Harry Piper (q.v.). Allen was employed by Doulton and painted all subjects with equal skill, although he became known for painting

Samuel Alcock Self Portrait

Copeland bone china vase, centre painting of classical lady by S. Alcock

Copeland Bone China Jewelled plate painted Shakespearean centre by Samuel Alcock

Arab villages, Nile views and Moorish mosques, and birds on Titanium ware. When Doulton created their well-known figures of graceful ladies in 1925, Harry was one of the first artists to hand-paint them, giving them life and personality. He sometimes used the pseudonym Richmond on litho-printed designs, which were later hand-coloured.

Allen, Robert, 1858 –1929

Painter who attended Burslem Art School, was first employed at Minton and then moved to the Pinder Bourne, Nile Street factory at Burslem. Here he studied under Art Director John Slater (q.v.) and eventually became his deputy. Robert painted all subjects with equal skill, often on Lactolain Ware (a type of pâte-sur-pâte), which was developed in 1899 using coloured slips production. He became Head of the Art Department and Charles Nokes' (q.v.) son Cecil became his apprentice. After 1893 Robert designed raised and acid gold borders that framed many of the hand-painted centres of dessert plates and cameos on vases. Little of his work was signed but some is marked with a number and accredited to him.

Allen, Thomas, 1831–1915

Figure painter and art director, born at Trent Vale, Stoke-upon-Trent, the son of a plumber and glazier. He served his apprenticeship at Minton and in 1851 painted a vase exhibited at the Great Exhibition, held at the Crystal Palace in Hyde Park, London. Thomas studied in the evenings at the newly opened School of Design in Stoke-on-Trent under Silas Rice, who taught him a sense of style and respect for drawing. In 1852 he won one of the first two-year National Scholarships awarded by the Governmental School of Design, South Kensington, London. Here he met John Simpson (q.v.), who taught him the discipline of technique. He was commissioned to paint a portrait miniature of Henry Cole (q.v.) and it is possible the T. Allen shown to have exhibited enamels at the Royal Academy in 1854 is this fine artist.

Thomas stayed with his brother in London and wrote *The Diary of Thomas Allen, Scholar 1852–54*, now in the Wedgwood archives, describing his life at art school and the trials and tribulations of living in London. Whilst studying in London both his parents died, but after finishing his course Thomas returned to Minton, where he worked with Thomas Kirkby (q.v.). He was involved in the important Minton commission of the hexagonal

Thomas Allen

Minton Bone china Vase painted by Thomas Allan c. 1860 Courtesy of the Potteries Museum and Art Gallery

tesserae decoration on the staircase leading to the ceramic court at the Victoria & Albert Museum. Thomas gained a reputation for painting figures in panels on vases in the Sèvres style, and specialised in allegorical subjects after Rubens, Etty and other masters. He and Henry Mitchel (q.v.) painted a pair of vases, standing forty-seven inches high, said to be the largest produced at that time. They were exhibited in 1867 at the Exposition Universelle in Paris and decorated with the Birth of Venus and the Toilet of Venus on the front and on the reverse a landscape decoration after *Boucher* (q.v.).

However, frustrated with not only by low wages (he earned little more than £3 a week) but by not being allowed to sign his work, in 1878 he left and went to Wedgwood as Chief Designer. Sometime after Emille Lessore left (q.v.), Thomas became Art Director, the first artist to hold this appointment. He partially retired in 1894 and fully by 1901, the census showing him living on his own means. His work at Wedgwood on decorated earthenware plaques and dishes with Shakespearean subjects was exhibited in the Exposition Universelle, Paris of 1878 and highly praised. Thomas introduced pâte-sur-pâte decoration at Wedgwood, assisted by modeller Charles Toft (q.v.) and by Frederick Rhead and William Palin (q.v.). His signed work was always in demand and very expensive. He died in 1915.

Allen, William, born 1861

Engraver, who trained in Burslem and joined Doulton in 1883. With Charles Vyse (q.v.) he engraved designs with great skill on copper plates, and they were able to create the depth that gave the engravings their detail. In 1881 he is shown as living at 37 Edward Street, Burslem, Staffordshire.

Armstrong, Annie Langley Nairn, active 1840s

Marine artist who married the London architect Robert Williams Armstrong (1824–84). He became Manager and Art Director of the Belleek Pottery In Ireland. The success of the Belleek designs was due to the collaboration between husband and wife. She created the fine designs on early Belleck ware inspired by shells, animals and botanical subjects. Annie was an accomplished artist who exhibited at the Royal Hibernian Academy from 1844 to 1847.

Arnold, William Henry Weston, 1816–1932

Artist, designer and illustrator who was trained at The Government School of Design, South Kensington, London and the Colorossia Atelier in Paris. He worked for Minton from 1876 to 1878, then became an independent artist. He exhibited at the Royal Academy and in America from c. 1907 to 1928.

Arnoux, Joseph Leon François, 1816–1902

Art director and chemist, born in Couloute, France, the son of Antoine Arnoux and Miette Fougue. He studied at L'Ecole Centrale des Arts et Manufactures. His father owned an important pottery at Valentine near Saint Gaudens, which manufactured marbled ware similar to the agate wares of Staffordshire. Although Arnoux had qualified as an engineer, during his childhood he had been involved in the making of agate ware. Combined with the experience he had gained when helping to manage the family business with his mother after his father's death, he therefore had management skills that allowed him to organise and direct a pottery workforce. He met Alexander Brongniart (Director of the Sèvres Porcelain Factory, Paris, 1800–49) who encouraged him and allowed him to gain experience in the Sèvres factory on the Rue de Rivoli, Paris.

Arnoux joined Minton in 1848 as a ceramic chemist to study manufacturing techniques and help with the development of encaustic tiles, and also to teach the art of pâte-sur-pâte decoration. He became Art Superintendent in 1849. By 1850 he had created an earthenware body used for tiles and slabs and some sculptured pieces. Just before the 1851 Great Exhibition he had designed a majolica body with colours vastly different to Italian majolica, and had mastered the technique of reproducing the fine colours of turquoise, bleu du Roi and rose du

Leon Arnoux 1816-1902

Barry after the Sèvres style. He also introduced Henri Deux ware. It was through his influence that many other foreign artists came to the Potteries.

The English Illustrated Magazine of September 1885 describes him and his team: 'During long years M. Arnoux has presided over the department of hand-painted china from original designs made by himself and his colleagues. These gentlemen go like other artists to Chatsworth and Rangemore, to cornfield, coppice, luxuriant riverside, yellow bog land and purple moor to seek inspiration for their subjects...

M. Arnoux with his able assistants produced work worthy of note in every department. The hand-painted dessert services are marvels of skill, and the number of richly decorated vases annually produced is very great.'

In 1878 he became a Chevalier of the Légion d'Honneur for his achievements as a ceramic chemist and writer. In the 1890s he developed the Minton down-draft kiln. In 1901 the Arnoux family were in The Villas, Stoke-upon-Trent, and also owned the house next door, which they rented to Leon Solon (q.v.). Arnoux retired in 1900 but was retained at Minton as a consultant. He was probably the most highly paid artist and art director in the ceramic industry. His salary is said to have been £1,200. He married Suzanne Serac and they had two sons and three daughters. His daughter married Solon's son Lucien. His sons, Ferdinand, born in St Gaudens, France and Albert, born in Stoke-upon-Trent became partners and co-proprietors in the firm of engineering, Hartley and Arnoux. *The Art Journal* of 1874 said of Arnoux: 'He will be remembered by his countrymen as one of the most skilful pupils of Brogniart and by Englishmen as the most talented and accomplished Frenchman who ever honoured our shores and aided us in the development of our Art Industries.'

Arrowsmith, John Bartlem (Johnny?), born 1862

Bird and flower painter, born in Hanley and shown in the 1881 census as living in Wesley Cottage, Stoke-on-Trent. His father James is listed as a potter and other members of the family of working age at the time were painters and paintresses. So far it has not been discovered where he trained. It is probable he entered Copeland's decorating department as a boy apprentice and stayed there the whole of his working life painting floral and bird subjects. Johnny signed or initialled his work and is especially known for his skill in painting The Mecklenburg Service, a copy of a Chelsea dessert service, originally ordered by Queen Charlotte in 1763 as a present for her brother, Duke of Mecklenburg Strelitz. The source of the bird decoration is thought to be *The Natural History of Uncommon Birds* by George Edwards c. 1743 (q.v.). W.T. Copeland reproduced this service

Bone china Copeland vases painted by J Arrowsmith c. 1900

three times, first for Thomas Goode of Mayfair, who exhibited it at the 1889 Exposition Universelle, Paris and where it was bought by the King of Greece. The second one was commissioned by the citizens of Norwich as a present to George V and Queen Mary on their marriage. The last service, again commissioned by Thomas Goode, was painted and signed by Arrowsmith, either with his initials or full signature. He worked for W.T. Copeland & Sons for over fifty years and is remembered with affection.

Arrowsmith, Samuel, born 1876 +

Gilder, born in Stoke, Staffordshire, brother to John (q.v.). He trained at Minton and was employed at W.T. Copeland & Sons c. 1899 to 1905 and Royal Doulton from 1907 to 1955. There are many entries in the Copeland black books that give an Arrowsmith (no initial) as gilding sanded scrolls and ornate gold work.

Askew, Richard, died 1798

Figure painter, a freelance artist who worked at both the Chelsea and Derby potteries. His influence on future pottery painting and design was immense and his life shows the importance such early artists. He worked for Nicholas Sprimont of Chelsea painting cupids in rose colour on crimson. In 1764 he was living on the King's Road, Chelsea and in 1772 was known to have lived at Derby. He succeeded James Banford (q.v.) painting cherubs, figures from allegories and classical legends. Askew is mentioned by Haslem as using the painting pattern number 180. In the centre of a plate is a cupid sitting on a cloud with trophies and a basket of flowers, which were painted by William Billingsley. In 1771 he painted for the Derby pottery, receiving commissions from William Duesbury; in 1795 he was being paid 4s 4d a day at Chelsea, and at Derby 5s 3d. It is thought he always worked from home as his name does not appear in either the regular painters list of Chelsea or Derby. He painted in the Boucher style and his paintings of cupids were unique, possibly using his children as models. His angel paintings were usually in rose or crimson, no two were alike and they had a spontaneity of design and drawing. Derby records show he painted figures on coffee and tea services. Askew returned to London in 1781, living at Coy's Gardens, Tottenham Court, where he set up as a miniature enamel and portrait painter. By 1786 he had moved to Dublin as an advertisement appears in *Faulkner's Dublin Journal* for 'Askew miniature enamel painter from London'. By 1793 he was living in Suffolk Street, Birmingham, describing himself as an enamel painter.

Askew, Robert, active 1772

Painter, the son of Richard (q.v.) who was apprenticed at the Derby factory. However, he terminated his apprenticeship and left, possibly to join John Laurence, a friend of his father's, working for Wedgwood in their Chelsea decorating business in London.

Astles, Samuel, c. 1792–1853

Flower painter who was employed by Flight and Barr at Worcester and possibly Chamberlain Worcester Porcelain after they amalgamated in 1840. He had been a pupil of Thomas Baxter, c. 1814–16, who specialised in groups of flowers especially on vases, which were remarkable for their detail and botanical accuracy. He exhibited a painting after Van Huysum (q.v.) on china at the Royal Academy in 1827. He died of typhoid fever at Spoon Lane, Smethwick.

Aston, Jabez (Jabey), born *c.* 1798

Fruit and flower painter, the son of George Aston and Ann, born in Ironbridge, Shropshire and trained as an apprentice at the Coalport pottery c. 1810–17. He possibly stayed there for the whole of his working life. Many references are shown in Coalport pattern books, where he is sometimes listed as J. Aston, sometimes as Mr Aston: '2/717 Flowers by Jabey Aston, 2/964 Jabey Aston's flowers, Fruit by Aston 3/195, 3/195 Save (Sèvres) group by Jabey Aston 3/421 plants painted by J. Aston, 3/433 Fruit by Mr Aston.' Jewitt describes him as one of Coalport's principal artists and he is known to have painted fine plaques in the Sèvres style.

Austin, Charles, born 1864

Flower painter, born in Hanley, Staffordshire, the son of a bricklayer who had his own business. He attended the local art school in 1879 and again 1884–86, where he won a free scholarship for a year. His work was entered for the National Schools competition and he won many prizes. In the 1881 census he is described as a flower painter potter living with his parents at 138 Leek Road, Hanley. He was employed as a floral artist by George Jones and Sons at the Crescent pottery Stoke-on-Trent and signed his work.

Austin, Jesse, 1806–1879

Artist Engraver, born in Longton, Staffordshire, the youngest son of twelve children. His father William was a tailor, born in Devonshire. Austin went to Longton Grammar School and studied drawing at night school. He was apprenticed at the Davenport pottery, where he learnt copper-plate engraving. In 1846 he went to F. and R. Pratt and Co. His designs are well known on pot lids. In 1859, after a disagreement with Thomas Pratt, he joined Brown-Westhead, Moore and Co. but returned to Pratts within a year as head of the engraving department. He signed or initialled over forty-three copper plates of his work. It is said he had a wide knowledge of ceramic colours and developed the multi-colour printing used by F. and R. Pratt so successfully. Austin was especially skilful when adapting large works, for example, those of Landseer (q.v.) to decorate pot lids, which are widely collected today.

Austin, Reginald (Harry), 1890–1955

Floral Artist and designer at Royal Worcester specialising in painting flowers, birds and fruit with his brother Walter (q.v.). He joined the Paragon China Co. as a designer but returned to work again for Worcester as a freelance artist. Most of his painting, especially of Australian birds and flowers, can be found on tea and coffee services. He signed his work.

Backstamp Royal Worcester Bone china Cabinet plate signed R Austin

Austin, Walter Harold, 1891–1971

Freelance flower, fish and bird painter, brother to Harry (q.v.). He worked for Royal Worcester as a freelance artist; some of his work can be found on their Sabrina ware. He was also a watercolour artist, specialising in painting delphiniums. He worked part time for a furniture manufacturer until 1948.

Ayrton, James John, 1877–1918

Painter who was apprenticed at the Royal Worcester pottery painting still-life designs. He left in 1915 for War service and was unfortunately killed by a horse after the armistice.

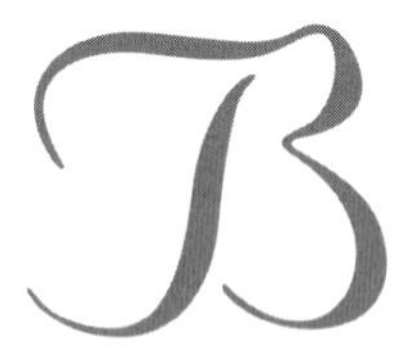

Bacon, Joseph Patrick, 1826–94

Landscape painter, born in Ireland but trained at the School of Design in Manchester. In the 1860s, he was employed by Minton on a freelance basis. He became Assistant Master at Stoke School of Art in 1856 and was appointed Head Master 1864–94. He also ran the Newcastle-under-Lyme School of Art from 1856 to 1894. By 1884 Stoke and Fenton School of Art had become one highly successful school, many of the students gaining positions in the local potteries. Bacon was highly regarded in the area as a fine teacher. He exhibited landscapes at the British Institution in 1865 and 1867. His painting *View of Trentham Hall from the Tittensor Monument* was exhibited in the Century Art Exhibition in Hanley in 1954.

Baggaley, Henry, active c. 1860

Modeller and manufacturer who designed and produced The Volunteer Jug and Jug of All Nations *c.* 1860 and the Prince Consort jug *c.* 1862. He was in partnership with Richard Moore manufacturing Parian. Unfortunately he became bankrupt twice.

Bagguley, active 1845–1848

Gilder, crest and heraldic painter, one of the premier gilders employed at Copeland and Garrett. Pattern number 6622 shows him painting a Motto and Lion and being paid 8d. His daughter Mary was born in Fenton and is shown in the 1881 census as a paintress.

Bagshaw, Thomas, active 1820s–1840s

Painter and gilder, born 1800 and employed at the Coalport pottery. It is thought he was a ground layer and involved in the development of ceramic colours. He married Mary Ann Jones in 1818 at Dawley Magna and their son James was born in Broseley in 1827. In 1859 he was employed at Coalport as a gilder.

Baguley, Isaac, 1794–1859

Gilder, born in Shropshire, first employed at Coalport then known to have been at the Derby works, eventually moving to the Rockingham pottery in Yorks where, according to a factory document dated 1829, he was in charge of all the gilding of both china and earthenware. Mankowitz and Haggar list Isaac Baguley, saying that after 1842 when the Rockingham Factory closed he leased part of the works at Rockingham (where his sons Alfred and Edwin had served their apprenticeship) to run a decorating establishment. They bought undecorated ware from Minton, Brown-Westhead, Moore & Co., and Powell Bishop and Stonier. His mark was Baguley Rockingham Works with or without the griffin crest.

Bailey, Ernest Tansley, 1911–1987

Modeller and watercolour artist, the son of a farmer, who trained at the Burslem School of Art. He won a travelling scholarship from the Potteries Federation to France and Italy. Bailey was an apprentice modeller at the Burgess & Leigh Middleport Pottery under Charles Wilkes (q.v.), eventually becoming the designer and modeller of many of their Art Deco shapes.

Bailey, William Willis, born 1806

Outside decorator and landscape, crests and butterfly painter, who is shown in the Militia lists of 1828 and 1831. He worked on the William IV Royal Dessert Service commissioned from the Rockingham pottery. An artist of great talent capable of painting all subjects with equal skill, Jewitt describes him as the principal butterfly painter. In the 1840s Bailey became an outside decorator at the nearby town of Wath-upon-Dearne, painting Rockingham and other pottery blanks. A signed example of his work on a dessert service inscribed 'Wath china works' was sold at Christie's. All the scenes were of contemporary paintings and taken from the literature of the day; some pieces of the service are exhibited at the Rotherham Museum.

Baker, Alfred, 1888–1928

Modeller who trained at the Cauldon Pottery then went to Doulton, where he worked with Charles Nokes. He designed and modelled many of the intricate vases, which were exhibited by Doulton at home and abroad.

Baker, F., active 1885–1889

Floral painter, employed by Copeland and shown in their records from 1885 to 1889. Many of the entries under his name do not give a pattern number, but the number 1/14892. In 1886 records show he painted plate floral centres. He specialised in painting primroses. Known to have painted flowers on some exhibits at the Exposition Universelle, Paris of 1889, some of his work was gilded by T. Hall (q.v.). He was later employed at the Crown Staffordshire Pottery.

Bakewell, James, active 1770s

Painter, originally employed by Wedgwood to paint their Etruscan vases. In May 1770, Josiah Wedgwood, writing to Thomas Bentley, states that Bakewell wanted to be a 'good enamel painter'. In April 1771 he was employed to draw flowers, which were engraved by Sadler and Green (q.v.). He was one of the artists who painted the landscapes on the famous Frog Service, commissioned by Catherine II in 1773 for the Palace of Chesme in Saint Petersburg.

Baldwyn, Charles Henry Clifford, 1859–1943

Artist and painter, the son of a professor of music. He lived at Chestnut Walk, Claines, Worcester and was employed at Royal Worcester from 1874 to the early twentieth century. Baldwyn specialised in studies of birds, especially swans, painting them in naturalistic surroundings. He also painted landscapes with country cottages or farmhouses. He signed his work. Eventually he left the ceramic industry to concentrate on painting watercolour studies. From 1887 to 1893 he exhibited watercolours at the Royal Academy and at the Suffolk Street Art Gallery, London and also at the New Watercolour Society.

Ball, Edward Oakes (Ted), born c. 1873

Landscape painter, born in Jackfield, trained at the Coalport pottery, becoming one of their principal landscape painters. In 1891 he is living with his widowed mother at the Trow Inn, Broseley, where she is described as an innkeeper. By 1897 he was married to Martha Jane James at Madeley and the couple were living at the Boat Inn, Tuckies Fields, Broseley; he described as a china painter and she as an innkeeper. He signed his work E. Ball, E. O. Ball or T. Ball and was working in the early 1900s. He succeeded Plant (q.v.) as chief artist and continued to paint many of his designs. His work is found on vases, dessert plates, small plaques, even small discs or buttons. Many of his landscapes have not the depth of those of his predecessor, possibly because he was expected to paint to a price.

Bone china Coalport seaux c. 1900, painted by E. O. Ball

Ball, James, born 1822

Painter, born in Westminster, London. It is not known whether he trained at Coalport or when he started to work there. In 1861 to 1881 he was lodging in Upper Church Street, Broseley, Shropshire and listed as a china decorator. He is shown in the Coalport pattern books as painting pattern numbers 5/358, 7/341, 7/408, 7/411, 7/414 c. 1861. When he retired in 1891 he moved to Russell Road, Madeley.

Ball, Percival, active c. 1860

Sculptor and modeller who trained at the Lambeth School of Art then attended the Royal Academy Schools and was trained under the sculptor Fontana and won a gold medal. In 1865 he was commissioned by Henry Doulton to design a series of oversized heads, sculpted in terracotta, specifically for the new Doulton Factory, which was built In the same year. He was praised for his statue *Elaine* exhibited at the Royal Academy. By 1881 the census shows him living at 6 Sloane Terrace, Chelsea, London, described as a sculptor.

Ball, W., born 1813

Landscape and floral painter employed at Copeland and Garrett. May have been one of the artists trained in Henry Daniel's decorating establishment on the Spode site in the 1800s., active 1840–50 painting all subjects. He is shown in the Copeland Special Order books as Mr Ball, possibly then foreman of the department. Over sixty entries are recorded under his name on pattern numbers from 7200–8500: these may be his designs and one shows he was paid 16s for painting a landscape. He painted a pierced Dresden-shaped dessert plate for the Great Exhibition of 1851 with flowers surrounded with raised gilding. Ball had a distinctive style, his leaves and small flowers painted with a single stroke of his paintbrush. The Special Order books show he painted on all types of ware from door furniture to large vases. None of his work to date has been found signed.

Bone china Copeland door knob c. 1830, by W. Ball

Ball, William, born 1813, active 1860–1880

Artist gilder, born in Penkhull, Stoke-upon-Trent and employed at Copeland. He may have been trained at Worcester but no evidence is available to support this view. William was the premier artist gilder of this period; he was chosen to decorate the painting of C. F. Hurten (q.v.), creating intricate jewelled designs on dessert plates and vases. Arthur Perry (q.v.) remembered a Mr Ball as working in the gilding department designing patterns and doing most of the jewelled gilding work. There are two fine examples of his work in the Spode Museum. He seems to have lived in Penkhull all his life and he married Sarah Arrowsmith on 13 February 1836. From1861–81 the family lived at Penkhull Terrace, Stoke-upon-Trent close to the Spode Works, where he was described as a china painter.

Porcelain plaque c. 1840, centre landscape attributed to Phillip Ballard

Ballard, Phillip, 1800–1890

Painter of figure subjects and landscapes. The son of an attorney in Malvern, Worcestershire, and brother to T. Ballard, R.A. He became an apprentice to John Bradley, a china painter of Pall Mall in the Parish of St James, London. His apprenticeship was a short one, lasting only two years and eleven months as Bradley became short of work and could no longer employ him. He joined the china and enamel painters, Silk, Muss and Essex.

Ballard was a competent painter in oils, exhibiting a picture entitled *Worcester* at the Royal Academy in 1823 when living at 26 Palace Street, Pimlico, London. By 1833 he was working with Thomas Randall (q.v.). His fine work included pastoral scenes after Watteau and cupids in medallions. Some survive in the Ballard family archives. His younger brother Stephen, an engineer to the Hereford and Gloucester canal, persuaded him to return home to join him in the canal company. Phillip died in 1890 after being attacked by a burglar.

Bancroft, Joseph, c. 1795–1857

Flower painter, born in Derby. In c. 1810 he served his apprenticeship at the Derby works, where he was influenced by the work of Thomas Martin Randall (q.v.). Haslem describes his work as excellent when painting flowers, shells and insects, but criticises his composition of larger groups. He said that the flowers seemed to have lost their highlights and were short of colour. By 1813 Joseph had gone to London but returned to the Potteries and may have been employed for a short time with Henry Daniel at the Spode pottery, but so far no documentary evidence has been found to support this view. In the mid-1820s he was employed at the J. & W. Ridgway pottery, then c. 1831 at Minton, where he became one of their premier artists, painting flowers, fruit, studies of feathers and Sèvres-inspired designs. Leading retailers asked specifically for his work and he stayed at Minton until he retired.

Banford, Berenice (née Glisson), active c. 1780s

Flower paintress who in July 1783 married James Banford. Berenice first worked for Wedgwood and Bentley's decorating establishment at Chelsea, London, where she met her future husband; they moved to the Derby factory. She worked from home, as male painters and gilders at the Derby works protested against the pottery employing women.

Banford, James, 1758–1798

Landscape artist and figure painter, born at Berkeley, Gloucestershire. His father Thomas was a mariner but the family were goldsmiths. In January 1773 James was apprenticed to Richard Chamberlain at Bristol as a flower painter. In August 1778, when the company became bankrupt, he left for London, working for the Wedgwood and Bentley's decorating establishment at Chelsea. From 1789 to 1795 he painted figures at the Nottingham Road works, Derby. His name is mentioned sixteen times in the old Derby pattern books. His style was influenced by the work of his friend Henry Bone (q.v.), who painted miniatures. James specialised in small cabinet pieces, decorating them with landscapes, figures and flowers, painting in a style very similar to Boreman (q.v.). He often painted little figures in the foreground of his work. He used bright colours – yellows, greens, blues and mauve, with a slant of light through the trees. Unfortunately Banford drank too much fortified wine, which made him quarrelsome and temperamental. He complained that he was not paid enough money for his undoubted skill. Letters c. 1790–95 exist from Banford and his wife asking William Duesbury for more money. Banford was in debt more often than not, obviously unable to arrange his affairs. He died at Bilston in 1798.

Bardell, active 1879

Bird painter at Copeland, known for painting birds and fine bird nests designs, particularly on earthenware plaques. May have been apprenticed at Minton 1862–68.

Barker, C., active 1900s

Bird painter. Known to have painted a signed series of game birds on Shelley China with a blue gilded ground. The bird design shows them in their natural surroundings or in flight. He was employed at Grimwades in about the mid-1950s but also did freelance work.

Barker, Ernest, 1890–1956

Painter trained at the Royal Worcester pottery by Harry Davies (q.v.). He specialised in painting sheep in the Davies style, but also painted flowers and garden birds, especially blue tits on pussy willow. His work is found on only small pieces of Worcester ware.

Barlow, Arthur B., 1847–79

Artist painter (brother to Florence and Hannah Barlow, q.v.). A childhood illness left him severely disabled but, encouraged by his doctor and taught by family friend W.G. Rogers, he learnt woodcarving. He joined Doulton's Lambeth Art Studio from 1871 to 1878 and studied at the Lambeth School of Art; and in 1872 he attended the Royal Academy. In 1871 he was living with his widowed mother at 48 South Lambeth Road, London, aged twenty-five and described as a sculptor.

His bold, stylised incised patterns of leaf scrolls in subtle colours, totally different from that of his sisters, were popular. He created all-over patterns, often repeating motifs of pointed leaves. In 1876 his work was exhibited at the Philadelphia Centennial Exhibition and is signed with an incised monogram ABB.

Barlow, Florence Elizabeth, born 1856

Artist and designer, born at Little Hadham, Hertfordshire to Benjamin and his wife Hannah. In 1861 the family, consisting of the parents and nine children, were living at Carters Farm, Hatfield Broad Oak, Essex. From 1873 she was employed at the Doulton Lambeth Art Studio, executing incised patterns of birds after the style of her sister Hannah. She was engaged on Doulton's marqueterie and faience ware. Florence created her designs from thick slip, often painting bird and foliage designs. John Sparkes described her work as covering a more extended field than her sister, as she incorporated ornament and animals in her designs. By 1881 she was living with her widowed mother, brother Hubert and sisters Lucy and Hannah. She exhibited in 1876 at the Philadelphia Centennial Exhibition and at the Louisiana Purchase Exhibition of 1904; also watercolours at the Royal Academy 1884–85, the Royal Society of British Artists, 1883–89, and at the Walker Gallery, Liverpool. Her work was incised FB or FEB monogram.

Barlow, Hannah Bolton, 1851–1916

Artist designer sister to Florence. In 1866 her father died and as one of the nine children Hannah needed a source

Doulton, Burslem handled large mug designed and decorated by Hannah Barlow. Courtesy of the M.O.H.Baker Collection

Doulton Burslem vase designed and decorated by Hannah Barlow

of revenue. Her family friend, Edith Rogers, introduced her to John Sparkes at the Lambeth Art School, where she became a student. She became fascinated by Japanese art, popularised in the 1870s, which influenced her style of design. She was at the Minton Art Pottery studio for a short time, but joined Doulton in 1871, the first woman to be employed there. Florence loved animals, which is reflected in her work. She brought frogs, mice and other small animals into the studio, an activity that was unpopular with her colleagues. By the 1880s her work was recognised and she had become a celebrated artist.

John Sparkes' notes, taken from *Nineteenth Century English Ceramic Art by J. F. Blacker*, record:'The artist who has given to the new Doulton ware one of its strongest characters is Miss Hannah B. Barlow. Miss Barlow's quick sketches of animals show an intense feeling for the spirit of the beasts and birds represented. These etched out figures are, so to speak, instantaneous photographs of the creatures. She possesses a certain Japanese facility of representing the largest amount of fact in the fewest lines, all correct, and all embodying in a high degree the essential character of her subject. Yet there is little tendency to run into a picturesque treatment, but the firmness of her work for the manufacture, the recognition of the limitations under which the designs are made, are all eminently kept in view in all her work.'

Hannah's sculpture and paintings were exhibited at the Dudley Art Gallery, Royal Society of British Painters, 1880–90, at the Society of Woman Artists and at the Walker Art Gallery, Liverpool. She exhibited modelled terracotta plaques at the Royal Academy in the 1880s. From 1895 her drawing became more detailed, with the borders becoming a more prominent feature. She won medals for her work in exhibitions at Nice in 1884, Paris in 1900 and St Louis in 1904. She retired in 1906. Her work is often incised with her monogram HBB.

Barlow, Lucy, born 1850

Artistic designer, initially working with her sisters Florence and Hannah in the same studio at Doulton, Lambeth. In 1881 she is described as an art student but by 1891 as an artistic designer. After some three years at the studio she decided to return home and keep house for her sisters. In 1901 she had moved to 33 South Side, Clapham, Wandsworth, now described as living on her own means.

Barnard, Harry, 1863–1933

Artist modeller and designer, born in Islington, London, the eldest son of a silversmith. He studied at the London Art School under John Sparkes, then gained employment at the Doulton Lambeth Studio, decorating ornamental vases and commemorative jugs under Mark V. Marshall. In 1884 he was appointed manager of the Studio but had a disagreement with Wilton P. Rix, then Doulton's Art Director, and left. In 1891 he was living with his wife and daughter at 38 Lilleshall Road, Clapham, Surrey described as artist, modeller and designer of pottery. In 1895 he joined J. Macintyre of Cobridge, where he introduced a form of pâte-sur-pâte decoration, which he called Gesso. In1901 he was shown in the census as living at Somerset Villa, Penkhull, and his occupation changed to ceramic artist and manager, Stoke-upon-Trent. Two years later he went to Wedgwood as a decorator of bone china and majolica tiles, becoming manager of the tiles department in 1899. However, by 1902 he had been moved to London to Wedgwood's retail branch, returning to Etruria in 1919 to help John Cook in the expansion of the works museum and to model in 1923 a new edition of the Portland vase. He continued to work on individual pieces and in 1927 modelled a large black basalt panel with designs of the potter at work and a quotation from Kipling's poem *The Rubaiyat of Omar Kal'vin*. He was the author of *Chats on Wedgwood Ware*, published in 1924. He became a well-known lecturer on Wedgwood and continued to design and model until his death.

Barratt, Robert, born 1876

Artist and painter, the son of George Barratt, an accountant and estate agent, who was apprenticed at the Royal Crown Derby manufactory about 1890 and continued to study at the Derby Art School in the evenings for fifteen years. In the 1891 census he is described as a designer apprentice living with his parents at 5 Victoria Terrace Street, Werburgh, Derby.

He became an artist and watercolourist, painting flowers with great skill. By 1901 he was living at 67 Macklin Street, Derby, described as a china artist (painter). He went to Australia with W.E. Mosely in 1932. Barratt left the factory to become a civil servant but continued to paint watercolours. He was a lover of sport, particularly of tennis, having his own tennis court, a keen gardener and a great friend of Cuthbert Gresley (q.v.). He died in 1940.

Barrett, active 1845-1850

Painter at W.T. Copeland, Stoke-upon-Trent, capable of painting all subjects with equal skill. Listed as Barrett, Barrett and Co and Barratt Leason and Co, and Glover and Barrett. The significance of these alternative names is not known, but the combination suggests that Barrett led a group of decorators. Barrett is shown to have painted only on highly decorated china dessert services and tea sets. There are over forty entries attributed to him with pattern numbers. Another Barrett is listed in 1893 as painting Game centres (central landscape depicting a game bird).

Barry, Alfred, active 1900s

Painter and modeller first employed with the Grainger Worcester pottery. He was their premier painter and modeller capable of executing and overseeing reticulated ware. In 1902 he went to Royal Worcester Porcelain Factory. He lived in Worcester at Cole Hill, later at 35 Stanley Road.

Bateman, Samuel, born 1850

Landscape and marine painter at Wedgwood, who painted tiles, vases and plaques. He was at Wedgwood when Frederick Rhead was experimenting with the Barbotine style of painting and the use of painted slip. Samuel was the only artist at the Pottery who mastered these techniques. In 1881 he was living as a lodger at 62 Penkhull New Road, Stoke-upon-Trent, described in the census as an artist painter. By the 1890s he left the ceramic industry, went to London and became a landscape oil painter.

Bates, David, 1842–1921

Artist and flower painter, born in Cambridgeshire and trained at the Royal Worcester Porcelain Factory, known for his floral studies but did not sign his work. After he left the ceramic industry he painted in watercolours and oils. In 1871 he is described as artist in oil and watercolour landscape. From then on he is described as a landscape painter living at Great Malvern and later in Edgbaston, Birmingham.

Bates, R. W., active 1900s

Landscape painter known to have decorated dessert plates at the Cauldon China Factory, Stoke-on-Trent. Usually the name of the landscape is on the reverse of the plate and it is signed.

Battam, Frederick, born 1818

Decorator, enameller and pottery designer, born in St Brides, Middlesex, son of Thomas and Louise, thought to have been employed in the family business but in what capacity is not known.

In 1859 he founded the Crystal Palace Art Union with his brother Thomas. The subscription was one guinea, for which the subscriber could choose his annual presentation piece from any of the Parian on exhibition instead of being allocated the prize selected by the union for that year. The Crystal Palace Art Union, patronised by Queen Victoria, was a success. Frederick and his brother Thomas ran it as a business and when Thomas died suddenly, Frederick became the sole director, changing the name to the Ceramic and Crystal Palace Art Union and operating from a new address, Regent Street, London. In 1861 he was living at 47 Notting Hill Square, Kensington with his wife Mary Ann and two children, described as artist for china manufactory. By 1891 the family had moved to Beckingham Cottage, Clarence Road, Bromley, Kent and he is described as a dealer in china and glass, living next door to his brother John H. Battam, who is described as a retired china decorator. He is probably the J. H. Battam shown in the last accounts of the Ceramic and Crystal Palace Art Union of 1882, who loaned then £111. 9s. 6d but was repaid when he took over the models of the Union.

Battam, Thomas, F.S.A., c. 1814–1864

Artist, painter and art superintendent. Born in London, the son of Thomas and Louisa (née Harrison), he was trained in his father's decorating business in London. Thomas became Copeland's Art Superintendent in 1835 at the age of twenty-five. The *Art Union Journal* of November 1846 described him as: 'An artist of classical taste, whose great natural abilities have been cultivated by assiduous study, and whose inventive genius is too powerful to be confined within the dull limits of ordinary routine.'

His ability to respond to market trends, particularly in the discovery and marketing of the new body Parian and to maintain the standard of design and quality of new ware decorated with innovative designs, was the secret of W.T. Copeland's success at the time. He exhibited their products at all the great exhibitions of the day, both at home and abroad. In 1851 he encouraged the potters to support the Great Exhibition, organising and speaking at meetings held in the six towns known as the Potteries. Thomas became a friend and mentor to the young Alfred Copeland (son of William Taylor Copeland) who ran Copeland's London business and wrote in his memoirs: 'Now in trade when I came on the scene Battam had done great things for W.T. Copeland... In 1855 Battam did well and in the International Exhibition, 1862 we did well.' However, the most important entry about Battam in Alfred's diary of 1895 was: 'After a while Battam had a shine [became annoyed] and he went, but a year or two afterwards I got him back...'. The disagreement was thought to have been due to the appointment of William Henry Goss, whose jewelled designs would not have been approved by Battam.

He married Mary Scarbrow in May 1845 and in 1851 they were living at Trent Vale with one servant, before moving to Heron Cottage in Great Fenton, about a mile from Stoke Station. But in September 1855 *The Staffordshire Advertiser* showed the coming sale of Battam's residence, a particularly fine house with stabling for four horses surrounded by gardens and pleasure grounds. The hall was twenty-seven feet in length and the principal room thirty-three feet long, and the mis-named cottage had nine bedrooms.

Battam's decision to leave Copeland was far-reaching. He went to London to manage the formation of the art department at the Crystal Palace, by then re-erected at Sydenham. He had persuaded many well-known dignitaries both at home and abroad to lend pieces. The collections traced the making of pottery from its inception, showing the work of British and Continental manufacturers.

In 1858 Thomas formed the Crystal Palace Art Union with his brother Frederick Battam (q.v.). He was one of the Jurors for the Pottery Class at the International Exhibition, 1862 and he became a Fellow of the Society of Arts. Eventually he returned to W.T. Copeland to resume his post as Art Superintendent but the exact date is so far not known.

Thomas was a fine artist who painted copies of masterpieces on large bone china plaques and was patronised by the Duke of Sutherland. He remained with W.T. Copeland until his sudden death at 5 Aubrey Villas, Notting Hill, London on 28 November 1864.

Baxter, Thomas, 1782–1821

Fruit, flower and landscape painter. Born in Worcester, son of Thomas who was a decorator and gilder at the Worcester Pottery. He trained with his father, learning how to paint with ceramic colours. The family moved to No 1 Goldsmiths Street, Gough Square, London, where they established a successful decorating studio. In October 1800 Thomas enrolled as a student at the Royal Academy School at Somerset House in the Strand, where he received drawing lessons from Henry Fuseli (q.v.), Professor of Painting who in 1804 was appointed Keeper of the Academy Schools. Thomas continued to work in the family business decorating white Coalport pieces and other English and Chinese porcelains. In 1801 it is said he painted vases with portraits of Emma Lady Hamilton that were probably bought by Horatio Nelson and, in 1802 he was invited to Merton, Nelson's country house, to make sketches of the surrounding neighbourhood. He became known as a painter of figure subjects and miniaturist and in 1802 exhibited at the Royal Academy and continued to do so until his death. His work was highly sought after in London. In 1808 he married Ann Roberts of Middlesex. They had one son Thomas (who became a school master and was a fine musician and naturalist) and four daughters. Baxter enhanced his reputation by engraving the plates for his book *An Illustration of Egyptian, Grecian and Roman Costume*, dedicated to Henry Fuseli and published in 1810, the year he completed his studies at the Royal Academy. In 1814 he was forced to leave London due to ill health and returned to Worcester, where the family lived in Edgar Street near to the Cathedral. He founded a school of art, teaching Astles, Cole, Doe, Pitman and Webster. His father joined him having closed the London decorating business. Thomas was decorating for Flight and Barr as an independent artist specialising in painting figure subjects; he also painted portraits and miniatures. His work is exhibited at the Worcester Museum.

In 1816 Lewis Weston Dillyn commissioned him to paint the fine porcelain produced at his Cambrian Pottery in Swansea, and as his relationship with the Worcester pottery had become strained he readily accepted. He was now allowed to choose the pieces he wished to paint and they were an immediate success, selling well in London. But by 1817 Dillyn was forced to transfer the pottery lease to the Bevington family because of a family trust and Thomas became redundant. He now advertised for business as a drawing master, miniaturist and portrait painter from his home in Goat Street, on the corner of which was the Theatre Royal. By 1817 Swansea had developed into a well-known seaside town and he hoped to attract commissions from the visiting gentry. He also spent many hours drawing scenes in and around the area. In 1818 he published six views of Swansea priced at 10s. 6d. Unfortunately he was not successful and having a family to support was forced to return to Worcester to seek more permanent employment at the Flight and Barr pottery. Again difficulties arose between him and the management and he moved to Chamberlain Worcester Porcelain, where his work was more appreciated. He stayed with this pottery until his early death at the age of thirty-nine.

Thomas is known for fine-detailed painting of figures, including scenes from Shakespeare or Scott's novels. He exhibited sixteen times at the Royal Academy 1802–21, being elected an Associate in 1801, the year in which he also painted enamels for George III. Slowly he established a reputation for producing enamels on metal, the best of which are in the Royal Collection at Buckingham Palace, such as the well-known *The Holy Family after Parmigiano*, 21 x 15 in, which was bought by George IV for £1,500. In 1815 the Nabob of Oude ordered a service from Worcester and Baxter is known to have painted dancers in a landscape setting. His landscapes had misty backgrounds with the figures and buildings painted in great detail. The painting by Thomas Baxter of his father' s studio at No1 Gough Street, London now in the Victoria & Albert Museum, which was exhibited in the Royal Academy in 1811, shows a typical decorating paint shop. Baxter was an artist of rare talent, mastering not only the use of oils and watercolours but also painting with ceramic colours.

Beard, John, 1787–1862

Painter and gilder who worked at the Nottingham Road, Derby Pottery. The 1851 census shows John Beard, born in Derby now aged 64, china painter and gilder, whose sons were Alfred, born in Stoke, and John, born in Derby in 1816. In 1851 he is listed as a china painter. However, in the Minton estimate book 1831to 1842 a John Beard is described as a landscape painter. It is therefore possible that John Beard trained and worked in Derby, left to go to Minton (his son was born in Stoke) then returned to Derby.

Beard, Sarah, born 1833.

Paintress employed at Minton for nearly seventy years. She was a daughter of John Evans and her son William (q.v.) was an engraver for Minton.

Beard, William, 1869–1950

Engraver son of Sarah (q.v.), first employed at Minton as an errand boy and feldspar washer. He then became an apprentice engraver who worked for Minton all his life. He was a fine swimmer and trained the Stoke-on-Trent swimming team.

Beardsmore, Evelyn Hope, 1886–1972

Paintress, known as Hilda, born in Stoke-on-Trent and trained at the local Art School. She first worked for Wedgwood, painting powder blue and lustre wares, and became head of the lustre department. During WWI she worked at the Bernard Moore decorating establishment at Wolfe Street in Stoke-on-Trent, a member of a team of painters and artists that included D.M. Millington and Hilda Lindop. Bernard Moore decorated the ware manufactured by the family firm and also took in decorating from other potteries. The decorations were influenced by the designs of William de Morgan, some having Middle Eastern themes. During the Bernard Moore period Hilda signed her work with a monogram.

Beddow, George, born 1813

Landscape and heraldic painter, the principal artist at Swansea and employed throughout the whole of their porcelain manufacturing period. He continued to decorate the residual stock after the factory closed c. 1826. George was a friend of William Pollard (q.v.) and is thought to have been employed by him c. 1844 in Swansea. Scarratt said he was at the Ridgeway Pottery again painting landscapes. He is shown in the 1851 census as living in Hanley, Staffordshire.

Bednall, Samuel, active 1880s

Artist gilder at the Osmaston Road, Derby factory, who worked on raised and chased floral sprays. He may then have moved to the Coalport Pottery c. 1890.

Bejot, Edouard, 1836–1885

Artist gilder, who worked first from his Paris studio but was persuaded to come to the Royal Worcester pottery. He is known to have gilded a pair of vases, a gift to Queen Victoria from a group of Worcester ladies, which are said to have cost £600. He returned to France and died in Paris.

Bell W., active 1860–1880

Artist gilder at Copeland, where he trained is not known. He executed intricate gilding designs and jewelling on all types of ware from vases to tea services. The only ones recorded in the Copeland Special Order books are pattern number D9369, a tea service, and pattern number D7941, a bon-bon dish, gilded and tinted. Recorded as decorating some of the fine work of the painter Golterman (q.v.).

Benbow, John, born 1813

Landscape painter, born in Broseley and shown in the Coalport Wages Book, pattern number 3/730, as painting landscapes. The wages book show he was paid £2.10s.0d for one week, denoting a skilful and valued artist, but whether he was allowed to sign his work is not known.

Bennett, Enoch Arnold, 1867–1913

Amateur painter, born In Hanley, Staffordshire, the son of a solicitor. He was a student at the art classes held at the Wedgwood Institute, Burslem. But he became famous as a writer, his novels including *Anna of the Five Towns*. His brother Septimus, born 1876, was a student at the Wedgwood Institute Burslem, 1886–88, and became a ceramic modeller.

Bennett, Harold R.I., NRD, 1893–1976

Landscape artist and designer, born in Congleton, Cheshire. He trained at the Hanley School of Art and taught for a time at the Leek School of Art. In 1929 he found employment at Burgess & Leigh, becoming art director after Charlotte Rhead left. His designs were inspired by nature and depicted country flowers in clear bright colours. He became a lifetime member of the Staffordshire Society of Artists, exhibited at the Manchester Academy of Fine Arts and was elected to the Royal Institute of Painters in Watercolour in 1956. He also exhibited at the Royal Academy, London.

Bentley A. F., 'Bert', active 1891–1936

Modeller at Wedgwood, Etruria, who trained under Harry Barnard (q.v.) and in the 1890s worked on the slip-decorated vases in the *Magnolia* range of wares. In 1919 he was associated with the production of the new edition of the Portland vase. He then worked chiefly with Jaspar, modelling portrait medallions with wreath borders. His initials and an elongated 'O' impressed in the clay can be found on some of his work. He also did portraits of Inigo Jones, who was mispelt as Indigo. He retired in 1935 having earned a reputation as a fine craftsman.

Bentley, Henry, active 1860s–70s

Parian figure-maker at the Minton pottery, son of Henry Bentley. He was apprenticed at Minton as a Parian maker but known to have left before 1882 (very few either model makers or Parian modellers are noted in any factory records).

Bentley, Leonard, active 1880s

Flower painter at Doulton, Burslem. He painted the floral designs of John Slater (q.v.), known as the Spanish style. When Cecil Nokes (q.v.) joined Doulton he studied under Bentley, who was a fine ceramic painter of great speed and accuracy, rare in those days.

Beresford, Charles, active 1895–1922

Landscape painter at the Royal Doulton factory, who painted lakes and mountain scenes. He may have either signed or initialled his work.

Betteley, Herbert, active 1886–1930

Artist gilder and designer, affectionately known as Harry. He studied at the Burslem School of Art and was employed at Doulton, but also worked freelance local potteries. He designed gold patterns, many of which were used to decorate the ware sent to the World's Columbian Exposition, Chicago of 1893. John Slater (q.v.), the Art Director, instructed him to train a team of artists and craftsmen. Friendly competition in the department worked well, producing excellent design. His work is signed HB with a number.

Besche, Lucien, active 1870s

Painter of figure subjects and outside decorator. He was trained in France and came to Minton in 1871, possibly because of the turmoil in France at that time. He soon joined Copeland, whether as a freelance artist is not known. In 1872 Besche is shown in the Copeland Special Order books as painting Watteau subjects and figures, mainly on dessert plates and vases, although his work has also been seen on large plaques. Unfortunately none of the entries show a pattern number but are descriptive of his creative style:

'1873 Mortimer shaped vase – large vase with perforated panels, Birds and Flies by Weaver, paid £10 guineas, Figures by Besche, paid £3/2/6d, gilding by

Porcelain dessert plate painted by L. Besche c. 1890

L. Besche signature

Owen; March 1873 Cecil shaped vase – large vase, Flowers, four days to paint, figures by Besche, paid £8.15.10, Muller 5 shillings'.

The entries also show he painted after the style of Rischgitz (q.v.); he did scenes from Aesop's *Fables* and from *Don Quixote*. Copeland sent many examples of his work to the 1873 Universal Exhibition in Vienna.

Besche and Charles Ferdinand Hurten (q.v.) became great friends and he married Emme Amelia, one of Hurten's daughters. They lived in Regent Street, Stoke-on-Trent, very near to the Spode works and owned another house in Milton Place, Stoke, which he rented to Hurten. Besche exhibited miniatures at the Royal Academy from 1883 to 1885; G. Wolliscroft Rhead wrote: 'He emigrated to London and confined himself to 'black and white' and painting in oils.' In London Besche illustrated books, and is known to have had a great interest in the theatre, possibly designing scenery and costumes for comic operas. By 1884 he had returned to the Potteries, renting a studio from a Miss Harvey on Trentham Road, Stoke-upon-Trent. He was an artist of rare creative talent, able to paint with skill not only on a ceramic surface but also in oils on canvas. He signed his work. L. B. or L. Besche.

Billingsley (Beeley), William, 1758–1828

Flower painter, outside decorator and manufacturer, born in Derby on 12 October 1758, the son of William, a flower painter at Derby, and Mary. He became an apprentice at the Nottingham Road Works, Derby at the age of sixteen for a period of five years at a salary of 5 shillings a week. His talent was soon recognised and he became the principal flower painter at Derby, succeeding Edward Withers (q.v.). Billinsley developed a naturalistic style, painting roses in his own special way by loading the brush with colour then slowly wiping it off, creating depth and naturalistic colours. He was allocated the painter's number 7, and lived at 22 Bridge Gate, Derby. The house had a small kiln in the lower storey. He became a great friend of Zechariah Boreman (q.v.), from whom he learnt painting, and together they experimented in making china bodies and new glazes. He left Derby in 1796 and it was said then that all his life he searched for a recipe for porcelain to equal that of the Sèvres manufactory in France, which was to cause him financial and personal problems.

In 1796, he and John Coke of Debdale Hall, near Mansfield (the son of the Rev. D'Ewes Coke of Brookhill Hall) established the Pinxton Pottery at the head of the Cromford Canal, with easy access to Mansfield. Billingsley mixed the clay himself but the quality of the ware produced varied greatly. The secret recipe he devised was not known even to his partner. In 1799 Billingsley left, but the Pottery continued to be run by John Coke until 1803 and then by Mr John Cutts. In 1813 Billingsley set up as an independent decorator at Belvedere Street, Stockwell Gate, Mansfield, Nottinghamshire. He bought white china from Staffordshire and decorated it along with fellow decorators George Hancock and Joseph Tatlow. In 1802, he and Henry Banks founded a porcelain works at Torksea Links near Gainsborough on the banks of the Trent, but it soon became bankrupt. The property passed to a group, which included Billingsley and his son-in-law George Walker. When Billingsley and Walker went to Flight and Barr's factory in Worcester looking for work in 1808, Billingsley was taken on only as a hired hand. However, between 1809 and1812 he and Walker were in the mixing room, experimenting with a new porcelain body and improving the kilns.

Briefly in 1811 he went to the Coalport factory, but in 1813 he started the Nantgarw Pottery with George Walker, in a small village was alongside the Glamorgan Canal, ideal for transporting not only the ingredients to make the pottery but also the finished goods to port at Cardiff, only eight miles away. Here for the first time he was his own master and had William Weston Young as a financial partner. Billingsley sold the entire output of the factory as white unfinished ware to outside enamellers in London, making mainly plates. In 1814 the business was sold to Lewis Weston Dillyn, owner of the Cambrian works at Swansea, where two new kilns were built to cope with the extra output. Walker developed a new soft-paste body, which became known as Swansea duck egg porcelain. Mr Dillwyn sold ware in London but kept some to be decorated at his pottery by Thomas Baxter, David Evans and Henry Morris, who had been apprenticed under Billingsley.

In 1817 Billingsley returned to the Nantgarw works and some manufacture was resumed. William Weston Young had raised more money and ten additional gentlemen subscribed another £1000; yet by 1822 this business had failed and Young was the sole owner of the Nantgarw buildings and contents.

By 1820 Billingsley and Walker again moved, entering into a seven-year partnership with Mr Rose of Coalport to manufacture their porcelains; they moved all their moulds and equipment to Coalport. This was a shrewd move on the part of Rose as he now produced patterns similar to those of both Nantgarw and Swansea and therefore effectively removed their competition from the marketplace. Billingsley died on 16 January 1828 and was buried in an unmarked grave at Kemberton, near Coalport. Many accounts have been written on this artist's life but that of John Haslem in his book *The Old Derby Pottery* records his turbulent life with sensitivity drawing on Billingsley's letters.

Billington, Dora, 1890–1968

Paintress, studio potter and teacher, trained at Tunstall and Hanley School of Art and in 1913 went to Bernard Moore's Pottery, were she painted flowers and foliage. She then went to the Government School of Design, South Kensington, London and in 1926 taught pottery, eventually taking charge of the art department at the Central School of Arts and Crafts in London. She designed for pottery firms, including J. & G. Meakin. In the early 1930s her work showed originality of form and treatment. She encouraged her students to develop their own individual ideas and standards through experimentation and a wide range of interests and techniques. Her work was widely exhibited and was respected in both academic and art circles. She became President of the Arts and Crafts Exhibition Society and was author of *The Art of the Potter.*

Bilton, Louis, active late 1800s

Flower and bird painter, trained under William Mussill (q.v.) at the Minton pottery. He then went to Australia where he painted watercolours of the local flora and fauna, which were published in the *Picturesque Atlas.* Returning to England, he joined Doulton in 1892 until 1911, bringing a portfolio of Australian flowers, which he used to great effect on their ware. In 1893 vases he painted with floral studies were sent to the Exhibition in Chicago. Many of his designs were lithographed. Examples of his work are in museums in both Australian and New Zealand. In 1900 he wrote an excellent article for *The Pottery Gazette and Glass Trade Review* on the decoration of pottery, speaking of the need for co-operation between those involved in art education and in manufacturing.

Birbeck, Alfred, born 1853

Floral and landscape painter, the son of Francis (q.v.) and cousin of Holland Birbeck. (q.v.) He trained at the Coalport pottery but went to Devon, living in Torquay 1878–88. Whether he painted as a freelance artist or was employed at the Watcombe pottery is not known. He signed his work.

Birbeck, Charles James, 1860–1933

Flower and fish painter, watercolour artist and art director, born in Stoke-on-Trent, Staffordshire and trained at the Hanley School of Art, where in the mid-1880s he became a part-time art master. He joined George Jones and Sons' Crescent Pottery, becoming their designer. In 1881 he was living at James Street, Stoke-on-Trent, a short walk to the Pottery. By 1895 he was appointed Art Director, continuing to serve the company for fifty-four years. Charles was a member of the first sketching club in Hanley in 1882 and he also painted in oils. He retired in 1931 and died two years later. His work is signed in full or initialled.

Birbeck, Donald Toulouse, 1886–1968

Bird and animal painter, the grandson of Francis (q.v.). He was trained at the Cauldon works in Shelton, Stoke-on-Trent and at local art schools. In 1931 he went to the Osmaston Road, Derby pottery as one of their premier artists, painting game and fish services. His work has a unique naturalistic look. Donald retired in the early 1960s.

Bone china Cauldon Vase signed D. Birbeck c. 1990 decorated with the Imperial Eagle (*Aquila Helica*)

Birbeck, Francis, born 1822

Artist gilder, born at Sutton Maddock, Shropshire, son of Joseph (1798). He was at the Coalport factory during the 1840s and again in the 1870s as an artist gilder. His work was shown in the Exposition Universelle, Paris of 1878, and was described by John Randall in his contribution to the *Victoria County History of Shropshire*: 'Mr Francis Birbeck was happy in the production of gems and in the art of gilding'. Many patterns are shown with either the initials FB or his name. In 1859 he is shown in the Coalport painters bills as being paid £5.10s.0d, a very large sum of money for those days. In 1881 he was living at 22 West Street, Stoke-on-Trent. The W.T. Copeland Special Order books show his painting of intricate gold designs on tiles and dessert services from 1882 to 1884. His artistic talent was inherited by his two children, Alfred and Joseph.

Birbeck, Henry Turner (Harry), 1888–1956

Painter and watercolour artist, the son of John Holland (q.v.). He worked at the Watcombe pottery, where his artistic talent was recognised and encouraged. In the early 1900s it is thought he left Watcombe to join Charles Collard, who had by then set up his own pottery. He played football and spent many happy hours with his friends sketching the bird life on the Devon coast and painting watercolours of the harbours. In WWI Harry enlisted with the Royal Engineers, serving in France. During the depression of the 1920s he worked as a qualified electrician, but painting was his true metier and soon he and friends Harry Crute and Tom Lemon opened a pottery at Daison. By 1929 the pottery had to close and Harry found employment with the local council. He had always hoped to return to his first love of painting but died aged 68.

Birbeck, John Holland, 1853–1898

Bird and flower painter, born in Coalport, the son of William (q.v.) and trained by his father at Copeland. He left to work for Brown-Westhead, Moore & Co. and Co. and then went to Torquay, Devon to work for the Torquay Terra Cotta Co. In 1878 they exhibited at the Exposition Universelle, Paris a pair of plaques painted and signed by JHB, one with storks and herons and the other a magpie, which were highly praised. From 1878 to 1888 he was one of the chief artists for the Watcombe Pottery, Devon, producing fine work, some of which is signed. He married Sarah Turner, daughter of the proprietor of the Royal Hotel, Babbacombe Downs in 1877. He gave private art tuition and some of his pupils won prizes at the local art festival. A bee or a butterfly is seen in many of his paintings, which are signed.

Birbeck, Joseph (Senior), 1798–1867

Painter, born in Worcester in the district of St Peters, and trained at Chamberlain Worcester Porcelain. In the 1820s he went to Coalport, where he painted floral studies and specialised in roses and fruit. In 1844 he became foreman of painters. His four sons Joseph, Francis, William and Thomas were also painters employed at Coalport. It is more than possible that Joseph was responsible for a team of painters, hence the entry in the Coalport wages book 'Joseph Birbeck and Co'. This team painted both his designs and other patterns. The entry 3/612 by 'Birbeck's girls' (the paintresses in his decorating shop) supports this view. His work is to be found on pattern numbers 2/242, 2/893, 3/108.

Birbeck, Joseph, born 1820

Ground layer and painter, the son of Joseph (q.v.). He was employed at the Coalport pottery and would have been part of his father's team of decorators. He worked from about 1851–80, eventually becoming foreman of an enamelling team, and was also responsible for all hand-painted, transfer-printed ware.

Birbeck, Joseph (Junior), born 1855

Landscape painter son of Joseph (q.v.), born in Coalport, Shropshire. He trained at the Coalport pottery, where he was at one time foreman of a painting shop. He is noted for painting fine landscapes after Turner (q.v.) He may have been employed at the Bodley pottery in Longton, Staffordshire before joining Copeland in 1881; he was then living at 15 James Street, Stoke-on-Trent. He painted fine landscapes signed and named on dessert ware. When at the Brown Westhead & Moore pottery he established his reputation as a fine artist, often painting fish services. In 1900–26 he joined Doulton, becoming one of their foremost artists. His underwater scenes provided a realistic setting for the fish studies he painted. His natural history interests were furthered by collecting birds eggs, fossils and butterflies.

Bone china Royal Doulton dessert plate painted and signed by J. Birbeck

Birbeck, Philip, born 1830

Painter and gilder who worked at the Coalport pottery from 1851–70s. He is shown in the Coalport painters' bills of 29 January 1859 as earning £3.10s.0d., a large amount of money at this time. He may have been part-owner of the Elephant and Castle pub in the High Street at Broseley, as he was often to be found there and the 1881 census records him as licensed victualler and china painter.

Birbeck, William (Senior), 1796–1870

Artist painter, born in Worcester and apprenticed at the Chamberlain's Pottery, he specialised in landscapes and bird painting. By1846 he was employed at the Minton pottery, where he is known for painting birds in the Dresden and oriental style. He also established himself as a crest and heraldic painter for china dinnerware. He is shown in the 1841 *Pigot's Royal National and Commercial Dictionary* as living at 84 Market Place, Hanley as a landscape and portrait painter. He is described by Scarrett as 'a fine figure of a man and esteemed by all who knew him'. He married In 1827 Mary Alabaster; then Anne Bella Alabaster in 1840. His son William Henry, born 1827, became an accountant but Charles James (q.v.) and William Albert Ernest (q.v.) became notable ceramic painters.

Birbeck, William, 1825–86

Artist painter, born in Broseley, the son of Joseph (q.v.). He was first employed at the Coalport pottery, living then with his parent's and elder brother, Francis. By 1851 he had married Harriett, a china burnisher, and they had one son, John Holland (q.v.). The last reference to him in the Coalport pattern book is no. 6/336 c. 1855. He is known to have painted many Scottish views at Coalport and was one of their premier landscape artists. The family went to France in the late 1850s, where it is possible William worked at Sèvres, as his future work shows this French influence. By 1861 he is listed in the Shelton census returns as an artist painter aged thirty-seven known for painting cupids and flowers. When he first went to W.T. Copeland, he specialised in painting landscapes, particularly Watteau subjects, and birds. One entry in their Special Order books of 1879 shows the costing of £9.10s. for twelve plates, the centres painted by Birbeck. It is possibly he is the Birbeck shown to have been lodging at 134/5 Old Market Square in 1861 when looking for suitable home for his family. Interviewed by Leonard Whiter (author of *Spode*), Arthur Perry told of his admiration for his teacher William. Many examples of his signed work can be found and command a high price. By the 1880s Mr R. F. Abraham, Copeland's Art Director, employed William Yale (q.v.) to paint landscapes as he worked fast, and William was then asked to paint Chelsea bird designs. Such was his skill that he soon became equally well known for the bird designs and again his work was greatly sought after. He lived with his family in 1881 at 16 George Street, Stoke-upon-Trent near to the Spode Works. All who knew him regarded him with affection.

Birbeck, William Albert Ernest, 1866–1952

Floral painter, the son of William Henry and his second wife Ellen, and half-brother to Charles William. He was trained at the Hanley School of Art and by 1881 was living with his parents at 11 Newcastle Road, Shelton and had joined his brother at George Jones and Sons' Crescent Pottery. An artist capable of painting all subjects, who signed his work, he was known especially for his design of a single rose surrounded by rose buds, the *Birbeck rose*. William was regarded as a good all-round painter capable of decorating in gold and ceramic colours. He was a likeable character and known to let foreign artists stay with him until they found suitable accommodation. By 1943 he had left the Crescent Pottery and applied for a job at W.T. Copeland, where he was interviewed by one of his old apprentices, Harold Holdway (q.v.), by then Art Director. Needless to say he got the job and decorated Copeland ware to the same high standard he had always set himself. He was eighty-five years of age when he died in 1952 at Stockton Brook, Staffordshire.

Bird, active c. 1840

Crest painter at the Copeland and Garrett pottery and, after the dissolution of this partnership, for W.T. Copeland until 1849. He is listed in the Special Order books as both Bird, and also Bird and Co, showing he had a team working for him.

Bird, Edward, active 1772–1819

Floral and painter of figure subjects who was apprenticed at the Old Hall, later the Ryton Works, Wolverhampton, which produced *papier-mâché* and tinware. He became well known for his painting on enamels in the late 1700s. Such was the delicacy of his work that his painted centres have been taken from tea trays and framed. He moved to the Japan and Pontypool Manufactory, Temple Back, Bristol.

Edward taught art and one of his pupils was Edward Rippingille, a supporter of the foundation of the Pottery Schools of Design. Bird turned to painting pictures, which were exhibited at Bath and at the Royal Academy. Examples of his work can be found at the Bantock House Museum, Wolverhampton.

Bone china Copeland dessert plate c. 1877. St Georges shaped plate painted with a view of Brunnen. Hand painted by William Birbeck. Courtesy of the Spode Copeland Collection, Trelissick, Cornwall

An unusual design of ceramic colour and polished gold by George Jones, Crescent Pottery, painted by William Birbeck

Birks, Alboin, born 1862–1941

Pâte-sur-pâte artist, born in Fenton, the son of Henry Birks (q.v.), a figure-maker and pottery manager of Pratt's pottery in Longton. Alboin went to the Minton pottery straight from school, where he was apprenticed as a surface modeller from 1876 to 1883. He specialised in pâte-sur-pâte decoration, training under Louis Marc Emmanuel Solon (q.v.), and spent all his working life at Minton. Tiffany's of New York, who requested a full signature on each piece, commissioned much of his work. He was known as being somewhat temperamental but kind-hearted. He lived at The White House, Clayton, near Newcastle-under-Lyme, Staffordshire. Birk's pâte-sur-pâte work is often signed. An artist of great skill, he was known in the area for his portraits painted in oils. He played cricket for the Trentham club and became captain of the Fenton cricket team; he was also was keenly interested in music.

Birks, Arthur Spode, 1833–1906

Modeller, the son of Isaac and Frances Mary (née Vigars). The family lived at Temple Street, Fenton, Staffordshire. He worked and probably trained at the Minton pottery. He was a man of considerable talent, who became chief modeller at Copeland. where he completed fifty-six years of service and on his retirement was presented with a large vase decorated with landscapes and finely gilded. He lived at 60 West Parade, Stoke-on-Trent, then moved to Dunwood Lane, a fine house near the shores of Rudyard Lake near to Leek in Staffordshire. He is listed in the 1881 census as a potters' modeller and a member of the Local Board of Health. He retired in November 1898.

Birks, Edward 1862–1889

Flower painter, the son of Joseph (q.v.), who trained at the Stoke School of Art 1875–89, winning a bronze medal in 1884 for flower painting and gold medals in 1885, 1886 and 1887. He was apprenticed at the Minton pottery from 1876 to 1883 and became a pupil teacher at Stoke Art School, where he specialised in flower painting. In 1875 he went to Pinder Bourne & Co. of Nile Street, Burslem, Staffordshire. John Slater (q.v.), the Art Director, thought very highly of his floral work painted in a traditional style. Signed examples are rare, but two of his floral studies were exhibited in the 1953 Century Exhibition in Hanley. After his death the committee of the Stoke School of Art made a donation of £10 to his widow in appreciation of his services to the School.

Birks, George (Junior), born 1819

Modeller, son of Joseph (q.v.). He was trained by his uncle (George Birks, a modeller, born in 1791) and was employed by the Minton pottery, modelling the figure *Literature* that was exhibited at the London 1862 International Exhibition. In 1865 his daughter Hannah married William Stanway, the son of John, an earthenware manufacturer.

Birks, Henry, born 1836

Pâte-sur-pâte artist, the father of Alboin and brother of Arthur Spode (q.v.). He is recorded as working in the tile department on studio tiles at the Minton pottery in 1876. He may well be the artist responsible for decorating with birds, flies, flowers and grasses a pair of vases recorded in the *Art Journal* for the London International Exhibition of 1862. In 1881 he was living at 111 Albert Road, Stoke-on-Trent and listed as a potter's foreman.

Birks, Lawrence Arthur, born 1857–1935

Pâte-sur-pâte artist, born in Fenton, Staffordshire the son of Arthur (q.v.). He served his apprenticeship as a modeller at the Minton pottery and was employed there from 1872 to 1894, working under Louis Marc Emmanuel Solon. He became a principal pâte-sur-pâte artist, signing his work. He left Minton to design and set up the Vine Manufactory with his brother-in-law Charles Frederick Goodfellow in Summer Street, off Corporation Street, Stoke-upon-Trent. They traded as Goodfellow Birks & Co., Staffordshire. However, five years later he designed a new factory with new partners, which traded as Birks Rawlins & Co. and which he managed for twenty-eight years. Lawrence designed and built the family home at Highfield House, Hanford, Staffordhire.

Bligh, John (Senior) (Bly), 1779–1833

Heraldic artist who in 1799 came to Chamberlain Worcester Porcelain from Lowestoft. He then joined Flight and Barr. It is thought he did the gilding and crests on the William IV service, also on the Lord Amherst Service in 1823. He died aged 54 at Carden Street, Worcester. His sons John and Jabez inherited his artistic talent: John painted landscapes and general subjects for Flight and Barr and Jabez became a freelance painter, exhibiting seventeen fruit studies at the Royal Academy from 1863–69, sixteen at the British Institute and six at the New Watercolour Society. A plaque with a scene of Worcester painted in a style similar to Grainger Worcester decoration has been attributed to Bligh (Senior).

Alboin Birks

Arthur Spode Birks

Lawrence Arthur Birks

Minton Vase decorated with pâte-sur-pâte decoration attributed to A Birks

Blore, Robert, 1812–1868

Modeller who was apprenticed at the Nottingham Road works Derby and joined the Minton pottery c. 1820, modelling animals, vases and ewers. He left to manage the Middlesborough Pottery, becoming an influential and popular member of the community until his death.

Booth, active 1890

Painter of birds of prey at Coalport. Some pieces with jewelled borders, decorated with birds, are known as *Hawking*. He may have been employed to paint only twelve patterns and possibly special pieces for the World's Columbian Exposition, Chicago of 1893.

Boothby, Harry, born 1873

Gilder, born in Fenton, Staffordshire, who was apprenticed at W.T. Copeland. He and Arthur Perry (q.v.) were lifelong friends. He was a gilder of great artistic skill responsible for many of the fine gilded borders of the 1920s.

Boreman, Zachariah, 1738–1810

Landscape and marine painter, born at Falconer Alley, Aldersgate, London. Possibly apprenticed to the Chelsea factory and worked for Nicholas Sprimont from 1755 to 1783, where he earned 5s.3d a day as chief artist. He was employed at the Derby pottery, where he signed an agreement with William Duesbury to stay for three years, earning two guineas a week but extra money for overtime. Boreman was one of the finest landscape artists known. He painted from nature; his paintings often had a winding river with minute figures in the foreground. He used soft colours, painting in the manner of a watercolour artist with wash backgrounds usually of a neutral tints and ochre-coloured skies. The sharp edges were wiped out with the wooden end of his brush. Paul Sandby (q.v.) is thought to have influenced his style. He also painted exotic birds and is thought to have been the artist who painted the Mecklenburg service, commissioned by Queen Charlotte from the Chelsea pottery as a present for her brother the Duke of Mecklenburg. Evidence from the weekly bills kept by Mr Barton (one-time London foreman for Mr Duesbury) shows that he also painted small models known as the Chelsea Toys. Boreman was popular with his colleagues and the management, becoming the friend, instructor and mentor of the young painter, Billingsley (q.v.). He taught him the art of ceramic painting and interested him in new ceramic bodies, which they fired in the kiln in the basement of Billingsley's house. Boreman left Derby to join Simms Decorating Establishment at 5 Fields Row, Pimlico, London, where he stayed until his death.

Bott, Thomas, 1829–1870

Painter and designer, born in Kidderminster and trained at the Richardson's Glass works at Wordsley, near Worcester in 1846. His paintings on glass were exhibited at the 1851 Great Exhibition. In 1853 he joined the Worcester Royal Porcelain Company, responsible for the so-called Limoges enamels, which were developed during the Kerr and Bins period, and painting plaques and portraits in white enamel on a dark grounds. He became one of their chief artists and foreman of the decorating department. Bott painted portraits, after Shakespeare, on the Midsummer Nights service exhibited at the Great Industrial Exhibition, Dublin of 1853. Prince Albert ordered a tray painted with a design after Raphael. Queen Victoria was delighted with the painting and ordered a large dessert service in a similar design. Bott exhibited two enamels at the Royal Academy, 1857–60. He signed and sometimes dated his work.

Bott, Thomas John, 1854–1932

Painter and outside decorator, the eldest son of Thomas (q.v.), a talented artist who inherited his father's ability, painting in the same style, especially Limoges enamelled ware. He became an apprentice at Worcester in 1866 and trained under R.W. Binns, eventually succeeding his father as principal artist. Sometime in 1875 Bott went to London to join the Brown-Westhead, Moore & Co. studio. After it closed, he remained in London as an independent decorator. By 1883 he had returned to Worcester, remaining a freelance artist and selling some of his work directly to Thomas Goode's of London. He painted fifty pieces for Brown-Westhead, Moore & Co. in the Limoges style, which were exhibited at the Exposition Universelle, Paris of 1889, where his work was awarded a silver medal. In 1881 he was living at Bath Road, St Peters, Worcester, described as an artist painter on porcelain. Bott spent the last years of his life as Art Director and General Manager for Coalport. He signed his work and some of it is dated. In 1892 he was living at 3 Princess Street, Stoke-on-Trent, Staffordshire. He died in 1932 aged seventy-seven.

The writer of his obituary in *The Pottery Gazette and Glass Trade Review* of 1 April 1932 tells of an interview with Bott in which he spoke with pride of his early days and his achievements. He described him as a modest man with a gentle demeanour, respected and revered by all his colleagues. Bott was buried at Broseley Cemetery and wreaths were sent from both the Cauldon potteries and the Coalport china works.

Bott, Thomas D., born 1861

Flower painter, born in Worcester. In 1881 he was living with his uncle, a shoe manufacturer, at 45 Sidbury,

Worcester St Michael. He met Charles Nokes (q.v.) at Worcester and they became great friends; he joined the Doulton pottery in 1889. His work was exhibited at the World's Columbian Exposition, Chicago of 1893. Signed pieces are rare.

Boullemier, Antonin Hilaire, 1839–1900

Artist and figure painter, born in Metz, France, where his father was a prominent artist at the Sèvres national porcelain factory. He served his apprenticeship as a painter of figure subjects at Sèvres, learning their style of decoration and use of colours. He studied under Hippolyte Evariste Etienne Fragonard (grandson of the famous painter) and trained in ceramic painting at the decorating establishment of Monsieur Dreyfus, a well-known ceramic artist. Antonin was a member of the National Guard and involved in the Siege of Paris. In 1870 he fled to England, joining the Minton pottery in c. 1872. Here he became famous for his fine figure painting of children playing games and of cupids. His work shows the influence of Watteau (q.v.), Boucher (q.v.) and Teniers (q.v.). In May 1873 the Prince of Wales bought a dessert service painted by Boullemier decorated with the adventures of Don Quixote after drawings by Gustave Doré.

Antonin enjoyed training the Minton apprentices and record books show he spent time touching up their work. He was a personal friend of Herbert Minton, but after a serious dispute with Colin Minton Campbell left and set up a decorating establishment in Penkhull New Road, Stoke-upon-Trent. But he continued to accept commissions from Minton. Leon Arnoux (q.v.) thought he was foolish, as his salary had been £400 a year, probably the highest paid at Minton at the time. In 1893 he received commissions from Brown-Westhead, Moore & Co. (which became Cauldon Ltd.), including the Shakespeare vase for the World's Columbian Exposition, Chicago. Between 1890 and 1892 he did some work for Coalport and in 1894 a pair of Minton vases, decorated in the old Sèvres style, were exhibited at the Imperial Institute, London, priced at £225 guineas. He exhibited miniatures at the Royal Academy c. 1881–82. His work was usually signed. The Rhead Brothers wrote of his work: 'It should be safe to say that in the whole of Staffordshire no person was more generally known or a greater favourite... his work will always obtain for him an honourable position in English ceramics...'.

Antonin was a bluff and jovial character; he rolled his own cigarettes, leaving a trail of tobacco wherever he went. He was popular and an accomplished bass singer, who had been offered the principal bass position at the Comic Opera, Paris – but he preferred to paint. His love of music was apparent when he conducted amateur performances and organised Penny Popular concerts at the Kings Hall, Stoke-upon-Trent. He died of a heart attack on 25 April 1900, just before his daughter's wedding. Yet the day before he had been

A Bone china Minton plate the centre painted by A Boullemier and portrait with signature. Courtesy of the Potteries Museum and Art Gallery

one of the judges of the art section of the exhibition of the Trentham Home Arts and Industries Society. In his address he advised the students who had exhibited to make a constant study of nature; and said that those who had not won a prize should not be discouraged, as though unsuccessful they must continue to work and persevere. They would find great satisfaction in work; in fact in work was the only satisfaction they would obtain in life and in it they would find a consolation for all their troubles.

Boullemier, Henry, active 1900s

Painter of figure subjects. Born in Stoke, from the age of thirteen he worked with his father Antonin (q.v.) at Minton, preparing colours. He painted in a similar style to his father. From 1901 to 1954 he obtained commissions from Doulton. He painted a rose bowl and cover with shepherdesses and sheep for the Crown Staffordshire Pottery in 1907. Henry succeeded his brother Lucien at the Minton factory after 1911, where he had his own studio. He served in the WWI in France and on his return went to the Royal College of Art before moving to France as a commercial artist. Eventually he returned to Stoke and it is thought he worked as a freelance artist, painting portraits, children, cherubs and female figures.

Boullemier, Lucien Emile, 1877–1949

Figure painter, born in Stoke, the son of Antonin (q.v.). He trained with his father at Minton, specialising in portraits and figure subjects. In 1905 he established a studio in Shelton and in 1911 was executing freelance work for Derby – ground-laid pieces were sent to him, which he decorated and returned to the factory, where they would then be gilded and fired. Lucian was a talented portrait artist; two of his portraits of Queen Victoria were bought by the Royal Family, and he painted the Duke of Windsor when Prince of Wales. Around 1904 he left Staffordshire to work for the Ceramic Art Company, Trenton, New Jersey, USA. Here he painted a set of four vases in the Sèvres style: the *Rose Vase*, *Woodland Vase*, *Grecian Vase* and the famous *Trenton Vase*, five-feet high and displayed at the Louisiana Purchase Exposition in St Louis in 1904. The views painted were taken from Emanuel Leutze's *Washington crossing the Delaware* and on the reverse was a winter scene of General Washington, possibly at Morristown. Lucien returned to England and in the early 1920s became Art Director for C.T. Maling and Sons Ltd, Newcastle-upon-Tyne, returning to the Potteries c. 1932. He was a fine athlete, enjoying water polo and was chairman of Stoke Swimming Club. He twice swam for the Staffordshire team and played football for Stoke City and Port Vale. He married and had one son and lived at 20 Eleanor Crescent, Westlands, Newcastle-under-Lyme, Staffordshire. During WWII he and his wife organised concerts for charity. When welfare officer at the Royal Ordinance Factory at Radway Green, staff formed their own concert party, called the Radway Jollies.

Portrait of Lucien Emile Boullemier Courtesy of the Potteries Museum and Art Gallery

Boullemier, Lucien, active 1940s

Painter and art director, son of Lucien (q.v.), who was trained by his father and succeeded him as Art Director of C.T. Maling and Sons, Newcastle-upon-Tyne in about 1956.

Boulton, active 1850–1890

Painter of figure subjects – cupids at Coalport, 1850–90, and cameo heads. Small finely painted studies, usually in profile and ornamented with jewel work.

Boulton, James, active 1880

Flower painter, who when thirteen years old was apprenticed to the Pinder Bourne and Co. pottery at Nile Street, Burslem, which in 1880 was taken over by Doulton. He painted dessert services, one of which was exhibited at the Chicago and other international exhibitions. He is known for painting rural scenes and children in underglaze blue colour.

Boulton, Sampson, born 1799

Artist and gilder who was employed at the Minton pottery from 1811–60. He became foreman of one the painters' decorating departments. His son Henry, who was born in 1822, became an apprentice at Minton aged twelve and eventually specialised in floral subjects.

Boulton, William, active 1878–1882

Painter of figure subjects at Copeland, on tiles and earthenware plaques. In 1881 he was living as a boarder at 21 Wood Street, Stoke-on-Trent. He copied the work of Sir Joshua Reynolds, *Miss Penelope Boothby*, on a china plaque in July 1880. No signed pieces have been found to date.

Boulton, William, born 1829

Artist gilder who worked at the Minton pottery. His work was shown at the Exposition Universelle, Paris of 1878. He became Superintendent of the earthenware decorating department at Minton. He is shown in the 1881 census as a foreman gilder potter living at 5 Park Terrace, Stoke-upon-Trent with his two sons: William, who was apprenticed as a gilder and Arthur, who attended the Stoke School of Art and served his apprenticeship as a painter at Minton 1877–1884.

Minton earthenware large Ewer, the painting attributed to Samuel Bourne c. 1845. Courtesy of the Potteries Museum and Art Gallery

Bourne, Samuel, 1789–1865

Freelance artist, landscape painter and designer, born in Norton-in-the-Moors, Staffordshire and trained under Wood and Caldwell of Burslem until 1818, when the firm closed. The Mason Pottery sales catalogue of 1822 shows 'Lot 1016 A, handsome Neapolitan Vase formed from the antique, beautifully painted in landscapes, enriched in burnished gold by S. Bourne', the reserve price being fifteen guineas. He is known to have painted a gouache and watercolour portrait of the Mason family at Wetley Abbey. In 1828 he joined the Minton Pottery, eventually becoming the chief designer. In September 1832, when living at Shelton, he held an exhibition of his paintings that was recorded in *The Staffordshire Advertiser*. Two of his paintings were used as book illustrations in *Teddesly Hall*, published by Bentley and Wear of Shelton in 1823 and in *Shelton Old Hall*, etched by J.F. Mullock. Some of his topographical paintings appear as engravings in *The Borough of Stoke-upon-Trent* by John Ward, published about 1843. One of his most interesting paintings was of a locomotive and train, one of the wagons being loaded with pottery, which was dedicated to the proprietors of the Birmingham and Liverpool Railroad. In 1847 he was appointed Professor of Ceramic Design at Marlborough House, London. He retired in 1863.

Bourne, Samuel, born c. 1822

Floral painter, son of Samuel (q.v.), who became a flower painter at W.T. Copeland. The first entry in the Special Order books at the Spode works for April 1858 records him painting cyclamen and hyacinths, and then later heaths and plants. But pattern number D 3626, c. 1864, painted by Bourne after Hurten, shows he had the ability to paint in the style of Hurten (q.v.) It is possible he left Copeland but which pottery he joined is not known. The 1881 census records Samuel Bourne and his wife living at living at 2 Ashwood Terrace, Stoke-on-Trent as an artist potter.

Bourne, active 1886–1891

Landscape painter at Copeland. There are eighteen entries in the Special Order books in the Spode archives showing Bourne painting landscapes; very rarely is there a record for floral painting. Whether he is connected to

Samuel Bourne (q.v.) is so far not known. Possibly he is the William Thompson Bourne, born 1847 in Hanley, in the 1881 census as living at 4 Prince Street, Stoke-on-Trent and described as a china painter.

Bourne, William, active 1880s

Known to have painted a Brownfield plaque, a portrait of a young girl, which is signed and dated 1881. Again family connections have not been established but the 1881 census shows a William Bourne, born in 1860, living at 151 Church Street, Stoke-upon-Trent, Staffordshire and described as a painter on china.

Bowdler, Arthur, 1842–1900s

Artist painter, born in Coalport, the son of Richard Bowdler, a china potter. In 1881 he was living at Park Street, Anstice Memorial, Madely, Shropshire. It is possible he was trained by William Cook and is known to have been a recognised artist at Coalport c. 1859, painting bird studies, beautiful landscapes and Sèvres-style floral studies on prestigious pieces. He became one of the Coalport's principal artists in the 1870s. Bowdler was especially noted for his simulated stones, particularly agates, on porcelain, which became fashionable for a short time. These stones were painted individually and their true effect depended upon the artists' skill in reproducing on the ceramic surface the varying tones of the stones chosen. When the fashion for this decoration faded Bowdler then switched to more conventional subjects. When sixty years of age, he again specialised, creating snowscapes of great beauty. He spent the whole of his working life at Coalport, surviving changes of style of both painting and management. Some of his work was signed.

Bowen, John, active 1760s

Painter, son of a Bristol watchmaker, who was apprenticed to John Weaver of the Limekiln Pottery Bristol in April 1734. He became an artist at the Joseph Flower Pottery, painting views with boats and scenery mainly in blue and white. He specialised in work free of the Chinese influence, which was rare at the time. His landscapes and figures and floral details were painted in the rococo style. One plate now lost did have a signature 'Bowen Fecit' on the reverse.

Bradbury, Richard, active1930s

Pâte-sur-pâte painter apprenticed to Alboin Birks at Minton. His work was either fully signed or initialled, mostly on dessert services. When Birks retired in 1937 Bradbury took over all his work and was the last pâte-sur-pâte artist employed by Minton. In 1939 he enlisted in the RAF.

Bradley, James (Senior), born c. 1810

Animal painter, employed at the Worcester pottery around 1852–60. He is known to have painted after Landseer (q.v.) and also Birket Foster (q.v.).

Bradley, James, born 1850

Painter of animals, flowers and figure subjects, born in Hanley, the son of James (q.v.). By 1881 he had moved to Worcester and was living at Green Hill, Bath Road, Worcester with his sister, Elizabeth. He was employed at the Worcester Kerr and Binns factory, specialising in painting dogs. He left the ceramic industry around 1891 to become an independent artist.

Bradley, John, 1786–1843

Artist painter, born at Buildwas near to Ironbridge. In 1812 he had a china warehouse at Coalbrookdale. Whether he was ever a painter at the Coalport manufactory has not been established. However, at the age of twenty-seven he enrolled in the Royal Academy School of Art. Some of Coalport, Swansea and Nantgarw designs have *J. Bradley and Company Pall Mall* printed on the reverse. *The Pottery Gazette and Glass Trade Review* of 1885 reported that the Bradley brothers had taught china decorating to the aristocracy and that they fired the work at Pall Mall. One of the brothers is known as being a painter on ivory, possibly the J. Bradley shown as exhibiting portraits in the Royal Academy 1817–43. In 1883 a James Bradley from Worcester is listed in Graves' *Dictionary of Painters* as exhibiting paintings of landscapes.

Bradley, (J.A.), active 1846–1859

Crest and armorial arms painter employed by Copeland and Garrett, and after the dissolution of their partnership, at W.T. Copeland at the Spode Works, Stoke-upon-Trent. He is listed in the Copeland Special Order books and is also known for painting musical emblems. A Mr J. A. Bradley, stated to be employed at Copeland, is reported in *The Staffordshire Advertiser* of 25 September 1851 as being awarded a medal at the Great Exhibition for painting ducks on china.

Bradley, Sarah, born 1833

Flower paintress, born at St Pancras, London who lived with her mother at 75 Pynest Street, Shelton. In the 1881 census she is shown as a potter's artist on china. Sarah decorated Brown-Westhead, Moore & Co. ware with birds and flowers, which was exhibited at the 1878 Exposition Universelle, Paris.

Brameld, John Wager, 1797–1851

Figure, landscape and flower painter and outside decorator. He and his brothers were partners in the Swinton Works (Rockingham). John collected floral specimens on all his travels and copied them as source material to create ceramic design. The vase depicting Don Quixote, now in the Rotherham museum, is an example of his work, some of which is signed. As a partner in the family business, his role was to see customers and manage the London shop and warehouse. His undoubted painting talent was not fully used, although he would have been heavily involved in the design of the King William IV dessert service, said to have cost £3000, and in other royal commissions. The service made for Queen Victoria was exhibited at Griffin Warehouse, Piccadilly, London. After the factory closed in 1842 he stayed in London, where he decorated and sold china from 7 Coburg Place, Bayswater. He exhibited Rockingham china at the Great Exhibition of 1851, where he is described as a manufacturer.

Brammer, active, c. 1820

A flower painter for the H. and R. Daniel pottery. Richard Daniel wrote to his father telling him of his successful trading in London. 'Do get some flower painters if possible,' he said. 'I have sold more than Pegg and Brammer and Ellis will do in six months.' Shown in the 1861 census as living at North Street, Penkhull, he is described as a potter china painter.

Brayford, Charles, active 1878–1887

Artist gilder at Copeland, Brayford's work was praised by Jewitt in 1883 as 'productions... of a high order of merit'. There are twenty-nine entries in the Copeland Special Order books showing Brayford decorated all types of ware from large vases and dessert services to tiles and slabs. He specialised in raised and chased gold designs of any subject, and shown as jewelling pieces. One entry on a shell-shaped jardinière reads 'Cupids by Birbeck and flowers by Brayford'. These would be gold painted flowers used to heighten the design. He painted marine scenes, and is recorded as a fish and seaweed painter. Whether he had a son who he trained is not proven, but the entry 'Bird on Branch by young Brayford' leads to this speculation.

Brentnall, Thomas, 1803–1873

Flower painter, born in Derby, who painted for the Derby pottery specialising in flower studies on plaques, after Dutch painter Jan van Huysum (q.v.). In 1821, due to failure in the business Brentnall was discharged from the Derby works and went for a short time to Coalport, where he was responsible for fine floral painting on their chinaware marked with The Society of Arts mark. He married Harriett, a Shropshire girl; their son Henry was born in 1824 and William Henry in 1828. By 1836 the family were living in Yorkshire, where Thomas was employed at the Swinton pottery, working on the William IV service. He is shown in the militia lists in 1831 as a china painter. By 1841 the family had returned to Staffordshire, where Thomas was a freelance decorator at the Ridgway factory. He went to France, but left in 1848 because of political unrest. Thomas delicately painted floral studies. So far no signed examples have been found, but he left a legacy to the ceramic surface that many artists have tried to follow.

Brewer, Francis, 1818–1897

Modeller and potter, born in Derby. He joined the Coalport pottery c. 1830s. In 1841 he is shown as living in Villa Terrace, Madeley, Shropshire, possibly then employed at Thomas Martin Randall's pottery, where he modelled fine vases and shapes, some with encrusted floral decoration. He left Coalport and by 1861 had started his own business in Fenton, Staffordshire making china and Parian ornaments. By 1881 the family had moved to Tamworth, where he is described as a designer and modeller of clay.

Brewer, John, 1760–1815

Artist painter, the son of a family of outside pottery decorators. His parents, John and Anne, were artists and from 1762 to 1767 had their own studios at Rupert Street, London. They moved in 1768 to Duke Street and finally by 1779 were living in Mercer Street. They exhibited their work at the Free Society and the Society of Arts. John first worked in watercolours and exhibited paintings of butterflies and insects. In 1793 he came to the Derby pottery from Chelsea and learnt the art of painting on ceramic surface. Brewer painted miniature studies on the ware, for which he was paid, in the first year, one guinea and a half each week, and thereafter two guineas a week. He painted all subjects with equal skill, but particularly figures and hunting subjects on all shapes of ware, eventually becoming a freelance artist. He was a successful drawing master in Derby, but continued to execute commissions for the Derby pottery. Between 1808 and 1815 he advertised in *The Derby Mercury* stating that an exhibition of his work would be held at his house, St Mary's Bridge, Bridge Street, Derby. Ladies and gentlemen were to be charged one shilling, children half price, but his pupils could see the exhibition free. He exhibited at the Free Society of Artists. He painted on ceramic views of shipping in watercolour style and in definite colours, using a palette of warm browns and reds with wiped out highlights, a technique he had seen in Billingsley's (q.v.) work.

Brewer, Robert, 1775–1857

Artist painter (the younger brother of John, q.v.). He was probably apprenticed to the Coalport pottery but became a journeyman painter to Flight and Barr at Worcester, an artist capable of painting in both oils and watercolours. It was then rare for an artist to be able to paint in both ceramic colours. Oils and canvas painting relies on bold strokes, whilst pure delicacy is needed on the ceramic surface. Robert was a pupil of Paul Sandby (q.v.), whose watercolour style can be seen in his painting. He exhibited landscapes at the Royal Academy in the late 1790s. Robert joined his brother at the Derby pottery in 1797, where his landscape painting was similar in style to that of his brother, causing difficulty in attribution.

On the service commissioned by the Duke of Devonshire, he painted local landscape views such as Bolton Abbey and Chatsworth. He followed his brother as an art teacher, advertising in *The Derby Mercury* in 1816. Robert's wife Mary was an accomplished artist, thought to have exhibited at the Royal Academy (an entry in Graves lists M. Brewer, subject Balloons, London 1785). By 1841 the family had moved to Shropshire and he painted for the Coalport factory. He is remembered for his fine landscape painting, especially his series of Irish views. He died at his daughter's home in Great Barr Birmingham in May 1857, aged 81.

Broad, John, active 1873–1919

Sculptor and modeller who worked in Doulton Lambeth studio, chiefly in terracotta. A pair of large vases, modelled by Broad and painted by J. Eyre, was exhibited in the World's Columbian Exposition, Chicago of 1893. He modelled candlesticks and other decorative pieces in salt glazed porcelain with carved, incised and modelled decoration, for example, of plants, insects and serpents. His ceramics were exhibited in the Arts and Crafts exhibitions of 1890 and 1910 and also at the Royal Academy 1890–1900. His work is signed with the monogram JB.

Brock, Joseph (Junior), 1816

Enameller and pottery manager who was born in Worcester (he may be the son of Joseph, shown as a gilder at many of the Worcester potteries). He is thought to have been employed first at Flight and Barr and later at Chamberlain Worcester Porcelain potteries. In the 1841 census he is listed as a china enameller, but in the 1881 census as Manager at the china works. He lived at 53 Henwick Road, Worcester St Cements, Worcester.

Brook, John, 1838–1906

Painter and designer who trained at the Sheffield School of Design. He was a draughtsman at the Crowley & Sons Iron Manufactory. In 1863 he won the Mayors prize, worth ten guineas, and the Montgomery medal; and in 1866 a National Scholarship to the Government School of Design, South Kensington; he also gained the Duke of Norfolk award. John joined William Morris, painting designs by Morris and Burne-Jones, then left to paint at the Minton Art Studio in Lambeth. He was chosen by the Manchester House Committee to report on the tile and mosaic section at the 1889 Exposition Universelle, Paris. He was popular with and held in high regard by his fellow artists. His daughter was a book illustrator. He died at 27 Camera Square, Beaufort Street, Chelsea, London.

Brookes, William

Engraver who supplied Wedgwood with engravings of the Ferrara pattern (an Italian harbour scene) and designed other patterns for transfer printing.

Brough, Charles Brayford, 1855–1922

Artist and gilder, born at Shelton New Road, Stoke, the son of Benjamin, a publican, and Elizabeth. He married at the age of 19 and had five children. He was employed at Copeland for over twenty years – an artist of talent capable of painting all subjects with equal skill. He is also shown in the Special Order books as creating many designs with raised gold.

It is possible the Brough family followed the common Victorian practice of naming one of their children after a special friend, hence Charles's middle name of Brayford. Brough certainly emulated his style of gilding, some of which he signed. There are thirty-three entries for him in the Special Order reference books but only one with a pattern number: 'April 1889, a Coventry shape comport pattern number C 309 decorated with raised gold flowers and gold edge'. A pair of dessert, St Georges-shape plates and a Derby-shaped vase decorated with birds of about 1890 are exhibited in the Spode Museum Stoke-upon-Trent.

Brough's work was exhibited by Copeland at the Exposition Universelle, Paris of 1889, which won him praise in *The Staffordshire Advertiser*. He kept a cutting from this paper recording the private visit of the Princess of Wales to the Copeland Spode works in 1897 which states: 'Mr C. Brough, who is a successful artist of the Sèvres School, was engaged upon a copy of the Windsor Vase, now in the possession of the Queen, a luxurious ornament, and typical of the artistic reproductions of the firm in this elegant porcelain. Mr Brough it may be mentioned was the painter of the valuable plaques that the Queen presented to the Czar as a wedding present.'

In 1903 he left Copeland to become one of Doulton's premier artists, and was given more freedom of design;

Charles Brayford Brough c. 1900s

again he painted for the Royal Family and Indian princes. He won the bronze medal at the Universal Exposition St Louis 1904. In 1881 he described himself as a potters' artist china painter, living at 22 Elgin Street, Stoke-on-Trent. The family moved from Stoke to Rhyl, North Wales in 1896, where it is said Brough was there only part of the time – a bit of a wanderer! Family records reveal that Brough was six feet tall with a waxed moustache. He was a keen cyclist and Captain of the North Staffordshire Wheelers, and he became a Wesleyan local preacher. His obituary shows he left Doulton to join Poulson Bros Pottery in the West Riding of Yorks as manager of their decorating department. The recently discovered photographs of his work shown here are thought to have been of work painted as a wedding present to Elizabeth Tams on her marriage to Arthur Peach (q.v.), fellow artists.

Brough, Joseph, died 1945

Painter who was trained by his father Charles (q.v.) at Copeland. He painted most subjects, especially Sèvres-style paintings in small cartouches on dessert services, but eventually was known for painting birds. He left Copeland to join Royal Doulton c. 1920, where he painted floral studies.

Minton earthenware plaque painted by E. Broughton

Copeland, Belinda Shape dessert plate decorated with enamel and gold by Charles Brough c. 1890

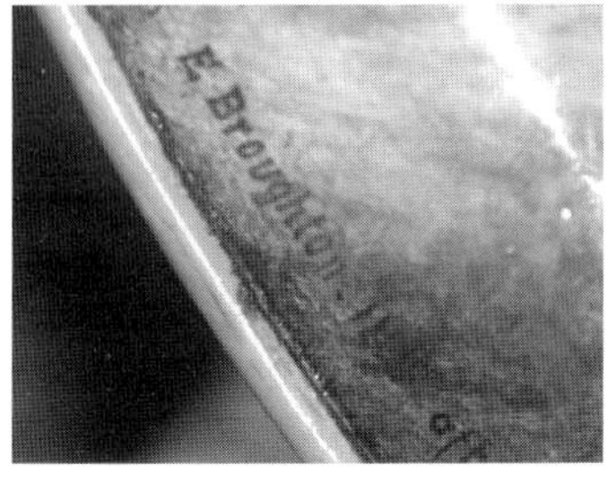

Signature on Minton plaque

Broughton, Edward, active 1870s

Artist painter employed at the Minton Art Studio, London. He painted after the style of Sir Joshua Reynolds on a Minton vase. Three Minton plaques are known, painted with the heads of Charles II children after Van Dyke, and some of his work is signed. The 1881 census shows an E. Broughton living at Bourne Street, Pownall Fee, Cheshire.

Broughton, Joseph, 1805–1875

Gilder and Japan painter. In 1816, at the age of eleven, he was apprenticed as a gilder and japan painter at the Derby Pottery. He and Haslem became friends and he contributed many stories and details that are recorded in Haslem's book *The Old Derby China Factory.* Joseph remembered the various numbers the painters used – for example, Billingsley (q.v.) was 7. He moved to the King Street Works at Derby and stayed until his death.

Brown, Reginald, 1909–1962

Flower and landscape painter, an apprentice at Doulton under Herbert Betteley (q.v.). By 1930 he was hand-painting figure and animal models, becoming foreman and manager of the department. In 1951 he was promoted to underglaze manager. He died in June 1962.

Brown, Wilmot, born 1866

Landscape painter and designer who was an apprentice at the Pinder Bourne pottery Nile Street, Burslem. His talent came to the attention of John Slater (q.v.), who trained him and encouraged him to attend the local art school. Wilmot became known for his historic buildings and landscape painting. He lived with his brother, who ran a Post Office in Stoke-on-Trent. He was always interested in nature, which shows in his flower painting. Later he painted flambé ware, many pieces of which are signed. Some his designs and drawings were engraved onto copper plates.

Brownsword, Henry, c. 1825–1892

Modeller, painter and designer. He was apprenticed at Wedgwood and attended the Stoke School of Art, studying under Prostat. From 1862 he worked closely with Emile Lessore (q.v.), colouring and retouching his designs. When Lessore returned to France, Wedgwood sent blanks for him to decorate and Henry often took and collected the finished work, acting as an important liaison between the artist and the pottery.

Brownsword, John Joseph, active 1900s

Painter and gilder at the Osmaston Road, Derby factory, painting all subjects. There are over eighty patterns which record his work in the Derby pattern books, for example: 'Pattern 998, Devonshire dessert plate maroon ground, painted flowers printed and filled figures of children by Brownsword'. He attended Derby School of Art in the evenings. After leaving Derby, he became principal of the Hull School of Art and designed the Ypres War memorial, a model of which was exhibited in Hull. He was a well-known BBC lecturer and broadcaster in 1930.

Bruce, Ellen, 1827–1907

Paintress at Copeland. Mrs Bruce was trained at Copeland and became a fine freehand paintress, eventually becoming foreman of the paintresses. She is well known for painting cornflowers and her skills were much appreciated by the Copeland family. In 1897 the Princess of Wales visited the Spode Works at Stoke-upon-Trent and *The Staffordshire Advertiser* reporter wrote of her encountering 'Mrs Bruce, who after fifty-three years of service with the firm, skilfully handles the camel's hair brush and was engaged in applying a cornflower decoration to some plates'. She is one of the few women paintresses who received recognition at this time in the Potteries. She was known as a formidable lady who controlled her department with skill and tact. She married Robert Bruce, a printer, but by 1901 was a widow living at 27 Penkhull New Road and described as a potters' paintress.

Bunker, Albert, 1875–1924

Gilder, born at New Tipton, Chesterfield. When fourteen years old he was apprenticed to Charles Rouse (q.v.), head gilder at the Derby pottery. He came to the notice of Leroy (q.v.), becoming his chief assistant. In 1914 Albert left the pottery to work for a better salary on the Midland Railway, but it is thought he continued to paint in oils.

Butler, Frank A., active 1872–1911

Designer and decorator at Doulton. He started his artistic career as a stained-glass decorator, becoming a decorator and designer of stoneware. John Sparkes comments: 'I introduced him to the new work and in a few months he brought out many new thoughts from the silent seclusion of his mind. A bold originality of treatment and the gift of invention, are characteristic of his work. He has struck out many new paths. A certain massing together of floral forms, and ingenious treatment of discs, dots, and interlacing designs indicate his hand. He not only produces designs for himself but also keeps three or four assistants busy, by designing forms and patterns for them to carry out. His best work, perhaps, is that where the ground is carved, leaving the pattern in relief, and he is facile principally in the treatment of the wet clay vessel, by squeezing it into shapes other than circular…'. Butler won a prize in the Society of Art's Art Workshop competition, which was exhibited by Doulton at the Philadelphia Centennial Exhibition of 1876 and the Arts and Crafts Exhibition of 1889. He marked his work with an FAB incised monogram.

Buttle, George Allen, 1870–1925

Painter of figure subjects and portrait painter. His father James was a commercial traveller in porcelain. He trained at the Wedgwood Institute, Burslem from 1893 to 1896 and worked for Bernard Moore and Keelings of Burslem, Wedgwood, Bishops and Stonier and finally Doulton (1905–11), then returning to Bishop and Stonier as Art Director. He is known for painting figure subjects, classical cupids and child portraits. A large vase painted by Buttle was shown in the Brussels exhibition of 1910. He painted cameos and miniature scenes on china dessert services. Classical scenes influenced many of his paintings. His *The Three Bays, South Coast of Anglesey* was exhibited at the 1953 Century Exhibition in Hanley.

Buxton, Samuel, 1790–1860

Engraver at the Minton pottery. He was born in Hanley and had two sons – John, born 1832, artist of floral subjects at Minton, and Samuel, born 1830, artist on china, who specialised at Minton in painting fruit, flower and butterfly subjects.

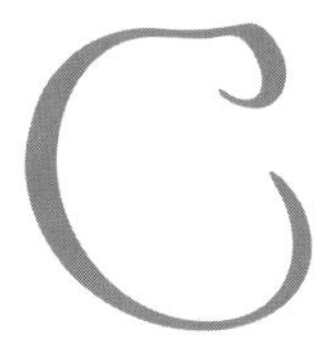

Callowhill, James, 1838–1917

Artist, painter and ceramic decorator, the son of a tailor in Worcester and brother to Thomas (q.v.). He was apprenticed at the Kerr and Binns pottery, Worcester in 1853 and attended the Worcester Government School of Design, where in 1851 he won a prize. At Worcester he produced experimental pieces of pâte-sur-pâte and became known for his individual style of painting with gold, creating unique designs, especially of storks, in both colour and raised gilding. James was known as a fine animal and flower painter in the Japanese style. In 1881 he was living at 4 Mount Pleasant, London Road, St Peter's, Worcester. He painted for the Royal Worcester Porcelain Company, staying in Worcester for thirty years. The date at which he and his brother may have come to the Potteries to work for the Doulton Pottery at the Nile works in Burslem is not clear; or they may more likely have been employed as outside decorators. However, it is said they incorporated a small insect in their designs. James's obituary shows he had success as a landscape artist, painting in oils, working in North Wales and the South of England.

Around 1885 the family decided that they would sell all their property and emigrate to America. James became a tile designer with the Willets Manufacturing Co. of Trenton, New Jersey, where he signed his work either with a signature or a monogram. He lived at 66 Java Street, Green Point, Long Island. When writing home he tells of a visit to the painting room of two ladies, who commented on how the painting was like that of Worcester. Mr Lycett (q.v.) said it ought to be as the brothers had done the best work at Worcester. Callowhill was among twenty-five skilful decorators assembled by Edward Lycett at the Faience Manufacturing Company at Green Point, Trenton, New Jersey. James Callowhill was also associated with William Thomson Walters of Baltimore, whose ambition was to publish a monumental book on his own collection of Far Eastern ceramics, using the lithographic firm of Louis Prang of Boston. Callowhill was to be one of the principal artists of *Oriental Ceramic Art*, which took nearly seventeen years to complete. Towards the end of the project his three sons assisted him and some of the colour plates in the book are signed. He made lithograph plates for the Baltimore & Ohio railway and worked for Rogers Art Gallery. By 1889 he was living in Boston, becoming well known as a landscape artist in both oils and watercolour and also working on other book illustrations.

Callowhill, Thomas Scott, 1840–1934

Figure portrait and landscape painter, the son of a tailor at Worcester and brother of James (q.v.). He was apprenticed to the Kerr and Binns Pottery, Worcester and worked in Worcester for the next thirty years. A well-respected artist of considerable talent, he was described as painting in the Limoges style. In 1870 he and his brother-in-law Josiah Rushton (q.v.) exhibited in the Workman's International Exhibition held in London, where their work was highly praised. Thomas was known for painting head cameos on china. In c. 1885 he painted classical heads on a superb, jewelled déjeuner service created by the company as a wedding present for the Countess of Dudley. There is no doubt the brothers' decision to leave pottery painting and try other forms of art is responsible for the three year gap in their biographies. They did spend some time trying to run their own businesses and then worked for the Doulton pottery, probably on a freelance basis. However, their decision to emigrate to America proved highly successful. By 1887 Thomas was living in Baltimore, designing tiles for the Chesapeake Pottery and also working for the Phoenixville Pennsylvania Pottery. At the Exhibition of American Art he won a bronze medal for freehand painting. When at the Provincial Tile Works of Trenton, New Jersey he designed the tiles for a wealthy Rhode Island citizen, Marsden P. Perry, who choose *Nymphs and Satyr* by Adophe by William Bouguereau (1825–1905) as the subject to adorn his large bathroom. These panels were signed by Thomas and won high praise. His sons Hubert and Ronald, both talented artists, had by now joined him. The Callowhill brothers were fine artists, able to use their talents in many forms, from ceramic colour to oils and watercolours. Whether the American companies they worked for employed them on a salaried basis is unclear, but they certainly became highly successful independent decorators and designers.

Cambridge, Arthur, born 1856

Painter, born at Spetchley, Worcester, son of Benjamin, a stationmaster, and his wife Susannah. From 1868 he was apprenticed to the Worcester Royal Porcelain Co., where he remained until 1875. After his father died he and his mother moved to the Queen Caroline Inn, Quay Street, Worcester and the 1871 census describes him as a scholar and his mother as an innkeeper. Although he remained at the Worcester factory until the 1890s, the 1881 census shows the family had moved to 4 Mealcheapen Street, Porter Stores, his mother now described as a publican and he as artist on china. By 1891 he and his brother were living at Walsgrove House, Spetchley Road, Worcester. Sometime in the 1890s he obtained employment at the Coalport manufactory, now not only painting but also gilding and living at Coalport Road, Madely, Shropshire.

Capes, Mary, active 1876–1883

Paintress who worked at the Doulton Lambeth studio. She painted mainly on faience ware. The designs were influenced by Japanese patterns, and painted with enamel colours on saltglaze ware. She marked her work with the monogram MC.

Carrier de Belleuse, Albert Ernest, 1824–1887

Sculptor who studied at L'école des Beaux Arts in Paris. In 1840 he established a studio for reproductions of eighteenth- and nineteenth-century sculptures. His assistants included Auguste Rodin, who stayed for seven years in his studio. Albert gained commissions for models for Parian reproductions from many of the Staffordshire potteries. The Wedgwood pottery exhibited his sculpture *Charity* at the 1851 Great Exhibition, and commissioned other models made from carrara and terracotta, which were exhibited at the London International Exhibition in 1862. In 1848 the Minton potteries chose his bust *Wellington* and other pieces produced in majolica. In 1852 Albert replaced Emille Jeanest (q.v.) as modelling instructor at the Stoke and Hanley Schools of Art. In 1855 he decided to return to Paris, as he preferred to work on much larger productions of sculpture, but continued to produce on a freelance basis for Minton and W.T. Copeland. The globe vase he designed for W. Brownfield was exhibited at the Exposition Universelle, Paris of 1889: it was eleven feet high, made of celadon green china and decorated with figures representing the seasons; it showed lines of latitude and longitude, and geographical outlines representing continents and seas. He also designed ironwork at Coalbrookdale in Shropshire. In 1876 he was appointed Art Director for Sèvres, but maintained a studio in Paris. Some of his original work went straight to auctions in Paris, London and Brussels. In January 1881 he agreed to do freelance work solely for Minton, but remained Art director at Sèvres until his death. He had a son, Louis Robert (1848–1912), who became Art Director of the earthenware factory at Choisy-le-roi (Seine) making amongst other pieces terracotta busts and mythological figures.

Carter, Truda (née Ellen Sharp), 1890–1958

Artist designer, born in Wilmington, Kent, the daughter of David Sharp MD, FRCS and Jessie Margaret Murdoch. In 1903 Truda studied for three years at the Royal Academy of Art, where she met teacher John Adams; they married in 1914.

John was appointed Head of the School of Art and Technical College, Durban, South Africa, and the couple returned to England in 1918 when John became a partner in the Carter, Stabler and Adams pottery at Poole in Dorset. Truda's designs for the company were influenced by Jacobean motifs and by the Art Deco movement. In 1924 the firm exhibited her design *Persian Deer* at the British Industries Fair. By 1929 the couple had divorced and she married Cyril Carter, a partner in the pottery, and Truda continued to produce innovative designs until 1950, when she retired due to ill health.

Cartlidge, John, 1807–1869

Flower painter, first at the Ridgway Pottery then at W.T. Copeland. His work was shown at the Great Exhibition of 1851. In 1861 he and his wife Harriet and their six grown-up children lived at 10 Endon Street, Penkhull, Stoke-upon-Trent. All his children were described as painters or gilders on china, but in the 1881 census Samuel is shown as an art student in London. Cartlidge's obituary in *The Staffordshire Advertiser* on 3 April 1869 is included here as it could well have been written of many of the unknown artists of the time.

'For many years he was a servant of the late Alderman Copeland and at the Exhibition of 1851 he shone conspicuously. At this period the firm gained for themselves high honour but nothing in those days nor indeed up to a recent date was heard of a workman's ability, or indeed how much he did to build up his employers reputation; but we are happy to be in a position to state, that now working men are considered more than human machines. With no apparent ambition (or at least the ambition of ordinary men) he made himself a position in the ranks of art, and maintained his stand for long against foreign competitors, the grace, variety and beauty of his outline was equalled only by the richness of his colouring marvellous in its natural sweetness and freedom. The late E. Baker of Worcester and formerly of the Potteries, who also made himself to the writer's knowledge, was a warm admirer of his countryman. I name this by the way merely as an instance of good sense and equally good feeling, so widely different from a few inferior men, who could never see anything particular to admire (but did to copy) in the studies of Mr Cartlidge. He never seemed to have the idea to make capital out of his great abilities, as some have done, and wisely not even in his hours of leisure and pastime; he never seemed to have time, only to make general studies; indeed he must not have had the remotest notion of money making. He was remarkable for his courtly demeanour, unassuming, firm in friendship in manners courteous, combined with an air of refinement, his real hobby was Music, in which, had he studied he would doubtless have excelled. I have no other motive in penning this brief sketch than simply as a friend to pay a tribute, which I consider due to his memory.'

Earthenware vase painted with the Ruskin pattern by George Cartidge

Cartlidge, George, 1868–1961

Artist and modeller, son of Lewis George, artist and designer, employed at the Ridgway pottery. George was trained at the Hanley School of Art and became an apprentice at the Sherwin and Cotton Tile works. Whilst working he continued his art education, gaining a full teacher's certificate, and in 1897 was in charge of the painting class at Hanley. By the early 1890s George had become Art Director at Sherwin and Cotton and invested money in the pottery. His two barbatine plaques of Francis Wedgwood and Dr Benjamin Boothroyd were mounted over the entrance of the old School of Art in Bethesda Street, Hanley.

By 1910 Sherwin & Cotton became bankrupt and George and his wife lost a considerable amount of money. He then joined with John Adams (q.v.), trading

Signed eartheware Sherwin & Cotton tile

as Adams & Barrett at the Vine Street Pottery, Hanley, which produced portrait and picture tiles designed by George; but by 1915 this company had gone into liquidation. Another business opportunity occurred when George joined J. H. Barratt & Co. at the Boothen works, Stoke-upon-Trent in an enterprise that lasted for about ten years. Throughout this time George designed from his studio at home near to Rudyard Lake, Leek and was also Art Director for Sampson Hancock & Sons, Bridge Works, Stoke.

In 1919 George was invited to model ceramic portraits of the Republican Federal candidate J. E. Stinton; they became friends and established a small studio in Newport, Kentucky. In 1921 he returned to England, designing for Hancocks and producing pieces in his studio and maintaining his American connections. He was a fine watercolourist and also painted in oils. He died aged ninety-two at his home Park House, Yeavesley in February 1961.

Chair, Henry, 1859–1911

Employed as a china painter at Worcester for forty-two years and known for his painting of rose studies and for decorating their reticulated ware.

Challinor, Edward Stafford, born 1877

Painter, the grandson of Edward Challinor, an earthenware manufacturer in Fenton, he trained at the Newcastle Art School and was possibly apprenticed at the Doulton pottery, Burslem. In 1903 the family emigrated to America, first employed at the Willetts Manufacturing Co., Trenton, New Jersey, before moving to Chicago, where he became the premier artist at the Richard China Co.

By 1905 the Pickard Company had moved to bigger premises, The Ravenswood Studio. Here the artists worked in ideal conditions, having a library of old and the latest books from which to gain design inspiration. During the holidays the company shut down, but the artists were expected to return to work with many new designs, which, if not accepted by the pottery, were given away to friends and family. Edwards wife and daughter had now joined him. His hobby was music and having a fine voice he enjoyed taking part in many of the amateur productions in the area whilst in the evenings holding musical evenings for his fellow artists and friends.

Chamberlain, Humphrey, 1791–1824

Artist and painter, the son of Humphrey Chamberlain, owner of the Chamberlain, Worcester Pottery. Little of his work has been found to date but a Worcester plaque dated and signed 1822 of Princess Charlotte shows his fine painting. He painted some of the scenes on the Prince of Wales service. His brother Walter also had artistic talent, painting figure subjects, but again only a few examples have been found.

Chamberlain, Robert, 1737–1798

Painter and outside decorator and possibly the first apprentice at the Worcester Porcelain Co. in the 1750s he became head of the decorating department but in 1786 left to start a decorating business, buying undecorated ware from the Caughley Pottery, which he sold in his shop at 33 High Street, Worcester. Thomas Turner of the Caughley works bought his ware and sent it to London.

Charol, Dorothea, 1889–1963

Modeller of German nationality but born in Odessa. She studied in Brussels, Dresden and Munich. She provided figure models for Max Pteiffer's workshop in Schwarzburg, Volskstedt Thuringia and the Rothenthal factory. Her marriage to the painter A. Koglsperger ended in 1930 and she then lived in Paris, but later came to London. Dorothea gained a reputation as a portrait modeller and is thought to have worked for Wedgwood. In 1937 she modelled the Prime Minister the Rt. Hon. Stanley Baldwin and the Royal Worcester pottery commissioned a portrait plaque of King Edward VIII to commemorate his Coronation. Between 1937 and 1939 she modelled ballet dancers, bathing girls, a Pierrot group and the figure *Repose* for Royal Worcester.

Chell, Edward, 1842–1884

Artist gilder, born in Hanley. He became known for fine jewelling work on china and was manager of the gilding department at W.T. Copeland in the 1870s.

Chivers, Frederick, 1881–1965

Fruit and flower painter, the son of Herbert Chivers, a baker. He worked for the Royal Worcester Porcelain Co., but by 1906 was employed at the Coalport pottery, specialising in fruit studies, which have a characteristic style. The background on his work was achieved by working the ceramic colour with a matchstick, giving a stippled effect. He served in WWI, and then returned to Coalport. By 1930 he had moved to first the King Street Pottery then to Royal Crown Derby Pottery.

Frederick painted the service for the Duke and Duchess of Devonshire. Examples of his work are also to be seen on Paragon China. He signed his work.

Clappison, John, born 1837

Artist designer, born in Hull, who trained first at the High School for Arts and Crafts then at the Hull

Regional College of Arts and Crafts, obtaining his National Diploma in Design. He designed for the Hornsea Pottery, East Yorks and in 1958 was appointed Chief Designer. He designed Hornsea's Home Décor range, then in 1961 keyhole-shaped bon-bon dishes. In 1972 he resigned to take up the appointment of Chief Designer for Ravenshead Glass at St Helens, where he worked until 1988; he then became group shape designer at Royal Doulton, Burslem until ill health caused him to resign in 1998.

Clark, Ernest Ellis, 1869–1932

Landscape and flower painter, who in 1883 was apprenticed at the Osmaston Road, Derby Pottery and trained at the Derby School of Art in the evenings. He won seven medals in national competitions, and became a part-time teacher of crafts at the School of Art, Derby; by 1902 he was teaching full time. He was a member of the Derby Sketching Club, living at Spondon.

Clavey (or Cleavey), Phillip, active 1800s

Painter and china dealer at Derby. He was a friend of William (Quaker) Pegg (q.v.) and Martin Randall. He was well known for his botanical studies of single plants, which are difficult to paint with accuracy and were very popular at this time. He left the Derby pottery to become a glass and china dealer.

Cliff, Clarice, 1899–1972

Paintress and designer, born in Meir Street, Tunstall, Staffordshire and educated at the High Street Elementary Summerbank School. She was first employed at the Lingard Webster Factory as an enameller, earning a shilling a week, but three years later as a lithographer at Hollinshead and Kirkham. By the time she was seventeen she worked for A. J. Wilkinson Ltd. She attended evening classes at the Burslem School of Art in 1924, and then went to the Royal College of Art, London to study sculpture. In 1916 she returned to A. E. Wilkinson Ltd, where she was given her own studio. Her talent attracted the attention of A.C.A. (Colley) Shorter, who allowed her to design under the name *Bizarre*. This new, exciting and innovative range of ware appealed to the market and by late 1929 the whole of the Newport works was making her designed ware. Colley Shorter encouraged her to produce new shapes and designs in bright bold colours, which were totally different from the competition at the time, being angular and in the Art Deco style. In the 1920s her *Tibetan* ware had attracted designs by well-known artists, including Frank Brangwyn, Paul Nash and Laura Knight.

In 1944 she married Colley Shorter and became a director of the Wilkinson works.

In 1951 she designed the *Confederation Series* depicting eight views of Canada. In 1961 Shorter died, and reluctantly in 1964 she sold the business to W. R Midwinter Ltd, who retained many of the staff. In 1966 she donated many pieces from her husband's collection of decorative arts to the Borough Museum, Newcastle-under-Lyme.

Clowes, active 1845–1851

Flower painter at W.T. Copeland known for his floral studies. He painted on all types of ware from vases to tea and dessert services. He is listed in the Special Order books as Clowes and Company, which leads to the supposition that Clowes was a floral artist of note who had painters working under him. He is recorded as painting, amongst others, pattern numbers 5512 and 7665.

Cocker, George, 1794–1868

Modeller, an apprentice in figure making at the Derby pottery c. 1808. After he finished his apprenticeship in 1817, he joined the Coalport Pottery, where he did raised flower work, but he also tried unsuccessfully to start a small pottery. He spent a short time at Worcester but returned to Derby in 1821, staying for about four years. In 1826 he and John Whitaker, Senior, started making china figures at the Derby New China Factory in Friar Gate, but the partnership with Whitaker lasted little more than a year and George continued alone in a shop in Derby. In 1840 he moved to Chenies Street, Bedford Square Road, London, making figures and flowers. He did some work for the Rockingham Pottery, whether actually at the factory or from his own establishment is not clear. In 1853 he left London and came to the Potteries, working for Herbert Minton amongst others. He exhibited his work at the Mechanics Institute Exhibition of 1839 and is known to have modelled *Roman Matron, Boy with a Bird, The Dying Drunkard*; and for Minton, *Boy with a Bird Cage, Boy at a Well, The Rape of the Sabines* and *The Queen*. He modelled figures of famous or distinguished people and figures with a moral or sentimental theme. George had a son Edwin, born 1834, who also became a figure maker; a D. Cocker is shown on some figures, possibly another son.

Coffee, William J., active 1794

Modeller, first recorded as an assistant kiln man at Coades Artificial Stone manufactory, Lambeth, London. It is thought he came to the Derby pottery as a kiln man, but he persuaded William Duesbury to let him model some figures. By late 1794 he was employed as a modeller at 3s.6d for a ten-hour day, or 7s. for a human figure standing six inches high. Coffee first designed the figure naked, and then clothed it, as all figures had to exhibit correct anatomical details. Coffee took the place of J. Spangler (q.v.) and by 1795 was paid the same wages. Sir Nigel Bowyer Gresley at his Church Gresley China Works near Burton-on-Trent (established in 1794) offered him higher wages. However, this move was not a success and he had to ask his father to get him his job back, even if only as a repairer. Still not content, Coffee persuaded a relative of William Duesbury to advance capital and together they operated a Pottery in Derby, trading and marketing under the name W. COFFEE DERBY and making terracotta and china; the exact details of their manufacture are not clear. This venture was taken over by Duesbury and Kean, but Coffee continued to model terracotta ornaments and figures. He next opened a shop in London, but this failed, and finally he emigrated to Albany, New York State, America. He exhibited eight animal paintings at the Royal Academy 1801–16. His figure *Tinkers*, c. 1795–1800, is exhibited at the Royal Crown Derby Museum.

Cole, George, 1863–1912

Flower painter at Grainger Worcester, then at Royal Worcester Pottery. He is known for fine signed rose paintings.

Cole, Sir Henry, KCB, 1808–1882

Designer, who studied watercolour painting with David Cox, designed the first ever Christmas card, and published a monthly *Journal of Design for Manufacturers*, the first periodical devoted to design. He is remembered mainly for his controversial re-organisation of the Government Schools of Design, and his influence on the Victorian ceramic art world was of paramount importance.

Cole was apprenticed in the Record Office; such was his administrative skill that he eventually reformed the office in 1838, becoming Assistant Keeper of the Public Records. In 1846 The Royal Society of Arts held a competition for designs of tea services and jugs. Cole designed pieces and persuaded Herbert Minton to manufacture them. Their entry won a silver medal and the products sold well. Two years later he established the Summerly's Art Manufactures, in which artists and manufacturers worked together. Cole met many of the manufacturers and began to be interested in the Schools of Design. In 1848 he enlisted Prince Albert's support to hold an exhibition in London, the first International Exhibition of All Nations, called now the Great Exhibition of 1851, to which manufacturers of all trades, both at home and abroad, were asked to bring their finest

bone china Worcester vase, signed G. H. Cole

work. This was the first time all sections of manufacture had seen the works of their foreign competitors. The exhibition depended on contributions and was not state aided, but was a great financial and popular success. When it closed, the Royal Commissioners, advised by Henry Cole, decided to use some of the profits to establish the South Kensington Museum, now the Victoria & Albert Museum.

In 1852, Cole started to reorganise the Government Department of Practical Art and the Museum of Ornamental Art, which by 1853 became the Department of Science and Art. He believed that art and manufacture should be closely linked together. He visited nearly all the Schools of Design in Britain, giving advice and allocating money. In 1855 he was appointed Secretary and Chief Commissioner of the British Section of the Exposition Universelle, Paris. In 1862 he was one of the principal advisors for the London International Exhibition and, in 1867, Secretary of the Royal Commission of the International Exhibition in Paris.

He retired in 1873 after fifty years of public service. Many of his ideas were controversial but his belief that a partnership between industry and art institutions was essential for the training artists and designers never faltered and had lasting impact.

Cole, Solomon, active 1821

Artist and landscape painter who worked for the Flight and Barr pottery at Worcester. By 1821 he and T. Lowe had succeeded Thomas Baxter as premier painters. Cole exhibited sixteen paintings at the Royal Academy but stayed with the pottery until it closed. He then went to London and established himself as a portrait painter.

Coleman, Helen Cordelia, A.R.W.S., 1847–84

A self-taught floral artist helped by her brother William Stephen (q.v.). She was employed for a short time at the Minton Art Studio in London, where she produced some fine work. After it closed she continued as a professional artist, exhibiting her work at the Dudley Gallery and c. 1866 at the Institute of Painters in Watercolour, becoming a member in 1875. She exhibited at the Royal Society of Painters in Watercolours, becoming an Associate member in 1879. She exhibited still-life paintings at the Royal Academy 1865–75. She married the artist John Angell. In 1879 she was appointed Flower Painter in Ordinary to Queen Victoria.

Coleman, Rebecca, died 1882

Artist and paintress, trained at the Heatherley's Art School and in Germany. She then worked with her brother and sister, William Stephen (q.v.) and Helen Cordelia (q.v.) at the Minton Art Studio, London. Here she became well known for her designing and paintings of heads, which depicted ladies from all countries. She designed a set of twenty-five drawings of girls' heads, which were used by Minton to decorate dessert plates. Rebecca exhibited professionally at the Howell and James Galleries, and paintings of domestic subjects at the Royal Academy 1867–79.

Coleman, William Stephen, 1829-1904

Artist, etcher, illustrator, writer and art director. Born in Horsham, Sussex, the son of a physician. He trained as a naturalist, etcher and illustrator. In the 1860s he wrote several works on natural history, including *British Butterflies* and *Our Woodlands, Heaths and Hedges*, and also contributed to *The London Illustrated News*. William began to experiment with pottery designs and worked briefly for W.T. Copeland, but he was dissatisfied with his working conditions and in 1869 joined the Minton pottery, where he was given a large studio at the end of the china works overlooking the town of Stoke-upon-Trent. He was made Art Director at the Minton Art Studio in London, where he encouraged amateur artists. As amateur painting became fashionable, the Studio became one of the showcases of such work in London. Here undecorated ware was supplied to students to paint and their work then fired. The Minton Pottery from 1870s–80s sold thousands of blanks impressed with the Minton mark and many were painted and signed by amateur artists, whose identities are so far not known. William was known for his designs of nude children playing sports, or other pastimes, often in the open air. After 1873 he left Minton and became totally freelance, designing for book illustrations and painting work that he often sent to Minton for firing. He exhibited at various London exhibitions 1865–79 and was on the committee of the Dudley Gallery until 1881. He died at his home in St Johns Wood, London.

Collard, Charles Henry Fletcher, 1874–1969

Artist, designer and decorator, apprenticed at the Aller Vale Art Pottery, where he showed great talent. In 1889 he exhibited at the Art and Crafts Exhibition, being now one of the best designers and decorators at the Pottery. In 1901 Aller Vale joined with Watcombe and became Royal Aller Vale and Watcombe Pottery; in 1902 Collard went to Hart and Moist in Exeter, then to Longpark Pottery Ltd. In 1905 he started a pottery at Poole in Dorset, Charles Collard and Co. Ltd at the Crown Dorset Art Pottery, but Collard left in 1915 and sold it in 1917 removing to Ilminster. By by 1919 he had another pottery at Honiton, Devon. He retired in 1947 to Torquay, where he still made studio pots.

Comolera, Paul, 1818–1897

Sculptor and modeller, born in Paris, a pupil of François Rude. He came to England in the 1870s and modelled many objects for the Minton pottery, including the famous peacocks and the majolica fountain (seventeen feet high) exhibited at the Exposition Universelle, Paris of 1878. He was an eccentric character and his studio was like a menagerie. When introduced to the Duke of Sutherland, who was visiting the factory, he asked him for the loan of a stag. It is said the Duke sent one to the factory, accompanied by four keepers, and Coleman made a life-size model of it. He eventually returned to Paris, where he died.

Complin, George, active 1785

Fruit and bird painter, known to have been enamelling at Battersea in 1765. He may have been asked by Sprigmont (q.v.) to join the Chelsea Pottery, but certainly worked for the Derby pottery c. 1791. William Duesbury's London agent, Joseph Lygo, in his letters to Duesbury, talks of a trial given to Complin and his name was found in the old Derby pattern books: for example, No 159, a plate *Birds and landscape* by Complin. He painted in bright colours, sometimes including small animals and authentic birds, such as tom-tits and chaffinches, often incorporating them in his fruit designs. He was one of the painters who would not sign the petition to stop women getting work at Derby. He had a soft spot for the opposite sex and stood up for his beliefs. There is an example of his painting on a coffee can in the Derby Museum.

Connelly, Anthony, active 1900–1950s

Flower painter, trained at the Stoke and Fenton School of Art, where he won a bronze medal in 1889; he worked mainly at Minton under Mussill (q.v.). Connelly was a bohemian character who wore an embroidered waistcoat usually covered in paint. In the early 1900s he came to the notice of the Grand Duke Michael, then living at Keele Hall, Staffordshire, who commissioned him to paint many floral studies. In the summer Connelly worked as a labourer – and is known to have been in charge of a gang of men who built a road at Cheddleton village in North Staffordshire – but in the winter came back to work to the Potteries. Such was his talent he was never out of work. He was always short of money and in the 1930s was living at the Salvation Army Hostel, selling watercolour sketches in the local pubs. When seventy years of age he answered a Copeland advertisement for men painters. His skill won the respect of the decorating department. His watercolour *Study of Lilies* was exhibited at the Centenary Exhibition of Art in the Potteries in 1953.

Cook, William, c. 1800–1876

Fruit and flower painter, born in Burslem and thought to have been employed by Robins and Randall in London and also by Acherman, the London colour manufacturer and living in Camden Town. But he returned to Thomas Martin Randall's decorating establishment in Madeley, near to the Coalport Pottery. By the 1840s he was one of the premier painters working for Coalport and is thought to have painted the coat-of-arms for the Emperor of Russia's service in 1845. His artistic forte was the superb painting of flowers and fruit in the French style. His paintings were bright yet delicate, having many tonal features. It was not until 1862 that he is recorded as working on exhibition pieces and that his work was truly appreciated. Very often his painting was combined with that of John Randall (q.v.) on the panels on vases, but is rarely signed. He was still painting in 1876, by now widowed and living with the Watkins family at 3 Railway Terrace, Coalport.

Cooper, Susie Vera, 1902–1995

Her family ran a successful oil-refining business and a farm in Milton, Staffordshire and her grandparents had a small pottery in Hanley. Her father died when she was only eleven years old and her mother was left to bring up eight daughters, Susie the youngest. Her mother encouraged Susie's undoubted artistic talent and sent her to evening classes at the Burslem School of Art; she later followed a full-time course there, and then in 1922 applied to study at the Royal College of Art but without sufficient experience, was rejected.

Gordon Forsyth (q.v.), principal of Burslem School of Art, recommended her to his old friend A. E. Gray and she joined his company as a trainee designer, first learning the skill of painting on pottery, particularly for the new Gloria lustre range. Two years later she became a designer and her back stamp was added to all the designs she produced, which were either abstract or floral. In 1929 she took the unusual step of founding her own company, financed by her family and brother-in-law Jack Beeson, who became her partner. Space was rented at the George Street Pottery, but that concern went bankrupt and she found other premises at the Chelsea Works in Moreland Road, Burslem. Here she produced modern, bright designs including *Polka Dot* and *Exclamation Mark*, which could be easily painted by the paintresses. She exhibited her ware at the British Industries Fair of 1931, and they were an immediate success, resulting in the firm of Wood and Sons offering her premises. Harry Wood manufactured her new, modernist shapes, inspired by architecture, in ivory earthenware. Susie introduced underglaze patterns created by the use of thin crayon sticks called *Crayon Lines*.

Susie Cooper was forthright in her opinions and a skilled debater, and in September 1932 was elected to the Council of the Society of Industrial Artists, North Staffordshire branch. By mid-1930 her wares were being exported to Europe, Scandinavia, South Africa, Canada and the USA. Despite the War and the ban on decorated ware for the home market, she managed to continue exporting and in 1940 she was appointed Royal Designer for Industry, the first women to achieve this honour. In 1938 she had married the architect Cecil Barker, and their son was born in 1943. Now with her husband as partner, she had difficulty finding a supplier of white ware, so in 1950 she bought the Jason China Co. of Longton and transformed the production methods and body recipes. In 1951 she produced a new shape for bone china, Quail Hand, shown for the first time at the Royal Paviion at the Festival of Britain. Ceramic painting had been superseded by lithographs but Susie continued to adapt to different trading conditions with equal success. But in 1959 a fire badly damaged her Crown Works and production ceased for nearly a year. In 1961 she merged her company with R.H. & S.L. Plant, which in 1966 was taken over by the Wedgwood Group, where she continued to design. In 1988 Wedgwood reintroduced her Kestrel shapes with three different designs. Susie Cooper had the rare talent of an artist but also the ability to produce, manage and market her wares.

Corden, William, 1797–1867

Landscape and portrait artist, born at Ashbourne, Derbyshire. He was apprenticed at the Nottingham Road, Derby Factory 1811–15, but left c. 1825. William was a brilliant colourist, excelling in the art of cross-hatching and stippling. He copied from Thurston's illustrations to Tegg's edition of Shakespeare's plays on a dessert service and painted views of continental cities copied from one of the Duke and Duchess of Devonshire's services. After he left the Derby pottery he still painted portraits on Derby plaques that met with some success. He painted the figure subjects on a dessert service ordered by Lord Ongley c. 1820–21. In 1824 William went to London and in 1829 exhibited the picture *Hebe* on porcelain. He exhibited figure paintings at the Royal Academy 1836–55, while he was living in Windsor with the Marchioness of Cunningham as his patron. By 1831 he was an acknowledged artist engaged to paint a service commissioned by William IV from Rockingham. It cost £3000, consisted of 144 plates and 56 large pieces. Queen Victoria commissioned him to paint miniatures on metal, which were not a success. However, in 1844 Prince Albert commissioned him to paint full-length, life-size portraits of his ancestors, using the portraits at the castle of Rosenau Coburg. William took his son, who was a competent artist and painter who also gained commissions from Queen Victoria and Prince Albert. In 1854 William returned to the Potteries and entered into an engagement with a Mr Scaife, a miniature painter and photographer. He was a good-humoured man, very chatty, known to have enjoyed a drink or two. He died in Nottingham in 1867 aged 70.

Cotton, William, active 1800s

Landscape painter at the Derby pottery, 1800–18. He is thought to have moved to the Potteries around the 1820s. He is known for painting hunting scenes and Dutch subjects.

Coxon, Charles, 1805–1868

Modeller, born at Longton, Staffordshire, the son of Francis Coxon, a potter, and trained under modeller Louis Bourn. It is thought he was employed in one of the Staffordshire Potteries until he and his family emigrated to America in 1849, settling in Jersey City, where his brother William was employed at the American Pottery Company. Charles found employment with Edwin and William Bennett in Baltimore and developed their range of relief-moulded designs, such as the *Rebekah at the Well* teapot, first produced in 1852. Bennetts never patented this design, which was widely copied. In 1858 Charles went to run the Swan Hill Pottery in South Amboy, leaving the Bennetts on friendly terms.

Two years later he was in Trenton, New Jersey where he built his own pottery, which had two kilns. This was so successful another kiln and more land were added to the original site. The *Ellsworth* pitcher he designed depicted Colonel Ellsworth and his troops crossing the Potomac River and reaching Alexandria in Virginia. Colonel Ellsworth climbed a roof to pull down the Confederate flag and was killed by a sniper. He was the first casualty of the American Civil War, immortalised in the Coxon design. Charles Coxon died in 1868 and the family then ran the business until 1883, when it was sold.

Craft, William Hopkins, 1730–1810

Enameller and miniature painter, possibly of Tottenham, London. He was employed in the porcelain works at Bow and used vibrant colours, particularly bright claret. He exhibited seventeen enamels at the Royal Academy 1774–95. He was a talented artist and painter who signed his work.

Crealock, Colonel Henry Hope, 1831–1891

Artist painter of animals and historical events. He was a friend of Clement Francis Wedgwood and from 1874 to 1877 contributed animal drawings and designs suitable for the new photographic process being perfected at the Wedgwood factory at Barlaston. He retired from the Army in 1884.

Creswell, John, active 1830s

Flower painter employed at the Rockingham pottery c. 1828–39. He was paid 7s.6d. a day for the first three years, 9s.3d. a day for the fourth year and 10s.6d. a day for the fifth year. A Rockingham plaque has been found that has painted on the back, *Creswell pinx No 15.* He painted in a similar style to Steele (q.v.).

Cresswell, William (John), active 1840s

Flower painter, an apprentice at the Nottingham Road, Derby works, but left in 1821 for the Coalport Pottery, where he stayed until 1841, when he it is thought he went to France. In c. 1848 he gave up painting and taught dancing.

Cristall, Joshua, 1767–1847

Figure and flower painter of Camborne, Cornwall, the son of Alexander Cristall, a master of small vessels who traded in the Mediterranean area. His mother was well educated and devoted herself to the education of her son's talent, which was not appreciated by his father, who wanted him to follow him into his trade. Eventually he left home, was recommended by a friend to Josiah Wedgwood and for a time worked in the Potteries, possibly serving his apprenticeship at Davenports in Burslem. He is known to have worked at the New Hall Works, Longton, Staffordshire. Joshua disliked the routine of painting pottery and returned to London, where he became a student at the Royal Academy, studying watercolour painting. He was one of the founding members of The Royal Society of Painters in Watercolour, becoming its president in 1821. He exhibited paintings 1803–47 at the Grosvenor Gallery in London, was a member of the of the Old Watercolour Society and recognised as a painter of figure subjects.

Croft, Stella Rebecca, 1898–1964

Artist modeller and sculptor. Born in Nottingham, trained at the Central School of Arts and Crafts and for one year at the Royal College of Art as a student of pottery and sculpture. She exhibited at the Royal Academy 1925–62, also in Venice, Toronto, Milan and Paris. In 1925 she won the silver medal at the Exposition des Arts Décoratifs and also that year set up her own pottery, managed by her father, in Ilford, Essex, later moved to Worsey Wood, Billericay. She modelled and painted all her work herself but having contracted bovine tuberculosis in infancy, which affected her hands, had difficulty throwing pots on the wheel. She is known for modelling fine groups of animals and was commissioned by Royal Worcester for seven models, including a group of giraffes. She painted animal studies in both oils and watercolours. She was a founder member of the Essex naturalists group.

Cundall, Charles E., born 1890

Floral painter who attended evening classes at the Manchester School of Art and Levenshulme Evening School. He was awarded the chief honours at the national competition of Schools of Art in 1908 for two vases and a punch bowl decorated in red and silver lustre. In 1907 he was employed by the Pilkington Lancastrian pottery, where he was influenced by the work of Gordon Forsyth (q.v.). After WWI service in the Royal Fusiliers, he returned briefly to Pilkingtons but left to study portrait painting at the Royal College of Art, London. He exhibited at the Royal Academy and became a member. During WWII he was an official war artist.

Curnock, Percy Edwin, MBE, 1873–1956

Flower painter, the grandson of a Warwickshire farmer, who served his apprenticeship at the Doulton pottery and studied at the Burslem School of Art, where he met Edward Raby, Fred Hancock and David Dewsbury and was influenced by their artistic style. He trained under John Slater (q.v.) and Robert Allan (q.v.), becoming the premier artist at Doulton. He is remembered for his paintings using flat wash colours, first initiated by Frank Slater. His work was exhibited at the Exposition Universelle, Paris in 1889. Many of his paintings were chosen as designs for lithographs. Although he is noted for his rose painting, he also painted landscapes, particularly Italian lake scenes after the style of Corot (q.v.) In 1953 he lent his sketchbook and two flower paintings for the Century Exhibition in Hanley, Stoke-on-Trent. He was awarded the MBE in 1954.

Currie, John, 1883–1914

Figure painter and artist, born in Newcastle-under-Lyme, Staffordshire. He trained at Newcastle School of Art, then at Hanley School of Art, where he won a

Painting by John Currie *'Some Later Primitives'* c. 1912. Courtesy of the Potteries Museum and Art Gallery

scholarship to study engraving at the Royal School of Art. He joined the Minton pottery in 1897 and trained under Camille Solo (q.v.). In 1901 he was appointed master of life drawing at Bristol School of Art. John painted fine figure subjects, mainly on china panels and plaques, at Minton but found teaching and London more exciting, completing his art training at the Slade School of Fine Arts. He exhibited his work with Mark Gertler, Vanessa Bell and Augustus John and enjoyed the patronage of Edward Marsh and Sir Michael Sadler. He was appointed Inspector of the Dublin School of Art and established a studio on Wicklow Street, Dublin. He was a man with undoubted talent, but his private life was not happy, culminating in him shooting his mistress, then killing himself.

Cutts, James, born 1811

Designer and engraver, son of John (q.v.). It is believed that he trained at the Ridgway pottery at the Cauldon Works, Shelton, Stoke-on-Trent, Staffordshire. He worked as an independent engraver for patterns used on ceramics, designing patterns for Job Ridgway with a skilfully engraved view in the centre and elaborate border designs. James sold his patterns to many potteries, including Davenport. Some have the back stamp *J. Cutts Desr.* The later engravings were signed. James lived at Snowhill Cottage, Shelton for many years. It is possible that Cutts Street, Snow Hill, Shelton, Stoke-upon-Trent is named after the family.

Cutts, John, 1772–1851

Landscape painter and outside decorator who became manager and part owner of the Pinxton pottery until its closure in 1811. In 1812 he started decorating with flowers and landscapes for Wedgwood: for example, Alder Valley, Derbyshire; Dovedale, Derbyshire; Longley Park, Kent; Ullswater, Cumberland. In 1816 he left to establish his own decorating shop in Lane End, Longton, possibly the location of the old Pinxton works. By 1834 his firm was trading as Cutts and Sons in New Street, Hanley, employing about fifty workers, enamelling and gilding pottery and porcelain. He married Derby painter Edward Rowland's sister. Their sons Rowland (1794–1841), John (1804–48) and Lindley all became partners of the firm. His daughter Ellen married a crest engraver, and their son Rowland James Morris became a sculptor. On his death the business at New Street, Hanley, described as china gilding business, was sold and *The Staffordshire Advertiser* of January 1852 reports all claims were to be made to James C. Cutts of Snowhill, Shelton.

Dale, John Joseph (Jack), 1864–1938

Artist gilder, an apprentice at the Osmaston Road Works, Derby. He became George Darlington's (q.v.) assistant and was influenced by Desirée Leroy (q.v.) when working on the Princess May of Teck's wedding service. Due to a wage dispute he left Derby and took over from his father as sub-postmaster of the old Normington post office. He was known to have been a fine singer.

Daniell, Henry, 1765–1841

Enameller, colour maker, designer, art director and manufacturer. Henry was the eldest son of Thomas, an enameller and colour maker, who had been apprenticed to Warner Edwards of Bell Bank Works, Shelton, Staffordshire. Thomas inherited Mr Edwards' colour recipe book, which he then passed on to his son.

In 1789 Henry was working for John Mayer, but by 1796 he and Mr Brown had set up a business, enamelling and potting. They supplied Worcester with cream coloured earthenware. But by c. 1805 Henry had dissolved his partnership with Brown and entered into a business deal with Josiah Spode II at the Spode Works, Stoke-upon-Trent. Here he designed and built his own enamelling kilns. By mutual agreement, he decorated Spode's white ware and then sold the decorated ware back to Spode. Henry employed John Hancock (q.v.) of Derby as a ground layer, but it was Hancock's knowledge of gilding that was to become invaluable. From 1805–22 Daniell and Josiah Spode created some of the most fashionable designs on the market. But by 1822 Henry decided to start his own business, not only decorating but also making ware, in London Road, Stoke-upon-Trent, virtually next door to the Spode Works. At the time he left Spode, in an amicable parting, he was employing over 200 workers. They were given the opportunity either to stay with Spode or go with him, but unfortunately there is no accurate record of who stayed and who went. By 1826–27 his business was successful, having obtained the order of a dinner and dessert service from the Earl of Shrewsbury. Henry now owned two factories – London Road and Bedford Row, Shelton. In 1841 he took his son Richard into partnership with him, shortly before he died.

Darlington, George William, 1872–1927

Artist gilder and flower painter, born in Stoke-on-Trent, Staffordshire, the son of John, a potters' printer, and his wife Eliza. He was an apprentice at the Minton manufactory and in 1891 was living with his parents at 16 George Street, Penkhull, Stoke-upon-Trent, described as a potters' gilder. By 1892 he was one of the premier gilders at Copeland. However, he left Copeland to join Royal Crown Derby, as Leroy's (q.v.) principal assistant. His work can be seen on the Gary Service, commissioned by Judge Gary, which was sold by the estate of Elbery Gary Sutcliffe Junior of Louisville, Kentucky by Sotheby's in New York in 2001. George gave painting lessons and his hobbies included gardening and singing. He was described by those who knew him as a kindly gentleman.

Davies, Margaret May (Peggy), 1923–1989

Modeller and painter who lived with her grandfather and won a two-year scholarship to the junior art department at Burslem School of Art. She nevertheless had to leave to earn her own living, and by 1935 was employed as assistant designer to Clarice Cliff at the Wilkinson manufactory. By agreement with the management, she completed her art course. At Wilkinson's she modelled figures and masks but after three years left to join the Midwinter Pottery, designing nursery ware, and finally joining Royal Dolton to model small animals decorated with the well-known flambé glaze. She served as a nurse in WWII, and subsequently married a teacher. When she then returned to Doulton it was as an independent artist under contract. During her nearly fifty years at Doulton she modelled over 250 figures.

Davis, George, born 1768

Painter and gilder. In 1793 he was known to have painted fine exotic birds at Chamberlain Worcester Porcelain. Evidence from the factory and wages books researched by Geoffrey Godden (see *Chamberlain Worcester Porcelain*) shows he was paid a high wage and listed as Mr Geo Davis, paid £3 for attending the gold grinding. Only faithful employees were trusted with gold preparation and were supervised by one of the pottery owners. From the entries recorded it would seem that he was one of the leading artists of his time, designing patterns and responsible for their accurate execution. By the early 1800s he is shown as working for Flight and Barr at Worcester, but then returned to Chamberlain Worcester Porcelain.

Davis, Harry, 1885–1970

Animal painter, born in Worcester, the son of Alfred Davis, a china potter. He started his apprenticeship in 1898 at the Royal Worcester Porcelain Pottery under E. Slater (q.v.). At a very early age he showed skill in painting any subject, and was to become foreman of the painters. He had his own studio on the site and worked there until his death. Harry is best known for painting sheep in a pastoral setting on all shapes and sizes of ware; but he was a versatile artist who painted two services, commissioned by Prince Ranjitisinji, with views of the Prince's homes in England and India. Some of his landscapes were copied from the paintings of Corot (q.v.). He carried out etchings of cathedrals and similar studies that became signed and hand-coloured transfer prints. After WWII Harry painted some of Dorothy Doughty's (q.v.) bird models.

Davis, Harry, active 1900s

Artist potter, trained as a thrower at Carter Stabler and Adams. He worked with Bernard Leach (q.v.) c. 1934 running the Leach Pottery at St Ives. He then took charge of the pottery at Achimoto College on the African Gold Coast. He and his wife May, also a potter, travelled widely gaining experience from the art of other countries. In 1946 they converted an old mill at Praze near Camborne, Cornwall into the Crowan Pottery, throwing highly crafted stoneware table and household pieces. In 1962 they emigrated to New Zealand.

Davis, Josiah, 1839–1913

Gilder designer and draughtsman (grandfather of Harry Davis, q.v.) who worked in the Worcester potteries for over sixty years He is best know for the gilding surrounding the work of Thomas Bott (q.v.) and his scroll work with Charles Henry Deakins (q.v.) on the Chicago vase. He had two sons who joined him in the ceramic industry – George, who specialised in raised work, and Alfred, who became a china painter.

Deakin, Henry, active c. 1878

Flower painter of great ability who is shown in the Derby Pattern books as painting flowers and birds, but especially roses; for example, No 721, a plate with a centre group of roses painted by Deakin. Some time in the 1890s he moved to the Potteries, but to which pottery is not known.

Deakins, Charles Henry, born 1861

Artist gilder born in Worcester, the son of Henry Deakins, a carpenter and joiner. Deakins worked at the Royal Worcester pottery for most of his life, responsible for intricate gilding. He is best known for his work on the Chicago vase, which was the centrepiece of the Worcester Stand at the World Columbian Exposition in 1893 and is now exhibited at the Dyson Perrins Museum, Worcester.

Dean, (? Albert), active 1878

Flower and bird painter employed at Copeland. No initial is recorded in the Special Order book, but there are 22 entries showing a Dean painting flowers and birds. He was paid 90 shillings for a Japanese-shaped dessert plate decorated with birds and flies. Unfortunately not one entry gives a pattern number. It is more than possible he was a relative of Thomas Dean (q.v.) and that he left Copeland to join the Forester's Pottery in Longton, Staffordshire, there known as A. Dean and becoming Art Superintendent. In 1907 he was living at 47 Carlisle Street, Longton, Staffordshire.

Dean, James Edwin (Teddy), 1864–1935

Artist. painter of landscapes, birds and flowers, the son of Edwin Dean, an actuary of the Savings Bank, Cheadle; the family lived at Bank House, Bank Street, Cheadle. He was employed at the Minton pottery for over forty years (1882–1925) painting animals, fish and game. He is recorded in the Minton pattern books as painting pattern number G. 9314, a marine scene; 6393, a Worcester shape dessert plate with a small bird study in the centre; G. 9402, a shipping scene; and G. 7782, a Newcastle pierced dessert plate with turquoise border with two small cartouche landscapes and a country house landscape in the centre, dated 24/2/94. He was known for his copies of Landseer (q.v.) subjects, and of castles and scenes of historical interest. When not actually painting customer orders, Dean was allowed to paint subjects of his own choice. He was one of the most popular pottery artists at Minton, remembered for helping the young apprentices. When Minton won the order from the Willow Refrigeration Co. of 18 Grays Inn Road, London for a painted tiled panel for their dairy shop in Harrow, they chose *The Hundred Elm Tree Farm, Sudbury* painted by Dean. Much of his work is signed. The Minton bowl painted and signed by Dean to commemorate the surrender of the German High Seas Fleet to Vice-Admiral David Beatty in the Firth of Forth, November 1918, is painted with a view of the Fleet and an airship, and within its rope-scrolled border are the words of Beatty's signal: 'The German Flag is to be hauled down at sunset today and is not to be hoisted again without permission. 21st November 1918.'

The bowl is a fine example of history recorded on porcelain.

'Teddy' Dean painting at the Minton factory.
Signature inset. Family archives,

Up to 1891 Dean continued to live with his parents in Bank House, described as a ceramic artist. His first wife Kate Wilkins, who he married in 1894, died in the spring of 1897. He met Elizabeth Astbury, a farmer's daughter from Stafford, at the Royal Oak Hotel in Cheadle and they were married on 6 November 1900; they had two sons and one daughter and lived at 8 Charles Street, Cheadle. Teddy, as he was affectionately known, was lame but a keen follower of cricket, becoming a well-known umpire in the area. He was also a keen fisherman, which is shown in the accuracy of his paintings of fish on ceramics. The family remember him fishing at the Hales Hall pond, where it is said he was pulled into the water by a giant pike – fortunately, he was rescued. Like most artists at the time, he sold his work in his local pub, the Wheatsheaf; some such examples, priced on the back at 2s.6d and 7s.6d., are still in the possession of the family. Teddy was a Freemason, becoming the Worshipful Master of St Giles Lodge, Cheadle.

Bone china jewelled handled vase

Dean, Thomas, born c. 1855

Flower painter, son of John Dean, a potter, and apprenticed at the Minton pottery 1869–76. In 1877 he was awarded the leading prize at the Hanley School of Art. He always painted naturalistic studies, his skills informed by visits to the Duke of Sutherland's orangey and estate at Trentham, Staffordshire, and by the surrounding countryside. In the 1880s he taught flower painting at the Hanley School of Art, and in 1881 his family were living at 34 Berrisford Street, Shelton, Stoke-upon-Trent, Staffordshire. Around 1885 the family moved to the Torquay Pottery in Devon, returning to the Potteries by 1887; by 1891 Dean had become an earthenware manufacturer. This venture was apparently unsuccessful as he was later employed at Wedgwood, and in 1901 is described as a pottery artist living at Belgrave Road, Dresden, Longton.

Reverse of the above vase initialled C.E.D.

Dean, William Edward James, died 1956

Landscape and marine painter, the son of a Derby manufacturer and an apprentice at the Osmaston Road Derby Pottery, trained at the Derby School of Art. Dean sailed on the Grimsby trawlers to the Dogger Bank fishing grounds to study the ships, taking photographs and sketching. This experience gave his paintings an accuracy of detail that many other marine painters lacked. Unfortunately, he had an injured knee and walked with a crutch, but remained active and jolly. He is also known for painting views of Derbyshire.

Deaville, Charles, 1868–1939

Artist gilder, premier artist gilder at the W.T. Copeland factory and shown in the Copeland Special Order books

1889–1907. He was one of the few artist gilders allowed to initial their work. He was the finest artist gilder Copeland ever employed, working only with the important artists such as Hurten and Alcock. Very rarely did he initial his work. By the 1930s he and Harry Hammersley (q.v.) were taking part in all the outside activities provided by the pottery – for example, the Copeland flower show, where Deaville won many prizes. He was a keen member of the Boys' Brigade, becoming Captain of the Stoke division. He had the honour of representing the workforce at the funeral of Mrs R. P. Copeland (Henrietta, Richard Pirie's wife), who was often to be seen on the factory floor and was well known to the workers as a formidable lady! Deaville designed many of the fine borders on Copeland plates, which were the secret of Copeland's success throughout the late 1890s and early 1900s. Charles was a happily married man whose son Leslie became one of Copeland's finest engravers.

Degg, W., active 1890–1898

Artist gilder at the Copeland factory known to have decorated the work of C. F. Hurten (q.v.). Degg's son Jimmy was also a gilder at Copeland, probably trained under his father.

De Junic (Juinnie), active 1800s

Artist gilder at the Swansea Pottery. A Frenchman who may have been trained at Sèvres as a painter, his name is recorded as Jiugne, Junie or Junnie. He was named by Henry Morris as one of the three main painters and possibly called Jenny at Swansea. Jewitt records Jenny as a tracer of gold. Possibly he was the fine artist gilder responsible for the gilding of Swansea ware.

Delatre, François, born 1830

Modeller, born in France and employed by Brown-Westhead, Moore & Co., where he modelled birds and flowers that were exhibited at the Cauldon showroom, Stoke-on-Trent. However, by 1881 he was living at 32 Spencer Street, Battersea, Surrey, described as a figure modeller in plaster.

De Morgan, William Frend, 1839–1917

Artist and designer, born in Fulham, Middlesex, the son of Augustus, Professor of Mathematics at London University. When studying at University College London William attended art classes, and then trained at the Royal Academy Schools from 1859 to1861. Henry Holiday, a fellow student, introduced him to William Morris and Edward Burne-Jones and he became associated with the Arts and Crafts movement. He first produced tile and stained glass designs for Morris and Co., but was unhappy with the way they were produced. In 1869 he set up a kiln to fire his work in his parents' house in Fitzroy Square, London. He bought blanks to decorate from Wedgwood and other potteries; he continued to design for Morris and Co.

In 1863–67 he exhibited scriptural subjects at the Royal Academy, British Institution and the Suffolk Street Art Gallery. In 1872 he started to reproduce Syrian pottery of the sixteenth and seventeenth century. Unfortunately experiments with lustres caused a kiln fire that destroyed the roof of the house and he abandoned the project. The kiln at the new house, built this time in a garden shed, produced fine pottery, which was very successful. He moved to bigger premises, again in Cheyne Row, Chelsea, making large panels of tiles, which were sold to shipping companies, particularly P&O – and he designed panels for Czar Alexander III's yacht. Wedgwood was interested in his experiments on lustre decoration and did some the trials for him at Etruria. He maintained his close friendships with William Morris and Edward Byrne-Jones, who encouraged his undoubted talent. Morris and Co. retailed his work and used his tiles in their decorations. He employed the painters Joe Juster and J. Hersey, also Charles and Fred Passenger, who mostly initialled their work. De Morgan developed a distinctive range of lustre colours based mainly on copper and silver. It is thought he decorated some Wedgwood dishes and basalt tiles. In 1881 he moved to Merton Abbey to establish another studio much nearer to William Morris's new workshops. In 1885 he married Evelyn Pickering, a talented artist.

In 1888 he entered into a partnership with the architect Halsey Ricardo and built a factory near his home in London – The Sands End Pottery, Fulham. His association with the Minton Pottery and friendship with Colin Minton Campbell resulted in a commission to design a stained-glass window for a Rochester church, the design for which is in the Minton archives. It is thought that their friendship may have influenced Colin Minton Campbell to develop the Minton Persian range of designs. William, who suffered from poor health, spent winters in Florence, returning to England for the summer months. In 1898, Ricardo, due to his developing practice as an architect, retired from the business and William took Frank Isles, Charles and Fred Passenger into partnership. De Morgan himself retired in 1905 but the company continued until 1911. In his later years he starting writing and also became known for humorous illustrations. He illustrated a children's book *On a Pincushion and Other Fairy Tales* in 1877. However it is for his designs and his pottery that he is best remembered. A fine example of his work can be seen on the walls of the Bishop Selwyn Mortuary Chapel in Lichfield Cathedral, Staffordshire.

Densley, Mary, active 1890s

Faience artist at Royal Doulton. Her painting was influenced by Renaissance and Classical designs. A large vase painted by her was exhibited at the World's Columbian Exposition, Chicago of 1893.

Dewsbury, David, 1852-1929

Floral artist and painter, born in Burslem, Staffordshire, the son of Thomas, a potters' fireman. He trained at the Burslem School of Art, winning silver and bronze medals from 1872 to 1874 for fine floral studies. He was first employed at S. Alcock and Co.'s Hill Pottery, Burslem but by 1889 had gone to Doulton, where he developed the style created by F. Slater (q.v.) of painting flowers on a flat wash of colour, firing each layer before painting another to give a misty effect. He painted mainly on vases and sample plates and was noted for floral design, but he did paint some landscapes. He specialised in painting orchids, which he studied in the conservatories of the Duke of Sutherland and Joseph Chamberlain. Dewsbury's paintings reveal the closest study of plants in their natural form, which he transferred to the ceramic surface with great delicacy. Some examples of his paintings of humming birds have been found. He often signed his work with a painted monogram or signature.

Bone china Royal Doulton dessert plate painted and signed by D. Dewsbury with the floral study *'Arachanthe Clarkei'*

Dexter, William, 1818–1860

Fruit and flower painter born in Melbourne, Derbyshire, the son of William Bull and his wife Jane. His father was a successful lace manufacturer and inventor who with John Dunnicliff patented the Jaquard warp lace machine. William must have shown artistic talent at an early age, as he is known to have been one of the apprentice boys at the Derby manufactory in 1832. By 1839 he and his brother Walter went to France and Haslem states that William worked at a manufactory in Paris for about a year, where there is little doubt he learnt the art of ceramic painting. He painted flowers, exotic birds and fruit, often in an oriental design, with great skill. When he returned to his family in Babbington Street, Nottingham he is described in the 1841 census as a china painter. He married Caroline Harper on 29 July 1841, an advantageous marriage, as she was the daughter of a jeweller and watchmaker. It is thought she had been sent to complete her education in France, where it is possible the couple met. After a short stay in London in 1842 they went to France, where they stayed until the mid-1840s, then returning to London. By 1847 Dexter had set up his own studio in Nottingham, sending out a circular styling himself China Enameller to Louis Philippe, King of the French and M.M.S.A.R. the Duke of Nemours. The circular also stated: 'In soliciting the patronage of the gentry of Nottingham and its neighbourhood William Dexter begs to submit for inspection specimens of painting executed by himself, in all the various branches of oil and watercolour, Viz.-Portrait painting in every possible style; landscapes, flowers, fruit, Etc. accurately copied from Nature or originals of the best masters, chiffoniers, worktables, fire screens and ornamental work of every description completed to order. Oriental and china imitated so as to match sets or services that have been broken. Enamel painting taught and materials furnished No 1 Milton Street'.

In 1848 the couple were living at George Street, Nottingham and he is now described as a portrait and animal painter and his wife as a language teacher. But London seemed to offer a much more interesting and possibly lucrative life and yet again the couple moved to the capital, where he painted watercolours, sold at Ackerman's and other artistic establishments as book illustrations – for example, *Birds and Nests* of about 1851, published by Paul Jarrard, London. In 1851 he exhibited the painting *Dead Birds* at the Royal Academy. William and his wife were known to have been somewhat eccentric. At a soirée given by the Academicians at the end of the season for exhibitors and patrons of art Dexter appeared in traditional Hungarian attire, although he had been requested to wear evening dress. His wife also dressed eccentrically and gave lectures on the 'bloomer costume'.

In 1852 Dexter again exhibited at the Royal Academy with the painting *The Lark and her Young, Aesop's Fables*. However, when William heard stories of successful gold mining in Australia he was tempted away from his artistic success in England. He actually took a course of construction in the neighbourhood of Holloway, where a railway was being laid, working with the navies and attempting to gain skills relevant to gold mining. In 1852 the couple emigrated; how successful they were is not known, only that he died in Melbourne around 1860.

Dixon, Thomas, born 1798

Flower painter, born in Birch Meadows, Broseley and apprenticed to the Coalport manufactory c. 1810-17. In 1819 he married Sarah, a burnisher, and they had four children between 1820 and 1835. Daughters Elizabeth and Ann became burnishers and sons John and William were china painters. The family lived at Queen Street, Brosely, where he is described as a china painter. Dixon became known for his specialised floral groups of passion flowers and pansies. As his name is on the 1859 wages list, and in view of the many entries recorded in the Coalport factory pattern books, it is more than possible he ran a decorating department and stayed at the Coalport manufactory the whole of his working life.

Dixon William, active 1820s

Figure painter who worked at the Derby pottery painting figure subjects, often of a grotesque and ludicrous character. He painted the satirical mug copied from *Human Passions Deliniate* and figures taken from *Droll, Satirical and Humorous* by Tim Bobbin. He also copied Hogarthian subjects from prints, which were used in some pottery designs.

Dodson, Richard, born c. 1795

Painter and outside decorator, son of William who was Overlooker of the Derby painting department from1810. Richard was apprenticed at the Derby factory. c. 1807–14. He painted fine naturalistic birds in bright colours placed in well-spaced groups in natural surroundings, using a great deal of paint. Haslem thinks they were carelessly drawn but they fetched high prices. One of the dessert services he decorated had arabesque borders gilded by Thomas Till (q.v.). In 1820, shortly after his father's death, he left the Derby manufactory and established a small decorating business on Nottingham Road, which by 1875 had become The Plough public house.

Doe Ernest (Enoch), born 1794

Artist painter and outside decorator born in Worcester, who served his apprenticeship at Chamberlain Worcester Porcelain. His worked in an oil-painting style using heavy colours. His landscapes had hazy distances, often with an effect of rain, with sheep in the foreground and sunlight shining on white walls. Doe did some work for the Flight and Barr factory, no doubt in a freelance capacity.

He joined George Rogers Senior in an outside decorating business at Clerkenwell Close in London, buying white ware from Grainger's; after 1835 he was established at 17 High Street, Worcester. He exhibited floral studies at the Royal Academy and Suffolk Street from 1823–48 and exhibited plates decorated with scenes from Shakespeare's *Richard II* at the Great Exhibition in 1851. An artist of great talent capable of painting in any medium and any subjects with great skill. The 1881 census shows him as a retired artist living at Bank Cottage, Whittington, Worcester with his wife, daughter, daughter-in-law and two servants.

Doe, James, died 1797

Bird painter born in Lambeth, Surrey, who may have trained in Staffordshire at Wedgwood. In 1789 he was employed at the Flight and Barr factory at Worcester, and is known to have been at Grainger Worcester in 1796. Although he returned to London and travelled to Scotland and Ireland, he ended his working days in Worcester. Jewitt tells of a J. Doe potter who committed suicide by drowning at Sea Mills docks two and a half miles from Bristol, quoting from an article written by Joseph James in the *Monthly Magazine* of 1797. No connection is so far proved.

Doe, William, active 1800s

Painter of birds, feathers, landscapes and figures. He was a pupil ofThomas Baxter and exhibited landscapes at the Worcester Society of Arts exhibition in 1818. He may have been related to the Doe family recorded above as it is said he worked in partnership with Rogers from Chamberlain Worcester Porcelain as outside decorators trading as Doe and Rogers. However, no William is recorded. William Doe was admitted a Freeman of Worcester in 1815.

Donaldson, John, 1737–1801

Figure painter, possibly a freelance artist, born in Edinburgh. He specialised in figure painting on vases in the style of Boucher and Watteau. He is thought to have trained under Thomas Hughes of Clerkenwell, who enamelled china for the potteries of Bow, Chelsea, Worcester and Derby. In 1760 he was living in London and listed in *Mortimer's Directory* as John Donaldson, a portrait painter at the lower end of Princess Street, Leicester Square. He painted children with chubby faces and limbs c. 1770 for the Chelsea pottery and painted classical pictures on Worcester porcelain c. 1770. A set of vases painted with *Leda and the Swan, The Birth of Bacchus and Europa and the Bull* in the Worcester Works museum is signed with his monogram. He became known as a skilled miniature painter in Indian ink, was a Fellow of the Incorporated

Society of Artists, and exhibited at the Royal Academy and the Free Society from 1761 to 1791. Although highly skilled, it is known that he died a pauper.

Doughty, Freda G., died 1972

Modeller, daughter of Charles, a poet and explorer, sister to Dorothy (q.v.).

When Colonel Clive, one of the directors of the Royal Worcester Pottery, was staying with a cousin of the Doughty family in 1930, he saw some of her figure work and commissioned four figures. Throughout her career with the Worcester pottery she designed one hundred figures, known as the Worcester children. She is well known for *The Days of the Week* and *Months of the Year* children and for *Grandmothers Dress* and *Boy with the Parakeet*. She and her sister Dorothy lived at Goudhurst in Kent; they loved children and their garden rang with the laughter of their many small visitors. In 1943 they moved near to Falmouth.

Doughty, Susan, 1892–1962

Modeller and painter of birds, flowers and plants, born in San Remo, Italy, the daughter of Charles, poet and explorer. Her mother was a fine watercolourist. Dorothy trained at the Eastbourne School of Art, and was particularly interested in birds and all aspects of nature. In 1935 The Royal Worcester pottery started producing limited editions of her studies of first American and later English birds. She also modelled floral studies. Her work was very popular in the USA, where she visited on many occasions. In 1943 the family moved to Falmouth, Cornwall.

Dresser, Christopher, 1834–1904

Artist, botanist, designer and author, born in Glasgow, trained at the Government School of Design, Somerset House. During 1852–68 he became a student-lecturer, encouraging students to progress from copying to an understanding of patterns fit for the purpose for which they had been designed. He studied botany at Goethes Jena University, gaining a doctorate. His wrote for the *Art Journal* 1857–58.

In 1861 he was living at 4 Swifts Cottages with his wife Thirza and four children, described as a Professor of Botany. He published *The Art of Decorative Design*, 1862, *Principles of Design*, 1873, *Studies in Design*, 1875–76, *Japan: its Architecture Art and Art Manufactures*, 1882 and *Modern Ornamentation*, 1886. When lecturing he believed that ornament should be treated as a fine art; that there was a need for a Royal Academy of Decorative and Applied Arts; and that knowledge of design involved the understanding of the elements of ornament, art botany, the study of type forms and the history of ornament in Western and Eastern cultures. The following of these principles can be seen in his own ceramic designs. By 1871 the family had moved to Tower Cressey, Aubrey Road, Notting Hill Grove, Kensington; he now had ten children and described himself as architect and ornamentalist. During the 1860s and 70s he was a freelance designer producing shapes and patterns for the Wedgwood and Minton potteries. In the 1860s he became associated with the Minton Art Pottery Studio, and many of his designs are still in the Minton archives. His work on Minton ware was first exhibited at the Exposition Universelle, Paris of 1867 – a match-pot painted with *Dog in the Spirit* on one side and *In the Flesh* on the other. He used stylised forms derived from plants and often the skeletal parts of insects, birds and other animals; combined with bright colours, this created a distinctive style which sold well.

He designed electro-plated tablewares and decorative pieces, usually of a severe and angular modernist design, for J. Dixon, which were totally different from the designs of the time. The work was produced by Elkington and Co. He also designed ironwork for Coalbrookdale, and wallpaper and textiles.

After a government-sponsored trip to Japan in 1876–77 he became a collector of Japanese art, and this influence can be seen in his designs. In the early 1870s Dresser designed shapes that could be thrown on the potters wheel appealing to the true potter and members of the Arts and Crafts movement. By 1879 he had initiated the establishment of the Linthorpe Pottery, taking the post of art director, with H. Tooth as pottery manager. In 1882 he established a Studio for designs in Sutton and 1892–96 designed vases, made by W. Ault of Staffordshire at Swadlincote. He was art editor of the *Furniture Gazette*. He retired aged seventy to Ventnor on the Isle of Wight.

Dudley, Frank, born 1860

Artist gilder born in Stoke-on-Trent, the son of Joseph Dudley, a potter. He was known for his fine jewelled work at Copeland. His signature is in the back of one of the black reference books in the Spode Archives and research has proved that in 1890 he did the fine gilding on a Coventry-shaped plate painted by S. Alcock (q.v.) that had been commissioned by Davis Collamore and Co. of Broadway, New York.

Duncan, Edward, 1803–1882

Marine artist and book illustrator born in London and trained under Robert Havell & Sons, aquatint engravers. In 1834 he became a member of the New Watercolour Society, but resigned and in 1847 joined the Old

Watercolour Society. When travelling the country he met William Taylor Copeland, owner of W.T. Copeland, Stoke-upon-Trent, and stayed with him for over six months painting pictures of racing and hunting. His rural scene designs were engraved to decorate Copeland ware, and the pattern became very popular and was registered in 1850.

He then returned to London and was well known as a landscape and marine painter.

Duvivier, Fidelle, c. 1740–1817

Flower and landscape painter born in the parish of St Brice, Tournai, France, the son of Jacques Joseph Francis and his wife, née Jeanne Laport. He may have been an apprentice at Peterinck's factory in Tournai.

Nicholas Sprimont of the Chelsea Pottery was employing artists from this region and asked Duvivier to join him. Duvivier also painted for the James Giles Studio in London, possibly decorating Chinese porcelain. c. 1769–73 he came to Derby, signing a four-year agreement with William Duesbury at a weekly wage of 24s. but with the prospect of 5 guineas as principal flower painter. He stayed until October 1792, after which he painted at the New Hall Pottery, Longton, where he was one of their most talented artists. He left when the pottery hit financial trouble.

Duvivier held the position of drawing master at the Orme School in Newcastle-under-Lyme, 1790–96, and also ran an art class in Stone, Staffordshire. Clearly he enjoyed teaching as when he wrote to William Duesbury asking for employment on a freelance basis he said he had three working days free; this offer was refused, no doubt because sending ware to be decorated in Newcastle would not have been profitable and the Derby pottery at this time had many gifted painters. However, it is possible that he obtained freelance commissions around 1787–1811 from the Minton pottery as his designs can be seen on some of their early ware.

He painted large bold figures, using a palette of reddish-brown, blue and green, Watteau subjects in landscapes, fables, exotic birds and landscapes in monochrome. Often foliage or roots are to be seen at the bottom of his landscape paintings. Although the biographical details are difficult to prove, there is no doubt he was one of the finest ceramic painters of his time. Some signed examples are known. He died in 1817 and it is thought he was buried at Hanley Green parish church, Staffordshire.

Duvivier, William, died in 1775

Artist born in Liège, came to England c. 1743 with his son Henri to work for the Chelsea Pottery painting porcelain. William designed the Fable patterns and is thought to have taught O. Neale (q.v.).

Eaton, Arthur Charles, born 1876

Landscape, flower and animal painter, the son of Benjamin Eaton, a carter and coal dealer. He studied at the Burslem School of Art from 1887 to 1892. He trained under John Slater (q.v.) and R. Allan (q.v.) at the Doulton pottery, where he worked from 1889 until 1932. He assisted Charles Nokes in the artistic development of Holbein and Rembrandt wares and designed patterns for flambé and sung ware. He became a part-time teacher at the Burslem and Tunstall School of Art.

Eaton, Mary, 1873–1961

Fish painter, known to have been painting at the Hadley factory, Worcester 1900–1908. Usually her work is signed M. Eaton but the signature is often hidden in the painting. Little is known about the life of this painter, only that she became an official botanical artist for the New York Botanical Gardens.

Eaton, Robert, born 1843

Floral painter born in Derby, the son of Robert Eaton, a ribbon weaver, and Sophia née Pedley, sister of Henry Pedley, the Derby gilder, who was an established ceramic artist at this time. Robert served his apprenticeship c. 1855 at the Coalport Pottery and he is in the wages list of c. 1859 as being paid six shillings. By 1861 he had moved to the Potteries, staying with his uncle Henry Pedley at Cliff Bank Square, now described as a china painter.

A marked Davenport plate signed by Eaton c. 1887 has been recorded. He left Davenport to become one of the premier floral artists at Copeland, shown in the Copeland Special Order books from 1890. The notable entries are No 48, Spode Octogan shape designed fruit; and No 64, a shell handled jardinière painted with fruit in 1899. Number entries denoted items, which were manufactured for the 1889 Exposition Universelle, Paris.

Edkins, Michael, active 1750–1760s

Painter on Delftware from Birmingham, where he was apprenticed to a house painter; but before he finished his apprenticeship, his master died. He is known to have been at the Redcliffe Road works, Bristol. He initialled his work, which is decorated in Chinese design. When the Bristol pottery failed, he worked as a coach and general painter and decorator. He painted glassware for Little and Longmands and their successors, Vigor and Stevens, next to the old Bristol pottery. The story is told that he and his fellow artists at Bristol made their own brushes using the fine hair pulled from the eyelids and nostrils of cattle. He painted a signboard for the Delft potter, Joseph Flower, for which he was paid 10s.6d.

Edwards, Emily J., died 1879

Paintress and designer who may have worked at the Coalport Pottery from c. 1823–27, but she is well known for her designs at Doulton's Lambeth Studio, 1872–76. She specialised in foliage patterns and was one of the first women to design and decorate her own pieces and to train other artists. Her work is described in John Sparkes' (from the Lambeth School of Art) notes: 'Her work is ornament made up of an ingenious mixture of classical and conventional forms with natural growths. There is usually great flatness of treatment in her work, with elaborately diapered backgrounds, which in no way interfere. The colour clings to the small stamped patterns, and flows into the deeper depressions, to the manifest enrichment of the piece. She often gave indication of close study of antique methods of decoration…'.

Her mark is the monogram EJE.

Elden, Mathew R., born 1837

Painter, modeller and designer born in Manchester. He studied at the Stoke School of Art under Mr Protat and in 1862 designed a parting gift from the students for his old headmaster on his retirement. In 1863 he won a scholarship to the Government School of Design, South Kensington, London. He was at Wedgwood for a short time, working for Emile Lessore. In 1873 he succeeded William Coleman at the Minton Art Studio in South Kensington, London. Elden was a friend and fellow student of Kipling (q.v.), and he was also a supporter of the artist Whistler. He is known to have been rather difficult, regarded as a wayward character with a lively inventive mind, whose designs were innovative. He was an artist of great talent, but suffered from mental illness and died in an asylum.

Ellis, J., active 1870s

Landscape artist and modeller born in Barlaston, Staffordshire and trained at the Hanley School of Art, where he won a £10 prize for a vase exhibited at the International Exhibition, London, 1871. The next year he won the gold prize for modelling. He was employed at Wedgwood c. 1875 on a weekly wage of 50s. and a pair of vases he modelled was exhibited in the Exposition Universelle, Paris of 1878. Ellis then worked for Brown-Westhead, Moore & Co. pottery. *The Pottery Gazette and Glass Trade Review* reporting on the Paris Exposition Universelle of 1889 commented on a pair of vases exhibited by Brown, Westhead and Moore, which were painted by Ellis; and *The Staffordshire Advertiser*, reporting on the same exhibition, noted that Mr J. Ellis had painted very skilfully a number of rural scenes on plates and plaques.

Emery, F. J., active c. 1860

Painter, who patented crayon painting on pottery. However, his claim was challenged by Joseph Thorley; Emery then stated his was for amateur use only. Yet the Minton pottery exhibited examples of his work at the London exhibition of 1862; some were known to have been shown at South Kensington Museum in 1865.

Evans, David, born 1795

Painter and freelance artist, first working at Swansea from around 1814 to 1819. He then became the premier artist at Grainger Worcester and was known for his wildflower studies and strawberry designs. There are three signed plaques known, probably on Grainger porcelain. After leaving Worcester his movements are difficult to trace. He may have become a freelance artist and is thought to have been at the Coalport Pottery c. 1823–27, but the evidence is not conclusive and he may have painted for Minton. There are entries in the Copeland Special Order book 1846–47 that list patterns painted by Evans. An article in *The Pottery Gazette and Glass Trade Review* of 1881 on enamelling records that Evans worked for Worcester, Swansea, Coalport, etc.; and at the great works of Minton and Copeland.

Evans, George, born 1850

Modeller son of Mathew Evans, a house painter. He was apprenticed at the Royal Worcester Porcelain factory in about 1864 and is known for modelling large vase shapes and possibly the series of Boer War Figures. He left Worcester in 1906.

Evans, George, 1899–1958

Landscape painter who served his apprenticeship at the Royal Worcester factory in the 1930s. He hand-coloured Mediterranean scenes from designs by W. Sedgely and painted landscapes after Corot (q.v.), which he signed H. George. In 1929, as there was little work at Worcester, he went to Doulton, but returned to Worcester in 1931. He was one of the first artists to paint the series of birds designed by Dorothy Doughty (q.v.), giving them life and realism.

Minton Bone china dessert plate commissioned by David Collomore & Co. Signed Evans c. 1880

Minton Earthenware charger detail painted and signed by J.B. Evans

Spode Bread and Butter Feldspar porcelain plate. Painting attributed to David Evans c. 1822

Evans, John Bishop, 1842–1887

Landscape artist who trained at the Stoke and Newcastle Schools of Design. *The Staffordshire Advertiser* of 21 April 1860 reporting the Stoke Art School prize day states that he won two prizes for nature studies and the Lind–Goldschidt prize. He was employed by the Minton pottery 1865–85. His work was exhibited at the 1867 Exposition Universelle, Paris: the costing book entry reads 'A14, No 1230,Vase with painted landscapes and marine views'. There are seven entries shown in the Minton pattern books from March 1880–July 1885 under the name of Evans, two shown as J. Evans. All are G pattern numbers and are dessert services painted with landscapes, one named as *Erskine River Waterfall*, another as *View on the Bulls Road*. Sources of inspiration for his work, which he signed, are Paul Marny's *Views of Lichfield Cathedral* and *Tintern Abbey*. He left Minton to join Wedgwood as a designer of tiles and tableware, but continued to paint. He is shown in the 1881census as a potters' artist with a daughter, Annie, a potters' art student and two sons, living at 15 Chatham Street, Stoke-on-Trent. He is known to have painted watercolours.

Evans, Joseph, active 1860s

Painter at Brownfield & Co., known in 1860 to have painted underglaze colours in the Italian style on a vase modelled by Carrier Belleuse of Paris.

Evans, William, active 1860s

Painter, son of David, apprenticed at the Grainger Worcester factory. He is known for his article 'Old Times at Worcester Porcelain Works' printed in *The Pottery Gazette and Glass Trade Review* of 1887, which tells of the men with whom he worked and his high regard for them.

Eyre, George, 1818–1887

Artist, painter, designer and art director born at Halstead, Leicester and trained at the Stoke School of Art, then from 1845–47 at the Government School of Design at Somerset House, London. He became one of the early pupil-teachers at Stoke Art School and in c. 1847 preceded Aaron Green as Superintendent of the Minton drawing office. He assisted in the development of the encaustic design process, and was known for his designs of ecclesiastical decoration on tiles. He designed the pavements for Queen Victoria's house at Osborne and in 1848 tiles for the pavements at the railway station at Stoke-upon-Trent. He may have worked for Hackwood at the New Hall Pottery, but by 1854 he was at S. Alcock and Co.'s Hill Pottery, Burslem and then worked for their successors, Sir James Duke and Nephews, where by 1860 he was the chief artist. Eyre designed a dessert service using both bone china and Parian that was shown in the 1862 London Exhibition. He was a fine figure painter, designer and draftsman, designing the ceramic insets on the trowel used by the Rt Hon. W. E. Gladstone when in 1863 he laid the foundation stone for the Wedgwood Institute at Burslem. In 1864, on the death of Thomas Battam (q.v.), Eyre was appointed Art Director at W.T. Copeland, but was soon succeeded by Robert Frederick Abraham (q.v.). After 1865 nothing seems to be known about this fine designer. Pure speculation leads to the theory that as both Eyre and Abraham were at the S. Alcock pottery in the 1860s he went to Copeland as Art Director, but soon left and found the life of a freelance artist more congenial and profitable. In 1881 the family were living at 6 The Villas, Stoke, now described as a potters' designer, where he died in 1887.

Amongst the exhibits at the Century Exhibition held at Hanley, Stoke-on-Trent in 1953 were an Alcock bone china jug, a Harding's oval dish and an earthenware jug painted by him with allegorical subjects.

Eyre, John, R.I.B.A, A.R.C.A., 1847–1927

Artist, painter, book illustrator, designer and teacher born in London, the son of George Eyre (q.v.), who trained at the Stoke School of Art, then at the Government School of Design, South Kensington, London. He became a pupil-teacher at Stoke School of Art, and was eventually appointed an Examiner in Art by the Board of Education.

He was employed at the Minton Art Pottery Studio in London from 1872 to 1875 as foreman and kiln superintendent. However, after a disagreement with Mr Elden (q.v.) he left and was for a short time at Copeland as a designer. John next established a studio at the well-known retailers Phillips of Oxford Street, London, giving painting lessons to young ladies. By 1883 he had joined the Doulton workshops, Lambeth, London, staying until 1897. He designed panels illustrating agriculture, commerce and Columbus's life for the World's Columbian Exposition, Chicago of 1893; and also panels illustrating the life of Beswick, which were described in the *Journal of Decorative Art* in May 1887.

In 1919 he was a freelance artist painting pottery scenes in watercolours for G. R. Ashworth's pottery, and examples of his work have also been seen on Brown-Westhead, Moore & Co. ware. He was a fine watercolour artist: he exhibited at the Paris Salon and the Royal Academy in 1877 and 1919; at the Royal Society of British Artists 1906–18; and also the Royal Institute of Painters in Watercolour. Sometime during this period he became an Associate of the Royal College of Art.

In 1953 an etching of a portrait of his father and a watercolour *Chelsea Pensioners* were lent to the Century Exhibition in Hanley, Stoke-on-Trent.

Fall, John, active 1850

Landscape painter, possibly trained at the Coalport pottery. He is shown in their pattern books c. 1850. In 1857 he painted *The Picnic* on a porcelain plaque, which was awarded a medal at the Wenlock Exhibition of 1858. After which nothing is known of this highly skilled painter.

Fenn, Joseph, born 1877

Painter, son of John Fenn, a potters' presser. He trained at one of the local art schools and worked at George Jones' Crescent Pottery in Stoke. He was very popular with his colleagues, who appreciated his skill. He signed his work at George Jones and at W.T. Copeland. In 1901 he was living with his parents at 7 Park Terrace, Stoke-on-Trent, described as a china painter. He died while painting at his bench at the Spode works, and was greatly missed.

Fenton, Harry, active 1900

Modeller. He modelled tableware and domestic pottery at Doulton, but left to go to America, working in one of the potteries around Trenton, New Jersey. On his return to Doulton he became Charles Noke's assistant, modelling character and Toby jugs.

Fenton Thomas, born 1832

China painter born at Penkull, Staffordshire. In 1861 he was living at Penkhull Square, Stoke-upon-Trent, described as a potters' painter. He is listed in the Minton archives as a crest painter, working from the 1870 to the 1880s. By 1871 he was living next door to Christian Henk (q.v.) in George Street, now described as a potters' heraldic painter. His work was exhibited at the Exposition Universelle, Paris of 1878. By 1881 he had moved to 11 Sheppard Street, a couple of doors away from Mussill (q.v.) and in 1892 to 13 Albion Street, Penkhull. Still described as a potters' heraldic artist, the 1901 census shows him living with his son-in-law at 3 Shelton Old Road, Stoke-upon-Trent.

Ferneyhough, Frederick, born 1858

Painter and gilder, the son of Thomas Ferneyhough, a cooper, and brother of George (q.v.), born in Audley, Staffordshire and apprenticed at the Minton manufactory. He trained at the Newcastle-under-Lyme School of Art from 1873 to 1879 and was employed as the Royal Doulton pottery in the late nineteenth century. In 1881 he was living with his parents at Earl Street, Newcastle-under-Lyme, described as a china painter; the next year he married Isabella Davidson and in 1891 the couple were living at West Street, Newcastle-under-Lyme. By 1901 he had left the ceramic industry – he and his wife were living at 9 West Street, Newcastle-under-Lyme, his occupation now given as self-employed joiner (carpenter).

Ferneyhough, George, born 1855

Painter and gilder born in Audley, Staffordshire, brother to Frederick (q.v.) and apprenticed at the Minton pottery 1869–76 as a painter and gilder. He taught evening classes held at Newcastle-under-Lyme Art School and would have succeeded Bacon (q.v.) as headmaster if he had not omitted to take his teaching certificate. His work was shown at the Exposition Universelle, Paris of 1878. He worked at Doulton c. 1887–1905, where he painted animals and hunting scenes. Some of his drawings were used as designs, engraved then reproduced in underglaze blue on dinner ware.

Fifield, William, active c. 1820

Flower and landscape painter born in Bath, who worked at the Bristol pottery in Water Lane for over fifty years. Known to have painted the four tiles dated 15 February 1820, which were on the office walls of that pottery in 1873. He painted rose bouquets and landscapes with buildings in a watercolour style. Examples of his work – landscapes and figure drawings and flower studies painted by him and his son – are in the Victoria & Albert Museum; sometimes he named the landscape or the view on the reverse of the piece. His son was known for painting landscapes and medallions.

Fisher, Alexander (Senior), born 1837

Painter and author, born in Glasgow, Scotland, who specialised in painting bird studies, Greek ornament and studies after Landseer (q.v.). In 1861 he lived at High Street, Mount Pleasant, Stoke-on-Trent, described as a landscape painter. Ten years later he had moved to 11 Lawrence Street, Shelton, where his occupation is now given as china painter. Vases painted by him were exhibited at the Exposition Universelle, Paris of 1878 and he did some work for the Brown, Westhead and Moore pottery. By 1881 he had left the Potteries and found employment at the Torquay Terra Cotta Co. and Watcombe Terra Cotta Co. He signed his work A. F. He wrote *Hints on Fine Art Pottery Painting*, published in 1881, and possibly taught art at the Torquay and Brixham Art School.

Forsyth, Gordon Mitchell, R.I., A.R.C.A., F.R.S.A., 1879–1952

Artist, designer, art director and teacher. He was born in Fraserburgh, Aberdeen, where he won a travelling scholarship to study art and design in Italy. He became Art Director at the Minton & Hollins Tile Co., Stoke-upon-Trent, then in 1906 went to the Pilkingtons Tile and Pottery Co. Here he encouraged the throwers to produce new and innovative designs, and ran a fine art department and give his artists artistic freedom, encouraging them to experiment with the new, exciting glazes that the company was producing. Forsyth used Gothic lettering in motifs and heraldic designs on tiles. In 1916–19 he served in the RAF as a designer. In 1920 he became Superintendent of Art Instruction for Stoke-on-Trent until his retirement in 1945. Forsythe taught and inspired many pupils who were to become well known in the ceramic industry, including Clarice Cliff, Susie Cooper, Arnold Machin, Eric Slater, Victor Skellern and Harold Holdway. He believed in relating art training to industrial manufacture – the need to train young students to recognise that their art must be commercially practical to be successful. Forsythe wrote *The Art and Craft of the Potter* and *20th Century Ceramics* and exhibited at the Royal Academy from 1922 to 1948. Two of his paintings, *The Banners Thaxstead* and *The Lawnmarket, Edinburgh*, were shown at the Century Exhibition in Hanley, Stoke-on-Trent in 1953.

Pilkington lustre vase designed by Gordon Forsyth, 1908

Foster, Herbert William, 1848–1929

Artist, painter and designer born in Endon, Staffordshire, who trained at the Hanley School of Art, where he won a bronze medal in 1865. In 1872 he won a National Scholarship to attend the Government School of Design, South Kensington, London and was awarded a silver medal by the Worshipful Company of Artists. He exhibited at the Royal Academy and in Europe. Foster worked for the Minton Art Pottery Studio. He specialised in painting portraits, including members of the Royal Family, but also painted animals and birds. A large panel, *Euphrone after a design by Fisk*, was shown at the Exposition Universelle, Paris of 1878. Foster studied in both Paris and Belgium but continued to work for Minton between his studies abroad. The panels he designed for the Victoria & Albert Museum in South Kensington, *The Triumph of Truth and Justice over Ignorance Superstition and Crime*, were recorded in *The Art Journal* in 1877. His work is often signed. He left the industry to teach at the Nottingham School of Art, where from 1893 he was in charge of the life class. The well-known artists Dame Laura Knight and her husband Harold Knight were his pupils. His wife, also an artist, whom he taught and encouraged, did some designs for Raphael Tuck and Sons.

Fungalstad, Thore, born 1856

Flower painter, born in Norway and came to England in 1881. Very little has so far been discovered about this talented painter, only that he was at Copeland and is known for beautiful studies of roses. Arthur Perry (q.v.) remembered him as painting only raised designs. It is thought he became a freelance artist and left the ceramic industry to start a studio.

Furnival, Frederick, 1905–1985

Landscape and floral artist, book illustrator. He worked at W.T. Copeland in the early 1900s. There are two examples of his work in the Spode museum: a bottle-shaped vase and a small Portland-shape vase painted with landscapes. His painting on Copeland china is signed and usually the scenes are named. A garden pot and cover are known, which he decorated with a copy of Constable's *The Haywain*. After leaving Copeland he went to Watford, Hertfordshire, travelling to London every day to work for the Carlton Studios in Great Queen Street, Kingsway.

Large rectangle earthenware plaque, decorated in polychrome enamels by Thomas Allen with the subject known as *Il Peneroso* c 1883. Courtesy of The Wedgwood Museum Trust, Barlaston, Staffordshire

Bone China Copeland Jewelled dessert plate painted by Samuel Alcock, c 1890s

Minton Centrepiece c 1900, the panels painted by Henri Boullimier after Boucher

Porcelain Dessert plate, factory unknown, painted and signed by Lucien Besche

Copeland earthenware plaque, scene from *Da Quiote* painted by Besche

Porcelain Plaque painted with a view of Thirwall Castle by William Wallis Bailey. Paul Collins Collection

Watercolour of the Ruins of Tittensor Old Hall painted by R.W.Buss. Courtesy of the Borough Museum & Art Gallery Newcastle under Lyme

Watercolour of St Margaret's Church, Wolstanton, painted by Harry Barnard. Courtesy of Newscastle under Lyme Museum, Staffordshire

Minton Vase pâte-sur-pâte.
Signed by Laurence Birks

Signed Water colour study of flowers by C.B Brough. Family archives

Painted by Samuel Bourne. Feldspar porcelain dessert plate with Armorial Crest

Detail from a bone china Cauldon Vase c 1900. Signed by Donald Birbeck. Private Collection

Bone China Copeland dessert plate c 1880 of Melrose Abbey. Signed by Joseph Birbeck

Bird of Paradise c 1900s painted by Anthony Connelly. Courtesy of the Newcastle under Lyme Museum, Staffordshire

Chamberlain Worcester Hunting Jug painted by Humphrey Chamberlain. Paul Collins Collection

Earthenware Vases painted by Walter Crane c 1867

Left: Minton Majolica Jardinière and Stand designed by Carrier De Belleuse for the 1862 Exhibition

Above: Penkhull painted by John Currie. Courtesy of the potteries Museum and Art Gallery, Stoke on Trent

Below: Royal Doulton Dessert plate painted and signed by P Churnock and commissioned by Tiffany's of New York *Prima Donna*

Minton earthenware large plaque painted and signed by J.E Dean, c 1890

Minton bone china Ships Vase commissioned by Thomas Goode of Mayfair, c 1880. The painting is attributed to J.E.Dean after Morin

Minton bone china pierced dessert plate, pattern no G 4128, c 1882 painted and signed by J.B.Evans. Named on the reverse *Ambleside*

Copeland bone china seaux painted with Irish scenes by F. Furnival

Royal Doulton bone china dessert plate, impressed cipher for December 1913, painted and signed by C Greasley

The Plaza Cinema, Nelson Place, Newcastle under Lyme, Staffordshire c 1943 painted by Gordon Forsyth. Courtesy of the Newcastle Museum and Art Gallery

Minton bone china Vase painted by C. Henk and exhibited at the 1862 Exhibition

Bone china dessert plate, the decoration attributed to Albert Gregory, c 1890

Above: Painting of Venice c 1839. Courtesy of the Potteries Museum and Art Gallery, Stoke on Trent, by James Holland

Above: Lad Lane, Newcastle under Lyme, 1969 painted by Reginald G. Haggar. Courtsey of the Newcastle under Lyme Museum and Art Gallery

Above: Minton bone china pierced dessert plate painted and signed by Henry Mitchell, after the painting. A *Distinquished Member of the Humane Society* by Edwin Landseer

Spode Copeland Tea plate and Cup and Saucer designed by Harold Holdway from the Audubon Birds Series *Cuviers Regulus* c 1960

Copeland bone china cup and saucer painted and signed by Charles Ferdinand Hurten, private collection

Copeland bone china cup and saucer Hurten, Paris c 1889

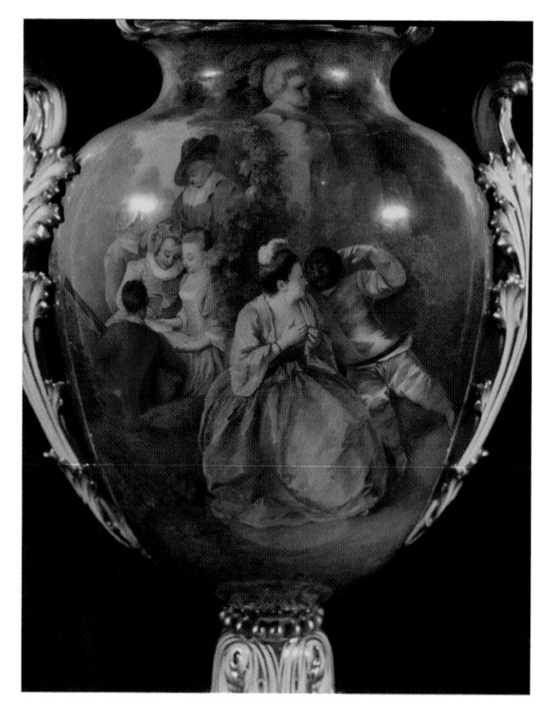

Left: Minton bone china Vase, c 1860 painted by L A Jahn

Right: bone china Baluster shape Vase c1920 with the 'Pillar Design' by Daisy Makeig-Jones. Courtesy of The Wedgwood Museum Trust, Barlaston, Staffordshire

Minton majolica vase, c 1850 painted by Tomas Kirkby

Above: Lessore Wedgwood earthenware plaque painted by Emile Lessore. Courtesy of the Potteries Museum and Art Gallery, Stoke on Trent

Minton bottle flask. Designed and painted by Stacey Marks, c 1877

Pair of Minton bone china Vases commissioned by Thomas Goode of Mayfair, painted by Henry Mitchell

Large Minton earthenware plaque decorated with flying parrots and signed by W Mussill

View of Trentham behind the Lake painted by Wenceslas Mussill, date unknown. Courtesy of the Newcastle under Lyme Museum and Art Gallery

Minton bone china pierced border dessert plate painted by Henry Mitchell c 1890

Copeland bone china plaque commisioned by Thomas Goode, c 1890. Centre decoration of Osbourne House, attributed to Erischgitz. Roses by W. Mussill

Royal Worcester Coral Clay Teapot c 1880s, painted in liqiud clay (Pâte sur Pâte) by William Pointon. Courtesy of the Worcester Porcelain Museum

Coalport bone china plate, painted and signed by J.H.Plant

Copeland large bone china plaque painted and signed by A Perry, c 1900

Painting in oils, *Red Lion Square* of 1854, by Hilton L. Pratt. Courtesy of the Museum and Art Gallery, Newcastle under Lyme

Design by Desiré Le Roi, c1880

Royal Worcester bud vase painted by Daisy Rea. Courtesy of The Worcester Porcelain Museum

Pair of Minton plates, the flowers painted by R Pilsbury and the flower containers designed and painted by E Reuter

W.T.Copeland & Sons fine cabinet plate, the painting by Thomas Sadler and the guilding attributed to Charles Deaville

Royal Doulton bone china plate, painted and signed by R Rushton

Left: Royal Worcester plate, decorated with butterflies, 1881, by James Sherriff. Courtesy of The Worcester Porcelain Museum.

Minton bone china ink set decorated by L. solon with pâte sur pâte. Courtesy of the Potteries Museum and Art Gallery, Stoke on Trent

The Sea Nymph painting by G. Speight, courtsey of the Potteries Museum and Art Gallery, Stoke on Trent

Detail of the Routen from the *Rivers of France* painting by Turner on a Copeland bone cina cup and saucer, from an early morning tea set, c 1892, by D. Lucas, Junior

Copeland large plaque painted by William Yale from the painting *Crossing the Ford in Summer Time* by Ansdell and Creswick

Painted on porcelain by George Speight. Paul Collins Collection

The Wedgwood family portrait by George Stubbs, c 1780. Wedgwood (also married Robert Darwin) can be seen mounted on horseback. She became the mother of Charles Darwin. Courtesy of the Wedgwood Museum Trust, Barlaston, Staffordshire

Copeland bone china plate painted in the centre with the landscape *Bregenz* by William Yale, c 1876

Minton bone china plate painted in the centre by W. Wise bearing the impressed mark for 1881

Terracotta panal depicting one of the months of the year from the façade of the Wedgwood Institute, Burslem, designed by Rowland Morris

Bone china seaux Copeland. Detail Londonderry landscape the signature is hidden in the trees below the house

Furnival created the Kensita's cigarette advertisement c. 1923 featuring the butler Jenkyn, which was based on the butler at Ramsdell Hall near Manchester. He illustrated for *The World Wide Magazine*, *Tit-Bits* and record companies. He became known as a painter of portraits and exhibited in the Royal Academy. Painting was both his work and his hobby and he enjoyed playing the piano. When he left London he went to Brighton and from there to Shoreham-by-Sea, West Sussex – and finally to North Harrow, Middlesex.

Gadsby, Thomas, active c. 1890

Flower and bird painter at Royal Crown Derby factory, who is recorded in their pattern books: for example, pattern book 1, No 625 Octagon shaped plate with bamboo border, spray of blackberry by Gadsby. He initialled his work.

Gallimore, William Wood, born 1841

Modeller and designer born in Burslem, Staffordshire, the son of William Gallimore, an engraver and colour maker. He worked for a solicitor in Burslem, but trained at the Stoke School of Art in the evenings, receiving some tuition from the French artist Louis Kremer. He became chief modeller at the W.H. Goss, Falcon pottery, Stoke-upon-Trent, Staffordshire. Around 1869 he was persuaded to join a group of highly skilled workers and their families, led by Goss's foreman William Bromley, to go to the Belleek Pottery in Ireland. Here Gallimore trained the Irishmen James and Edward Cleary, who managed the pottery from 1884–1920, in the manufacture of eggshell porcelain. In Ireland he was involved in a shooting accident that affected his right arm, but he learnt to achieve the same high standard of modelling with his left hand. However, the unrest in Ireland worried the workers and they returned to the Potteries around 1876, where they were welcomed back and again employed by William Henry Goss. Gallimore modelled the bust of *Charles Dickens* and developed over five hundred designs. He was commissioned by Thomas Forrester of the Church Street majolica works to model a St Bernard dog owned by Messrs Bayley of Shooters Hill, London. The dog model was life-size and decorated with accurate markings. Gallimore then lived at 9 Prospect Place, Stoke-on-Trent. Around 1900 the family emigrated to America, where Gallimore succeeded I. Broome at the Trent Tile Company, Trenton, New Jersey. He is also known to have designed vases for the Ceramic Art Co., owned by W.S. Lenox, and he worked for the American Encaustic Tile Company in Zanesville. He was noted for his cupids and boy models. Two of his sons, William (possibly), born in America, and Jesse, born in Hanley, eventually ran a design and modelling workshop, supervised by their father. His daughters Flora and Marian, born in Hanley, became modellers of floral relief patterns.

Gallimore often worked from home and Adeline Goss, in her biography of her father, wrote: 'I was charmed to see things of beauty grow under his magic touch. He never appeared to take any care, but a lovely form, or perfect portrait would appear to grow out of a series of hurried and apparently careless dabs with various tools at the wet clay'.

Gandy, Walter, active 1880–1932

Artist designer, son of Walter Gandy, a joiner, and whose brother Henry was an artist and art teacher. Walter was associated with the Doulton Lambeth pottery, where his advice was sought on all colour specifications; the painters submitted their work to him for approval. In 1881 he and his brothers and sisters were living with their parents at 63 Harleyford, Kennington First, Lambeth, London, his occupation was then 'draftsman, art pottery'; his sister Jessie, then aged fifteen, is described as a decorator at Doulton pottery. Two years later Gandy married Ada Dennis, who was working in the Doulton faience department 1881–94, where she designed for faience, carrarra and marqueterie ware, inspired by the work of Kate Greenaway (q.v.). Walter had a wide knowledge of ornamental and historical art and Henry Doulton often consulted him. His pottery designs were shown at Arts and Crafts Exhibitions in 1889 and 1916. He was a fine artist and watercolourist, exhibiting at the Royal Academy 1910–13 and the Society of British Artists, 1893–94. He won a gold medal at the Louisiana Purchase exhibition of 1904 and a prize in the Society of Arts' Art Workmanship competition for a jar decorated with seaweed.

Gauron, Nicholas Francis, born 1736

Modeller born in Paris and apprenticed to his uncle, Jacob, who was a silversmith. He worked at Mennecy and 1758–64 as chief modeller at the Tournai factory. He is shown in the Chelsea work lists of 1773 as being paid 8s.9d. daily. His son Nicholas worked with him and they modelled classical and allegorical figures at the Derby works. His allegorical group, representing Charles d'Oultremont, Prince Bishop of Liege, was presented to the Prince Bishop on his consecration in 1764. His style influenced the pottery shapes of the nineteenth century.

Gertner, Frederick Martin, R.C.A., 1886–1960

Modeller born in Worcester, the son of a carpenter. He trained as a wood carver with his father but studied art and sculpture in the evenings at the Victorian Institute, Worcester. Here he met painters from the Worcester pottery and became interested in ceramics. Gertner won a bronze medal at the Institute and a scholarship to the Royal College of Art School to study sculpture. In 1914 he became an assistant art master at Llanelli, Wales.

Gertner became chief modeller at the Royal Worcester pottery. His duties were to adapt the models, commissioned from freelance sculptors, for factory production. He modelled two sets of figures in carefully researched historical costumes. In 1956 he started the series 'Officers of the Papal Guard', researched with accurate detail. He retired because of ill health and his son Paul, who took over the department, and Neal French completed the series, which was issued as a limited edition.

Gladstone, Mary S., active 1880s

Portrait artist of Laurencekirk, Scotland. She designed a series of twelve female heads with Tennyson quotations, which were used by the Minton pottery for dessert plate designs. She was a well-known portrait painter, whose work was exhibited at the Royal Academy in 1879.

Glover, Josiah, born 1802

Floral artist, gilder and designer at the Copeland and Garrett pottery (after 1847 Copeland). He is shown variously in their Special Order reference books as Glover, Glover and Co, Glover Swetnam and Co., Glover Pedley and Co., Glover Ferrington (? Farrington) and Co., Glover Barrett and Co. Swetnam, Pedley and Ferrington were gilders, but Barrett was an artist, so possibly they combined to decorate services. The combination of names suggests Glover was in charge of a group of decorators. Glover's work was on tea services and dessert services, but he also painted vases and scent jars and the like on pattern numbers ranging from 4719 to 8034. Entry 20–2–1851 was a Pompeian-shaped double-handled vase, with blue dip richly gilt 'for exhibition' (the Great Exhibition of 1851). Many of the pieces had crests and mottoes with sprigs of flowers and floral groups. By 1881 the family were living at 26 Albert Street, Stoke-on-Trent, and he is described as a potters' gilder.

Goldermann, active 1870–1879

Flower painter at Copeland. He painted floral, grass, flies and bird studies, and is known to have painted china vases and dessert services. Wild flowers were his specialty. The entries for the Vienna Exhibition of 1873 show his work: 8–2–1872 China Gordon Can and Tray no 16, and no 17 Wild roses and flowers Exhibition. Muller (q.v.) gilded some of his work, as did Owen and Bell.

No biographical details are known but his sketchbook in the Spode archives dated 1856 includes floral studies in pencil and colour. Goldermann was a friend of gilder Edward Goodwin (q.v.).

Pattern book entry c. 1870. Courtesy of the Spode Museum Trust

Goode, William James, 1831–1892

Artist, painter and designer born at St Georges, Middlesex, the son of Thomas Goode, owner of the famous china warehouse at South Audley Street, London. He was a talented artist, often painting on pottery blanks. Many of his ceramic designs were influenced by the artist William Coleman (q.v.) and were produced by the Minton pottery on dessert services. *The Art Journal*'s catalogue of the International Exhibition, London of 1872 devotes a whole page to a majolica ewer and plateau contributed by Messrs Goode. It was made by Minton but designed and painted by William. The design was taken from the work of Ellen Montalea and consisted of three figures representing epic, tragic and lyric poetry. William designed a golden wedding plaque that was presented by Queen Victoria to the Emperor and Empress of Germany in 1879. He and Colin Minton Campbell developed a method of etching decorative designs on porcelain, examples that were exhibited at the Exposition Universelle, Paris of 1878. When Thomas Goode's commissioned ware from Copeland, William not only brought some of his own designs to the task but also changed their existing designs with great effect. He signed, dated, monogrammed or initialled his work and is known to have painted some five or six pieces a year. In 1878 William travelled to Russia, showing his designs to the Empress and other Royal customers; he stayed for four weeks, observing Russian tastes and culture. William was an avid collector of antique jade carvings and porcelain from Sèvres, Chelsea and Dresden. He trained his two sons, Minton and Herbert, to follow on the company's tradition. In 1881 he was living at Haverstock Hill, Belmont, Hampstead, London. He died aged sixty-one, leaving an artistic legacy unparalleled at this time.

Goode, William, born 1867

Artist gilder born in Ironbridge, Shropshire, the son of Edward Goode, an iron pattern fitter. He was apprenticed at the Coalport pottery c. 1882–90. He is known to have executed the gilding around the floral decoration on clock cases. He is also recorded as painting agate jewel stones on fine pieces. In 1891 he was living with his parents at Viaduct, Madeley, Shropshire, described as a china painter, but he seems to have done mainly fine gilding on signed pieces – for example, an 'ink stand, painted by Walley, flowers with agate stones and scroll gilding by Goode'.

Goodsby (Goadsby), James, active c. 1820

Modeller, who is shown in the list of employees at Derby in 1832. Possibly he also went with William Billingsley to Swansea. He modelled raised flowers on plaques, vases and small baskets and his work was of the highest artistic skill. After the Swansea pottery closed it is thought he returned to Derby.

Goodwin, John Edward, 1869–1949

Artist gilder, designer and art director, the son of John Goodwin, a grate maker. He was apprenticed and then employed at Copeland between 1887 and the 1890s and was responsible for the gilding on eggshell porcelain, vases and dessert services painted by Hurten (q.v.), Alcock (q.v.) and Yale (q.v.). Only two pattern numbers are listed under his name: 1/6034, a table plate with wreath ribbon; and 1/5997, table plate with gold scroll panels. His was the fine gilding on the *Midsummer Night's Dream* service painted by S. Alcock and exhibited at the 1889 Exposition Universelle, Paris. He joined the Wedgwood design team in 1892, then succeeded Thomas Allen as Art Director at Wedgwood in 1902 until 1935, at a time when the company was trying hard to cope with the change in marketing strategy. Due to American, Spanish and South African wars, they had lost lucrative markets. Godwin knew that the way forward was to aim for the middle market and produced more toy, nursery wares and tableware with safe, proven patterns. He was an excellent manager and developed his own small team of painters and gilders with whom he developed 'fairyland' and powder colours. His designs were popular and kept Wedgwood in the forefront of the marketplace. Goodwin travelled to America on behalf of Wedgwood on a fact-finding mission to assess market trends. In 1913 he modelled the shape *Edme* for the French-based firm of Pannier Frères. In notes compiled in 1935, Godwin wrote retrospectively: '*Edme* shape was commissioned by M. Pannier Frères of Paris, well-known architects and furnishers, very select, they would only accept commissions when given carte blanche. They furnished as an idea for a 10-inch plate with six scallops on the edge and vaguely showing the idea of flutings. This plate was soon discarded in favour of the plain edge which was made.' Eventually the shape was discovered by American consumers and is still marketed today. Goodwin retired in 1934 and was succeeded at Wedgwood by Victor Skellern (q.v.).

Goss, William Henry, 1833–1906

Artist, designer and pottery manufacturer, born in London. He was trained at the Government School of Design, South Kensington, where it is said William Taylor Copeland of the Copeland pottery sponsored him. Goss joined Copeland c. 1855, working mainly on the design of Parian figures and statuettes, and on new designs for the Copeland jewelled ware range that had first been exhibited at the Great Exhibition in 1851. In 1858 he left Copeland to start his own pottery in Stoke-upon-Trent. His heavily ornamented ivory body was awarded a medal at the International Exhibition in London in 1862. In 1870 Goss was established at the Falcon Works, Stoke-upon-Trent, producing jewelled ware for trinkets and costume jewellery and openwork baskets decorated with flowers, which became very popular. William Bromley was his foreman until 1863, when Joseph Astley succeeded him. By the 1880s the Goss pottery had become known for their heraldic designs on small items. These were ordered from holiday resorts all over England. Goss was known as a practical chemist and a writer on many subjects. He died at his home from heart failure but the business was continued by his sons, Victor Henry and William Huntley, until eventually it became part of the Cauldon Pottery.

Bone china jewelled vase designed and decorated by William Henry Goss c. 1880

Gould, active 1830s

Flower painter at the Davenport pottery. He is credited with painting some of the floral groups on the William IV service. A letter from William Davenport to his brother Henry about the 1832 Royal service noted that 'the floral bouquets should be well done and all by Gould '.

Gould, John, born 1882

Flower and fish painter at Copeland, born in Barlaston, Staffordshire. At Copeland there are eight entries under his name in the Special Order books, showing he painted on all ceramic surfaces with great skill. In 1881 he was living at Tan Yard, Barlaston, Staffordshire, described as an artist; in 1891 he was living in Tunstall, Stoke-on-Trent, described as an artist designer of Tile Panels, but for which manufactory is not known.

Goutard, Leonce, born 1836

Artist and designer born in Mamers, France, who was commissioned c. 1870 to design and paint dinnerware for Wedgwood, and by the London Retailers Borges and Co. In 1881 he lived with Pierre and Jeanne Mallet (q.v.) at 1 Hope Cottage, Acton, Middlesex, described as a painter.

Grace, William Edmund, active 1900s

Artist, painter and designer who studied at the Burslem Art School under Stanley Thorgood, and where he won the King's prize. He became an apprentice at the Doulton factory, trained by H. Piper, and under R. Allan produced ornamental ware. He designed lithographs and worked closely with Charles Nokes, designing patterns for underglaze printing. Grace painted jugs and loving cups issued in limited editions and stayed with Doulton until 1959. He was a fine pictorial draftsman and a painter in oils; some of his paintings were shown in local exhibitions.

Gray, George, active c. 1850

Painter of figure subjects, first trained at one of the Potteries' art schools, then at the National Art School, London. He painted two china plaques, a Titian head and a portrait of Princess Alice (one of Queen Victoria's children) after Landseer (q.v.). They were lent to the Longton Museum c. 1913 by the South Kensington Museum. His work was said to be reminiscent of oil painting and of a high standard.

Gray, Robert Bix, born 1803

Painter and outside decorator at Epsom, Surrey. In c. 1817 he was apprenticed to his uncle, Thomas Martin Randall, in London, painting many Watteau-style decorations. In the 1850s he started his own business at Northwood, near Hanley, Staffordshire, which lasted five years. Gray was next employed as a glass painter at Pilkington and Co., St Helens, until poor health forced him to retire. An artist capable of painting all subjects with equal skill, his ability to imitate the French style of decoration to perfection was one of his notable assets. His son Robert Edward, born in 1825, became a gilder and groundlayer at the Minton pottery.

Spode feldspar porcelain comport the painting attributed to Richard Greatbach c. 1840

Greatbatch, active 1845–1860

Artist gilder and painter at W.T. Copeland. Shown in their Special Order books as Greatbatch; R. Greatbatch is listed after 1848, and Greatbatch and Co. There are 112 entries for these craftsmen. From the entries Greatbatch was apparently the artist and R. Greatbatch the artist gilder. They painted and gilded designs of floral studies, birds and landscapes with equal skill. Their work was exhibited at the Great Exhibition of 1851. The floral groups have a distinctive style, but unfortunately there are no examples with signatures, so the work can only be attributed to them. Greatbatch and Co. can be interpreted as either Greatbatch overseeing the work of other artists on a pattern he designed, or 'the company' may have been his apprentices.

Greatbatch, Robert, active 1800s

Modeller and engraver who was an apprentice of Thomas Wieldon. He later set up his own business in Fenton, Staffordshire, where it is known he was associated with Thomas Radford, a fine engraver. He was employed at Wedgwood as a modeller.

Pattern book. Courtesy of the Spode Museum Trust

Greatbatch, William, active 1875–1882

Artist and gilder, an apprentice at the Minton pottery. He became chief engraver at W.T. Copeland, but whether related to R. Greatbach (q.v.) is not known.

Green, Aaron, 1820–1896

Painter, heraldic decorator and gilder born in Etruria, near Hanley, Staffordshire. At the age of eleven he became an apprentice at the S. Alcock Pottery. After he had reached his majority, he went to the Minton pottery, where he stayed until he retired. He was a painter of great skill, who worked on landscapes, portraits and flowers. He had the ability to do cloisonné decoration and to work with raised paste. Scarrett described him as a clever decorative artist. Green became principal designer in charge of the drawing office at Minton in the early 1850s. From 1861 to 1891 he lived at 12 George Street, next to the Roebuck Inn, described as an artist and china painter. He is noted in 1871 for his design on encaustic tiles for the Hall of Assembly, Washington. He was awarded the Co-operators Medal at the Vienna Exhibition of 1873. Green stayed at Minton for over forty years, and was chosen as the artisan to report on the ceramic court at the Exposition Universelle, Paris. His son William Alfred, born 1863, trained at the Newcastle School of Art and became an apprentice at Minton from 1876 to 1883.

Gregoire, Charles, active 1860–1866

Floral artist of great skill, possibly of French origin, who was employed to paint raised studies of roses on Parian ware at Copeland. He also worked for Minton and may have been a freelance painter.

Copeland Parian Bottle Vase painted by Gregoire. Courtesy of the Spode Copeland China Collection, Trelissick, Cornwall

Gregory, Albert, born 1874

Flower painter born in Derbyshire, the son of Martin Gregory, a hosier and draper, who served his apprenticeship at the Crown Derby factory at Osmaston Road. He trained at the Derby School of Art, and became famous for his painting of roses. He signed or initialled his work. Gregory painted flowers in a naturalistic style, becoming especially known for the large, full-blown rose, found in many of his paintings. He was regarded as one of the finest floral painters at Derby. After some time in America c. 1908, he returned to Derby, where he painted the flowers, fruit and fish studies on the famous Gary service, gilded by George Darlington (q.v.).

Gresley, Cuthbert, 1876–1963

Landscape and flower painter, the eldest son of Frank Gresley and grandson of James Stephen Gresley, both of whom were talented artists. He worked for Royal Crown Derby under John P. Wade in 1893. He was regarded as one of their finest artists, painting landscapes and floral subjects, including the service presented to Princess Mary of Cambridge on her marriage. He was also known for painting watercolour rural landscapes. Gresley had a great love of music and was a fine singer. He had a business interest with Miss Eunice Maud (Sybil) Francis, a leading embroiderer, in the 'Travellers Joy' Café, Chellaston Road, Shelton Lock (which was noted for good food and where he displayed his sporting trophies). He lived at Chelleston and Shelton Lock.

Gresley, Harold, B.W.S., N.S.A., D.C.M., 1892–1963

Artist and teacher, the younger son of Frank Gresley and brother to Cuthbert. (q.v.) He was educated at Chelleston School and at the Derby School of Art, where he won a National Silver Medal (1912) and a year later a Bronze Medal. Harold worked very briefly for the Royal Crown Derby Co., but preferred teaching to painting. He enlisted in the Sherwood Foresters in WWII, where he won the Distinguished Service Medal. On his return he studied under Arthur Spooner R.B.A. at the Nottingham School of Art. He became assistant art master at Repton School.

Griffin, Thomas, born 1797

Modeller at the Derby pottery, known to have modelled the figure *Grimaldi as a Clown*; he succeeded Edward Keys as head of the modelling department. In c. 1826 he left and went to Rockingham, where it is thought he modelled some of the comports for the William IV service, and also a series of continental peasant figures.

Hackwood, William, 1757–1839

Sculptor and modeller born in Sandwich, Kent, the son of John, a soldier.

Josiah Wedgwood wrote to his partner Thomas Bentley on 20 September 1769: 'I hired an ingenious boy last night for Etruria as a Modeller. He has modelled at nights in his way for three years past, and never had any instruction, which circumstance considered he does things amazingly, and will be a valuable acquisition. I have hired him for five years, and with Denby and him I shall not want any other constant Modeller at Etruria' (Finer and Savage, *Wedgwood Letters* page 80). Hackwood became chief portrait modeller for Josiah Wedgwood 1769–1832, known for his work on ornamental ware, especially Jaspar, and for adapting busts and reliefs from the antique, used on Wedgwood medallions. He also modelled local celebrities and members of the Wedgwood family.

In 1774 Wedgwood said 'Hackwood is of the greatest value and consequence for fine small work', yet later complained to Bentley that Hackwood was becoming very expensive. In 1802 there is evidence that Josiah Spode II was trying to persuade Hackwood to join his pottery, but he did not succeed. It is thought he did sign some of his work, but Josiah Wedgwood told him very firmly not to do so, believing the only mark should be that of the factory. His output was prodigious; amongst the most notable *bas-reliefs* in Jaspar are *The Birth of Bacchus* and the companion piece *The Triumph of Bacchus*. In 1776 he modelled his portrait medallion of Edward Bourne, the bricklayer at the Wedgwood Factory, caused Josiah to comment: 'Old Bourne is the man himself with every wrinkle and cranny in the whole visage'. When Hackwood retired from Wedgwood he had served two generations of the Wedgwood family and completed sixty-three years of service. He died in 1839 and is buried with his first wife Ann in St Peters Churchyard, Stoke-upon-Trent, Staffordshire.

Haddock, Albert, 1889–1971

Artist gilder, an apprentice at Royal Crown Derby Pottery in 1902 under George Hemstock. He left to join Minton in 1912 and enlisted in the Army in 1914; he returned to Derby in 1935. Haddock was a superb artist gilder who trained boy apprentices. Much of his finest work was decorating services for Middle Eastern rulers. His portrait, donated by Michael Crawley, is in the Royal Crown Derby Museum. He retired aged 79.

Hadley, James, 1837–1903

Modeller and designer born in London, the son of Richard Hadley, a hairdresser. By 1841 the family had moved to Worcester, his father working at 72 High Street. James was first apprenticed to his father but never completed his apprenticeship, preferring to join the ceramic industry. He trained at the Government School of Art in Worcester, where he won in 1852 two prizes, one the book *Memoirs of the Early Italian Painters* by Mrs Jameson and a case of drawing instruments for ornamental modelling. He was first employed at the Kerr and Binns pottery and eventually became chief designer and modeller for the Worcester Royal Porcelain Co. Hadley was mainly responsible for the Japanese style of work shown in Exposition Universelle, Paris of 1878 and the Vienna Exhibition of 1883. He experimented with pâte-sur-pâte decoration (two plaques by him are in the Dyson Perrins Museum, Worcester). He designed a series of children after Kate Greenaway (q.v.), which became very popular. In 1875 he left the Worcester manufactory to work as a freelance artist from 95 High Street, Worcester.

By 1891, the family of four and a domestic servant had moved No 1 Beechwood, Worcester, and Hadley is now not only described as an artist in ceramics but also as an employer, and his son Louis N. Hadley as an artist in the business. In 1896 he had produced his own pottery, *Hadley Ware*, with his three sons, Howard, Louis and Frank in Diglis Road, Worcester. After his death in 1903, the firm continued and in 1905 the Worcester pottery bought the business.

Haggar, Reginald George, R.I., ARCA, MSIA, FRSA, 1905–1992

Artist, designer, art director, teacher and author, born in Ipswich and studied at the Ipswich School of Art, then at the Royal College of Art, London. In 1929 he was appointed as an assistant designer at Minton but after six months became Art Director. He was responsible for organising the Minton exhibits at the English Pottery Old and New exhibition at the Victoria & Albert Museum and in 1935 at the Royal Academy of British Design. He favoured modernistic design, popular at this time, and designed new shapes and patterns to meet this market. In 1935 he left Minton to become head of Burslem School of Art, where he remained until 1941 and then moved to the School of Art in Stoke. Haggar left full-time teaching to become a lecturer, writer and freelance painter. Now he held art classes teaching his pupils to use his unique palette of greys, blacks and greens with a little orange, ideal for the pictures he painted of the Potteries. He wrote many books, including *English Pottery Figures* (1947), *English Country Pottery* (1950) and *The Masons of Lane Delph* (1952). He was a member of the Royal Institute of Painters in Watercolour, President of the Society of Staffordshire Artists and an exhibitor at the Royal Academy. An obituary notice remarked: 'The selfless encouragement he gave to others' research has been instrumental in widening our knowledge of the history of ceramics, and we all who are his students, as well as his friends, will remember him always with gratitude.'

Hague, Reuben Ernest, 1883–1968

Freelance artist and designer, the son of Frederick Hague, a joiner. He was an apprentice at the Royal Crown Derby manufactory and possibly trained at the Derby School of Art. He painted tiles and panels with mermaids and other fabulous subjects, also designing patterns for transfer printing for the Thomas Hulme Universal Company. He was a competent landscape watercolourist who signed his work. Hague became well known for his fine painting on plaques of old masters and for royal portraits. He painted

Bone china Crown Staffordshire tea plate decorated with exoctic birds by R Hague

exotic bird designs for the Crown Staffordshire China Company, which he signed on the reverse, and which were of a very high quality; they were possibly made for the American market. Hague's son Douglas was trained at the Hanley School of Art in 1937 and painted for Royal Crown Derby in a similar style to his father. He became a ceramic designer for Thomas Hulme and later for the Ben Capper transfer manufacturer.

Hall, Sidney, born 1877

Painter, son of James Hall, a civil servant. In 1891 he served his apprenticeship under F. Salter at the Doulton pottery, and was living with his parents at 26 Kings Street, Newcastle-under-Lyme, described as a student (Arts). He painted all subjects with equal skill on many fine dessert services. He became head of the decorating department and was responsible for training young painters and for the hand-painted services. He stayed at Doulton until 1952. Much of his work is signed.

Hall, William, c. 1800-1861

Flower painter. He worked first at Derby but was discharged in 1821 and went to the Coalport pottery; he then became painter and overlooker at Messrs Alcock. A plate painted with a basket of flowers, dated 1822, was presented to Mrs Thomason Haslem's aunt with the artist's initials on the back; it is now in the Haslem collection. After leaving Alcocks it is thought from the reference in *The Staffordshire Advertiser* July 1838 that Hall became a colour maker, but was now insolvent. Haslem says he was at Copeland.

Hammersley, Harry, born 1875

Flower painter and designer, the son of William (q.v.) and possibly an apprentice at Copeland, trained by his father. He attended one of the local art schools, probably Stoke, where he won a medal engraved 'Harry Hammersley subject 23D National Medal for success in Art awarded by the Department of Science and Art 1897'; it is now in the Spode Museum archives. He painted floral studies on the ceramic surface and fine watercolour studies and was a contemporary of Arthur Perry (q.v.). He lived through many important changes in Copeland's art department but was never given the status he so richly deserved, employed always a piece-work painter and never a member of the staff. He followed the Spode tradition of designing a different floral study on each piece, a practice that demanded great skill in design. His pattern *Gainsborough*, c. 1930s and designed for the American market, became a bestseller. The floral studies were transfer printed under glaze and painted by girls.

In 1931 Prince George, Duke of Kent visited the Spode works. The tour of the factory included a visit to the artists' room, where he saw Hammersley engaged on elaborate drawings similar to those that he had inspected in the Museum (*The Pottery Gazette and Glass Trade Review*, August 1931). Hammersley signed his work H.H. Harold Holdway (q.v.), who was to become Art Director at Copeland, wrote in his unpublished memoirs about the help and advice he received from Hammersley,

Courtesy of the Spode-Copeland China Collection Trelissick Cornwall

who he describes as a slight, short man with greying hair, a fine conversationalist, extremely generous and mild in character. He was happily married and had moved to 74 Penkhull New Road, Stoke-upon-Trent.

Hammersley, William, born 1837

Flower painter, who was trained at one of the local art schools. He won the students' prize from the Department of Science and Art at South Kensington, London in 1853 and two more in 1854. The prizes are in the Spode Museum archives, as he painted for Copeland's for over twenty years. The Special Order books in the Spode archives record many patterns by Hammersley from 1890, mainly fine floral studies, but whether they are by William or by his son Harry (q.v.) is not proven. William lived at Boothenwood Terrace for at least forty years, within easy walking distance of the Copeland manufactory. He was described as a potters' porcelain painter from 1861, and in 1901 as a retired china painter.

Hammond, Edward, born 1848

Painter and engraver employed at Minton Art Pottery Studio, London c. 1870, painting medieval subjects on tiles and slabs. He was known to have been rather a wayward character and a friend of Mathew Elden (q.v.). He etched the outlines on copper plates from which transfer patterns were made.

Hancock, Frederick, active 1879–1913

Freelance painter of flowers, fish, game and landscapes. He was employed as a clerk in an office, but then went to the Pinder Bourne & Co. pottery, training under John Slater (q.v.), and stayed after the company was taken over by Doulton. He was noted for a variety of subjects. He painted quickly to an excellent standard. After he left Doulton he continued to receive commissions from them.

Bone china Doulton Burslem dessert plate signed, with the impressed mark Jan 1896

Hancock, George, c. 1780–1850

Artist, ground layer, painter and outside decorator born in Stoke-on-Trent, the second son of John Hancock. In 1805 he is known to be painting with Billingsley at the Pinxton pottery, and is then thought to have joined the Ridgeway pottery at Cauldon Place, Stoke-on-Trent. By 1819 he was employed at the Derby pottery, where he encouraged paintresses to paint flowers, which was not a popular move and caused great unrest. He supervised a new method of ground laying, in which powdered colours were laid through stencils. George was a floral artist with a bold, compelling style that had been influenced by his time with Billingsley. He left Derby and found employment at Burton-on-Trent, where his skill was used in the production of china. But in 1836 he returned to the Potteries, and may have decorated for the Minton pottery. Briefly in 1839 he was employed in a factory in Lyons in France; it is said he had his own decorating firm in London; and then he decorated glass at Stourbridge. He painted watercolours, some of which are held in the Derby Museum. His hobbies included angling, at which he was expert. He died at Wordsley in Staffordshire.

Hancock, George, born 1812

Colour maker born 14 May 1812 at Dawley Magna, Shropshire, the son of William (q.v.). He was an apprentice at the Coalport manufactory, where he became responsible for the ceramic colours, notably turquoise, which was similar to the Sèvres Bleu Celeste. In 1850 he succeeded in producing a Rose Du Barry colour from a suggestion by the London retailer Mr Daniell. The colour was very popular and used for expensive services ordered by not only Daniell but also by the well-known London retailers Mortlock, Phillips and Thomas Goode's. Although Hancock was not a painter or gilder, his contribution to decoration at Coalport contributed greatly to their success. A service displayed at the Great Exhibition of 1851 was noted in *The London Illustrated News* as 'having great beauty and richness of tone even the Jurors commented on the dessert service the imitation of the original Sèvres colour they said it was remarkable…'. By 1881 Hancock had left the ceramic industry and was shown as an Innkeeper living in Bridge Street, Madeley, Shropshire.

Hancock, Harry Sampson, 1817–1898

Flower painter, the grandson of John Hancock (q.v.). He worked as a flower painter at the Nottingham Road,

Bone china Royal Doulton dessert plate signed J. Hancock and with the printed mark for May 1902

Derby pottery and in 1848 became joint founder of the King Street works. He taught Henry Sampson (died 1934) who specialised in flowers and landscapes and by 1900 had become the premier landscape artist at Derby.

Hancock, James, 1791–1865

Colour maker and ground layer. The son of John Hancock (Senior, q.v.), he trained as a colour maker and ground layer at Worcester; his son Sampson became owner of the King Street, Derby Factory, and his cousin James manager of the Royal Porcelain Works at Worcester in 1862.

Hancock, John (Senior), 1757–1847

Flower painter and colour maker who was apprenticed at the Nottingham Road, Derby factory. He used to walk to Nottingham, where he father lived, and then back to Derby to work. He was a good floral artist, who worked briefly for the Cambrian pottery in Swansea, then came to Staffordshire, where he worked for Turner at Lane End. Simeon Shaw states: 'Hancock was employed by Messrs Turner of Lane end prior to 1800, where he is credited with the method of gilding with burnished gold. The practice originated with Mr William Smith of Slack's Lane, Hanley, who knew the secret of water gilding practiced at Birmingham, which suggested the application of gold in a liquid state (amalgamated with Mercury) in place of gold leaf used upon size; and the attempt being made the result passed all expectations.' Hancock was subsequently with Henry Daniel at the Spode Works 1805–07 as an enameller and ground layer, and is credited with the development of gilding and the introduction of silver lustres based on platinum. In 1816 he left and went to Wedgwood as a colour maker and manager of the enamelling department.

Hancock, John, 1777–1840

Painter, the second son of John Hancock (Senior, q.v.), a colour maker and ground layer. He was also employed with H. Daniel at Stoke in 1805, and then went to Derby, working under his brother George (q.v.), painting birds in the Sèvres style. At the time of his death from consumption he was living at Blackfiord Bridge, described as a designer.

Hancock, John, 1804–1839

Painter and designer born in the Potteries, the eldest son of John Hancock (Senior, q.v.), a colour maker and ground layer at the Derby manufactory, although the date of his joining is not known. Haslem says he painted a large bowl with jug to match in about 1823 or 1824; they were decorated with bold flowers and kept as show pieces. He says Hancock painted flowers, birds and heraldic crests at Derby from 1823 to 1836, and may have painted the armorial bearings on the Earl Ferrers Service. In 1830 he married Mary Harrison at St Peter's, Derby and their son George was born a year later. The couple were living in Traffic Street and he is described as a china painter. In 1836 he left Derby for the Messrs Cowsels at Blackford Bridge, near Bury, now employed as a designer. His designs were used for waistcoats, ladies' dresses and toilet tablecloths, which were very successful. One toilet cloth design was of the young Queen Victoria, and sold extensively. He died of consumption in April 1839 at the early age of thirty-four.

Hancock, Joseph, born 1876

Landscape, fish and game painter. He became an apprentice at Doulton when fourteen years old, training under Harry Piper (q.v.) and Charles Noke (q.v.). Hancock was noted for his painting of game, fish, birds and landscapes after Corot (q.v.). He remained at the Doulton factory until 1926 and returned there 1942–45. He was a slow painter and is known to have taken fourteen days to paint a vase.

Hancock, Robert, c. 1729–1816

Artist, designer and engraver thought to have been born in Burslem, Staffordshire. In 1746 he was apprenticed to George Anderton of Birmingham. He was a pupil of Ravenet, the French artist, who managed the Battersea establishment for S. Jansen. Hancock designs are known on Birmingham enamels but it is thought he worked at the Battersea Enamel Factory, York House under the direction of John Brookes c. 1753. He moved to the Worcester factory. In 1772 Hancock bought a share in the Worcester works, but he sold it two years later, being unable to agree with the other partners. It is said he invested his money in a bank, which failed. He joined Turner at the Caughley Pottery c. 1775–80, then moved around the country and was in Birmingham 1791. When in Bristol in 1796 he drew small portraits; his *Samuel Taylor Coleridge*, dated 1796, was engraved. He lived in London in 1808. Hancock contributed many designs to *The Ladies Amusement Book*, published 1762, which were used as source material by many well-known potteries into the twentieth century. He was a mezzotint engraver of great talent, influenced by Sir Joshua Reynolds and Joseph Wright of Derby.

Hancock, William, born 1828

Painter, son of John Hancock (q.v.). He was one of the last apprentices at the Nottingham Road, Derby works. He may have decorated for the Coalport Pottery, and examples of his signed work have been found. He is known to have worked for Sampson Hancock at King Street, Derby. He married and had three sons, all of whom became painters in the ceramic industry.

Handley, A., active 1881–1882

Painter of figure subjects at Copeland. He is shown in their records as painting figures and copying the work of old masters onto tiles and plaques, but he also specialised in painting cupids, bathing figures and heads. His work is signed.

Harper, George, 1856–1892

Landscape artist and outside decorator born in Broseley, Shropshire. He served his apprenticeship at the Coalport manufactory c. 1868–75 as a china painter. However, by 1881 the family were living at Salthoude, Broseley, his occupation is given as landscape painter (artist), and he is shown in the Coalport pottery pattern books. Some time after 1888 he had left to work in the Potteries. He may be the same artist who was painting castles in Thomas Allen's Studio at Wedgwood in the late nineteenth century.

Harper, John, born 1842

Landscape painter born in Broseley, son of John Harper (born 1812), a china painter. He was apprenticed at the Coalport manufactory c. 1854–61. Father and son were employed at the Coalport pottery from 1870s, where John Junior painted landscapes and was also thought to have been responsible for some of the 1890 to 1895 patterns.

Harradine, Arthur Leslie, died 1965

Modeller and freelance designer who was apprenticed to Doulton, working at the Lambeth Studio 1902–12. He studied under Albert Toft, the modeller, at the Camberwell School of Art. He was a modeller of great skill and responsible for a series of limited editions of salt-glaze characters from Dickens and of the politicians of the time, such as A.J. Balfour. He modelled figures of birds in stoneware with decoration in coloured slips. In 1912 he went to Canada to join a Canadian Regiment and in WWI fought in France. On his return he became a freelance designer. Many of his designs were produced by Doulton, including *Top of the Hill*, *Autumn Breezes*, *Fruit Gathering* and *The Old Balloon Seller*. His modelling is noted for its feel of movement and liveliness; he marked some of his work LH. He sent at least one new model a month, sometimes two or three, to Doulton. He died in Gibraltar.

Harris, Charles, born 1876

Flower and bird painter born in Appleby, Leicestershire

and apprenticed at the Royal Crown Derby manufactory. He is known for painting small delicate sprays of flowers and brightly coloured birds in the Chelsea style. He was a contemporary of Cuthbert Gresley (q.v.); they worked together decorating the wedding service for Princess Mary of Cambridge. By 1911 it is thought he emigrated to America.

Harrison, C., active 1890s

Flower painter at the Brown, Westhead and Moore pottery. He may have been at the Coalport pottery in the late 1890s, before joining Doulton 1906–08. Here he painted misty roses and many fine floral designs and signed his work.

Bone china Cauldon dessert plate signed Harrison c. 1900

Bone china Royal Doulton dinner plate c. 1930s signed by C. Hart

Hart, Charles Holloway, born 1867

Artist painter born in Burslem, Staffordshire and in 1880 started his apprenticeship under John Slater at Pinder Bourne and Co. He studied at the Burslem School of Art and worked for Doulton 1880–1927. He specialised in flower painting, creating the misty effect that was a hallmark of Doulton at the time. He could paint fish, game, lakeside scenes and castles with equal skill. His work sold well in North America. His son, also Charles, born 1908, joined Doulton as an apprentice in 1922 and trained under his father, painting fish and game, but later helped in the development of underglaze painting of figures.

Hartshorne, active from 1849

Flower painter who is listed in the Special Order books at W.T. Copeland, painting pattern numbers 8084, 7523 and D 6352. He specialised in floral studies: an entry shows a Hartshorne painting orchids on a Richelieu-shape dessert service, the gilding done by Coxon. However, in 1870 a flower painter of the same name is known to have worked at William Brownfield & Sons, Cobridge, Staffordshire. Two of the vases he painted, designed by Protat or Mollart, were exhibited at the Philadelphia Exhibition of 1876. The 1881 census records a William Hartshorne, son of John Hartshorne, who was a potters' manager out of employment, as being a china painter living at 149 Flint Terrace, Wolstanton, Staffordshire.

Hartshorne, James Edward, born 1841

Animal and flower painter born in Broseley, Shropshire and apprenticed at the Coalport manufactory around 1853 to 1860. He then may have been employed at the Royal Worcester Porcelain Co., until he returned to the Coalport manufactory from 1870 to 1878, painting animals, principally cattle. His work was exhibited by Coalport in the International London Exhibition of 1871. After Robert Frederick Abraham (q.v.) left Coalport to become Art Director at W.T. Copeland, Hartshorne took over his work, which he painted with great skill, becoming one of Coalport's premier artists. When the new Crown Derby manufactory opened at Osmaston Road he became the first foreman of the painters and gilders department. In August 1878 his name appears in the pattern books, on numbers 597, 598 and 786, as painting fish, dogs and birds, but also responsible for the gilding of the ware. There are other references of 1878: pattern number 791, painted birds, fish and dog Mr Hartshorn; number 1008, Regal Dessert plate, salmon ground fish and bird centre, painted in Hartshorne's room. It is thought he stayed about five years and in 1881 the family were living at

70 Byron Street, Normanton, but his occupation now reads foreman decorative department and china works, teacher of drawing and painting professor. The first evidence that his life outside the ceramic industry may be more rewarding appears in *The Wreckin Echo* of 1881, which says he was assistant art master at the School of Art, probably the Derby Art School, and that he had left Coalport to join Derby, where he painted animals, fish and birds. The 1901 census returns describe him as an art Master and farmer living with his wife and four children (Albert is described as a china painter) at Benthall Lane, The Lea, Shropshire.

Haslem, John, born 1808–1884

Painter and writer born at Carrington Bowden in Cheshire, but went to Derby to live with his uncle, James Thomason, the commercial manager at the Derby pottery. In 1822 he became an apprentice at the Derby works under Robert Bloor and worked with many of the foremost china painters and modellers of the period. The Duke of Sussex was so impressed with his work that in 1836 he sent him to London to study under E.T. Paris, a historical painter, who did some painting for Queen Adelaide. Haslem became known for painting portraits but still did special work for the Derby pottery. During 1836–65 he exhibited at the Royal Academy. In 1844 he won a Society of Arts medal for his enamelled portrait of the Duke of Wellington and from 1845 he gained commissions for portraits of their family from Queen Victoria and Prince Albert. It is thought he may have been Queen Victoria's art tutor. An enamel of the Queen was exhibited at the Great Exhibition of 1851. By 1857 Haslem left London and returned to Derby to live again with his uncle at 7 Nottingham Road Street, Alkmund, Derby, described in the census as an enamel painter-artist. At this time he wrote articles for *The Derby Reporter* and his book *The Old Derby China Factory: the workmen and their productions* describes the life of many of the artists employed in the pottery industry at the time. In the 1881 census he is listed as a retired enamel painter.

Hassall, Josiah, born c. 1850

Floral and bird painter and designer, the son of Joseph Emery Hassall, a china manufacturer. He trained at Stoke and Fenton Art School, where in 1865 he won a year's free tuition at the Science and Art Department in London. He returned to W.T. Copeland and served the company for the next thirty years. Joss, as he was known, was an unusual character, but because of the quality of his painting was allowed his eccentricities. According to Arthur Perry, speaking to Len White 'He was a Falstaff, a great friend of Brushy Beardsmore, whose wife kept a fish shop, and if he met Brushy on his way to work he'd just go off with him for two or three days and help sell his brushes (which Brushy made) from his horse and cart and get drunk with him.' Joss was a good artist though; an entry of 5 October 1880 in the Copeland Special Order books shows that he was paid 24 shillings for a set of seventeen tiles painted with laburnum and birds.

Hassall, Joseph, born 1876

Engraver, the eldest son of Josiah (q. v.), who worked in the engraving department at Copeland, becoming foreman by the 1930s.

Silhouette drawings by Joseph Hassall

Hassall, Thomas, 1878–1940

Flower painter and art director, the younger son of Josiah (q. v.). At the age of fourteen he was apprenticed to Charles Brough and then to Thomas Sadler at the Spode works. He studied at the Hanley and Stoke School of Art, and worked at Copeland 1892–1940. In 1892, at the

Thomas Hassall in his office at Spode

Study of fish by Thomas Hassall

early age of twenty-three, he returned from his studies at the Government School of Design, South Kensington, London to become foreman of one of the decorating departments. In 1910 he was made Art Superintendent. In 1931 he designed a coffee service for the Prince. Hassall had two sons: one became a representative for Copeland and the other worked in the factory. In 1935 Hassall was appointed a director of the Company, the first art director in the history of Spode to be given this appointment. His sudden death at the age of sixty-two was a great shock to workers and management alike.

Hawkins, William, 1858–1930

Fruit flower and figure painter, the son of a commercial traveller. He was employed at the Royal Worcester Porcelain Factory from 1874 to 1928, becoming foreman of a painting shop, and was one of the premier artists of his time. He either initialled or signed some of his work. Hawkins copied famous paintings onto the ceramic surface: for example, Gainsborough's *Blue Boy*, Reynolds' *Mrs Carmac* and Meissonier's *The Cavalier*. He also painted fine miniatures. By 1901 he was shown as foreman of the decorating department.

Heap, Samuel H., born 1873

Fruit, flower and freelance painter, son of Samuel Heap, a tobacconist. In 1891 he was living with his parents at 45 Queen Street, Tunstall, described as a flower painter. He trained in the Potteries but emigrated to America. He was employed on a freelance basis at many of the thirty-eight Potteries in Trenton, New Jersey. He was known to have been at the Pickard China Co. c. 1905, and he then went to the Stouffer Studio, where he stayed until the 1920s.

Heath, Richard, born 1835

Painter and gilder born in Shelton, Staffordshire and worked for H. and R. Daniel of Stoke-on-Trent. Scarratt says that he painted for Ridgeway's Cauldon Works, and that one of his sons was a gilder. From 1861 to 1871 he was living at Stoke Road, Penkhull, Stoke-upon-Trent, described as a china painter; but in 1881 he was living at 82 Stoke Road, his occupation changed to painter and gilder.

Heath, William, born 1843

Painter born in Burslem, Staffordshire, employed at the Minton pottery. In 1861 he was living with his parents at 103 Liverpool Road, Burslem, described as a potter; but by 1871 he had married and moved to George Street, Stoke-on-Trent, now described as a potter china painter. He was a successful ceramic artist whose work was exhibited at the Exposition Universelle, Paris of 1878. Ten years later he had become a freelance designer, as the census shows him living at Minton Place, Stoke-upon-Trent (next door to Samuel B. Furnival, described as Managing Director at Pottery Works), his occupation now given as designer in pottery (own account).

Hemstock, George, born 1867

Artist gilder in Derby, the son of a baker and an apprentice at the Crown Derby manufactory. He assisted Desire Leroy on the dessert service made for the Duke of York and Princess May on the occasion of their marriage. His daughter Kate, although a talented watercolour artist, was also employed in the gilding department at Derby.

Henk, Christian R.H. (also known as Carl), 1822–1905

Figure and landscape painter born in Coburg and worked for Tielch and Co., Silesia before moving to Minton c. 1848, where he stayed for nearly thirty years. He

Majolica dish modelled by C. Henk after a Japanese Ivory c. 1875

Bone china Minton dessert plate painted by C. Henk Courtesy of the Potteries Museum and Art Gallery Stoke-on-Trent

painted mainly figure subjects and landscapes after Watteau (q.v.), Sèvres style portraits and cupids. His work was included in the International Exhibition, 1862 and in the Exposition Universelle, Paris of 1867. He is listed in the Minton factory books as painting No 176: Dessert plate, Sheep and Cattle scene, by Henk. He applied for British naturalisation and bought four new housing plots on George Street, living in number 41. His son John (q.v.) joined him at the Minton manufactory and his daughter Elizabeth, born in 1844, married Louis Jahn (q.v.), the well-known Minton artist.

Henk, John, 1846–1914

Modeller, son of Christian (q.v.), born in Cologne and trained from 1863 to 1868 at the Stoke-on-Trent School of Art, where he won the silver medal for modelling and was a pupil of Protat (q.v.). In 1871 he married the girl next door, Laura Thekla A. Muller, the daughter of Adam Muller (q.v.), one of the premier decorators at the Minton manufactory. John modelled many fine animals, which were exhibited in 1889 at the Exposition Universelle, Paris, and he is noted for his work with T. Longmore (q.v.) modelling elephants. He was awarded a medal at the Vienna Exhibition of 1873 and was eventually responsible for all the modelling at Minton. By 1881 he had moved to 19 West Parade, Stoke-on-Trent with his family and two servants and was still there ten years later, described as a potters' modeller.

Hewitt, John Pilson, 1855–1930

Painter of figure subjects, the son of a railway engine fitter. He was trained at the Minton Art Studio in London under William Coleman. He worked for Minton in the mid-1870s and Copeland 1878–82 painting figures, subjects, particularly heads, on plaques and tiles. His style was fashionable and copied by other Copeland artists, such as J. Arrowsmith and H. Lea. In the 1880s he joined Wedgwood, where in 1882 he painted a charger of *Petruchio*, a character in Shakespeare's *Taming of the Shrew*, in the style of T. Allen (q.v.). Hewitt was an assistant to William Palin (q.v.) before working at Royal Doulton 1885–93. In later life he became a representative for Harrison and Son, the ceramic colour manufactures. He was a man of great charm and thought to have been one of the best painters of figure subjects of his time. His hobby was skating, at which he excelled, winning a bronze medal for roller-skating in the international style. He judged many local roller skating competitions.

Hill, Albert, born 1840

Artist, painter, gilder and outside decorator born in London. In 1859 he became an apprentice at the Royal Worcester Porcelain Co, where he stayed until the 1870s. Initially he coloured figures and painted birds, but was also a competent gilder. Eventually Hill acquired his own muffle kiln and decorated for E. Locke. He became a teacher of painting and exhibited his work at the Howell and James Gallery, London. In 1881 he was living at Green Hill, London.

Hill, James, 1791–1854

Flower painter, gilder and modeller. He was an apprentice at the Nottingham Road, Derby works and stayed with the pottery until its closure. The pattern with a large rose and scattered flower sprigs became known as 'Hill's flowers'. He modelled small animal figures, using a penknife instead of a modeller's tool. He joined W. Locker in forming the King Street Factory at Derby and was known as an amiable character and much respected by his fellow artists. On 3 May 1854 *The Derby Mercury* reported his death: 'On Tuesday week in Parker Street Mr James Hill in the 64th year of his life, an artist of considerable ability. The numerous specimens of flower painting produced by him in the china works in the town are characterised by an almost inimitable delicacy and beauty.'

Hill, Thomas (Jockey), 1753–1827

Landscape painter, the son of Thomas Hill, portrait and landscape artist of Battersea, London. Hill went to Derby in 1795, after working at Chelsea, replacing Zachariah Boreman as a landscape painter. He was paid two and a half guineas a week for not less than 54 hours work or 7s. a day. Jockey was an artist of great talent, although he had lost three fingers of his right hand: he held the brush between the stumps of his fingers. His work influenced by Paul Sandby (q.v.) and is characterised by the inclusion of brightly painted small figures in the foreground, often agricultural workers at rest with their animals. He became known affectionately as Jockey because of his love of horses. He rented two fields, and owned sometimes as many as thirty horses. His pony Bob used to take him to work each day, return home by himself, and was trained to return at the end of the day to collect his master. In c. 1800 he returned to Paradise Walk, Chelsea, London and in 1801 joined his father at 53 Great Marlborough Street. He exhibited at the Royal Academy between 1805 and 1808 and later became a dealer for Government stores. Haslem gives the impression that although talented, Jockey was not too unhappy to stop painting and earn his living in another way. He died in Marylebone aged 74.

Hillman, Frederick, born 1862

Flower painter born in Bovey Tracy, Devon, the son of William Hillman, a potters' printer who almost certainly worked at the Torquay Pottery. By 1881 Frederick and his widowed father had come to the Potteries, living at 42 John Street, Shelton, Stoke-on-Trent. He worked for Taylor Tunnicliffe and Co. Ltd, Hanley, then at Brown Westhead & Moore; his work for them was exhibited at the World's Columbian Exposition, Chicago of 1893. Examples of his signed work have been found, which show the skill of this fine artist.

Hindley, J., active 1900s

Pâte-sur-pâte artist who was employed at the Doulton factory at Nile Street, Burslem, Stoke-on-Trent, Staffordshire. Some of his signed work has been found.

Hinley, Charles, active 1890s

Figure painter and designer who trained at the Government School of Design, South Kensington in the 1870s. He was employed as decorating manager at Wedgwood from 1893 to 1898 on a salary of £500, and must have been at Brown-Westhead, Moore & Co. prior to that date, probably as a departmental manager, as they complained to Wedgwood about poaching their staff. Examples of his work are in the Museum of Applied Arts and Sciences, Sydney, NSW, Australia.

Histwood, Haigh, died 1854

Painter, retailer and outside decorator born at Royds Hall, Huddersfield in the late 1770s. He was apprenticed at the Rockingham works and considered to be the best painter of fly designs. He was permitted by Lady Milton of Wentworth House to draw over 500 insects from her

Bone china Brown Westhead Moore & Co dessert plate c. 1891, painted by Fredrick Hillman

collection. Hirstwood is recorded in the 1821 census but known to have moved to York by 1827 to manage the Brameld's shop, until it closed in 1833. He started a china decorating business in York, buying in white china from Sampson Bridge and Co. of Longton and firing it in his own kilns with his son-in-law William Leyland. When the partnership ended, William Leyland went to London, where he painted and decorated lamps. So far no signed examples of Histwood's work have been found. He had two sons, Joseph (1813–31) and William, both of whom were apprentices at Rockingham and are known to have worked with their father on dessert services for King William IV and the Duchess of Cumberland. He died in York.

Hodgkiss, James, 1867–1937

Landscape and bird painter, son of Thomas Hodgkiss, a potters' clay manager. He became chief designer at Wedgwood from 1900 to 1923. He was closely associated with Daisy Makeig-Jones (q.v.) in the design of fairy lustre decoration around 1900. He worked with the art director John Edward Goodwin and the chemist George Adams in the development of powder colours, designing patterns for china bowls with printed gold on a powder-blue background. He signed his work, painting birds in landscapes and designing scenes of birds in their natural landscapes for bone china dessert sets. By 1900 he had married Ada Mary Hobson at Stoke and in 1901 the couple had set up home at 5 Clive Street, Hanley, Staffordshire and when he was described as a potters' decorator.

Hodkinson, Fred, active c. 1895–1949

Artist gilder, son of William (q.v.), who was apprenticed at the age of thirteen under Herbert Bentley at the Doulton pottery, learning to work with acid gold and raised paste. He became manager of the acid gold department, and was responsible for many fine important services.

Hodkinson, William George, born 1857

Artist gilder, landscape and flower painter born in Derby and trained at the Hanley and Stoke School of Art. He was an apprentice at Minton under Leon Arnaux (q.v.), then living with his parents at Boothen Penkhill, Staffordshire. He left Minton in 1877 to join Doulton, where he stayed until 1920. William painted floral subjects in widely different styles and landscapes, often including sheep and cattle. He decorated panels with raised gilding and moulded effects and with Charles Nokes designed for Doulton flambé ware. His work was influenced by the Art Nouveau style. He was a talented artist with the rare ability to paint in both ceramic colour and gold. His work was exhibited at many exhibitions, for example, in Chicago, St Louis and Paris.

Hogg, Herbert Warrington, born 1863

Modeller, born in Salisbury Wiltshire. He trained at the Derby School of Art in the evenings and worked at the Crown Derby factory. He also exhibited his paintings at the Royal Academy, 1883–85. In 1886 the Derby pottery was concerned about his health, gave him leave of absence and paid for him to go on a Mediterranean cruise. Examples of his fine work are to be found in the Royal Crown Derby Museum.

Holdcroft, George, 1884–1951

Engraver who at thirteen became an apprentice at the Doulton pottery. He was one of seventeen members of the Holdcroft family to work there. He stayed sixty-seven years with Doulton and deserved his reputation as the finest etcher of the six towns.

Holdcroft, Harold F.R.S.A., M.S.I.A.D., active 1920s–1960s

Artist, designer and art teacher who trained at the Burslem School of Art in 1921. In 1929 he became Works Designer at the Royal Albert Pottery, Longton, where he designed the popular pattern *Country Roses*. From 1944 to 1948 he was master in charge of the Longton Art School. Holdcroft was appointed director of the Thomas Wild & Sons pottery.

Holdway, Harold, 1913–2002

Designer and art director, born in Stoke-on-Trent, the son of a railway worker. He was educated at Cauldon Elementary School and won a two-year art scholarship to the junior department of Burslem School of Art; after this he was awarded a bursary to continue his senior art education. During his final art school days he was fortunate to get a part-time placement with the George Jones, Crescent Pottery in Stoke. In 1933 the management changed and Harold was employed to design lithographs, which he hated. In 1934 he joined Copeland, where he was to remain for the rest of his working life. By 1940 he had become Chief Designer. In 1943 he joined the Fleet Air Arm, returning to Copeland after the War. By the 1950s he was producing modernistic designs, such as *Moon Drop* and *Soft Whispers*. Holdway was appointed Art Director in 1956 and became a member of the Spode Board of Directors in 1976. His best-known designs are *Reindeer*, *Queens Bird*, *Rhododendron* and *Christmas Tree*. Holdway had one son, Paul, who became chief engraver at Spode.

Bone china Spode Copeland plate designed by Harold Holdway, c. 1952. Source: the Audubon bird prints

Harold Holdway (left) Len Whiter (centre) and Arthur Perry (right) in the W.T. Copeland showroom, presenting Arthur Perry with a pair of Copeland china flying ducks c. 1970

Hollins, Henry Plant, born 1857

Modeller born in Hanley, Stoke-on-Trent, the son of an innkeeper, bandmaster and Professor of music. He was apprenticed to Solon (q.v.) at the Minton pottery c. 1873 and worked on pâte-sur-pâte decoration. An example of his work, a cabaret set, can be found at the Manchester City Art Gallery. He initialled his work with a monogram of joined H.H. He left the Potteries in the 1900s to become an artist in London.

Holloway, John, born 1847

Landscape painter born in Hanley, employed at the Minton pottery painting scenes with figures after Boucher (q.v.). His work was shown in the International Exhibition, 1862. He joined Thomas Allen at the Wedgwood pottery, again specialising in painting landscapes, marine, animal and bird subjects. By 1881 the family were living at 70 Seaford Street, Hanley, where he is now described as a china painter and beer seller.

Holmes, Robert Lea, born 1877

Flower painter, who came from Derby and lived at Grosvenor Avenue, Trent Vale, with his wife and children – Harold, born in 1904, and Bernie, born 1907. He was a student at the Stoke School of Art, eventually becoming a teacher in the junior department, and also at the Burslem School of Art. He worked at Copeland and is recorded in their Special Order books c. 1891 as painting tea services. When he was demobbed after WWI, there were very few vacancies for artists at Copeland and he went to the Grimwade pottery in Burslem. His oil painting *Aston by Stone* was seen at the Century of Art Exhibition in Hanley, Stoke-on-Trent in 1953.

Holtzendoff, Count Georg von, active c. 1878–1888

Landscape and painter of figure subjects born in Dresden, the son of Hans, courtier to the King of Saxony. He was educated at the Military Academy. When at University, he realised he had artistic talent and went to the Dresden pottery. He came to England to escape from the Franco-Prussian War, working at Derby about 1878–80. His work is rare but if found is initialled G. H. By 1905 he returned to Dresden to take over the duties as head of his noble family.

Hopewell, John, 1834–1904

Bird painter at the Royal Worcester Porcelain factory, who was succeeded by C. Baldwin (q.v.).

Hopkinson, Edward (Senior) 1788–1868

Gilder apprenticed at the Derby factory under William Smith. He had several sons who were trained in the ceramic industry. By the early 1840s the family came to the Potteries, where they started a small business making figures, vases and ornaments.

Hopkinson, William, born 1808

Modeller born in Derby, the son of Edward (q.v.). He was apprenticed at the Derby pottery, working in the same room as Gadsby (q.v.) and Lucas (q.v.). He and his father started a small business making figures, vases and other ornaments, using raised flowers. William left the Potteries and is known to have been in London in 1875, where his daughters Agnes and Alice were born. The story is told of his meeting William Gladstone, MP at a dinner, at which Gladstone took some of the guests to see his collection of paintings and china. He had two unmarked vases, which were thought to have been produced by the Derby pottery. William recognised the decoration and was able to authenticate them; Gladstone was delighted and displayed them with his other Derby pieces. Hopkinson is listed in the 1881 census as a china pottery figure maker, living at 22 Townmead Road, Fulham, London.

Howell, Thomas, born 1845

Artist gilder at Copeland. Their Special Order book shows entries for Mr Howell, Howell and S. Howell. He decorated a large Coventry-shape plate with a richly jewelled border for the 1889 Exposition Universelle, Paris. In April 1889 he is shown as working on an order for Queen Victoria, a table plate with the head of her Majesty, six panels of roses and shamrocks and a Star of India centre. From the records it is possible that Howell was also employed as a crest or heraldic painter. In 1881 he was living at 4 James Street, Stoke-on-Trent, Staffordshire.

Howells, Edwin, 1821–78

Bird painter and gilder born in Broseley, Shropshire, who painted at the Coalport pottery from c. 1840 to 1860. He is thought to have introduced the Chelsea bird designs that were popular in the 1840s. When forty years old, he was described as an artist gilder, living in Broseley.

Hoy, Agnete, born 1914

Studio pottery designer born in London, the daughter of a pharmacist and bacteriologist. She was educated in Denmark, at the School of Arts and Crafts in Copenhagen and at the Royal Copenhagen Porcelain Company. 1937–39 she was employed at Gerhard Neilsen's Holbaek Stoneware; however, when she came to England to visit her family, war broke out and she stayed with her brother. Agnete applied unsuccessfully for a job at Wedgwood, but met Gordon Forsyth at the Burslem School of Art, who introduced her to Guy Harris, one of the directors of Bullers. In 1934 Harris had opened a small studio in the factory at Milton, and put Ann Potts in charge. She was responsible for designing figures, and the studio then produced vases, bowls and dishes with unusual glazes; but Potts left in 1939 to get married and the studio closed. Agnete experimented with the Bullers hard paste porcelain and was appointed Bullers' designer, on £6 a week, to open up the studio again and to design coffee sets, cooking ware and tea ware. The studio produced hand-turned pieces, which they then decorated. Hoy eventually had a team of ten, each essential to the product and allowed to sign their work. In 1950, when Bullers closed, Agnete returned to London with her husband as a designer at the Doulton Lambeth Studio. By 1956 the studio closed and she set up her own studio at home and became a teacher at Richmond and West Surrey Colleges of Art.

Huggins, Vera, active 1923–50

Became one of Royal Doulton's best-known designers and throwers of stoneware. Her decorating techniques included *sgraffito*, intaglio and under-painting; also tube lining. She preferred soft blues, greens, beiges and yellows. Her designs were first shown at the 1925 Exposition Universelle, Paris, followed by display in the British Exhibition at the Royal Academy in 1935. Her wares were very popular in the United States, Australia and New Zealand.

Hulme, Frederick, born 1867

Artist gilder, son of a terracotta finisher. He did very fine gilding, and sometimes put his initials on the back of a piece in red. This was not a signature, but a factory identification mark. Many more initials like this may come to light in the future; even as late as the 1930s gilders were not allowed to sign their work. Fred lived in Shelton and walked to work at the Spode works, Stoke each day.

Hulme, Jesse, 1789–1852

Portrait artist, engraver and designer. He is thought to have been at Swinden in Yorkshire c. 1816, and then moved to Staffordshire around 1825 to start a pottery – but this was unsuccessful. He was employed at Wedgwood 1842–44 as an engraver.

Hundley, Henry, born 1841

Flower painter born in St Peters, Worcester, known for gilding and raised enamel work that showed a Persian influence. In 1881 he was living at Sansome Place, Claines, Worcester with his family; son Ernest, aged 15, was a china decorator and his daughter Alice worked in the engraving department.

Hurten, Charles Ferdinand, 1818–1906

Flower painter born in Cologne, where he studied at the Municipal School of Art. When eighteen years old he went to Paris, gaining commissions from the Sèvres pottery and other Parisian decorating establishments.

His work was shown at the Exposition Universelle, Paris of 1858, and seen by William Taylor Copeland, who persuaded him to come to Stoke-upon-Trent by offering him a salary of £320 a year and his own studio. He also promised that if at any time Hurten and his family wished to return to their native land, he would pay for their journey. Hurten accepted, becoming the premier floral artist at W.T. Copeland 1857–97. He was the first artist in Britain to paint floral studies from nature. He visited the gardens of Chatsworth House and Trentham Hall, and also the private gardens of the Copeland family at Oulton, near Stone, Staffordshire. At the Great Exhibition of 1851 Hurten was described as one of the best flower painters in Europe. He had an imposing manner and a genial temperament and was popular with his fellow artists; it is said that he ordered food hampers from Fortnum and Masons, which arrived by train at Stoke Station. Hurten was often to be seen in consultation with the kiln fireman, thus ensuring his work was placed in the most suitable spot in the kiln. Hurten's work was displayed in the Showroom at the Spode Works. He had many private commissions, one of which was to design panels for the Duchess of Devonshire's grand drawing room at Chatsworth. He signed his work either C. F. H. or C. F. Hurten.

In 1873 he lived in Swinton Terrace but by 1881 had moved to Lucien Besche's (his son-in-law) house at Minton Place, Stoke-upon-Trent, with his wife and four grandchildren, Antonin, Amelia, Charles and William Besche. It is possible his daughter and son-in-law were at this time living in France. His obituary in the *Evening Sentinel* of 7 January 1901 read: 'Mr Hurten was a most industrious and prolific artist. His productions were a notable feature of the Copeland's exhibits at the London International Exhibition in 1862, the Exposition Universelle, Paris of 1878 and the Exhibitions of Vienna, Berlin, Philadelphia Melbourne, Sydney and Chicago, and it is not to much to say that there is scarcely a Royal Palace or National Museum in Europe which does not contain specimens of Mr Hurten's craft.' The reports of these exhibitions praise his work and there is little doubt Copeland's success was in no small part due to his unique talent.

In the late 1890s times had been changing and Hurten had lost a great friend when the art director Robert Abraham died in 1895. In 1897 he was tempted to leave Copeland to go to Kilburn in London and live with his daughter, having been offered work from various book publishers. Unfortunately his health was failing and he could not take advantage of this work, and for the last few years of his life he received an annuity from the Pottery and Glass Trade Benevolent Fund.

Below: Copeland Arms pattern book No 2. Courtesy of the Spode Museum Trust

Jahn, Albert Christian, A.R.C.A, born 1865

Artist, son of Louis (q.v.) who trained at Hanley Art School, Staffordshire, where in 1884 he won the gold medal for life drawing in a national competition. He then studied at the Government School of Design, South Kensington. 1892–1907 he was Headmaster of the Wolverhampton School of Art, and then went to the Sheffield School of Art.

Jahn, Ludwig Hartmann Adelbert (Louis), 1840–1911

Painter of figure subjects born in Oberweissbach, Thuringia and working in Vienna. In 1862 Colin Minton Campbell and Leon Arnoux asked him to come to work for Minton. He painted vases in the Sèvres style with cupids and children, and was influenced by the paintings of Watteau (q.v.) and Raphael. Some of his first work for Minton was shown at the London International Exhibition of 1862. He married Elizabeth, daughter of Christian Henk, and they had three children – Henrietta, Albert and Francis. However, aged forty-one he is recorded as a widower, living at 15 Church Street, Hanley. He became Art Director for William Brownfield and Sons c. 1873–93 and was responsible for a great globe vase created from tinted porcelain. He was succeeded by Frederick Rhead (q.v.). In 1895 he returned to Minton to succeed Leon Arnoux as Art Director.

Jahn's final employment in 1900 was as curator of Hanley Museum, Stoke-on-Trent, a post he thoroughly enjoyed. He had a vast knowledge of ceramics and was an avid collector; he was also a naturalist, spending much of his free time at Dovedale, hunting for rare beetles. He joined the North Staffordshire Field Club in 1871 and became an authority on lepidopteran and coleopteran. In 1908 he became a Vice President of the Field Club, and in 1909 was awarded the Garner Medal for his studies on coleopteran in North Staffordshire. He died on 20 April 1911 and was buried in Hanley cemetery.

James, Harry, born 1860

Painter and gilder born in Merthyr, Glamorgan and trained at the Government School of Design, South Kensington, London. In the 1890s he came to the Coalport factory as a decorator.

Jeannest, Pierre-Emile, 1813–57

Sculptor, modeller, ceramic and silver designer, the son of Louis-François, a French bronzelier and a pupil of the sculptor Pierre Delaroche. He probably worked in the studio of the Count D'Orsay and was in England for some time before coming to Minton around 1845. He replaced Samuel Bourne, who had left to join the National School of Design, Kensington, London. In 1850 he worked on the Emperor of Austria service. His figure models include *Hawking*, *Fishing* and *The Rose of England* and he also designed allegorical figures. Minton produced his designs in terracotta, majolica, Parian and china. He left the Potteries to join Elkington and Co. silversmiths, but still created designs for Minton on a freelance basis. His first work for Elkington was a silver group of *Queen Elizabeth I entering Kenilworth Castle*, which was exhibited at the Great Exhibition of 1851. In 1853 he was appointed supervisor of the French workers at Elkington. He became modelling instructor for the Stoke and Hanley School of Art and for a short time at the Birmingham School of Art. He died on 7 February 1857 at the early age of forty-four.

Jessop, George, 1882–1944

Flower painter and apprentice at the Derby factory, where he specialised in painting flowers in loose bunches, often incorporating a rose. During WWI he worked at a munitions factory in Coventry; after the War he returned to the Derby factory, then took up an appointment as a railway sign writer in the 1930s. By 1935 he was again painting for Derby. His wife Annie was a gilder at Osmaston Road, Derby.

Jinks, Samuel, born 1852

Painter and gilder born in Newcastle-under-Lyme, Staffordshire. He attended the Newcastle School of Art in 1867 and joined Minton as an apprentice 1870–77,

Signed plate by Jinks, no factory attribution

eventually specialising in painting portraits. By 1878 he was employed at the Brown-Westhead, Moore & Co. pottery. *The Staffordshire Advertiser*, reporting on wares exhibited by the pottery at the Exposition Universelle, Paris in 1889 said: 'Mr Jinks will be represented by a considerable number of pieces painted on china – chiefly highly finished figure subjects and there are several handsome vases enriched with bouquets of delicately modelled flowers both bisque and coloured after nature.' In 1881 he was living at 16 Broad Street, Newcastle-under-Lyme, listed in the census as an artist painter.

Johnson, Arthur Leslie, 1870–1940

Portrait artist and ceramic painter, the son of William Johnson and Mary (née Sneddon). After Mary's early death, her sister Sarah came to look after the family. She and William started Johnson and Sneddon Furriers, Burton-on-Trent.

Leslie, brought up at Beresford House, Rolleston, Leicestershire was made to join the family business, which he hated. By 1891 he had moved to Burslem and married Ellen Hortense Carpenter. Family recollections state that the couple were given a bakers shop and a manager to run it. Leslie took no part and continued to paint as a freelance artist. He painted historical portraits and figures in the style of Watteau (q.v.) and Fragonard for some of the well-known factories in the area, including Bishop and Stonier. In 1903 he painted vases for the Crown Staffordshire Pottery decorated with scenes of *The Cries of London*. Leslie is known for his work with Doulton 1905–37. The dessert services he painted throughout this period often have intricate gilded borders. His work is finely executed and has a distinctive delicate manner related to the Art Nouveau style. It sold well in America and Australia.

Johnson, George B., 1859–1931

Bird painter, known to have been at the Royal Worcester Porcelain Company 1875–90, specialising in painting game birds and exotic flamboyant birds such as storks and flamingos. He painted landscapes in the style of the Chamberlain Worcester Porcelain period and signed or initialled his work; he also painted in watercolours and oils.

Jones, Cecil, active 1800s

Flower painter thought to have been born near to Coalport in the late 1700s. He was shown in the 1841 census as a china painter. He married and had at least three sons. He was a floral artist of some merit working for Coalport, demonstrated by many entries in their pattern books. It is thought he left Coalport in the 1840s to go to Wordsley, near Birmingham, to paint on glass. Examples of his signed work have been found.

Jones, Horace Overton, 1856–1928

Artist and designer, the fifth son of George and Francis, who trained at the Government School of Design, South Kensington and in 1877 won a silver medal and a book for painting flowers from nature. After his training he was sent on a world tour, ending in America. He then returned to join the family business of George Jones at the Crescent Pottery, Stoke-on-Trent, Staffordshire. In1889 he became a partner in the business. Many transfer-printed patterns were designed by him and are signed H.O.J. They are floral studies and sold well, having a different style from the usual pottery designs of

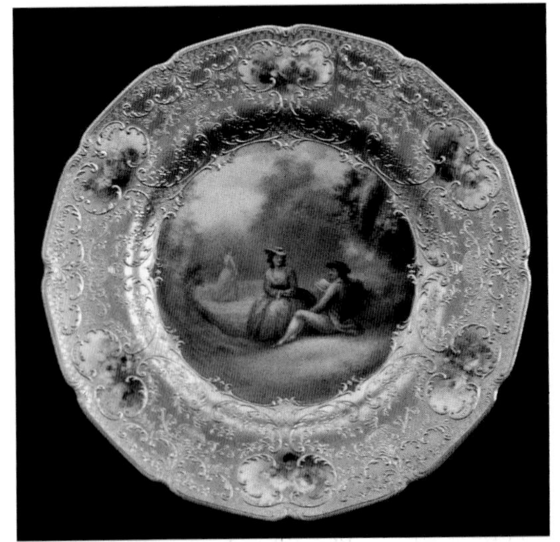

Above: Bone china Royal Doulton Cabinet plate signed A. L. Johnson, c. 1900

Left: A. L. Johnson photograph from the family archives

Above Left: Family portrait painted by A. L. Johnson

this period. By 1895 he had left the company, whether by design or necessity is not known. He then painted in oils and watercolours. In 1894 he exhibited his work in Birmingham at the Royal Society of Artists. The average price for his work at this time was between ten and fifteen guineas. In 1916, his painting *Showery Weather* was accepted by the Royal Academy. In 1918 he painted a series of local buildings and views, which were reproduced as postcards. In 1925 he and his wife Constance decided to join their second son Raymund in Wellington, New Zealand. Horace held exhibitions of his work and in 1928, the year he died, three of his paintings were exhibited at the New Zealand Academy of Fine Arts, Wellington.

Joyce, Richard, 1873–1931

Painter and designer born in Derbyshire. He studied at the Swadlincote School of Art, where he won the Queen Victoria prize for art. He became an art teacher at the Burton-on-Trent School of Art. Richard worked briefly for the Bretby pottery and Moore Bros, and then went to Pilkingtons, where he designed and painted Lancastrian ware, which was exhibited at the Arts and Crafts Society Exhibitions in 1910, 1912 and 1916. At Pilkingtons he painted work designed by other artists, including Walter Crane, and helped with the modelling of Gordon Forsyth's (q.v.) panel depicting *St George*. He became known for his own modelling of animals taken from his observations at Belle Vue Zoo, Chester. These were mainly painted in lustre. He signed his work with either a monogram or a signature.

Pilkington large lustre vase decorated by R. Joycec. 1920

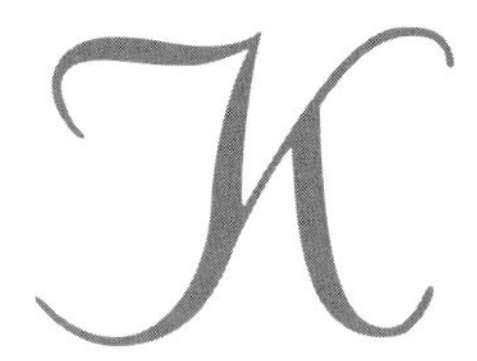

Kean, Michael, 1761–1823

Miniature painter and designer born in Dublin and trained at the Dublin School of Art, where in 1799 he won the gold medal. He studied under Edwin Smith, the sculptor, and then went to London to study at the Royal Academy School. Here he turned to miniature painting, and learning the art of drawing in crayon. He exhibited crayon portraits at the Royal Academy 1786–90 and won a medal for Fine Arts. By 1779 he had become a miniature painter and designer of great skill. In March 1795 he painted a miniature of Elizabeth Duesbury and about this time visited the Derby warehouse, where he gave advice on a service they were producing for the Prince of Wales. Eventually he became a partner in the Derby works with William Duesbury.

Keates, Alfred, active 1880s

Artist, floral painter and designer born in Stoke-up-Trent, but in 1902 emigrated to America with his family. He worked there for the Pickard China Co. painting beautiful stylised flower designs. In 1910, with Marker and Gibson, he started the International Art Studios, but in 1912 formed his own decorating establishment, Keates Art Studio, Chicago, where he decorated china but also provided a firing service for those artists who did not have a kiln. By 1922 he had an art and gift shop, which survived the Depression, and by 1937 he was listed as a lamp manufacturer. His daughter Madelaine, a flower painter, was trained by him and helped in the running of the business.

Keates, Norman, active 1907–14 and 1920–61

Flower and landscape painter, one of the last bound apprentices at Royal Doulton under David Dewsbury (q.v.), and trained at the Burslem School of Art, where he gained his teacher's certificate. After service in WWI he returned to Doulton and when Dewsbury died in 1929 painted many of his original designs.

Keeling, Richard, active 1880s

Landscape painter born in Longton, Staffordshire, the son of Moses, a china kiln fireman. He was employed by the John Aynsley & Son factory at Longton and in 1881 was living at 4 Forrister Street, Stoke-on-Trent. However, he may be the same painter shown in *The Potteries Newcastle and District Directory* of 1907 as living at 66 Oxford Street, Longton, Staffordshire.

Bone china Royal Doulton dessert plate signed and with the impressed mark for December 1914 decorated with a study of *Cypripedium Argus*

Keeling, Thomas, born 1864

Figure painter, son of Thomas, a potter's overlooker. in 1881 he was living at 3 James Street, Stoke-on-Trent, Staffordshire. He is shown in the Special Order books at Copeland 1882–84 as painting figure subjects on tiles and slabs; some of the designs were after Hewitt (q.v.). Thomas is known to have been at Coalport in the early 1900s painting fruit, animal studies, figures and portrait heads with great skill. He became one of their principal artists, but it is thought that in 1909 he left Coalport to open a china shop in Kidderminster. He was an artist of great talent who signed his work.

Keene, Alfred John, 1864–1930

Watercolour artist and painter born at 7 Keddlestone Road, Derby, the son of a printer, bookseller and picture dealer. He trained at the Derby Central School of Art and was employed at the Derby factory c. 1880. There is a plaque of his work in the Royal Crown Derby Museum. Owing to an arm disability, which made it difficult for him to hold the porcelain pieces, he became a watercolour artist, painting landscapes and animals. Alfred was a founder member of the Derby Sketching Club in 1881 and was President at the time of his death.

Keys, Edward, 1798–1861

Modeller, the son of Samuel Keys (Senior), (q.v.) who trained at the Nottingham Road, Derby factory. He modelled farm and domestic animals and figures, including the Dr Syntax series. They were a great success, becoming collectors' items. Edward became foreman of the figure making department in 1821, then left and went first to Henry and Richard Daniels and then to Minton, where in 1831 he was earning thirty shillings a week. He and his brother Samuel were possibly responsible for developing china figure making there. In 1842 he left to start his own factory, but it failed and he became bankrupt. He then joined Wedgwood, where it is thought he modelled many items for their Carrara range until 1853.

Keys, John, 1798–1825

Flower painter born at Derby, the eldest son of Samuel (Senior, q.v.) and an apprentice at the Derby pottery. His work was neat and delicate, and he used natural colours when creating his botanical studies. He painted quickly and also produced many watercolour drawings. Examples of his work can be seen in the Derby Museum.

Keys, Samuel (Senior), 1771–1850

Artist gilder, apprenticed to William Duesbury at the Derby Nottingham Road factory, where he worked 1785–1831. He was regarded as one of the finest gilders in the industry, excelling in gold arabesque scrolls into which he sometimes introduced colour. He decorated china figures with great skill. For sometime between 1831 and 1850 he may have worked at Minton. In 1838 John Simpson (q.v.) painted a miniature of him. He and Thomas Steel (q.v.) were great friends and worked at the same table. He died on the 8 October 1850 in Derby.

Keys, Samuel (Junior), active 1830s

Modeller and repairer, son of Samuel (Senior, q.v.) and brother to Edward (q.v.), an apprentice at the Nottingham Road Works at Derby. He became known for modelling theatrical figures and was foreman of figure production, but left c. 1830 and joined his brother at Minton.

By 1833 he was living at Upper Cliffe Bank and later moved to Liverpool Road, Stoke-upon-Trent, Staffordshire. Samuel entered into partnership with John Mountford, trading as Keys and Mountford from John Street, Stoke-on-Trent, producing Parian figures. Their wares were shown at the Great Exhibition of 1851 and given a honourable mention. By the 1860s he produced earthenware with another partner, Briggs, trading as Keys and Briggs, Stoke-on-Trent, using drawings designed by his younger brother John. The company modelled ornamental and useful wares in terracotta and majolica. Samuel was one of the original members of the North Staffordshire Society of Arts, founded in 1842. From 1851–64 he had another interest, the Cock Inn in John Street, Stoke-on-Trent. It is said he went to France to the Peterinck factory in Tournai at the age of seventy-two.

Kipling, John Lockwood, 1837–1911

Architectural sculptor and book illustrator born in Yorkshire, the son of the Rev. Joseph Kipling, a Methodist minister. He was educated at Woodhouse Grove School, Bradford, West Yorks. Kipling visited the Great Exhibition of 1851 then became a student under Sir Phillip Cunliffe-Owen, and was employed by Godfrey Sykes modelling dinner plates at his Bourne pottery. He continued his art education at the Stoke-on-Trent Art School and in 1863 won joint prize with Robert Edgar for terracotta designs for the façade of the Wedgwood Institute. He married Alice McDonald and in 1865 was appointed Sculptor of the Bombay School of Art, India. Ten years later he became curator of the Central Museum and Head of the School of Industrial Design, Lahore. When he retired in 1893 the family returned to England. He wrote *Beast and Man in India*, published in 1891 and illustrated an edition of his son Rudyard's book, *Kim*. Kipling died at his home The Gables, Tisbury, Wiltshire.

Kirk, William Boyton, born 1825

Modeller born in Dublin and trained at the Dublin School of Art in 1845; the next year he won a prize at the Society of Arts. Mr Binns of the Kerr & Binns pottery Worcester commissioned him to model figures for a dessert service called *The Midsummer Night's Dream*, the shapes of which were designed by Charles Toft (q.v.) and Edward Locke (q.v.) and was exhibited at the Dublin Exhibition of 1853 attracting the attention of Queen Victoria, who is reported to have spoken to both Binns and Kirk. By 1881 he had taken Holy Orders and was the clergyman at Holy Trinity, Birkenhead.

Kirkby, Thomas, 1824–1901

Painter of flower and figure subjects born in the village of Trentham, Staffordshire. He joined Minton as an apprentice in 1837 and stayed until his retirement in 1890. He is remembered for his painting of figures after Watteau (q.v.) and of cupids, which became synonymous with the Minton designs of this period. He was also noted for his decoration on tableware, modelled by P-E. Jeanest. Kirkby's painting on a dessert service was exhibited at the Great Exhibition of 1851 and the Exposition Universelle, Paris in 1855. His plaque portraying Queen Victoria surrounded by grotesques in a Renaissance style was highly praised. In 1867 he was chosen as one of the twelve British workmen sent to Paris to report on the Exhibition. The Minton archives show he was paid £13 for one month's work by 1879, and that in his later years he worked from home. His last years at Minton were spent as Art Curator. In 1881 he was living at Ash Green, Trentham and in 1887 he retired.

Minton plaque painted by Thomas Kirby. A reproduction of the plaque in the South Kensington Museum depicting a soldier after the battle of Mantegna c. 1860

Labarre, Charles, active 1890s–1900s

Painter who may have been trained and employed at the Sèvres manufactory. He joined John Slater at the Doulton pottery, where he painted vases for the World's Columbian Exposition, Chicago, 1893. He painted *The Columbus* vase modelled by C. Noke and one of the four *Diana* vases, again modelled by Noke, and also worked in conjunction with George White on the original *Dante* vase.

Lambert, George F., born 1850

Painter and gilder born in Chichester, Sussex. He studied at the Derby Central School of Art, where in 1879 his majolica ware designs won a bronze medal at the National Art School competition. George worked at Derby in the 1880s, specialising in painting and gilding eggshell porcelain. His name appears often in the Derby pattern books from 1878, and there are examples of this work in the Derby Museum.

Lamunby, Walter, 1884–1952

Marine, landscape and possibly freelance painter, who was an apprentice at George Jones and Sons Ltd, and attended Stoke School of Art. Examples of his signed work have been found on a pair of china dessert plates, impressed *Collingwood*, painted with fine marine views; he may have been employed at Collingwood's Crown Works, Longton, Staffordshire. From there he went to John Aynsley and Sons, before joining S. Fielding and Co. Ltd., Devon pottery, Stoke-on-Trent, Staffordshire in about 1912. He became their premier artist and stayed for forty years. Walter used other signatures for his work: for example, Coleman, Hinton, Cox and Marsh. The reason for this strange practice has so far not been discovered.

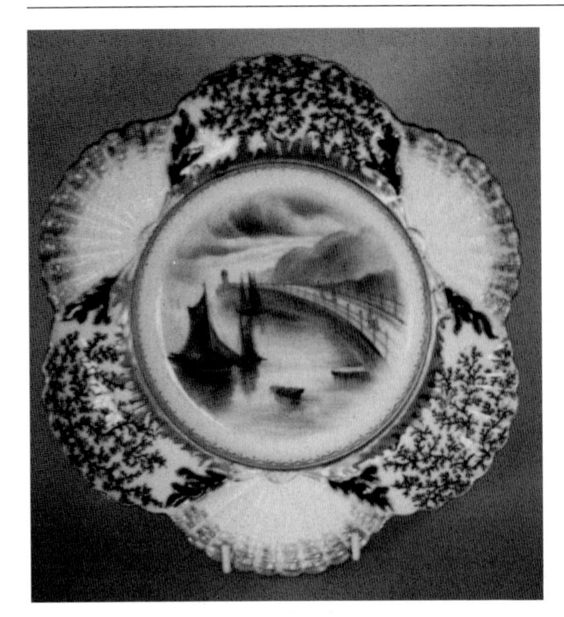

Bone china plate produced by Collingwood Bros c. 1900 painted by W Lamumby

Landgraf, G., active 1841–1882

Painter of figure subjects born in Bavaria, a contemporary of Count Holtzendorff (q.v.) He was first employed at Brown-Westhead and Moore in the 1860s, whether at their London studio is not known, and exhibited at the Staffordshire Industrial Exhibition held in the Mechanics Institute, Hanley in 1866. He returned to Germany and was premier artist at the Berlin porcelain factory c. 1878. Next he was employed at Crown Derby from 1878 to 1882. In 1881 he was boarding at 26, Melbourne Street, Derby, the home of Henry Denman (a signal inspector for the Midland Railway).

Langley, Leonard, 1868–1916

Painter and designer who was an apprentice under John Slater (q.v.) at the Pinder Bourne Co. factory, Burslem which was taken over by Doulton. He became a designer and head of the department, designing wares decorated with transfer prints and lithographs.

Lardy, Lucien, born 1856

Artist gilder born in Chalon, France and working at Coalport c. 1890. He created artistic raised, jewelled designs. In 1894 references are made to Mr Lardy's room that leads to the assumption that he was in charge of the jewelling and highly expert gilding at Coalport. This type of decoration was used on many vases painted by their premier artists.

Latham, John, born c. 1801

Flower and bird painter and outside decorator born in Coalport, who may have painted for both Worcester and Nantgarw before 1820. The Coalport pattern books show him painting birds and Sèvres-style groups. It is thought he painted butterflies and floral groups on white ware at Coalport before going to Minton, where he worked 1840–65. A Minton plate dated and painted with butterflies and foliage is in the Victoria & Albert Museum. The 1861 census shows him living in Shelton, Staffordshire.

Lawrence, Stephen, active 1820

Painter of all subjects, thought to have been born in Broseley, Shropshire c. 1797. He worked at Coalport, painting landscapes and bird studies. Later he is known for fine floral studies, but left around 1847 to work at the Wordsley Glass factory, Birmingham.

Lawton, Cuthbert, active c. 1800

Painter of landscapes, said by Haslem to have also painted hunting and figure subjects at Derby. He was a painter of great skill. Although his work is rarely found, examples can be seen in the Derby Museum.

Lea, Henry (Harry) C., born 1861

Artist painter born in Burslem, Staffordshire, the son of a traveller for Copeland, who painted all subjects with

Bone china W.T. Copeland & Sons plate commissioned by David Collamore & Co., New York

equal skill and signed his work H.C. Lea. He was listed as painting hawking subjects, marine landscapes and flowers, particularly roses. One entry in the Copeland Special Order books of December 1880 shows he painted a déjeuner tray with marine views, the gilding by C. Deaville. Nine dessert plates decorated with a poppy design have been found in America (Pattern number R 146, impressed mark for 1900), specially commissioned for David Collamore and Co., New York and bearing their backstamp. Only one of the plates was signed H.C. Lea. They are fine examples of his work. He was known as a true Victorian gentleman, rather superior but a very pleasant character. In 1892 he was living at 3 Princess Street, Stoke-on-Trent and by 1907 had moved to 25 Frederick Street, Stoke-on-Trent, Staffordshire.

Leach, Bernard, 1887–1979

Studio potter, designer and author born in Hong Kong. He studied at the Slade School of Fine Art 1903–07, and also learned etching at the London School of Art under Frank Brangwyn. In 1909 he returned to the Far East and by 1911 was living in Japan, studying the work of other potters and learning Raku and stoneware pottery from the Sixth Kensan. He built a kiln in his home in Tokyo. When he returned to England c. 1920, he set up a wood-burning kiln and started to design and produce pottery at his home in Cornwall, founding the St Ives pottery. He had many pupils, including M. Cardew, K. Pleydell-Bouverie, N. Braden, David Leach, Margaret Leach and S. Hamanda.

His publications include *A Potter's Outlook*, 1928 and *A Potters Book*, 1940. He believed that the pot should be the work of the individual potter, from the start of its production to the end, a view that revived the attitude of the Arts and Crafts movement. Exhibitions of Leach pottery have been held in the UK, Sweden, Norway and Denmark. Leach made useful domestic wares at a reasonable price, but more importantly, individual pieces showing art and originality. Unfortunately his pottery works was damaged by a land mine in WWII. His son David became an apprentice under his father 1930–33. He ran the Leach pottery for a number of years, until he established his own in Devon.

Lead, Leonard, 1787–1869

Flower painter born at Pinxton, the son of a charcoal burner at the Derby pottery who moved to the Pinxton pottery as a woodcutter. Leonard was apprenticed at Derby as a flower painter c. 1800. At the age of nineteen he became a member of the Fox and Owl Club, where he met many of the well-known Derby artists of this period. He painted fine floral studies for Derby for over forty years. His obituary in the *Derby Reporter* said: 'He was one of the last of the staff of artists at the old Derby factory, by his energy and industry he brought up a large family in a creditable manner, he died at the age of 82.'

Obviously a well-known member of the local society and highly regarded, his paintings are rich and varied, done in vibrant colours. Haslem says he spent the later years of his life painting Derbyshire spar ornaments in varnish colours. He had a brother, John, who worked for Pinxton at some time and is thought to have been a gilder.

Leason, George J.P., 1841–1911

Flower painter and managing director. He started work as an errand boy when only ten years old. He had only a limited education but went to Newcastle Art School in the evenings. By 1900 he had become Managing Director at Minton.

Ledward, Richard Arthur, active 1880s

Modeller who trained at the Wedgwood Institute, Burslem, Staffordshire and was employed by Wedgwood, but left to become a teacher at the Government School of Design, South Kensington, London.

Leger, Armand, born 1855

Artist gilder born in France and by 1881 was living at 46 Havelock Street, Stoke-on-Trent, Staffordshire. Possibly the artist gilder who worked for Minton from 1872 to 1882 and decorated the cups decorated with Japanese groups and embossed with gold that were exhibited at the Vienna Exhibition of 1883. He became head of the Brown-Westhead & Moore pottery's art department and his work was exhibited at the Exposition Universelle, Paris of 1889. He left to succeed Charles Hindley (q.v.) as decorating manager at Wedgwood in the late nineteenth century.

Leonce, Georges, active 1870s

Flower painter born in France, who had glowing reviews in art magazines in the 1870s. One writer claimed he was a prince amongst flower painters. When John Slater (q.v.) was sent to France by Henry Doulton to study the work of the European factories, he met Leonce at a party, after which, as Slater tells the story, he woke up in a hut in Brabizon, near to Fontainebleau. He and Georges became great friends and Slater wagered his French friend £50 that he could not paint as well on English bone china as on the hard paste porcelain of France. Slater sent him a Bodley dessert service to paint and the result was superb. Georges gained commissions from Minton and Brown-Westhead & Moore.

Leonce, Gustav, active 1870s

Freelance designer and watercolour painter who supplied designs and drawings of fish and chickens for Minton for use on dinner services, which were engraved by William Wise (q.v.). He also designed for Wedgwood and Brown-Westhead & Moore. He and Georges Leonce (q.v.) may in fact be one and the same artist.

Leroy (or Le Roi), Desiré, 1840–1908

Flower and bird painter born at Les Loges, Commune d'Arrou, France, the son of a Sèvres painter, who was apprenticed from the age of eleven at Sèvres. He came to the Potteries in the 1870s and was employed by Minton from 1874 to 1890, living in Richmond Terrace, Stoke-on-Trent, Staffordshire. He painted many important services, specialising in birds and flowers in the style of the Limoges enamellers. His work was exhibited at the 1878 Exposition Universelle, Paris and highly praised. Leroy was paid by the day at Minton: an entry for 3 October 1874 items six days, patterns white enamel on turquoise, some done at home, for drawings of cups and

D. Leroy

Royal Crown Derby plate c. 1900 commissioned by Davis Collomore & Co., New York, c. 1900

plates white birds and flowers on turquoise – fifteen shillings. In 1890 he left Minton to become art director and designer for Royal Crown Derby, where he had his own studio and two assistants, Jack Dale and George Darlington. He is shown in 1890 on the wages list as being paid £225 per year.

In 1894 P. Taillandier came from France to join Leroy and together they produced some truly fine work. Leroy stayed at Derby until his death. *Pall Mall Magazine* of December 1906 described his artistry by saying that 'every line of it is harmonious, even when the colour scheme is daring and unconventional. Every detail of the rich but never over weighted ornamentation, from the heavy gold chasing to the tiny turquoise jewelling of which he seems especially fond, is typical.' Like many of the continental artists who came to the Potteries, Leroy created studies of each and every one of his paintings. He was obviously popular with his fellows, often only working two or three days each week. He was an impressive figure in his top hat and carrying a cane – a true gentleman, yet not too proud to play whist with his fellow workers. He designed and painted the dessert service for the Duke of York and Princess May of Teck commissioned by the Derby Corporation as a wedding gift for 6 July 1893. It is said that only when the commission for a dinner service of too many pieces for him to complete arrived did he have other artists helping him, preferring to complete an order himself. He died on 17 May 1908 and was buried in Old Normanton Cemetery, Derby.

Lessore, Elaine Therese, born 1844

Artist, designer and painter, the granddaughter of Emile Lessore (q.v.) and sister of Louise. She trained at the Slade School of Art, where she met her first husband William Bernard Adeney. They were associated with the Bloomsbury Group of artists and founded the London group of artists in 1913. They divorced in 1920 and she then moved to Hampstead, near to her sister, who introduced her to the world of pottery designing and painting. In 1926 she married the painter Walter Richard Sickert, with whom she had shared a studio. Her designs and paintings on Wedgwood are found dating into the 1930s. In 1927 she held an exhibition of watercolours at the Saville Road Gallery, amongst which were some of her pottery designs and painting. Although never employed directly by Wedgwood, she introduced many artists and designers from the Bloomsbury Group to the company.

Lessore, Emile Albert, 1805–1876

Artist painter, the son of a notary, who studied law but soon turned to art. He was trained to paint with oils and watercolours in the studio of Jean Auguste Dominique Ingres. His paintings were exuberant and florid, totally unlike those of Ingres. He exhibited his first picture, *Le Frere Malade*, in the Paris Salon in 1831. His work was popular and fetched very high prices, and he continued to exhibit watercolours and oils paintings until 1850. His ceramic training was at Laurin's manufactory at Bourg de Rheine, near to Paris. By 1851 he had joined the Sèvres factory, where he painted after the Old Masters. His landscape painting revolutionised the ceramic world of the time, as it was done with majolica glazes and described as impressionistic. The Emperor of Russia paid 1,000 guineas (£1050) for a pair of his vases. It is thought he left Sèvres because of the jealousy his original work created with the other artists. His style showed great freedom, very different to the stipple technique of his colleagues. In 1858, after his wife died, he came to London with his three children, specialising in freehand majolica paintings. After six months he joined Minton, who exhibited his works in the International Exhibition in London in 1862.

After many disagreements with the Minton management, Lessore accepted an offer from Wedgwood, where he was given everything he asked for and his talent was recognised. Lessore began to concentrate on designs of contemporary life, such as children with their pets and family groups in outside settings. He worked at the factory 1863–68, but the inclement weather and smoke of the Potteries gave him rheumatism. He and Godfrey Wedgwood came to a happy compromise. Lessore would spend the summer in London at the showroom entertaining buyers and in effect acting as an agent for Wedgwood, and the winter in Paris. By 1867 Wedgwood had increased their share of the contemporary design market and the demand for Lessore's type of design declined. He returned to France to live at Marlotte, near Fontainebleau, where he had a kiln in the grounds. Here he experimented with lustre glazes, and remained in constant touch with Wedgwood, accepting commissions, which he sent back to the pottery for firing. Pieces, often signed, were included in the Wedgwood exhibitions in London, 1862, Paris, 1867, and Vienna, 1873. He is known to have designed blanks for the Davenport pottery. Lessore survived the Siege of Paris in 1870 by successfully hiding his work. His artistic talent was passed on to his children and granddaughters Louise Powell and Therese Lessore.

Lessore, Jules R. I., active 1870s

Landscape artist, son of Emile (q.v.). He exhibited landscapes regularly at the Paris Salon, the Royal Academy, the Suffolk Street Art Gallery, New Watercolour Society and the Grosvenor Gallery 1879–92. He decorated some of the Wedgwood pottery that was sent over to France, in the style of his father.

Lewis, Esther, active 1877–1897

Landscape artist, the daughter of Robert Lewis, a cotton broker, who may have trained at the Lambeth School of Art. She became a faience artist at the Doulton Lambeth Studio, painting usually on tiles and decorating carrara and impasto pieces. She was one of the most accomplished painters of woodland, mountain and marine views. She marked her work with EL or a signature.

Lewis, Florence E., died 1917

Flower painter employed at Doulton from 1874 to 1897. She painted flowers, foliage and birds, and did some pâte-sur-pâte decoration. She trained many of the Doulton artists and her work was shown at the Vienna Exhibition of 1873, in Paris, 1878 and at The World's Columbian Exposition, Chicago in 1893; and again at the Paris International Exhibition of 1900. In 1883 she published a book on china painting. Florence travelled widely, but in 1897 received an inheritance and no longer painted on pottery. She continued to exhibit her work in oils and watercolours at the Royal Academy 1881–1915, the Royal Society of British Artists 1892–94 and the Dudley Art Gallery 1873–1917. Her work is marked FL in a monogram. Florence's sister Isobel was noted for her exotic flowers and painted with her at Lambeth 1876–87. In 1881 they were living together at Stockwell Park, London.

Lewis, Frank E., born 1865

Artist gilder born in Worcestershire, who came to Coalport c. 1890 and stayed into the twentieth century. He was probably the designer and foreman of a decorating shop. There are many entries allocated to him in the Coalport books, showing that he did fine jewelling work. Examples can be seen at the Ironbridge Museum Trust, Coalport China Museum. His elder brother James was also employed at Coalport as a gilder.

Lindner, Doris Lexey Margaret, 1896–1979

Sculptor and modeller born in Llanyre, Radnorshire. She studied sculpture at St Martins School of Art, London and the British Academy School in Rome. She was employed for a short time by Minton in the 1930s. However, it is for her work for Worcester that she is known. Doris spent many hours studying animals. In 1931 she designed a range of dogs, followed by another of animals at play. In 1936, having watched many performances by the Bertram Mills Circus, she designed groups of circus horses. In the 1940s she designed racehorses and a Santa Gertrudis bull, modelled from life. Doris did some modelling for Wedgwood but spent forty years with Royal Worcester. She spent her last years in the Cotswold village, Broad Campden, where she displayed some of her modernistic stone and bronze sculptures, which were influenced by the work of Henry Moore and Barbara Hepworth.

Linnell, John, 1792–1892

Landscape and portrait artist who in 1805 became a pupil at the Royal Academy Schools and trained under John Varley, painting portraits and landscapes. He is known to have decorated Minton pottery for Summerleys Art Manufacturers.

Lock(e), Edward, 1829–1909

Painter and potter who was apprenticed at Grainger Worcester in 1845. His work included the pâte-sur-pâte treatment of floral subjects; he became a manager of the pottery department in 1889. In 1895 he started his own pottery, Locke and Co. Ltd, Worcester with his sons and Arthur and Walter Stinton, but in 1904 the business failed. His daughter Kate specialized in pâte-sur-pâte painting and there are examples of her work in the Dyson Perrins Museum, Worcester.

Longmore, Thomas, born 1847

Modeller of tiles and ornamental wares who worked at Minton 1860–1900. He lived in the Hartshill Minton cottages, Stoke-upon-Trent, Staffordshire. His work was exhibited at the Vienna Exhibition of 1873, where he was awarded a co-operators medal. Thomas also worked with John Henk on the famous Minton elephants. In 1889 he became an assistant master at the Stoke School of Art, but resigned in 1888. His brother Joseph was apprenticed at Minton as a painter 1860–67.

Lovatt, William, active 1822

Modeller, enamellist and miniature painter at the Herculean Pottery, Liverpool, who in 1817 was living at 38 Hill Street, Liverpool. The minute Book of 4 June1822 of the proprietors of the Herculaneum Pottery records that William Lovatt was engaged as a modeller and painter for a further term of six months at a wage of £2.5s.0d a week. In 1817 he modelled an Adam and Eve plaque.

Lovegrove, John, 1795–1873

Gilder at Derby who trained under William Smith. When the factory closed in 1848 he went to London, gilding china in leaf gold for a shop in Tottenham Court Road. He later came to the Potteries and eventually returned to Derby. John's son William also worked at Derby, painting birds and flowers.

Lowe, Robert, born 1842

Artist gilder born in Broseley, Shropshire, an apprentice at Coalport. He is shown in the 1881 census as living at 10 George Street, Stoke-on-Trent, Staffordshire. He was employed at Copeland, their Special Order books showing entries under his name for fine jewelled gilding. It is thought he was in charge of one of the gilding departments and stayed at Copeland for the rest of his life. It is not known whether this is the same R. Lowe known to have been at Coalport.

Lowe, Thomas, active 1840s

Painter of figure subjects who was a pupil of Thomas Baxter and Solomon Cole. He succeeded Baxter as the figure painter at Flight and Barr, Worcester. Later he worked in London, and a signed plaque of a young woman, dated 1834, was sold at Sotheby's in London in 1971. Thomas exhibited at the Royal Academy in 1845, then living at 40 Ely Place, London, and he is known to have entered exhibits of painted porcelains to the Great Exhibition of 1851.

Lucas, Daniel (Senior) c. 1788–1867

Landscape painter who trained at Davenport's Longport Pottery. He came to the Nottingham Road factory, Derby, c. 1820, where he became the principal landscape artist. He moved to the Potteries, where he was employed at Minton in about the 1840s, and it thought he also did work for Coalport in 1841. Lucas used the following ceramic colour combinations in his painting. For the sky, light blue, old tile blue and azure blue. The cloud shadows were achieved by combining two blues, grey, black, purple and rose. For shadows for the landscapes and for finishing the distant shadow, two blues, black, yellow, rose and olive brown. For finishing the middle ground, grey, black, purple, orange and olive brown. He would glaze the whole with orange, yellow or transparent greens as required. He used the oil painter's technique of strong, thick paint like enamels, covering the service so often none of the porcelain is seen.

In 1841 Lucas is known to have been living at the Sytch, Burslem, as the sale of his furniture is recorded in the *Staffordshire Advertiser* of July 1841. It included valuable oil paintings by Rhodes, Price and Lucas in gold frames. Lucas left the Potteries for Birmingham, where he worked as a painter of Japan patterns until his death. He is said by Haslem to have painted in oils and done some of the best public house signs in Derby: for example, Jolly Toper near St Mary's Bridge, The Plough and The Peacock, both on Nottingham Road. He became a founder member of the North Staffordshire Society of Arts. His hobby was fishing and he was an expert angler. He had three sons, all apprenticed at Derby. His son John (1811–33) went to the Swinton Pottery in 1832, where his paintings of *The Plains of Waterloo* and of *Chatsworth House* were found on two plaques. Examples of his work can be seen in the Royal Crown Derby Museum. William, born 1812, was an artist gilder who stayed at Derby until the pottery closed, then worked for Minton 1840s–50s, producing work of the highest quality.

Lucas, Daniel (Junior), 1819–1898

Landscape painter and outside decorator born in Derby, son of Daniel (Senior, q.v.) apprenticed at the Derby pottery and employed there 1835–45. Lucas left Derby and came to Coalport. In 1862 he was painting for Copeland, then moved for a short time back to Coalport, and finally returned to Stoke-on-Trent. The entries in the Copeland Special Order reference book show that he painted rustic subjects, and in 1862 a tray with the painting *Passing the Brook* after the Belgium artist, M. Verboeckhoven, depicting sheep and cattle in a pastoral setting. In 1862 Copeland exhibited a vase decorated by Lucas with Italian scenes after Turner, which was

Derby plaque c. 1820s attributed to Daniel Lucas, Senior

Above: Bone china jug W.T. Copeland. The Scenes are taken from Turner's *Rivers of France* Series painted by Daniel Lucas Junior c. 1860

Above: Unmarked small china plaque signed Lucas Thought to have been produced by one of Lucas's sons in his decorating business. Private Collection

Aove: Bone china Copeland handled Ewer thought to have been commissioned by the Honorable Company of Goldsmiths, landscape decoration by D. Lucas

highly praised. Many of the fine landscapes on Copeland ware that have been dated to the late 1850s have been attributed to Daniel Lucas (Junior).

He is known to have painted exhibition pieces for the Great Exhibition of 1851 and the Exposition Universelle, Paris of 1868. Only three entries in the small black books, in the Spode archives record his name: pattern numbers D 2338, D2132 and D2070. Pattern number D 2609 c. 1862, with miniature paintings taken from *The Rivers of France* after Turner, is also attributed to Lucas. This, as other landscapes by him, is named on the back in gold on the bottom. All paintings on pieces attributed to Lucas lead the eye through the painting to the fine architectural buildings depicted. Another service, known as *The Rivers of England*, may have been done at the same time by this artist, but so far no pieces have been found. In 1866 he exhibited paintings at the Second South Staffordshire Industrial Exhibition, to which he also sent examples of his new patented process of transferring and printing in gold and colour on china.

By 1870 Lucas had established an independent workshop in Longton, probably assisted by his son, where he painted landscapes and decorated china for many potteries. By 1879 he lived at 37 Sutherland Terrace, Longton, where he had a studio. His signed painting of *The Bay of Venice* is exhibited at the Potteries Museum and Art Gallery Stoke-on-Trent.

Lunn, Richard, active 1870s

Designer and Art Director at the Osmaston Road, Derby factory, appointed 2 August 1882. He designed Venetian vignettes for raised gold plates and vases. In 1887, the ladies of Derby commissioned a service to present to Queen Victoria on her Jubilee, which he designed, as he did the service made for Gladstone, which was commissioned by the Liberal Working Men's Derby Committee. This service consisted of twenty-six pieces – eighteen plates, four low and four large comports. Count Holzendorff's (q.v.) sketches of local scenes were used in the decoration and floral arrangements were painted by James Rouse (q.v.). The committee only paid £60 for it but it is known it cost the factory much more. Lunn was criticised as Art Director for being no more than competent when working on expensive and elaborate pieces, and he left in 1889. He was at one time headmaster of the Sheffield Art School and is also known for some of the terracotta designs on the South Kensington Museum and also on the Albert Hall.

Lycett, Edward, 1833–1909

Painter, gilder and outside decorator born in Newcastle-under-Lyme, Staffordshire. He trained at the Newcastle School of Art and then at the Thomas Battam decorating china establishment in London. He was employed at Copeland for a short period. The entry in the Copeland Special Order books, pattern number 6286, a royal shape dessert plate, is 'gilded by EL'. His work was shown in the Great Exhibition of London 1851.

Lycett emigrated to America c. 1861; he and Warren (of whom nothing so far is known) opened a decorating workshop in Green Street, New York. They employed thirty to forty artists to gild and paint furniture and plaques with Greek patterns, similar to those Lycett had worked on in London. After the Civil War, c. 1865, he moved around the country to St Louis, Missouri, Cincinnati and East Liverpool, Ohio, providing teaching facilities for amateur artists. By 1877, leaving the business in the hands of his son, he taught ceramic decoration at the School of Design in St Louis. He opened a decorating studio in East Liverpool, working on blanks provided by American potteries. Lycett founded the Faience Manufacturing Company at Green Point, New York 1884–92. Here he worked to improve glazes, bodies, shapes and decoration, being particularly fond of using superb yellow and pink roses in his designs. He was described as 'the pioneer of china painting in America'. In 1890 Lycett retired from the Faience Co, but joined William Lycett's decorating studio in Atlanta, Georgia, and continued his research, notably into the use of metallic lustres. His sons Francis and Joseph were modellers and decorators. He is regarded as an important figure in American ceramic decoration. He invented a unique method of applying gold to china, the secret of which he never revealed, that has never been duplicated. His work can be seen in Dearborn, Michigan.

Machin, Arnold, OBE, A.R.A., A.R.C.A., 1911–1999

Sculptor, modeller and painter, apprenticed at Minton and trained at the Stoke School of Art. He studied modelling under Eric Owen, the head modeller at Minton c. 1925–29. He left the Potteries c. 1930 because of the Depression and was employed at Derby. He became a full-time student at the Derby School of Art, winning a scholarship to the Royal School of Art in London 1937–40. He exhibited at the Royal Academy. Machin returned to the Potteries, becoming the first full-time figure modeller at Wedgwood, working in a secluded studio in the Barlaston factory. He

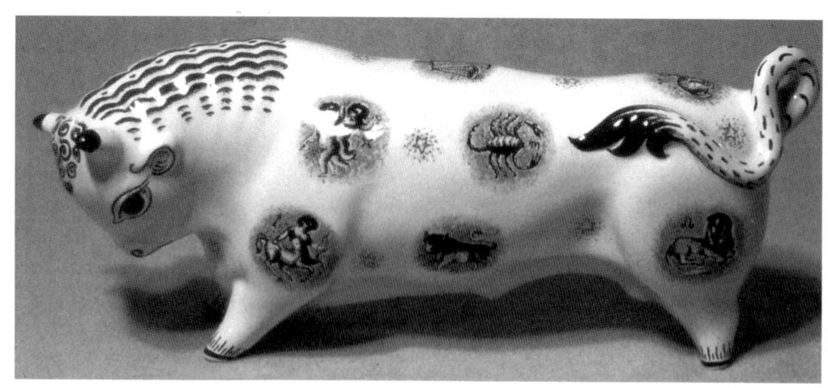

Ferdinand the Bull. Modelled by Arnold Machin when at Wedgwood

modelled *Taurus*, *Ferdinand the Bull*, *Penelope* and *Courtly Lovers*, amongst others, and some flat-back figures. In 1953 he modelled cameo portraits for Coronation ware. He became Master in Charge of Stoke-on-Trent Art School, 1941–42. Machin was an instructor at the Royal College of Art, London, elected an ARA in 1947 and RA in 1956. In 1964 he designed new coins, for which he was awarded the OBE.

Makeig-Jones, Susannah Margaretta (Daisy), 1881–1945

Painter and designer born in Wath-upon-Dearne, a mining village in Yorkshire. The family moved to Torquay, Devon, where her doctor father hyphenated his name to avoid confusion with another medical practitioner. Daisy was educated at home, at a boarding school in Rugby and completed her education at the Torquay School of Art and the Slade School of Fine Art, London. In 1909 she wrote to her brother's father-in-law Cecil Wedgwood, who recognised her artistic talent and gave her an apprenticeship at the pottery. Two years later she was appointed a member of the staff and was employed from 1915 until her retirement in 1932. Daisy became known for her designs on nursery ware: for example, *Rabbits*, *Chickens*, *Mao* and *Yellowstone Zoo*. Her name is synonymous with the Wedgwood fairyland lustre range of designs, which were first produced in 1915. In 1931 she was asked to retire in response to falling markets for her work and she reluctantly agreed.

Wedgwood footed bowl designed by Maykeig-Jones

Mallet, Pierre M., born 1836

Freelance painter and designer born in Tussey, France. He was a friend of Leonce Goutard (q.v.), and may have come to the Potteries around 1870. He gained commissions from the Brown-Westhead, Moore & Co. pottery, painting flowers and fruit, and from Wedgwood. His designs were commissioned by the London retailers, Borgen and Co. In 1881 he was living at 1 Hope Cottage, Acton, Middlesex.

Pattern book Cord Edged dessert plate c. 1860 pattern number D 2221 painted by Mansfield. Courtesy of Spode Museum Trust

Mansfield, Joseph, born 1803

Artist gilder born in Madeley, Shropshire. He was employed at Coalport 1820–29 and may have served his apprenticeship there. He then moved to the Rockingham Works. From 1849 to 1860 Mansfield was employed by Copeland at the Spode Works, where he became one of the premier artist gilders of this period. The Special Order reference book in the Spode archives show he worked on all types of ware, from candlesticks to vases and dessert services, on *Louis, Regimental, Royal* and *Queen Anne* shapes. His work can be found on pattern numbers ranging from 5877–8614. It is possible that his son succeeded him as in September 1860 a Mansfield J. (which usually denotes junior) is shown as gilding a Berrisford vase painted by Hurten (q.v.).

Marks, Marguerite Heymann (Grete), born 1901

Paintress and freelance designer born in Cologne and trained at the Cologne and Berlin School of Art and the Weimar Bauhaus. At Weimar she was taught by Johannes Itten. During the six-month course he allowed the students to be creative, to experiment in differing materials and to learn the principles of design. In 1923 Marks started her career at Hael Werkstatten for Artists Ceramic Co. in Marwitz, where she designed stoneware bowls using vivid glazes and unusual colour combination. Grete married the owner of the company, Gustav Loebenstein, in 1924; after his death she managed the company of ninety employees.

By the early 1930s, frightened by ant-semitism, she left Germany for London. Ambrose Heal, head of Heal's retail shop, introduced her to Gordon Forsythe (q.v.). She exhibited her work at the Burslem Art School and taught there for one term in 1937. Grete was then employed by Minton, where a special modern department was created and her designs were alloated the backstamp *Grete Pottery at Minton*. In 1938 she married Harold Marks, an extra-mural tutor for Oxford University, and started the Grete Pottery at Summer Street, Stoke-on-Trent. She bought biscuit ware from Wedgwood and Goss and employed six part-time workers, selling the decorated ware to Heals and the John Lewis Partnerships stores. The pottery closed in WWII, and in 1946 the family moved to London, where she set up a studio at home and taught at Camberwell School of Art, where she threw and handcrafted her work.

Marsh, James F., 1817–1874

Modeller who exhibited a terracotta wine cooler designed in the Revivalist style at the Great Exhibition of 1851. He worked at Davenport, but by 1865–69 he had became a freelance modeller with Rowland Morris, working on the Wedgwood Institute sculptures. At the1865 Industrial Exhibition in Hanley, Staffordshire he exhibited terracotta wares and an adaptation of a medieval jug.

Marshall, John, born 1831

Flower painter, designer and art director trained at the Government School of Design, South Kensington. He became Art Director at Harvey Jones and Co., Longton, Staffordshire, where his work shows the influence of Chinese, Japanese and Persian art. He is recorded in the 1881 census as living at 21 South Street, Stoke-on-Trent, manager of a decorating department.

Marshall, Mark Villers, 1843–1912

Sculptor and modeller born in Cranbrook, Kent and trained at the Lambeth School of Art, London. He first worked for his friend R.W. Martin (q.v.) at his studio at Pomoma House, but when his hopes of a partnership were dashed around 1874 he went to the Doulton's Lambeth Studio, where he stayed until he died. He is known for his designs of reptiles, lizards, salamanders, dragons and frogs. Lewis Carroll's *Jabberwocky* verses were the inspiration for his Borrogrove vase, which is modelled in the form of an animal, half hedgehog and half fish. He was influenced by the Art Nouveau style, using bright flowing colours and almost always incised outlines. His work was exhibited at the Arts and Crafts exhibitions of 1889–1912 and at the World's Columbian Exposition, Chicago in 1893. Marshall designed three large vases for the International Exhibition in Paris in 1900 and signed his work MVM.

Martin, Charles Douglas, 1846–1910

Merchant and businessman born in Hoxton, Kent, son of Robert Martin and brother of Robert, Walter and Edwin Martin (q.v.). He ran the Martin Brothers family warehouse and showroom at Brownlow Street, Holborn, London. He was a true gentleman, affable and knowledgeable, who got on well with the customers. He listened to their thoughts and ideas, sending back diagrams and instructions to his brothers. Charles also controlled the firm's finances. After the showroom burnt down, he became depressed and never recovered.

Martin, Edwin, 1860–1915

Painter, the youngest of the three Martin brothers, who trained at the Lambeth School of Art c. 1872 and also took lessons from H.P. Fawcett. Edwin's abstract designs were not appreciated by his brothers. He met the architect Sidney Greenslade (exhibited 1893–98, Royal

Academy), who recognised his ability, and his work found favour with the art critics of the day. When his brother Walter (q.v.) died, he became responsible for the throwing and firing of the family pottery, R.W. Martin and Brothers in Fulham and later at Southall, London.

Martin, Robert Wallace, 1843–1923

Sculptor, modeller and manufacturer, elder brother to Edwin (q.v.). Robert was the son of a large family and he took many jobs to supplement the family income. After falling and breaking his wrist, he spent time drawing, and one of his father's friends showed his work to John Birnie Philip, a sculptor, who designed and produced architectural ornament in the Gothic style for many church restorations and was known for his work on the Albert Memorial. He offered Robert an apprenticeship, costing £50 but giving no salary. Although his mother was happy to provide the money from her small income, he knew the financial strain it would cause the family, so refused.

The wholesale stationers, Barry and Hayward in the City of London, employed him and his father. He was offered employment with Mr Thomas, Augustus Welby Pugin's chief assistant, who was in charge of the stonemasonry at Westminster. It was this period in his training that gave him a love and understanding of the Gothic style, which is prominent in his designs. In 1860 he went to the Lambeth School of Art in the evenings, now working with sculptor Alexander Munro at Buckingham Palace Road. In 1864 Robert went to the Royal School of Art, and joined the Society of Arts, winning a competition in ornamental carving and still thinking his future lay as a sculptor. However, it was at the Lambeth School of Art, under headmaster John Sparkes and when training with Edward Bale (who later became better known as a watercolour artist), that he became fascinated with experiments in clay and glazes and turned his artistic skill to modelling in terracotta. In 1864 Robert won a free scholarship to the School and met George Tinworth (q.v.). In 1871, after working for a short time at the Farmer and Brindley masonry yard, he went to the Watcombe Terra Cotta Company, modelling large vases, jugs and statuettes. He soon returned to London to C.J.C. Bailey and Co., where he was allowed to have his own work fired in their kiln.

By 1873 Martin had established a home for his family and a business at Pomona House, Fulham, London, which he rented for £50 a year. He was joined by his brothers Edwin and Walter, who had completed their training at Doulton. Usually Walter threw the pots and Edwin decorated them. In 1879 a writer in the *Art Journal* described Robert as an artist but also as a workman, manufacturer and merchant. Therein lay his

Martin Brothers tile

Martin Brothers grotesque jug

Martin Brothers in their studio. All courtesy of the Potteries Museum and Art Gallery Stoke-on-Trent

success. Pomona House was fashionable situated, so that many people stopped and bought the goods on display and told their friends. By 1874 C.J.C. Bailey would no longer fire their ware, so they found an old soap-making plant and started production again. By 1881 the brothers were employing three men and two boys making earthenware, and trading as R. W. Martin and Brothers. By the late 1880s they had a showroom in Holborn, London.

Martin, Walter Frazer, 1858–1910

Potter and colour maker, brother of Robert (q.v.) who trained at the Lambeth School of Art. Walter joined Doulton as a colourist, but George Tinsworth, by now a family friend, advised him to learn the art of throwing the ware. This he achieved and he was also in charge of firing the ware produced by the family firm. He continued to experiment with ceramic colours thus giving the firm a wide colour range from which to choose. Unfortunately the secret of these colours died with him when he fell from a ladder in 1910.

Mason, Robert, born 1868

Flower painter born in Newcastle-under-Lyme, Staffordshire. He married a gilder at Coalport and they lived in Madeley. He was employed at Coalport in the 1890s. He was a painter of great talent who was able to adapt to any ceramic surface. He painted small floral plaques, which were used on metal boxes. He also painted roses on buttons and miniature china discs. His work was used for large, heavily jewelled vases painted with floral sprays. He is also known to have painted for the Crown Staffordshire Pottery c. 1903.

Mclaughton, Mary Louise, 1847–1937

Amateur painter and author working in America, known for her underglaze Limoges decoration *Cincinnati Limoges*. She worked with the Cincinnati Pottery Club and in 1879 founded the Women's Pottery Club, which used the Rookwood Pottery kilns (founded in 1880 by Maria Longworth Nichols) for a time to fire their ware. Mary devoted the next period of her life to writing about ceramics and ceramic decoration. In 1895 she was working with inlaid decoration and by 1898 designed Losanti ware. Her work was exhibited at the Philadelphia Centennial Exhibition of 1876, and in New York and Paris in 1878.

Mclennan, John H., born 1852

Painter of figure subjects born in London, who became a student at the Lambeth School of Art and was then employed by Doulton Lambeth as a Faience artist. During 1880–1910 he painted murals, tiles, plaques and vases, and designed panels for the Great Ormond Street Children's Hospital. Some of his ornamental tile patterns, inspired by Malory's *Morte d'Arthur*, were exhibited in 1904 at the Louisiana Purchase Exhibition in St Louis, USA.

Mellor, George, 1776–1861

Gilder and Japan painter who was apprenticed at Derby. In 1776 he went to Pinxton and by 1779 was employed at Coalport, where he stayed until 1811. George returned to Derby from 1815 to1830, but by 1841 was a china dealer in Victoria Street, Derby. He was known for his floral studies and insects, which were painted with great delicacy.

Mellor, Thomas, born 1856

Modeller and pâte-sur-pâte painter born in Hanley, Staffordshire, the eldest son of William, a figure maker, and Angelina, who trained at Minton. In the 1880s he went to Wedgwood, working on inlaid decoration in the style of Saint Porchaire, examples of which were shown in the World's Columbian Exposition, Chicago of 1893. He also worked as a Jaspar decorator, sometimes signing his work with his initials. In 1881 he was living with five brothers and a sister at 27 George Street, Stoke-on-Trent, Staffordshire.

Micklewright, Frederick, 1868–1941

Landscape and flower painter. The family came from Dudley, where his father was a well-known bell ringer. They may have had connections with the Micklewrights of Shrewsbury, who were coachbuilders and artists known for armorial painting. He was employed by many potteries and it is difficult to clearly state his early career.

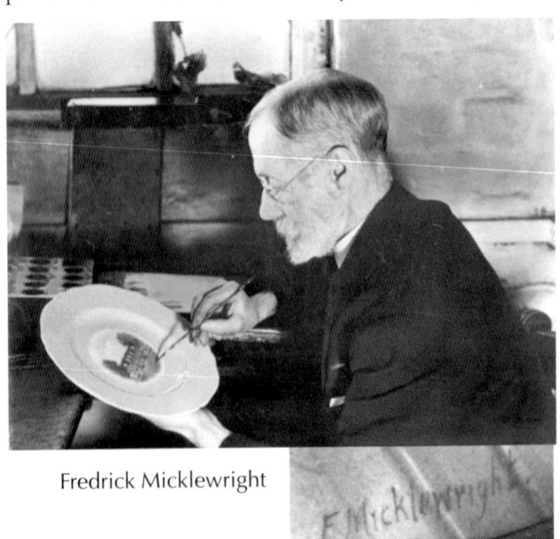

Fredrick Micklewright

Painting of Hanley market, 1840, by Fredrick Micklewright

It is possible that the Micklewright shown in W.H. Brock's notebook as leaving Derby in 1890 is the same artist who came to the Potteries. Frederick lived in an age when hand-painting was no longer financially viable and employment was hard to find. He is known to have got one job by showing a plate painted with game birds to a pottery manager, possibly at the Brownfield Pottery, and he also worked for John Aynsley and Sons, Portland Works, Longton, Staffordshire. The family remember him leaving the Potteries for Dumfries, Scotland to manage a factory. He was unable to control the workforce there and returned to Staffordshire. Examples of his work have also been found on Paragon China Co. Ltd plaques (originally the Star China Company) painted with *The Cavalier and the Musketeer* after J.L.E. Messionier (1815–91, q.v.). In the 1930s he became one of Copeland's premier artists, and retired on a company pension.

He painted landscapes by using stippling to achieve light and shade and signed his work. An example is shown in the Goode's Special Order Book of 1 March 1929, pattern number C 1387 *Eton College* centre and C 1387 *Iona Abbey*. The entry in 1931 reads 'pattern number C2564 on Royal Embossed shape dessert plate, the centre *Holywood Castle* painted by Micklewright'. Later in his career he painted landscapes of famous places, which were engraved and then printed on the ware and hand-coloured. The family remember Frederick as an unworldly gentleman who loved to paint in both oils and watercolour When work was scarce he painted at home, and if a visitor admired his work he would very happily give it to them, totally oblivious of the financial state of his household. He was a quiet, dignified Victorian gentleman, with a little white beard, who wore a white wing collar. When sitting at his bench he was so absorbed in his painting that he did not hear the noise of the young apprentices who worked nearby. He was one of the last true pottery artists. He is shown in the *Potteries Newcastle and District Directory* of 1907 as living at 22 Butler Street, Stoke-on-Trent, Staffordshire.

Midwinter (née Wyse), Eve, born 1926

Artist designer, the daughter of a colonel serving in the Indian Army. When she was seven years old she attended the co-educational school at Huntingdon, where she met Roy Midwinter. After War service in India she went to live with the Midwinter family in the Potteries, training at the Burslem School of Art. Eve married Roy Midwinter and became involved with the family business, bringing back from London examples of contemporary designs as inspiration for the Midwinter designers. By 1960 her talent was recognised and in 1962 she designed the Midwinter stand at the Blackpool Fancy Goods and Gift Fair. After the failure of her marriage she joined her friends Susan and Euan Cooper Williams-Ellis at their Portmeirion Pottery, working with unusual glazes; but she continued to design for Midwinter. The next years saw change and amalgamation of many potteries and Midwinter became part of the Wedgwood group. Eve continued to design for Wedgwood until 1986, when she resigned and became a freelance designer. She supplied designs for Maw & Co and Barratts of Staffordshire, always recognising the market trends and designing within its limitations.

Milward, Harry C., active 1900s

Artist gilder who served his apprenticeship at Derby factory and came to Doulton aged twenty-eight in 1898. He is known for executing some of their finest jewelled and raised gold work. One service, commissioned by an Indian maharajah, was said to have cost £30,000. He is last known to have been employed at Doulton in 1918.

Millward, William, active 1882–1890s

Artist gilder at Copeland known to have decorated a Chelsea-shaped dessert plate with a rich jewel design, which was exhibited at the Exposition Universelle, Paris of 1889. He decorated many of the works of well-known artists at Copeland and may well have been head of the gilding department. He was a contemporary of Goodwin (q.v.) and Deauville (q.v.).

Mitchell, Henry T., 1824–1897

Artist painter, born in Burslem, Staffordshire, a pupil of George Speight. He may have trained and worked at John Ridgway's Cauldon Place works before he joined Minton c. 1860. His work was exhibited in the International Exhibitions held in London 1862, Paris 1867 and Vienna 1873. A coffee set with animals on the cup and grasses on the saucer exhibited in Vienna was bought by Charles Pense on the 19 June 1873 for 48 florins. Mitchell is known for his fine paintings after Landseer (q.v.), including a service for Queen Victoria,

Bone china Doulton plate signed by H. Mitchell

which is now at Balmoral. In 1877 Mitchell left Minton for Harvey Adams and Co. of the Sutherland Road Works, Longton, before joining Doulton c. 1893. Jewitt obviously thought very highly of this artist: 'Mr Henry Mitchell, medallist of the Paris and Vienna Exhibitions, celebrated as an animal, landscape and figure painter and whose works are remarkable for their finish, their modelling and their delicacy of treatment and whose greys and flesh tints are of a peculiar purity and beauty.' Mitchell's work at Doulton was exhibited at the World's Columbian Exposition, Chicago of 1893. Charles John Noke, Art Director, said of his work: 'There are few more beautiful sights on ceramic painting than the silver grey tones of Mitchell's landscapes.' Scarrett said: 'I have seen some of his work. His deer amid bracken are exceedingly nice.' He lived at 40 Hill Street, Stoke-on-Trent and had five children. His son William Henry is shown in 1881 as an apprentice china painter aged seventeen. Mitchell was a popular man and when he died his fellow artists, as a mark of their respect, sent a wreath to his funeral.

Back stamp

Mitchell, Mary, born 1849

Painter born in Shoreditch, Middlesex, the daughter of Frederick A. Mitchell, an artist and wood engraver. She painted at the Doulton Lambeth Studio, London, 1874–87, and is known for her portrayal of rustic subjects with incised decoration. She marked her ware with the monogram MM. Her brother became an apprentice copper engraver.

Moorcroft, Walter, 1917-2002

Artist designer and potter educated at Rugby public school. Despite winning a university place, he joined the family business at Stoke-on-Trent learning his father's working methods and his designs and becoming a Master Potter. Walter served in WWII but was released in September 1945 from active service on compassionate grounds as his father had had a severe stroke. He rejoined the British Pottery Manufacturers Federation, who represented the potters, and helped with the various government controls that had been imposed whilst running the factory.

Although still producing the old successful designs he incorporated his own style, preferring exotic flowers, which were a great success. He continued experimenting in Flambé ware, which soon represented ten per cent of the Moorcroft output. The fine Moorcroft tradition of distinctive quality and innovative designs was maintained.

Moorcroft, William, 1872-1945

Artist, designer and potter, son of Thomas Moorcroft, who was born in Derby 1848 and was a floral artist at E. J. D. Bodley's Hill Pottery, Burslem, Staffordshire. William trained at the Wedgwood Institute, Burslem and at the Government School of Design, South Kensington, London, where he was awarded his art master's certificate. He designed printed patterns for James Macintyre and Co. Ltd, Burslem; in 1897 he became designer and in 1898 manager of the ornamental ware department. He signed each piece and kept severe control of the art department. When in 1912 Macintyre's decided to stop art and tableware production, he decided to start his own pottery at Cobridge, having kept the sole right to his designs. Thirty of the workers came with him to W. Moorcroft Ltd, an innovative pottery. William designed single flower and nature studies: for example, iris, poppy, peacock, feather, rose, and harebell in numerous colours and with metallic glazes. All his vases in different shapes were hand-thrown, designed from contemporary Art Nouveau, Ancient Greek and eighteenth-century Chinese models. After his death, the business was taken over by his son Walter, who continued to produce innovative designs that appealed in the marketplace.

Morley, George, born 1862

Painter and gilder, son of William, a potter's labourer, who in 1881 was living at 23 George Street, Newcastle-under-Lyme, Staffordshire. He was an apprentice at Minton and studied painting at the Newcastle-under-Lyme Art School. His work was shown at the Exposition Universelle, Paris of 1878. George and his brother William emigrated to America, decorating for the Ceramic Art Co., which was founded in Trenton in 1889 by Walter Scott Lenox and Jonathan Coxon Senior. They targeted the top end of the market and sold through the well-known retailers Tiffany's of New York and Banks and Biddle of Philadelphia. It Is possible George also worked for Knowles, Taylor and Knowles of East Liverpool, Ohio, painting gold decorations on their Lotus ware range.

Morley, William, born 1866

Flower painter, brother of George (q. v.). He may have been employed at Doulton as his fine floral painting has the same misty, unique quality of the Doulton decorations of this time. By 1890 he was a well-known and respected artist in America. It is thought he was employed with his brother at Knowles Taylor and Knowles of East Liverpool, Ohio. He worked for the Ceramic Art Company in Trenton, where he painted many fine dessert services and ornamental wares and became very well known. Walter Scott Lennox paid good wages and gave his artists every encouragement. William's rose painting was used in many of the designs, and his ability to paint soft greys and pastel tones on Lennox bone china of the early 1900s appealed to American buyers. The Company's advertisements told of a different design for each piece. William was an artist capable of painting bird and fish subjects to an equally high standard. He signed his work.

Morrey, Harry, 1884–1944

Painter apprenticed to Doulton when fourteen years old. He was trained to paint all subjects but became known for his rural and farming scenes. Harry spent several months in Australia sketching all aspects of sheep rearing and other farming subjects such as ploughing, harvesting and milking. He is known to have painted and designed some of Doulton's Holbein range of ware.

Morris, Henry, 1799–1880

Artist, flower painter and outside decorator who joined the Cambrian Pottery as an apprentice to Lewis Weston Dillyn in 1813. He painted brightly coloured garden flowers and is known to have painted on the Lysaght service. He was employed by T. & J. Bevington, decorating Swansea white porcelains. He is then thought to have worked in London and Staffordshire, but returned to Swansea in 1841 to live at Pleasant Street, where he erected a decorating kiln to decorate white ware. His signature or initials and date are on some of his pieces. Morris also painted in oils and colours. He was a competent musician and interested in astronomy and astrology. He is buried in the Dan-y-Graig cemetery at Swansea.

Morris, Rowland James, died 1898

Modeller who became freelance. He studied at the Hanley School of Art under Protât (q.v.) and at the Government School of Design, South Kensington, London. It is thought that he lived in London and was at the Minton Art Studio with Michael Elden (q.v.). By 1873 he was at Wedgwood, concentrating on majolica ware. He and Mathew Elden were chosen to create designs for the terracotta façade of the Wedgwood Memorial Institute. He modelled a life-size terracotta statue and two series of terracotta panels called *The Months*. Elden, although brilliant, was unreliable and Morris did most of the work that made his name. Morris worked for the Powell & Bishop Pottery of Hanley and also Samuel Alcock of the Hill Top Pottery, Burslem. During 1885–91 he was employed by Bernard Moore at the St Mary's Works, Longton and part time at James Stephen Wilson's St Gregory Works, Longton. In 1891 he established his own studio in Hanley.

Morton, Thomas, born 1848

Artist gilder who may have been at Minton but was known at Doulton as the artist specialising in raised paste gold work. He was also responsible for the fine gilding on vases painted by Curnock, Tittonsor and Eton. Examples of his work are in the Worcester Porcelain Museum.

Mosley, William Edwin, died 1954

Flower painter, an apprentice at the Osmaston Road, Derby factory c. 1893. He left in 1912 to work at the King Street factory, but in the early 1930s he and Robert Barratt (q.v.) went to Australia, returning to King Street around 1933. Two years later he returned to Osmaston Road, where he stayed until his death. William is noted for painting miniature portraits and delicate flower arrangements, which often included roses and forget-me-nots. He was a keen gardener and a member of the Derby Sketching Club.

Mott, J.H., active 1880–1950

Designer and painter who worked at the Doulton Lambeth Studio and succeeded W.P. Rix (q.v.) as Art Director from 1897 to 1935. He then became a consultant, having had a wide knowledge of glazes and ceramic bodies. He designed simple shapes for matt-bodied and flambé ware. He nearly always marked his experimental and other pieces JHM.

Mountford, Jesse, 1799–1861

Landscape painter, brother to John and the son of Thomas. He was born in Hanley but trained at the Nottingham Road, Derby pottery, although in 1821 he was discharged by Mr Bloor. From 1821 to 1833 Jesse designed tableware for Coalport and from 1835–60 was at Davenport. He used a fine stippling effect for his drawing of buildings and rock. He was a keen fisherman and lived about two miles from the Davenport Pottery, near the River Severn. He died at Longport, Staffordshire.

Mountford, John, 1817–1906

Figure maker and potter born at Back Sytch, Burslem, Staffordshire, the son of Thomas Mountford, an enamel kiln fireman and colour maker at the Nottingham Road Works, Derby. He was apprenticed as an ornamental potter and then went to Copeland in Stoke-upon-Trent as a figure maker. When trying to find the recipe for the old Derby biscuit figures, he discovered a new marble-like body that was first called statuary porcelain but became known as Parian. This was ideal to mould into the famous sculptures of the day and became a great success. Both Minton and Copeland claimed credit for its invention, an argument that has lasted into the present century. After John left Copeland, he went into partnership with Samuel Keys, producing Parian ware at a factory in John Street (now called Leese Street), Stoke-on-Trent. To celebrate the partnership, forty of the Copeland workers gave them a dinner, wishing it every success. The company exhibited some of the ware at the Great Exhibition of 1851. Unfortunately the partnership failed, John became bankrupt and he returned to the Crown Derby Works to assist Sampson Hancock. He is shown in the 1881 census as a dealer in glass and china living at 12 Burton Street, Derby.

Muller, John Adam, born 1820

Artist gilder born in Deutz, near Cologne. He was employed by Copeland to work on fine china dessert services and vases for the London 1871 and 1872 International Exhibitions. He is recorded in the Copeland Special Order books in November 1870 as gilding a vase with birds on one side and a landscape on the other. These exhibits were not given a pattern number, but a number only: for example, Cup and saucer No 46, rose sprays jewelled gilded and chased; Vase on claw feet, Winthrop shape jewel borders by Muller. There are twenty-eight entries of his work during this period. He left Copeland c. 1875 and joined Minton as one of their foremost gilders working in raised gold. An entry in the G. Minton pattern book series show he was paid £1 for two hours work when working on pattern number G 2621 – twelve Winchester-shape plates described as gold-blue landscape centres. There is an entry in the Minton wages book of 4 January 1877 for gilding a pair of pâte-sur-pâte vases painted by Solon (q.v.) and also a pair of vases painted by Mussill (q.v.). His work is mentioned in the *Art Journal*'s report of the Exposition Universelle, Paris of 1878.

Murray, Keith, MC, RDI, FRIBA, 1892–1981

Architect designer of pottery, glass and furniture born in New Zealand and educated at Mill Hill School, London, then trained in New Zealand at King's College, Auckland. He was a freelance designer for Stevens and Williams, glass manufacturers, at Brierly Hill. The range, called Keith Murray Glass, attracted Wedgwood who commissioned work in 1932–39; some of it is etched with his signature. He designed exciting shapes for such products as inkstands, ashtrays and jugs in moonstone or matt green glazes. His work was recognised when he won a gold medal in the Fifth Triennial, Milan in 1933, and in 1976 a travelling exhibition of his work was shown at the Victoria & Albert Museum. After a distinguished War service Murray returned to Wedgwood in the capacity of architect. He and his partner C.S. White designed the new Wedgwood factory at Barlaston, Staffordshire.

Muss, Charles, 1779–1824

Artist and enamel painter, son of an immigrant Italian house painter and enamel painter in Newcastle-upon-Tyne. He painted for both Caughley and Coalport, usually landscapes and figures in sepia and purple monochrome, but no signed examples have so far been found. By 1800 he was in London living at 46 Castle Street, Oxford Market. In 1802 he had moved to 12 Michael's Place, Brompton. Finally he moved to Warren Street. Muss painted for William Collins, who was listed as a glass manufacturer. In 1806 Muss sent for his father, Bonifacio Musso, and they started a decorating shop, painting enamels, in Great Windmill Street, which unfortunately failed. He submitted paintings to the Royal Academy from 1817; *Waters of Oblivion* sold for 50 guineas He was to paint many more popular works, such as *Fall of Ninevah*, said to be the largest on metal at twenty-one inches high and fifteen inches wide, which George IV bought for £1500. He could be the Muss of the Silk, Muss and Essex decorating business, but to date no evidence has been found.

Mussill, Wenceslas (William), 1829–1906

Flower and bird painter born in Austria near Carlsbad, Austria. He studied in Paris and had paintings exhibited in the Paris Salon. Mussill met C.F. Hurten (q.v.) in Paris, and no doubt through this connection came the Potteries. Sometime in the 1870s, on the recommendation of Christian Henk (q.v.), he went to Minton, where he was offered a weekly salary but refused, wishing to be paid separately for each piece. The Minton records show that

Bone china Minton dessert plate painted by Mussell

on 2 October 1873 he earned £22-15s-0d for painting three pairs of vases, one dish and one ten-inch tile in a week. Other entries show weekly earnings of £21-10s-0d and over £9. His work was greatly admired and had an influence on the students in the local art school. Mussill was the leading artist capable of the barbotine technique of painting with either thick ceramic colours or coloured clay slips. Unlike most painters, whose work would need possibly three firings, his was only fired once. He spent hours creating his studies, first on paper, before they were used on the ceramic surface. He kept the original drawings and painted copies for the potteries that employed him. He was influenced by the work of John Bateman of Biddulph Grange, who published the book *Mexican Orchids*. Until this publication the flower was not known and Mussill painted many orchids studies. He spent all his spare time painting, often on the Duke of Sutherland's estate at Trentham Gardens, Staffordshire and at Biddulph Grange, but is known to have travelled as far as Manchester and Liverpool. He was a small Victorian gentleman, who always wore a scarf or a muffler to protect his throat. He was a bachelor and had a housekeeper, Frederika Halinal, who was born in Prussia. After her death he lived alone, cooking and looking after the house. He became a wealthy man, maintained a studio and taught painting. In the late 1880s he did some work for Brown-Westhead, Moore and Co. that included pieces for the Exposition Universelle, Paris of 1889. When Thomas Goode commissioned two plaques from Copeland the order stated the gilding was to be done by Copeland but the centre decorations of Windsor Castle and Balmoral were to be painted by Mussill. He was regarded with great affection and known to have been a genial host, but became rather reclusive before his death.

Mycock, William Salter, born 1872

Painter and designer, originally a tile painter, who first worked for Wedgwood while studying at art school in the evenings. He joined the Pilkington Pottery sometime in 1906, where his designs included florals, gothic, heraldic and ship subjects, and also sgraffito of a fine unusual design. His work was shown at the Arts and Crafts Exhibition in 1906. He signed his work with a monogram.

Pilkington lustre vase decorated by William Mycock after Walter Crane

Nabney, Robert, born 1849

Crest painter born in Fenton, Staffordshire and studied at the Stoke School of Art. He was at employed by Minton and became head of one of the decorating departments from 1902 to 1920.

Neatby, William. J., 1860–1910

Designer and freelance modeller who worked for an architect before working for the Brumanstoft Co. 1880–90. Doulton employed him from 1890 to 1907, where he became head of the architects department, modelling cararra ware, friezes, masks, and caryatids in an architectural style. His work was influenced by the Art Nouveau style. In 1896 he designed a set of life-size terracotta female figures for the Winter Gardens in Blackpool, Lancashire. He designed circular plaques with hunting and pastoral scenes for Harrods' Food Hall, and the façade for a Bristol printing works. After leaving Doulton he worked freelance, designing stained glass, influenced by C.F.A. Voysey (q.v.) and other manufacturers associated with the Arts and Crafts movement. His work is often initialled.

Nixon, George, born 1862

Painter born in Burslem, Staffordshire. In 1881 he was living at 23 Hope Street, described as an earthenware painter. He is known to have been employed at the Brown-Westhead, Moore & Co. Pottery, where he painted exhibition pieces for the World's Columbian Exposition, Chicago of 1893. He was working still at the Cauldon factory in 1906.

Nixon, Harry N.A.D, born 1886

Flower painter and designer, an apprentice at Doulton in 1900, training at the Burslem School of Art in the evenings, He won many medals in national competitions for plant and pottery designs, and after his training he taught part time in the evenings at the Burslem School of Art. Nixon painted flowers on table and ornamental ware. He became chief collaborator with Charles Noke on the designs for Titian and Flambé ware and was involved in the development of the hand-painted figures for which Doulton was to become to well known.Those pieces manufactured before 1913 that have on their base 'HN' preceding a number were Nixon's design. He was involved in the creation of Chang ware, named after the southern Sung potter Chang, which had a crackle-glaze effect. Away from work Nixon was an active church worker in the Stoke area and designed the twenty-one inch high flambé vase made for Lichfield cathedral. Three of his watercolours floral studies were shown in the Century Exhibition in Hanley, Stoke-on-Trent in 1953.

Noke, Cecil J. (Jack), died 1954

Painter, designer and art director, son of Charles Noke (q.v.), educated at Newcastle High School. He was apprenticed to an architect before serving as an officer in WWI. In 1920 he joined the Doulton and was trained to fully understand the art of painting both under and over the glaze by L. Bentley and R. Allen. In the evenings he studied at both the Stoke and Burslem Schools of Art. Noke assisted Harry Nixon and his father in the creation of flambé, Sung and Chang Wares. He became head of the engraving department, and on the death of his father was appointed Art Director. He was a modest and popular man who although officially retired in 1936 at the age of seventy-eight, continued to go to his studio at the pottery until his sudden death.

Noke, Charles John, 1860–1941

Modeller and pâte-sur-pâte painter born in Worcester, son of a collector and retailer of ceramics. He was apprenticed as a modeller and designer at the Worcester Pottery, living at Sparrowfields Farm, Red Hills, Worcester as a boarder. He studied at the local school of design, and stayed with the Royal Worcester Co. for sixteen years. In 1889 he was appointed chief modeller for Doulton. The figures *The Jester, The Moorish Minstrel, Henry Irvine* and *Ellen Terry* are examples of his fine work. He and Cuthbert Bailey were responsible for the new glazes and bodies produced at this time. He also initiated the Holbein and Rembrandt range of wares. Noke enjoyed his freedom to design at Doulton and took great pleasure in the success of the product. He became assistant head with John Slater (q.v.) of Doulton's Art Department, and in 1914 he was appointed Art Director. His team created new and exciting products, which were totally different from those of the established pottery factories at that time.

Nunn Walter, active 1900s

Painter and designer. After studying at the Government School of Design, South Kensington, London, Nunn came to the Potteries. He had a rare ability to create scenes and characters from Shakespeare's plays, which appealed to the buying public. The designs had historical authenticity and were fresh and appealing. Nunn stayed at Doulton for thirteen years and contributed greatly to their success in the 1900s.

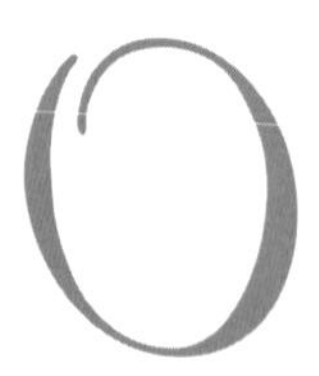

Olsen, Erling B., 1903–1992

Designer and modeller born at Drammen in Norway. Eric, as he was affectionately known at Copeland, studied at the Oslo at School of Art, St Martin's School of Art, London and the Faience studio at Sèvres. He first joined Wedgwood, where his work was very popular, but in 1932 went to Copeland, where he was offered

A group of fancy ware designed by E. Olsen and produced by Copeland in their new grey glaze *Onyx*

Art Deco cat designed by E. Olsen

a studio of his own and the opportunity to experiment with glazes and new shapes. The animals he designed at this time reflect the Art Deco style of the period and his fancy goods range, totally different to the normal Spode style, brought a much-needed fresh approach. In 1942 Eric was called up and went to join the Norwegian Quartermaster General, where he became a camouflage expert. After the War he became chief designer for Haeger Potteries, Illinois, USA.

Right: Eric Owen

O'Neale, Jeffryes Hammet, 1734–1801

Artist, painter and freelance decorator, thought to have been born in County Antrim, son of a landowner. He studied with William Duvivier, who originated fable subject designs, and worked for the Chelsea and Worcester Potteries on a freelance basis, 1770–75. O'Neale is associated with painting animals in landscapes and large classical subjects with fine detailed brushwork. He also worked with and for James Giles (q.v.). When employed by Wedgwood in the 1770s, he was paid £3 a week, much to Josiah Wedgwood's disgust, who thought it was excessive; but he was known to have said that O'Neale worked quickly. His fable subjects consisted of animals full of life, be they mythical or real. His figures were always anatomically correct, although their clothing could be curious. His landscapes had blue rivers with waterfalls and punt-like boats and his trees were characteristically gnarled and broken with green or red leaves. O'Neale's classical subjects depicted ruins and obelisks with banks of cumulus clouds. His use of bright colours added a special touch to his work that made it distinctive. He is known to have signed his work 'O' Neale pinxt' or ONP. He painted the watercolour *Taken from behind ye China House at Bow*, which shows the approximate position of the Bow manufactory. In 1765 he became a Fellow of the Incorporated Society of Artists, where he exhibited miniatures. His signature can be found on the stonework of his paintings. He returned to Ireland c. 1784 to paint scenery for *The New British Traveller*. There he was described as the most capital painter in Ireland.

Owen, active 1860–88

Artist gilder at Copeland, Stoke-upon-Trent. He gilded the ware painted by C.F. Hurten (q.v.) and C. Weaver (q.v.).

Owen, Eric Raymond, 1902–1974

Modeller born in Stoke-on-Trent and trained at the Burslem School of Art. He was apprenticed at a Minton Hollins tile works under Arthur Emery and in 1922 went as a modeller to Minton, staying for twenty-five years. In 1928 he was appointed Chief Modeller, producing the figures *Mimosa*, *The Bridesmaid*, *Jack*, and *The Dutch Girl*. He left to join Wedgwood, where he became Chief Modeller 1946–47. His work for Wedgwood included heat-resistant tableware and portrait medallions. Owen was a part-time instructor at the Longton and Stoke Schools of Art 1929–44.

Owen, George, died 1917

Modeller and designer of reticulated ware born in Worcester and living at 12 Wood Terrace in the Arboretum for many years. He worked at Grainger Worcester. His pieces were exhibited at the International Exhibition, 1862 and were described as true masterpieces the by the *Art Journal*: 'Grainger's perforated Parian has fine qualities, but it was cut mechanically on a pattern applied to the unbaked clay; a man or boy without special gifts could do the piercing after some training. Not so that of Mr Owen; after marking of the body of the piece into sections, the ground is either pierced or reserved for a delicate application of colour. The pierced ground, all cut by hand, is largely in a honeycomb pattern divided by bands of reticulations in endless variety. These bands of diapers are seldom duplicated; the astonishing skill of the artist is displayed in the variety of his combinations, the sharpness and geometrical accuracy of their execution so that the walls of the vases only a fractional part of an inch thick resemble nothing so much as lace, lacework in porcelain of a beauty and delicacy beyond description.' Owen signed his work.

Palin, William Mainwaring, R.B.A.,1862–1947

Painter born in Hanley, the son of William, an engraver of copper, apprenticed at Wedgwood (1875–80). His undoubted ability to paint all subjects to a very high standard soon came to the notice of Thomas Allen (q.v.), who appointed him his assistant. In 1880 William went to London to study at the Government School of Design, South Kensington, continuing his studies in Rome and Paris. In later life he became known as a genre and mural painter. He became Vice President of the Royal Society of British Artists in 1914.

Palmere, Charles P., born 1830

Portrait and figure painter born in Paris. He was first employed at the Flight and Barr, Worcester pottery, then from (1865–73), having acquired a reputation as a fine artist, he worked at Coalport as one of their premier painters. Palmere painted a number of pieces for the 1871 London International Exhibition, including portraits after Greuze, Shakespearean subjects and some views of Mentmore, the home of Baron Rothschild. Two years later, his portraits of the Emperor and Empress of Austria on a pair of vases shown at the Vienna Exhibition were highly praised. In 1880 it is thought he returned to Worcester to the Royal Worcester Porcelain Co., where he painted figure subjects after Teniers (q.v.).

Pardoe, Thomas, 1770–1823

Painter and outside decorator born in Derby. In the 1780s he was apprenticed at the Derby Factory under William Duesbury (q.v.). His paintings were noted for their freshness of design and versatility. He painted animals, landscapes, flowers and oriental designs. At some point he moved to the Potteries, possibly to John Turner of Lane End, Longton, but from 1795–1809 he became chief painter at the Cambrian Pottery, Swansea, painting superb floral studies. Many of the excellent paintings on Swansea porcelain of this period are attributed to him. He was one of the rare painters happy painting with gold, and his work has many favourite motifs, such as insects and borders of intersecting ellipses. From 1809–15 he is recorded as an outside decorator in Bristol, using mainly Coalport ware. Some examples have been found marked 'Pardoe, 28 Bath Street, and Bristol'. Pardoe is known to have sold ceramic colours and taught painting to young women. The actual date on which he left Bristol is not known. However, when W. W. Young (q.v.) took over the Nantgarw Pottery he employed Pardoe and his son to decorate the stock left by William Billingsley and Walker when they left for Coalport. He decorated this ware with flowers, fruit and butterflies. His favourite flowers were open pink roses and tulips in full bloom. Pardoe's sketchbook is now in the Victoria & Albert Museum. He died at Nantgarw.

Pardoe, William Henry, 1803–1867

Flower painter, outside decorator and potter trained by his father William (q.v.). He specialised in conventional flowers and leaves in small yellow urns and in brightly painted bouquets. It is possible he set up his own decorating business, first at Neath then in about1826 in Cardiff. He is shown in Pigot's *Directory* for 1830 as a dealer in china and glass at St Mary's Street and High Street Cardiff. Some pieces have been found marked 'Pardoe Cardiff'. In 1833, using part of the old Nantgarw works, William made red ware and tobacco pipes. He added a stoneware department and also, it is thought, decorated Rockingham ware. After his death his widow and family continued the business until 1920.

Parker, John

Painter born in Shropshire who went to Coalport about 1830–40, painting feather and flowers but specialising in still life groups of shells.

Parnell, Gwendoline, active 1916–1935

Portrait painter and modeller of Irish origin, with an aristocratic and artistic family background. Her great aunt Emily Farmiloe was a book illustrator and her grandmother was lady-in-waiting to Queen Victoria. Gwendoline became a well-known portrait painter during WWI. At an exhibition at the Goldsmiths Hall, London of *Enemy Crafts*, badly painted German toys caught her interest; she enrolled at the Camberwell School of Craft and was taught under Professor Lunn, the ex-manager of the Royal Crown Derby Factory. At the British industries fair in 1917, Queen Mary bought her figure of Henry VIII. In 1918 she started her own small pottery in Upper Cheyne Row, Chelsea, London, designing and making figures influenced by those of Chelsea. The business was very successful and in 1925 she exhibited her work at the Exposition Universelle, Paris and was awarded a gold medal. In 1927 Parnell was elected first President of the Guild of Pottery. In 1935 she moved to work for the Royal Worcester Porcelain Co., living at Edgar Street near to the factory, where the workers gave her the affectionate nickname 'The Duchess'. Her work included models of *London Cries* and chinoisserie child figures. She retired to The Old Rectory, Grafton, Flyford, near to Worcester.

Parry, Edward Ernest, active 1880

Painter employed at Dolton, Burslem, Staffordshire 1887–93. He is known to have also worked at both the Cauldon and Grimwade factories.

Patten, Joseph, 1800–1870

Flower painter apprenticed at Coalport about 1820. He is one of the first artists to be named in their pattern books (pattern numbers 934, 935 and 937), listed as painting groups of flowers and later crests and wild flowers. He became one of the premier painters at Coalport and spent the whole of his working life there. His son Samuel eventually became decorative foreman of one of the departments at Coalport.

Peach, Joseph Arthur, born 1864

Flower painter born in Derby and trained at the Osmaston Road Derby Pottery. He moved to the Potteries, first to Minton and then to Copeland. He is shown in the Copeland Special Order books as a floral artist, from 1885–89 painting on the 1/over series of pattern numbers. He painted mainly on dessert services and occasionally is shown as painting tea services, but there is no record that he painted on vases. To date no signed pieces have been found. His work was shown in Paris in 1889. Peach married Elizabeth Tams (Lizzie, born in 1865 at Stoke-on-Trent, daughter of Thomas Tams, q.v.) a paintress at Copeland. In 1890 the family returned to Derby, and Peach advised the whole Tams family to follow, saying 'there were always Italian skies in Derby, unlike kiln filled Stoke-on-Trent's notorious five towns'. He worked at the Osmaston Road factory, Derby and is shown in their pattern books; for example, pattern number 1883, 'Dessert plate, butterfly and flowers by Peach, acid border'. In 1895 the family left for Sydney, Australia, hoping the sunny climate would be beneficial to his health (he had contracted tuberculosis). They bought a hardware shop in Sydney and Peach taught at the local School of Art and sent paintings back to his relatives in England.

Pearce, Arthur E., active 1870s–1900s

Artist and painter who studied architecture, first at the Government School of Design, South Kensington, London and later in Paris at the Julien Studio. In 1873 he was employed at the Doulton Lambeth Studio, specialising in tile designs and using his vast knowledge of historical styles and ornaments for inspiration. Pearce designed Doulton's exhibition stands and advertising wares, particularly spirit bottles. He stayed at Doulton for fifty-seven years, signing his work with a monogram of his initials, AEP. He was an artist of considerable talent whose paintings were exhibited at the Royal Academy in 1901 and the Royal Society of Artists 1882–83.

Pedley, Henry, born 1806–1880

Bird and crest painter born in Derby and an apprentice gilder at the Derby manufactory in 1818. In 1832 he is shown in the wages list under the gilders section. He moved to the Potteries, where he had a successful career as a painter, specialising in birds. He was employed at the Copeland and Garrett manufactory as their Special Order books show H. Pedley painting from 1846 to 1851: for example, July 1846, pattern number 5800 'china bottle birds each side'; 1848 'China dishes with Crest and arms'; and December the same year 'Muffin dish', pattern number 3302. The family then lived at Vale Street,

Stoke-upon-Trent, and two of his children were then in apprenticeships: Harriet as a burnisher and Harry as a modeller. Pedley left Copeland for Coalport, where he is shown on the 1859 painters wages list receiving high pay. Coalport pattern book number 6/416 shows 'Two Birds by Pedley'. He died at West Street, Stoke-on-Trent, his death certificate stating he was a crest painter.

Pegg, William, 1795–1867

Flower painter and outside decorator, an apprentice at the Nottingham Road, Derby factory c. 1810–19; he then went to Swansea. He painted single flower blooms, perhaps influenced by works in the collection of Sir Hans Sloane. In the 1820s William may have worked for Daniels of Stoke-on-Trent, painting fine floral studies. A letter from Richard Daniel to his father c. 1824 states: 'Do get some good flower painters if possible. I have sold more than Pegg and Brammer and Ellis will do in six months'. Pegg left the Potteries for Manchester, possibly to join the textile company Thomas Hoyle in South Manchester as a pattern designer. Finally, he established a successful calico printing business with Mr Taylor and Mr Hampton at Heaton Norris, Stockport.

Pegg, William Quaker, 1775–1851

Flower painter born at Whitmore, near Newcastle-under-Lyme, Staffordshire, the son of a gardener at Etwell Hall near Derby. He entered a five-year agreement with Derby to be employed as a floral painter, succeeding Billingsley (q.v.). Using his observations from nature and botany books, Pegg painted flowers that were botanically accurate, writing their names on the undersides of the pieces. In 1800 he joined the Society of Friends, his strong religious principles now conflicting with his art, as he came to believe that painting was sinful. He left the factory and retired to a village, where from 1801–13 he tried to earn a living, unsuccessfully, as a framework knitter, working a wool loom. Mr Bloor of the Derby pottery persuaded him to return, and his subsequent work was popular and sold for a high price. His signed and dated sketchbook of July 1813, discovered by John Twitchett, shows Pegg's artistic talent. In 1822, again on religious grounds, he left the pottery and started a general store on Nottingham Road, Derby with his wife Ann, which he ran until his death.

Pennington, John, 1765–1842

Figure painter, son of James, a potter of Copperas Hill, Liverpool, whose business failed; the family then moved to Worcester. John was an apprentice painter at Wedgwood. It is thought he worked in the Wedgwood Chelsea Studio with his brother Robert (1765–1842). John moved to Worcester and became one of the chief artists at the Flight and Barr factory, specialising in monochrome painting and figure subjects. He painted the figures depicting Hope on the Duke of Clarence service in 1792, now known as the Hope service.

Penson, Henry Swift, 1868–1951

Artist, painter and designer, an apprentice at Minton 1881 under William Mussill (q.v.). He studied at the Stoke School of Art 1882–90 and in 1890 won a scholarship to the Government School of Design, South Kensington, London. On his return he became a teacher at the Stoke School of Art. In the early 1890s he exhibited mythological subjects at the Royal Academy. Eventually he became a designer and draftsmen for Minton Hollins Ltd and the Campbell Tile Co.

Perling, Robert, 1834–1893

Landscape and animal painter known to have been working at the Kerr & Binns Pottery, Worcester during the 1850s. He copied the work of Landseer (q.v.) with great accuracy onto dessert plates and vases. By 1881 he and his family had moved to Castle Green Street, Owen, Hereford, where he is shown in the census as an artist (landscape).

Perry, Arthur, 1872–1973

Painter, son of George Perry (born 1822, a mould and figure maker) and Elizabeth. He trained at the Hanley School of Art, where his work, examined by representatives from the Government School of Design, was awarded medals of excellence. As a small boy he had said he wanted to learn to paint and was delighted when his father's friend, William Birbeck, took him as an apprentice at

Copeland earthenware plaque painted by Arthur Perry

Bone china Copeland centre piece painted with a view of Scarborough Castle. Courtesy of the Spode Museum Trust

Copeland. Birbeck died a year later and Perry completed his apprenticeship under Charles Brayford Brough (q.v.), who taught him not only painting but also gilding. He left Copeland for Coalport 1899–1908. There are many examples of his signed work on Copeland, Coalport and Doulton ware. After a time he returned to Copeland, where he was remembered with great affection, a man with a lively wit and razor-sharp mind, always ready to help the young apprentices. He was proud to boast that he had never been short of work, having the ability to paint any subject with consummate skill, such as heraldic designs, landscapes, fish, game and flowers. Perry designed copper-plate engravings.

His best example was in 1929, when he created designs from the paintings of twenty-four hunting scenes by Lionel Edwards, which became best-selling patterns. Perry and Thomas Hassall, Copeland's Art Director, disagreed and at the age of fifty-five he left Copeland's for the last time and joined Doulton, where he stayed until he retired. He was regarded as the foremost fish and game painter of his day, and he also painted landscapes in the style of Birbeck to meet the demands of Doulton's American market. On 8 September 1965 he was interviewed on radio, on *Women's Hour*, describing ceramic painting. He said it took many hours of diligent study, great dexterity of hand and keenness of the eye, and that many good artists left as their pay was so poor. Perry retired due to poor eyesight and lived with his daughter in the village of Eccleshall, Staffordshire. He continued his hobbies of gardening, walking and swimming. He often said he had enjoyed every minute of his career and would not have changed any of it.

Phillips, Ernest John, active 1876–1932

Flower painter apprenticed at the Royal Worcester Porcelain Co. who specialised in painting small groups of flowers in the old Worcester style. He was a keen gardener and painted watercolour studies of the flowers in his garden.

Phillips, Thomas, born 1862

Painter and designer apprenticed at the Worcester Royal Porcelain Co., but by 1888 joined Doulton in Burslem. Phillips decorated examples of Spanish ware and his work was exhibited in Paris and Chicago. Later he painted designs and patterns under glaze and became responsible for a team of decorators.

Pillemont, Jean, 1727–1808

Artist, landscape and marine painter, born and educated in Lyons. He trained in Paris and Vienna then came to London in 1763. He worked in oil and pastels, but is better known for his watercolour paintings. He was a fashionable painter of his day. His chinoisserie designs, published in London and Paris, provided the Staffordshire potters with source material for design. The design book *The Ladies' Amusement*, compiled by Robert Sayer, shows designs after Pillemont, which were then engraved by Robert Hancock. Both Wedgwood and Worcester used this source for some of their designs. Pillemont styled himself painter to the King of Poland and to Marie Antoinette, Queen of France. He died in Lyons.

Pilsbury, Richard (Senior), 1831–1897

Floral painter born at Newcastle-under-Lyme who served his apprenticeship at the Samuel Alcock and Co., Hill Pottery, Burslem. He studied at Burslem School of Design under W.J. Muckley 1853–58, specialising in flower painting. He was awarded twelve medals from the Government School of Design, London and became an art teacher there for a short time, before returning to work in the Potteries. He is remembered as one of the premier painters at Minton from 1866–92. Solon (q.v.) said of his work in the *Art Journal* of 1897: 'Pilsbury may be said to have witnessed the dawn of a new era which was to change the face of English decorative art and to have been one of those whose artistic work has materially assisted in bringing about the revolution of public taste… he turned to nature, the only guide which never misleads, and by his untiring work in the greenhouses, his conscientious reproductions of the best models he found there, he gained experience and the skill he wanted to emerge from the swamp of the old routine and bud out as a true and complete flower painter.' He is shown in the 1881 census as living in Regent Street, Stoke-on-Trent. Pilsbury left Minton for a short time around 1892 to work at the Osmaston Road, Derby factory, but later accepted the post of Art Director at the Moore Bros, Longton.

Pilsbury, William Heath, born 1869

Painter, son of Richard, born in Stoke-on-Trent, an apprentice painter at the Minton factory from 1883–90.

THE

LADIES AMUSEMENT;

OR, WHOLE

ART of JAPANNING

MADE EASY.

Illuſtrated in upwards of Fifteen-Hundred different DESIGNS, on Two Hundred Copper Plates;

CONSISTING,

Of Flowers, Shells, Figures, Birds, Inſects, Landſcapes, Shipping, Beaſts, Vaſes, Borders, &c.

All adapted in the beſt Manner for joining in Groupes, or being placed in ſingle Objects.

DRAWN BY

PILLEMENT and other Maſters,

And excellently ENGRAVED.

To which is added, in LETTER-PRESS,

The moſt approved Methods of JAPANNING; from the Preparation of the Subject to be decorated, to its being finiſhed:

WITH

DIRECTIONS for the due Choice of COMPOSITION, COLOURS, &c. &c.

The SECOND EDITION,

N. B. *The above Work will be found extremely uſeful to the* PORCELAINE, *and other Manufactures depending on* Deſign.

LONDON:

Printed for ROBERT SAYER, Map and Printſeller, at the Golden-Buck, oppoſite Fetter-Lane, Fleet-Street.

Pages out of the book *The Ladies Amusement* by Robert Sayer. Above, the first page, below, illustrations by Jean Pillemont

Bone china Minton pierced border dessert plate year cipher for 1881 painted and signed by R. Pilsbury

He painted tiles and panels in the 1880s. However, the 1901 census shows he had become a wallpaper designer on his own account.

Piper, Arthur, born 1837

Painter and artist gilder born in Madeley, Shropshire, possibly trained at Coalport. After 1871 he went to Osmaston Road, Derby, where he executed fine raised jewelling decorations.

Piper, Enoch, born 1834

Heraldic, crest and flower painter born in Madeley, Shropshire. He worked at Coalport 1850–90. At the age of fifty-five he left Coalport to join Doulton, becoming their premier crest painter. He painted the crests on the service commissioned for Edward VII.

Piper, Henry E. (Harry), 1859–1906

Flower and bird painter, son of Enoch (q.v.), born in Madeley, Shropshire, first employed at Coalport then at Doulton painting flowers. Henry created the Doulton rose, which he painted on dessert plates that were exhibited at the World's Columbian Exposition, Chicago, of 1893. His work was in great demand, particularly by the famous retail house of Tiffany's of New York. His death at the age of forty-seven was a great loss to the industry.

Pitman, John

Painter, a pupil of Thomas Baxter (q.v.). He is listed in the Worcester 1841 directory as a painter of animals. His work was exhibited at the Royal Academy, the Suffolk Street Art Gallery, London and at the British Institute 1820–27.

Planche, André, 1728–1805

Modeller born in London, the son of Paul and Marie Planche, who had a coffee shop in Soho. Marie was a relative of Louis Fournier of the Chantilly Pottery, where possibly André learnt to make porcelain. He was apprenticed to a Soho goldsmith, Edward Mountenay. He and his wife moved to Lodge Lane, Derby, where André was making finely modelled small animals and figures from china and firing them at Mr Woodward's pipe kiln in Willow Row, Derby. However, there is another view that he worked in a small factory at St Mary's Bridge, funded by a son of Louis Henri de Bourbon, Prince of Condé, who was also associated with the Chantilly Pottery. His models came to the notice of John Heath and William Duesbury (q.v.) of the Derby, Nottingham Road, China Works, and they entered into a business agreement with him, which failed. André next become associated with a French count, an illegitimate son of Prince Louis Henri of Bourbon, but this venture also failed. He then went to Bath, where he became involved

Bone china plaques painted by J.H. Plant

with the theatre. Many of the early Derby figures and animals have been attributed to Planche.

Plant, active 1845–1851

Landscape painter at Copeland and Garrett, shown as painting pattern numbers from 5594 to 8557, particularly landscapes. For example, December 1846 'Victoria shape china dessert plate pattern number 7547, landscape centre named view in gold letters'; there is another entry without pattern number of Goodwood House. It is possible that many of the fine landscapes of the late Copeland and Garrett period were painted by Plant, but to date no signed examples have been found.

Plant, James, born c. 1780

Heraldic crest painter born in Staffordshire and worked at Chamberlain Worcester Porcelain for over forty years. He remembered Lord Nelson's visit to the works in 1802. His son Alfred, born about 1813, was a painter at Worcester. Mr Binns of Kerr and Binns recalled a heraldic artist named Plant working in 1852.

Plant, James, active 1800s

Landscape and figure painter. In 1803 he was doing work for Simms and Muss, the outside decorators, painting groups of children playing and snowballing on Nantgarw ware. It is possible that he is the same freelance artist who lived in London painting portraits and small enamels on silver and gold for Rundall and Bridges. Queen Victoria is said to have commissioned work from him. He was a very nervous man, who in his later days painted very slowly but with great accuracy.

Plant, John Hugh, born 1854

Landscape painter born in Stoke, Staffordshire, the son of a publican and in 1881 living at 65 High Street, Stoke-on-Trent with his family. Plant trained at the Cauldon pottery during the Brown-Westhead, Moore & Co. period and at the Hanley School of Art. Sometime in the 1880s he was painting marine and landscape views and also decorating buttons with stags' heads at Coalport. In 1890–1902 he was employed at Wedgwood, specialising in landscape and topographical views. Durinf 1902–17 he was at Doulton. He was a prolific painter, one of the few able to paint quickly but with great skill and accuracy. He copied ships after J.M.W. Turner, painted scenes of Venice and was able to capture the prefect blue of the sea, the soft Italian skies and the colours of the buildings.

Pointon, William, 1861–1941

Modeller employed at Royal Worcester c. 1880, as a pâte-sur-pâte artist of animals and landscapes, sometimes in coloured clay. He modelled figures of soldiers that realistically depicted their life in WWI. He signed his work and examples are in the Dyson Perrins Museum in Worcester.

Pollard, William, 1803–1854

Flower, fruit and landscape painter born at Landore, near Swansea. He was first sent to work in a solicitor's office but it was soon apparent that he had a natural artistic talent. He became an apprentice painter at the Swansea Pottery from 1815. David Evans (q.v.) had a great influence on his style of painting. William is known for his wild flowers, fruit and landscapes with a characteristic soft and delicate look achieved by the ceramic colours chosen. After leaving Swansea he was a freelance artist, painting Bebbington white ware; he worked on the Bebbington-Gibbon service. In 1822–27 he was employed by H. & R. Daniel in Stoke, then returned to Wales for by 1830 he had set up as a china dealer at King Street, Carmarthen. He traded as a china dealer, porcelain painter and as an auctioneer and appraiser. By 1846 Pollard was living with his sister and brother-in-law in Burnham Spa, Somerset. Pollard was a fine artist whose work can be found on pieces from other well-known potteries. He used a spray of thick-stemmed heather as a trademark and was noted for loosely arranged floral sprays, the gaps in between the blossoms filled in with a dusky black colour.

Pope, Francis C. (Frank), active 1880–1927

Modeller at Doulton noted for vases with natural forms, grotesque animals in relief and vases modelled in the shapes of gourds. He worked with M.V. Marshall and H. Simeon on the production of mottled brown, leopard-skin slipware. His work was shown at the Arts and Crafts Exhibitions 1899–1916 and at the Louisiana Purchase Exhibition in St Louis in 1904. His ware is marked F.C.P. or signed in full.

Pope, Stephen, 1842–1928

Flower painter, an apprentice at Cauldon, studying in the evenings. He worked at the Cauldon pottery, owned first by Ridgeway then by Brown-Westhead, Moore & Co., for seventy-four years. Pope decorated vases for the World's Columbian Exposition, Chicago of 1893. His work is seen on a Cauldon marked vase of the 1900s, which shows a floral composition delicately achieved, in a style different to those of his contemporaries. In 1900 his work was shown to the Chinese Envoy when he visited the pottery as an example of one of their premier artist's work. When a tea service was produced for Princess Mary on the occasion of her marriage in 1922, Pope was included in the presentation party. Again, when the Prince of Wales

Bone china Cauldon rose bowl c. 1900. Signed S. Pope

visited Staffordshire in June 1924 he had the honour of being presented to him. At the end of his career, Pope claimed to be the oldest ceramic artist in the country. He signed his work and in 1881 is shown as living at 62 Harley Street, Stoke-on-Trent, Staffordshire.

Potts, Ann B., born 1918

Modeller who trained with Gordon Forsyth (q.v.) and W. Ruscoe (q.v.) at the Burslem School of Art 1933–37 and 1934–39 ran the newly opened studio for Bullers Ltd. She modelled animal figures but rarely vases. Ann married in 1939 and shortly afterwards left Bullers to work at the Fulham Pottery 1940–41, selling her work through the London retailer Heal's. Sometimes she signed her work with her full name.

Potts, B., active 1872–1897

Artist gilder at Copeland shown as gilding the work of the premier artists on vases, baskets and jardinières, but not on tea or dessert services. He worked with Alcock (q.v.), Hurten (q.v.), Brough (q.v.) and Besche (q.v.), but no pattern or ornamental shape numbers are given. There is one signed plate known in the Spode-Copeland china collection at Trelissick, Cornwall.

Powell, Ada Louise (née Lessore), 1882–1956

Painter, designer, calligrapher, daughter of Jules A. Lessore, a well-known landscape and marine artist (q.v.) and granddaughter of Emile Lessore (q.v.), who trained at the Central School of Art, London. She married Alfred Powell in September 1906. Together they designed new patterns for Wedgwood, which the company badly needed at this time to maintain their share of the market. They first submitted designs to Wedgwood in 1904 and their collaboration lasted for forty years. Using the Wedgwood pattern books, the pair created a range of simple sprigs of flowers and foliage, but also rich designs of foliage in bright, daring colours and platinum lustre. These included animals and birds inspired by the designs of William Morris. They trained Wedgwood artists, for example, Millicent Taplin (q.v.), to interpret their designs and assisted in the establishment of hand-painting in the1920s.

After WWI, Louise studied calligraphy and illumination at the Central School for Art. Alfred designed plaques in the 1930s and 40s with designs of Barlaston Hall, ships, animals and birds. Wedgwood encouraged them and helped them set up a London studio in Millwall and afterwards at Red Lion Square, Bloomsbury, sending biscuit ware to them from Etruria, which they often had fired by J.L. James. They also painted furniture for Ernest Grimson and Sydney Barnsley. Their work was exhibited at the Arts and Crafts Exhibitions from 1906 to 1926. Louise was a member of the Society of Scribes and Illuminators and her work was exhibited at the Arts and Crafts Exhibitions of 1910 to1935. They marked their designs with a heart-shaped leaf and with the initials AP or LP.

Powell, Alfred Hoare, 1865–1960

Architect, designer and pottery painter born at Bisham, near Marlow, the fifth son of the Rev. T.E. Powell. The family were related to the Powells of Whitefriar's Glass and were second cousins to Lord Baden Powell. He was educated at Uppingham School and trained as an architect at the Slade School of Art, London. He worked in the office of John Sedding, a church architect. Alfred became fascinated with the Arts and Crafts movement and decided to practice as a painter. He exhibited at the Royal Academy in 1890 and in 1891 at the Fine Art Society. In 1903 he wrote articles for *Connoisseur* and *Studio* magazines. Powell knew the Wedgwood family and had no hesitation in submitting some designs to them, which were approved. He and his wife Louise (q.v.) became an important part of the Wedgwood decorating team. He was a member of the Art Workers' Guild from 1916–41 and again in 1943. Alfred continued to create designs for Wedgwood until his death.

Powell, John, active 1800s

Painter of figure subjects and outside decorator, known to have been at Chamberlain Worcester Porcelain; by c. 1802 he was ordering white ware from the factory. He moved to 91 Wimpole Street, London, decorating Chamberlains white ware, Nantgarw, Swansea blanks and French porcelain. By 1812 he had moved to 53 Great Marleybone Street, London. He exhibited paintings on porcelain at the Royal Academy c. 1811–30.

Powles, Richard, c. 1764–1807

Landscape and marine painter born in Lowestoft and employed at the Lowestoft Pottery from 1776 to 1784, painting marine subjects. He was also a good watercolourist.

Pratt, Henry Lark, 1805–1873

Landscape painter apprenticed at the Nottingham Road, Derby factory. He painted plaques in a style influenced by Daniel Lucas (Senior) (q.v.), but used a softer range of colour. Whilst employed at Derby he also worked as a picture restorer, as an advertisement records: 'HENRY L. PRATT, Landscape and animal painter, Paintings

Wedgwood Queen's Ware charger decorated with a view of St Paul's Cathedral by A Powell.
Courtesy of the Potteries Museum and Art Gallery Stoke-on-Trent

carefully cleaned and repaired, 8 Larges Street, Friar Gate, Derby'. From 1830–40 he worked at Minton as a landscape painter. He received a commission from publishers Chapman and Hall of London to sketch views of Staffordshire, Cheshire and Derbyshire for their 1848 *The Baronial Halls and Mansions of* England. It is thought that by 1851 he returned to Derby, but possibly not for very long, as from 1861 he worked freelance on Minton china. Three of his oil paintings are at the Derby Art Gallery and his *View of Penkhull* is in the City of Stoke-on-Trent collection.

On 8 March 1873 the *Staffordshire Advertiser* published his obituary:'Our obituary contains the name of Mr H. L. Pratt whose connection with art in the district deserves more than a mere mention. Mr Pratt was born in Derby and served his time as a landscape painter, at the Old Derby china works. In 1830 he came to the Potteries and was employed at the works of Messrs Minton. In 1844–45 he was employed by Messrs. Chapman and Hall of London in taking sketches of the Baronial Halls of Staffordshire, Cheshire and Derbyshire and devoted himself during his leisure hours in acquiring the skill of painting in oil. Of this branch of art he became passionately fond and in Derby, Birmingham and Coalport left evidences of his skill. Many of the Galleries of the noblemen and gentlemen of the midland counties contain paintings by him, Mr Pratt having been employed by amongst others the present Sir Robert Peel, the late and present Dukes of Devonshire and the late Dowager Duchess of Harrington. He had also some years ago the Honour of her Majesty's patronage who was pleased to purchase a Tete déjeuner service on which were views of Windsor Castle, Balmoral etc. There was scarcely a picturesque nook in Staffordshire Derbyshire, Shropshire and part of Cheshire that he had not seen and sketched and of Dovedale he was especially fond. The love of art permeated his nature and in the true sense of the word he was an artist.'

In 1871 he exhibited his painting *The Lodore Falls* at the London International Exhibition. Henry was living at Penkhull Terrace, Stoke-upon-Trent the year he died and he is buried in the Stoke-upon-Trent churchyard with his wife Margaret, who died 1886.

Pratt, Henry Lark (Hilton), 1838–1875

Artist, son of Henry Lark Pratt (q.v.), who adopted the name Hilton to avoid confusion with his father. He probably trained with his father, as there is one entry in the Minton wages books for him. Hilton became a landscape artist of great repute, exhibiting his work at the Royal Academy from 1867 to 1873. He is buried with his parents in Stoke-upon-Trent churchyard.

Price, Horace, 1898–1965

Flower painter known to have worked at Worcester from 1912. He painted flowers in the style of J. Hadley (q.v.) and became foreman of the apprentices in 1945.

Price, John (Jack), 1881–1949

Floral painter born in Newcastle-under-Lyme, an apprentice and then working at Doulton 1894–1932, where he specialized in floral subjects, before leaving for Grimwades. Sometime in the 1940s he was employed at Copeland to paint flower, bird and game subjects. He was a handsome man, tall and thin, always wearing a white overall, which was unusual in those days. In 1945 he was appointed decorating manager at the Royal Crown Derby factory, working on plates that were presented to Princess Elizabeth on her marriage. Each plate had a landscape of Derbyshire in the centre, a coloured print signed 'J. Price'.

Prince, Edwin (Edward), 1827–1896

Landscape painter, one of the last apprentices at the Nottingham Road, Derby pottery, staying until it closed in 1848. He may have spent the next two years in London but returned to Derby to the King Street pottery 1850–55. His painting was influenced by the work of Daniel Lucas (Senior) (q.v.), as he used similar warm brown tints. He is next known to have found employment at Messrs Wailes establishment in Newcastle-upon-Tyne. Here he painted on glass, which was used in ecclesiastical windows. He left the Tyne in 1878 and spent his last years at Overstrand, Cromer, continuing to work as a freelance china painter.

Protât, Hughues, active 1835–1871

Sculptor, freelance modeller and art teacher born in France, who exhibited at the Paris Salon 1843–50. He was originally a stone carver but found employment with Jackson & Graham, London, who made furniture in the French style. Protât came to Minton as a modeller around 1845, staying until 1858 and also teaching modelling in the evenings at the Hanley and Stoke Schools of Art, 1850–64 and at the Minton Memorial Institute in Stoke-upon-Trent. He gained commissions from Wedgwood 1851–63 and did work for the Sir James Duke & Nephews and W. Brownfield & Sons potteries. By 1863 he had left the Potteries and established a studio at 14 Great Smith Street, Westminster, London, but continued to model for the pottery firms. His models for Minton included candlesticks, candelabra groups and statuettes, which were produced in Parian. Wedgwood continued to commission his work, which was exhibited at the International London Exhibition of 1871. He then returned to France.

Raby, Edward John, 1863–1940

Flower painter born in Staffordshire, the son of Samuel Raby, a flower modeller.He was trained at the Worcester Art School and at the Worcester pottery. He took his inspiration from nature, creating floral studies with great skill. His sketchbooks were full of watercolour paintings of flowers, which he had studied in greenhouses and gardens. His work was influenced by Art Nouveau designs. Edward developed a special secret colour, Raby Mauve. He joined Doulton about 1892 where he specialised in rose painting. It is said of his work that he achieved a floral design of perfect flower forms and that his painting had depth of colour, especially when using red ceramic colour, which was unusual and unequalled in his day. John Sparkes comments: 'A great painter of flowers on pottery. Rich combinations show him to be adept at nature study, a master indeed, one of the first flower painters of his times. His rare skill and knowledge, the beautiful colour blending of lovely forms, and the excellence of each individual bloom are alike remarkable.'

Raby usually signed his work with the monogram EJR or in full. He retired in 1919. He was a religious man, a member of the Salvation Army and would often go down the coal pits in Staffordshire to talk to the workers before he went to work. He spent his retirement painting and making studies for future work on the river Severn.

Royal Worcester plate commissioned by Theodore Star of New York painted by Edward R. Raby c. 1884

Raby, Enos, 1795–1861

Painter,and ground layer, born in Madeley, Shropshire. He was employed around 1830 with Thomas Martin Randall (q.v.) at Madeley but in 1851 joined Coalport, where he stayed until his death.

Raby, Samuel, born 1827

China potter and painter.He is thought to have first worked at one of the Bristol potteries. From 1860–70 he manufactured plaques with hand-applied flowers, thought to have been decorated by the Callowhill brothers (q.v.). In 1881 he was living at Cherry Orchard, Providence Terrace,Worcester St Peter.

Radford, (?J.), active 1869–1889

Flower painter at Copeland.There are thirty-five entries under this name, but only six listed as J. Radford from 1877. Radford painted flowers, especially begonias and blackberries, and fruit on all surfaces, from tiles to fine china vases. His work was gilded by Bell. Two entries show he painted 'after' Hurten (q.v.) and there are three showing his work which were exhibited in the London International Exhibitions of 1871 and 1872. Some pattern numbers are shown: for example, February 1871, pattern number D 7857, cup and saucer with an ivory ground painted with festoons of flowers for the Exhibition.An entry for the 4th Dragoon Regiment reads 'Paris shape dessert plate, Pattern number D 8916'. He decorated tiles with painted wreath of ferns, which were commissioned by Cubitt and Co., London. The 1881 census shows his occupation as 'potters' overlooker of painting department', and he was then living in Stoke-upon-Trent.

Randall, George, 1821–1907

Bird painter born in London, the eldest son of Martin and Hannah Randall, educated at Ackworth Quaker School. He painted for his father and became a partner in the family decorating business in Staffordshire in 1853, then living in the nearby town of Fenton. In 1860, when the business failed, George went to Minton. His work was influenced by the Sèvres style of painting and although he was known mainly as a fine bird painter, a pair of vases decorated with birds and landscapes was shown at the London International Exhibition of 1862. In 1869 he joined Copeland and is shown in the factory records as painting birds on pattern numbers D 7201 and

D7936, and he is also listed with the number 8 on a pair of vases that may have been exhibited at the International Exhibition in London in 1871. Exhibition pieces were often listed with only a number. George left the ceramic industry to become a professional photographer. The 1881 census shows the family with a servant living in Occupation Street, Stoke-on-Trent.

Randall, John, 1810–1910

Bird painter born at Ladywood, Broseley,Shropshire and trained by his uncle T. M. Randall (q.v.). John started his career at the Rockingham Pottery c. 1831,then came to Coalport in 1935. He stayed for forty-six years until his sight failed. He originally painted birds in the Sèvres style but later developed his own unique style. A vase painted with a copy of John Gould's Peruvian humming bird paintings was exhibited at the International Exhibition in 1862 and highly praised. In 1867 the Society of Arts sent some artists to the Exposition Universelle, Paris and John was chosen to write reports on the ceramic and iron exhibits. During this time he visited the Sèvres Factory, where he saw their painters using botanical and zoological specimens for inspiration, working in excellent conditions, very different from those of his English contemporaries. In 1868 he read a paper to the Society of Arts on technical education, no doubt based on his experiences at Sèvres. In 1879 he again visited the Exposition Universelle, Paris as a reporter. He was keenly interested in geology and in 1863 was President of the Geological Society. John had a fine collection of minerals and fossils, which was exhibited at the Great Exhibition in 1851 and then bought for the nation. After he retired from Coalport he became postmaster at Madeley and continued to write; his literary output included *A History of Madeley and the Clay industries on the Banks of the Severn* and *The Severn Valley and the Willey Country.* When ninety-five years old he was given the Freedom of Wenlock, Shropshire.

Randall, Thomas Martin, 1786–1859

Artist gilder,outside decorator and potter born in Broseley, the son of a barge master, an apprentice at the Coalport works. From 1803-1813 he worked at the Nottingham Road, Derby pottery, where he became friends with Phillip Clavey and William Pegg (q.v.). It is thought he did some work for the Pinxton pottery in Mansfield around 1812. Thomas next moved to London, where it is thought he worked for Robins and his partner Stevens at their business at 33 Hatton Hall, in the parish of St Andrews, Holborn. However, when in 1815 this partnership was dissolved Randall probably became a partner with Richard Robins, trading as Robins & Randall, outside decorating establishment, and specialising in finishing Swansea, Nantgarw and also imported French porcelains. The company had a high reputation, known as one of the best outside decorators operating in London about 1810-1830. Their main customer was Mr Mortlock, the well-known retailer of fine porcelain. In 1818 Robins and Randall and their families were living at Eaton Street, but moved into new houses adjacent to each other at Barnsbury Row,Spa Fields, Islington. It is thought their decorating kilns were situated in a mews area behind the Row.

In 1825 Thomas's partnership with Richard Robins ended on a friendly basis and the family returned home to Madeley, Shropshire. He founded his own pottery at Park Lane in which he produced soft-paste porcelain, Madeley China, very much like the early Sèvres body. Randall employed some excellent painters, including Philip Ballard (q.v.), who painted landscapes after Watteau (q.v.) and Boucher (q.v.). His nephew John did the bird decoration and in 1853 he employed Robert Bix Gray (q.v.), who specialized in flower painting, and Christian Henk (q.v.) and Louis Jahn (q.v.) painted special commissions for him. Randall's decoration included shell studies. His ground colours were extremely fine, especially turquoise and deep blue. In 1840 he moved his business to Broad Street, Shelton, where his work so impressed Herbert Minton that he tried to persuade him to join Minton, but did not succeed. In August 1858 he put up for sale a small Parian pottery, which had once been his gilding shop at St James Street, Shelton, Staffordshire, and auctioned his furniture and books prior to leaving the district. The Randall family were active members of the Quaker community and their sons attended the Ackworth Quaker School. Thomas was an active promoter of the Temperance societies. When he retired he lived at Shallowford, near Norton Bridge, Staffordshire, but died in Southport. Randall was a potter and artist of great talent whose influence on pottery design lasted into the next century.

Ravilious, Eric William, 1903–1942

Designer and book illustrator,born in West London and trained at the Eastbourne and Brighton Art School. In 1922 he won a scholarship to the Royal College of Art, where he was taught by Paul Nash. Eric went to Italy and on his return to England held his first watercolour exhibition, from which he received many commissions.

It was not until 1933 that he became interested in ceramic design. E. Brain & Co. and A.E. Wilkinson Ltd asked twenty-seven artists to produce a tableware design and their work was shown at a special exhibition of pottery and glass at Harrods, London. Eric now received commissions, including one from Wedgwood to design an arrangement of garden implements. It was produced in 1957 on pottery with matching textiles. He designed more tableware patterns – decorated with domestic garden scenes or letters of the alphabet, for example – and also Coronation mugs and bowls decorated with the Boat Race. He also designed furniture and glass. He was one of the few artists able to paint as an illustrator and on canvas yet also produce superb designs for ceramics. He became an official war artist in 1940 and was lost on air patrol in Iceland when serving with Coastal Command.

Rea, Daisy, 1894–1984

Flower paintress at the Worcester factory from 1909. She was trained in the Handley Worcester style and known for painting wild flowers. In the 1930s she started to paint Worcester figures using the mark 33.She and her sister Grace hand-coloured the Freda Doughty children models. Daisy was put in charge of the paintresses of the figurine department.

Reed, Thomas Amos, born 1869

Painter and art director, an apprentice at the Osmaston Road, Derby pottery. He became Art Director and was responsible for all designs on Derby ware except the work of Desiré Leroy, (q.v.). He left in 1926.

Remnant, Charles, active 1890s

Marine painter ,who trained as an industrial evening student at the Derby School of Art and was employed by the Osmaston Road, Derby factory. His marine paintings were unique; he painted in blue and white, showing great artistic skill. Charles was a member of the Derby Sketching Club but left Derby in 1899.

Reuter, Edward G., 1845–1912

Flower painter born in Geneva, the son of a botanist. He studied floral design in Paris in 1864 and visited Egypt in 1868. In 1870 he came to London to study at the Government School of Design, South Kensington. He was influenced by the work of William Morris, who employed him as a book illustrator, illuminator and calligraphist. He was given commissions by the Minton Art Studio and after the fire there he moved to Minton in Stoke-upon-Trent, being appointed assistant designer under Leon Arnoux (q.v.) in 1866. Edward signed his work and was paid by the day, but unusually was allowed travelling expenses. He designed Minton ornamental ware, including tiles and vases, and his work was shown in the Exposition Universelle, Paris of 1878. He established a reputation as a versatile designer and watercolour artist and painted illuminated addresses. Known as a quiet man who rarely spoke, he lived at 6 Harding Terrace, Regent Street, Stoke-on-Trent in 1881. After Leon Arnoux died in 1895, he returned to Switzerland but by 1901 was persuaded to return to Minton, where he introduced a range of new designs influenced by his stays in Egypt and India.

Edward Reuter

He designed *Persindo* porcelain for his friend Lawrence Birks of the Birks Rawlins & Co. Vine Pottery, Stoke-on-Trent. This was advertised in *The Pottery Gazette and Glass Trade Review* in 1909 as an ivory porcelain with a design influenced by early Persian artists, and it became very popular.

Reynolds, Alfred, 1818–1891

Inventor designer and litho printer,employed by Minton and Hollins c. 1848.

He invented the Collins and Reynolds process for transfer colour printing on flat surfaces. He was awarded a first-class certificate at the Exposition Universelle, Paris of 1855 and at the Vienna Exhibition of 1873. He was listed as a printer on pottery and won a co-operators medal. By 1880 he was described as a manager and earned the large salary of £350 a year.

Rhead, Charlotte Antoinette Adolphine (Lottie), 1885–1947

Painter and designer born in Burslem, Staffordshire, the daughter of Frederick Alfred and Adolphine Leononie, née Hurten. She was educated at Longport School and

Hanley Higher Grade School and trained at the Fenton School of Art. She was first employed at Keeling & Co, Burslem, making hotel and hospital ware. When her father went into partnership with F.H. Barker (trading as F.H. Barker & Rhead Ltd) she joined his decorating team, but the venture was unsuccessful. Charlotte worked then for T.& R. Boote, who were producing tube-lined tiles. About 1913-1914 she joined her father, now Art Director of Wood & Sons, where she trained a team of decorators in the tube-lining technique and designed new patterns. The first was *Poppy Seed.* By the 1920s her work was recognised and some potteries included *Lottie Rhead Ware* on their backstamp.

Her father persuaded Harry Wood to buy the Crown Pottery near to Wood & Sons and moved his studio to the new site. This company, called Bursley Ltd, developed the art ware side of the business and in 1922 Charlotte joined her father and was given her own studio. In 1926 the Crown Pottery was severely damaged by fire and production virtually ceased. Charlotte, now aged forty, joined Burgess and Leigh at Middleport, where again she trained a team of decorators to use the tube-lining technique for her innovative decorating designs. Here she was addressed as Miss Rhead and took her little dog with her to the studio. In 1931 she joined A.J. Richardson's Crown Ducal Pottery, where she designed the patterns *Foxglove*, *Wisteria* and *Byzantine.* Owing to the fall in the market in WWII, Rhead left but was offered a position as designer for H.J. Wood Ltd at the Alexandra Pottery, Burslem until her death.

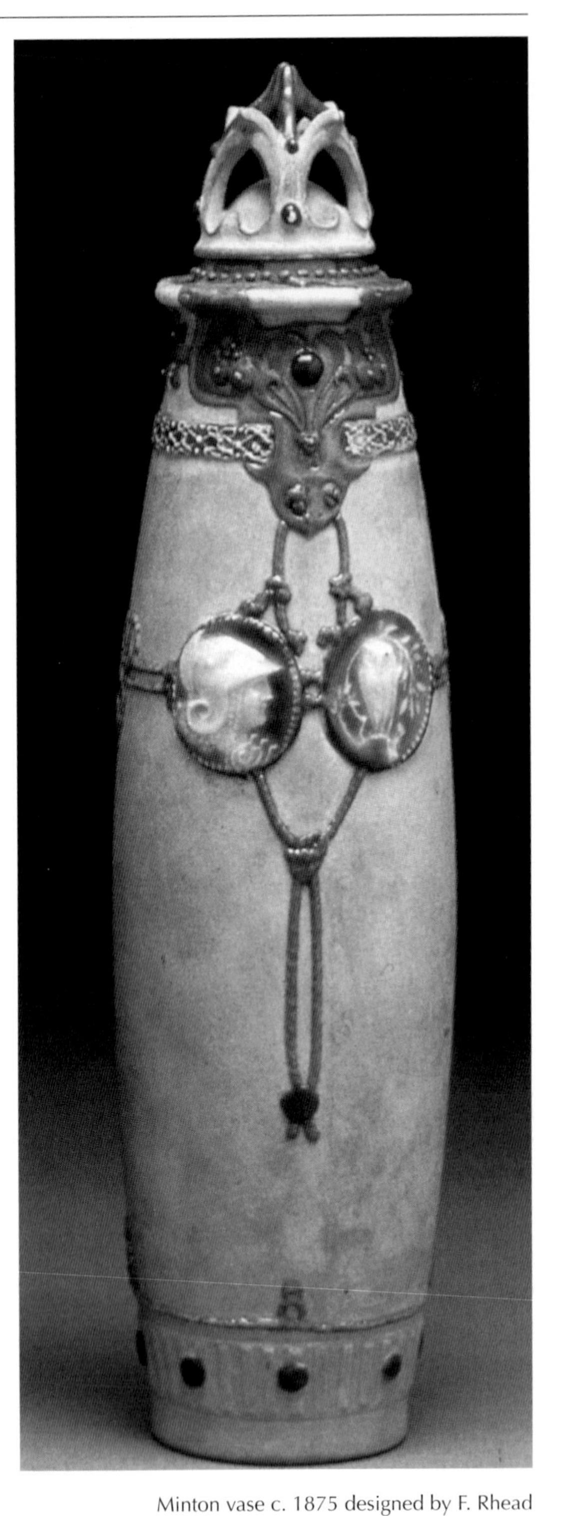

Minton vase c. 1875 designed by F. Rhead

Rhead, Frederick Alfred, 1856–1933

Painter and pâte-sur-pâte artist born in Newcastle-under-Lyme, Staffordshire, the son of George Wooliscroft Rhead (q.v.). He trained at the Newcastle, Stoke, Hanley and Burslem Schools of Art, later becoming an art teacher. Frederick joined Minton as an apprentice painter in 1868 under Leon Solon (q.v.) and became a fine decorator of their pâte-sur-pâte designs. In 1878 he went to Thomas Allen's (q.v.) studio at Wedgwood, where he designed sgraffito and slipware. His work was exhibited at the Exposition Universelle, Paris of 1878. In 1894 he became Art Director of the Brownfield Guild Pottery and in 1896 moved as Art Director to Wileman & Co., introducing the extensive *Intarsio* line of art pottery, which was influenced by Dutch design. He remained there until 1905. He is known to have designed for Burgess & Leigh and was a great friend of their head modeller Charles Wilkes, with whom he set up a small business in William Clowes Street, Burslem making ornamental wares, but it was not a success. His other business venture, with his friend F.H. Barker at the Atlas Tile Works, also failed and was sold in 1910.

Frederick then went to America for a short time but by 1913 had become Art Director at Wood and Sons. In 1929 he left and joined the Cauldon Pottery. He was a book illustrator and wrote articles on pottery as well as the book *Staffordshire Pots and Potters* with his brother Frederick. He was a founder member of the Pottery Manager and Officials Association and whilst President served on the National Council of Pottery Design.

Rhead, Frederick Hurten, 1880–1942

Painter, designer and author trained at the Schools of Art in Stoke, Hanley and Fenton. He joined his father at Brownfield's Pottery and then at Wileman & Co. In 1899 he became Art Director at the Wardle & Co. Ltd pottery and taught art in the evenings. By 1902 he decided to emigrate to America, where he had a distinguished writing career, his opinion revered. He never returned to the Potteries. In 1910 he was at the University City Pottery, Missouri. He was the acknowledged expert on American clays, working with Kathryn E. Cherry, designer and paintress, and Taxile Doat from France, a well-known Sèvres ceramist; together they produced some stunning designs and shapes. His work influenced Adelaide Alsop Robinea, the well-known American potter and porcelain-maker who 1909-1911 worked at the University City Pottery alongside Rhead. He recognised her talent and encouraged her to experiment with stone bodies and glazes, which were very successful and are collected today.

Minton Large charger painted in the Jean de Court Style by G. W. Rhead. Courtesy of the Potteries Museum and Art Gallery Stoke-on-Trent

Rhead, George Wolliscroft (Senior), 1832–1908

Heraldic painter, and designer born in Stoke-upon-Trent, the son of a modeller and potter. He studied at the Newcastle and Stoke Schools of Art, winning several national medals, and trained as a designer at Brown-Westhead, Moore & Co. before joining Minton. Here he became the principal heraldic artist. George was a fine art teacher, holding the posts of Assistant Master at Newcastle School of Art 1869-1879, and 1879-1900 was Master of Art at Chesterton (Newcastle, Staffordshire), Fenton and Longton, Stoke-on-Trent, Staffordshire. He started the Fenton School of Art in 1889. His talent was passed down to four of his eleven children. In 1881 he was living at Stoke Old Road, Stoke-upon-Trent, but died at The Laburnams, Clayton, Newcastle, Staffordshire.

Rhead, George Wooliscroft (Junior) R.E., 1855–1920

Painter, artist and etcher of genre, classical and topographical views born in Stoke-on-Trent, the son of George (Senior, q.v.) and apprenticed at Minton under W.S. Coleman (q.v.). He won a scholarship to the Government School of Design, South Kensington, London, where he was awarded silver medals. He went to the Minton Art Pottery Studio, London, where he adapted subjects from Japanese paintings with great skill and accuracy. George studied with Alphonse Legros and Ford Maddox Brown. He contributed several plates to *The Portfolio* magazine and etched views of Eton and Cambridge colleges and others subjects. By 1882 he had returned to the Potteries, working at Doulton before joining Wilman & Co, Staffordshire. He was a fine artist, exhibiting paintings at the Royal Academy 1882–96, was a member of the Art Workers Guild and an Hon ARCA. He then turned to teaching, becoming a director of the Southwark Polytechnic Institute. George designed murals and stained-glass windows and became well known as an etcher. He was elected to the Royal Society of Etchers in 1883. He wrote and illustrated many books, including *Staffordshire Pots and Potters* with F.W. Rhead, *Pottery Marks* and *The Earthenware Collector*. In 1881 he was living at 2 Phene Street, Chelsea, London. In 1914 he married Annie French, an accomplished painter, etcher and illustrator of children's books.

Rhead, Louis F., 1858–1927

Painter and designer born in Newcastle-under-Lyme,Staffordshire. He became an apprentice at Minton, whilst training at the Newcastle School of Art and at Somerset House, London. When his brother Frederick Alfred (q.v.) had a disagreement with the management at Minton, Louis's indentures were cancelled. He joined his brother at Wedgwood, first as a freelance designer but from 1882 as a member of staff. Louis emigrated to America, where he became a successful poster designer and illustrator, but he returned to the Potteries in 1896.

Rhodes, William (?), active 1845–1851

Flower painter and designer at Copeland, listed as Rhodes and Mr Rhodes. There are one hundred and thirty-nine entries under the name, eighteen for Mr Rhodes. When comparing the entries from the Special Order reference books and the pattern books, no true picture emerges as to the exact role of this fine painter or gilder, as some entries say 'gilded by' and others 'painted by'. The work shown can be divided into three categories: beautiful floral studies on china dessert plates of all shapes; sprigged and swagged festoons of flowers on tea wares; and a series that could be transfer-printed and hand-painted. Although no definite conclusion can be reached, Rhodes was a superb floral artist. Mr Rhodes was an artist gilder, listed as early as 1845, and shown as having painted armorial crests.

Rice, Silas, 1821–1873

Painter and art teacher. He was a student at the Government School of Design, South Kensington, London, where he was described as one of Mr Wilson's most successful and meritorious pupils. In 1844 he was one of the painters decorating the Queen's summerhouse with William Etty (q.v.) and Edwin Landseer (q.v.). Rice first went to Edinburgh as an assistant teacher but in 1849 came to Stoke-on-Trent as headmaster of the Art School. When J.C. Robinson left the Hanley School of Art he became headmaster of both schools. He was a successful teacher and had many famous pupils, including John Salter (q.v.), Albert Wright (q.v.) and Thomas Allen (q.v.). In 1864 the art education of the six towns was reorganized and Rice retired on a pension of £150. He married Frances, fifth daughter of Thomas Bourne Poulson; they lived first in Penkhull, Stoke-upon-Trent and on his retirement moved to Clifton, near Ashbourne in Derbyshire.

Rice, Thomas H., born 1863

Painter, the son of Silas (q.v.), born in Stoke-upon-Trent. He was apprenticed to Leon Solon (q.v.) at Minton to learn pâte-sur-pâte decoration. By 1893 he had joined Doulton at Burslem. He signed some of his work.

Ricketts, William Albert, 1862–1930

Fruit and flower painter,who was at the Worcester Pottery from 1877 into the 1900s. He signed his work. He was also a watercolour artist and his work was exhibited at the Royal Academy.

Ridgway, Richard, 1888–1930

Artist gilder, who studied at the Stoke School of Art and served his apprenticeship at Minton.He joined Doulton, where he worked with William Skinner (q.v.). A gilder of great talent, known to have worked on a tea service for Queen Mary, he eventually became responsible for all gilded ware, making sure the high standard of Doulton was maintained.

Rischgitz, Edouard, 1831–1909

Landscape painter, and artist born in Switzerland, who became a pupil of Jean-Baptiste Camille Corot in Paris. He learnt to paint natural landscapes with great architectural accuracy; in later life his landscapes became more misty and ethereal. He went to Minton c. 1864 to supervise their exhibits for the Exposition Universelle, Paris of 1867 and execute some Barbotine painting. By 1871 he was at Copeland and is shown in their Special Order books as painting landscapes and subjects after Aesop, although he was always known for his architectural painting. His last entry in the Copeland Special Order books is for 6 July 1871, which records him painting a dinner service with landscapes of London.

Bone china Minton pierced border dessert plate painted by E. Rischgitz c. 1864

Bone china Minton vase painted and signed by L. Rivers c. 1895

Rischgitz moved to London to teach painting and drawing, still specialising in landscapes. His pupils included Prince Christian, Princesses Victoria and Marie Louise of Schleswig-Holstein. It is thought that he became art master to Queen Victoria's children. Rischgitz exhibited at the Royal Academy 1878-1881, the Grosvenor Galleries 1878-1881 and also contributed work to the magazine *Good Words*. Two of his children inherited his artistic talent: Alice 1856–1937 became a floral artist of great ability and Mary painted landscapes, miniature portraits and also taught painting. Their work was exhibited in many art galleries throughout the country, for example, in Liverpool, Dudley and Manchester. Rischgitz died in London at Mary's home, Cambridge Lodge Studios, 42 Linden Gardens, Bayswater.

Rivers, Leonard, 1863–1939

Flower, fish, game and landscape painter,the second son of Leonard and Ann. In 1881 the family of were living at 2 Berkeley Street, Stoke-upon-Trent and it is possible he was trained at the local art school. His work has been found on Brownfield's, Crown Staffordshire, Minton and Copeland ware. When in 1895 William Taylor Mountford Copeland announced his retirement he was presented with an address recorded in a leather-bound book, which all the employees had signed. Leonard Rivers had signed it under the heading past employee. In 1900 the Chinese Envoy visited Minton and was impressed with his work. It is interesting to note that Rivers is shown as painting fish and game subjects for Copeland again in 1901. William Fowler Mountford Copeland (nephew of the above) sent him to the family home, Kibblestone Hall, Oulton, Staffordshire to paint the new species of daffodils that he had propagated. They were exhibited at the Royal Horticultural Society, where they were awarded prizes. Rivers was known for painting roses that had a dewdrop painted on one of the flowers. He also gained commissions around this time from the Vine Pottery, which he signed in either pink or green. Family records show he left the Potteries c. 1916 and lived in Warwickshire, where he continued to paint watercolours.

L. Rivers

Rix, Wilton P., active 1860s

Painter and art director employed at the Doulton Lambeth Pottery from 1868. Examples of his signed work have been found. He served as Art Director 1870-1997. Rix developed the range of colours that withstood the high firing of salt glazing. In 1887 he was the joint patentee with Doulton on the technique of Marqueterie ware. By 1901 he had moved to the Potteries, living on Liverpool Road, Newcastle-under-Lyme, described in the census as pottery expert specialist (on own account).

Roberts, Ellis William, 1860–1930

Painter and artist, son of Thomas Roberts,a pottery manager, who was an apprentice painter at Minton in 1874. Ellis studied at the Stoke School of Art under Joseph Bacon (q.v.) 1874-1882, then won a two-year scholarship to the Government School of Design, South Kensington, London, and from there a travelling scholarship to Italy. He went to Paris to study at the Atelier Julien, living in poverty. On his return to England he acquired the patronage of Joseph Shaw of Derby, the mineral manager of the Midland Railway, and by 1889 he had become a member of the British Pastellists. He exhibited a pastel portrait of Lady Hilda Keppel at the Grosvenor Gallery and her family association with the Prince of Wales led to further commissions. Ellis became a fashionable painter and his studio a meeting-place for ladies of fashion, many of whom commissioned work from him. Amongst his patrons were Millicent, Duchess of Sutherland and Sir Henry Doulton. He was elected an A.R.C.A. and a member of the Royal Society of Portrait Painters. In 1898 he returned to the Potteries to speak at the Stoke-on-Trent School of Art, and his success was an inspiration to the students. Ellis died at his home, 12 Wexford Road, Wandsworth Common, London.

Roberts, Frank, 1857–1920

Flower and fruit painter, son of Edward Roberts, an engine fitter, who was an apprentice at the Royal Worcester factory. He left Worchester in 1881 and it is thought he went to Stourbridge to paint on glass. He had returned to Worcester by 1901.

Robertson, George, 1777–1833

Artist, landscape and marine painter born in Ayrshire. He married Ann Yates in 1798. He painted detailed landscapes in autumn colours and specialised in naval engagements and stormy seas, copied from marine paintings or engravings. Mr Bloor commissioned George to paint two large oil paintings, one of the Nottingham Road, Derby factory frontage and the other showing the large warehouse and buildings with hogsheads of china and figures. They were hung in the Derby china showroom at 34 Old Bond Street, London but are now lost. After he left Derby, Robertson became a successful drawing master, although he spent the last three years of his life in Nottingham County Asylum.

Robins, Richard, active 1820s

Painter and outside decorator who trained at the Pinxton Pottery, Mansfield. From 1812 to 1825 he and Thomas Randall (q.v.) ran a decorating business at Spa Fields, Islington, London.

Robinson, active 1845–1850

Flower and crest painter at Copeland. He is recorded in their special reference books as Robinson, Mr Robinson, Robinson Junior and Robinson and Co. as painting crests, mottoes in gold and pretty floral patterns in the style of Sèvres. The Robinsons painted on all types and bodies of ware, including curtain holders, door furniture and bon-bon stands. It is more than possible that they were members of one family.

Tile painted by Rochfort photo courtesy of Rosemary Pulver

John Downes Rochfort Photo courtesy of Rosemary Pulver

Rochfort, John Downes, 1825–1885

Painter and amateur artist of great talent, whose signed and often dated work can be found on Wedgwood and Minton blanks. He was descended from an old Irish family, the son of Colonel John Staunton Rochfort of Clogrename, Ireland. No records survive to describe his artistic training but he is known to have been associated with the Minton Art Studio. He painted portraits of his sister Margaret Ann (Nina) Hildyard and her family on Minton blanks. John admired the work of Emille Lessore, which he copied on Wedgwood blanks. He had a long and lasting relationship with Ruth Louisa Herbert, an actress and theatre manager, painting her portrait on two plaques. Although not working in the industry professionally, he could well be regarded as one of the best ceramic artists of the Victorian era.

Rodgers, Gladys M., born 1887

Paintress, born in Bedale, Yorkshire. She studied at the Salford School of Art and joined Pilkingtons Pottery, mainly working on lustre patterns. She won a gold medal for her work, which was exhibited in Paris in 1935, signed with an R on a shield in a square.

Rogers, George (Senior), active 1790s

Painter employed at Chamberlain Worcester Porcelain painting pattern numbers 271, 272, 282 and 308, and also crests. He and Edward (Enoch) Doe (q.v.) established a decorating business, buying white ware from the pottery. The sales book of 1822 shows he bought a small vase for 15s.0d a basket for 2s.6d and two match pots, which were decorated with topographical views, for 4s.0d. This partnership was dissolved in 1835, perhaps due to his death.

Rogers, George (Junior), died 1877

Painter, son of George Rogers (Senior, q.v.).He trained at Chamberlain Worcester Porcelain c. 1 820. He was an artist of great talent, working in the style of the watercolour painters of the day, using broad washes of colour and delicate designs. He is also known to have painted stained glass. A Roberts is listed in the Worcester trade directories of 1841 as a china, glass and earthenware dealer.

Rose, active 1800s

A French artist who worked for the Lowestoft pottery becoming their chief artist. He is thought to have introduced the rose flower in many of their designs. He painted a small rose under the handles of the ware as a signature. His career ended when his eyesight failed and he died in poverty.

Ross, James, born 1811

Fruit painter apprenticed at the Rockingham Pottery. He is shown in the Militia Lists of 1829-1932 as an apprentice china painter at Swinton. A plaque painted with grapes and signed 'J. Ross 1829' is known.

Rothwell, Thomas, 1740–1807

Painter, engraver and topographical artist.He may well have been trained in one of the Staffordshire potteries, then moved to Birmingham, but he is known to have been the principal painter at the Cambrian Pottery, Swansea before Thomas Pardoe (q.v.). In 1794 he lived in Swansea and published a series of engravings of the area. His work was influenced by British painters such as George Stubbs and he certainly used designs from *The Ladies Amusement* by Robert Sayer. His work has clarity and fineness of detail.

Rouchard, François, active c. 1880

Figure painter and designer who came from Montereau, France. He was a pâte-sur-pâte artist at Minton. He designed menu holders and other wares and is known to have experimented with clays to produce Barbotine and impasto work. He signed his work with a monogram.

Rouse, James (Senior), 1802–1888

Flower painter born in Derby, the son of a gardener, an apprentice at the Derby factory under William (Quaker) Pegg (q.v.), who also gave him drawing lessons at his home. He is the only artist to have been employed at all the Derby factories. James's early work showed great artistic skill: he created fine floral studies from the anemones, auriculas, tulips and other flowers, which he saw growing in his garden. Mr Bloor, proprietor of Derby, ordered him to paint three large vases: the centre vase was twenty-five inches high, the other two twenty-one

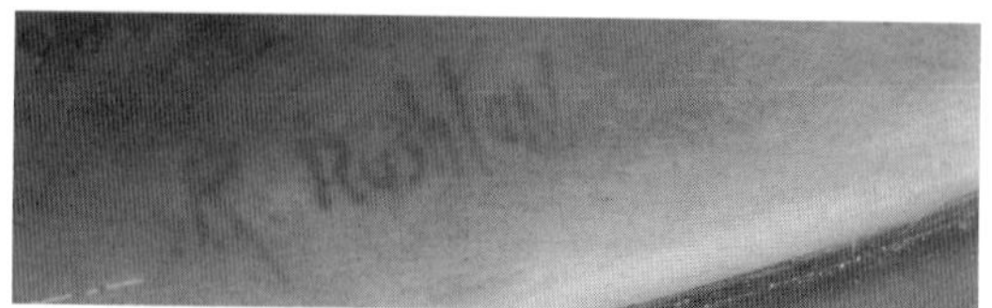

Royal Worcester earthenware dish reg mark 651926 printed mark for 1919 painted and signed by R. Rushton

inches, and they were known as 'long toms', decorated with flowers intermingled with fruit. John Keys (q.v.) said they were owned by a Mr Pope of Bonchurch on the Isle of Wight and valued (when Keys wrote his book in 1895) at three hundred guineas. After James left Derby c. 1826 he went to the Potteries, joining Coalport in the 1830s, where he worked on miniatures and figure painting in Sèvres style. His work was exhibited at the Great Exhibition of 1851 and the London International Exhibition of 1862. He left Coalport c. 1871 to work at the Ridgway Pottery, Cauldon Place Works, in Hanley. He then painted enamelled jewellery in Birmingham but was persuaded by Sampson Hancock to return to the King Street, Derby pottery in 1875. His last work was on the service commissioned for William E. Gladstone in 1888, but whilst engaged on this work he had a stroke and some of the pieces where finished by other artists. James signed some of this work. He had three sons employed in the ceramics industry. Charles became head of the gilding department at Derby pottery at the end of the nineteenth century. James was a fine figure and landscape artist, known to have worked for Coalport c. 1859 and at Minton 1860-1870, painting white china as an outside decorator. William was born in 1824 and was an apprentice gilder at the Derby factory, then employed at Coalport 1840-1860.

Rushton, Josiah, born 1836

Painter of figure subjects, who worked for the Worcester Royal Porcelain Co.1852-1871 painting figure subjects, portraits and copies of Gainsborough pictures on plaques. He painted a series of famous ladies at the Court of King Charles. He exhibited landscapes at the Royal Academy and the Suffolk Street Gallery, London 1875-1881. He marked his work with the monogram JR with three dots. By 1881 he had moved to Gloucestershire, where he became an artist and art teacher.

Rushton, Raymond, 1886–1956

Landscape painter,who worked for the Royal Worcester Porcelain Co. He painted brightly coloured country houses and cottage gardens, and also seascapes. He hand-coloured engravings of castles and cathedrals that were designed by H. Davis. He retired in 1953.

Sadler, Thomas, active 1892–1906

Floral painter employed by Copeland at the Spode Works, Stoke-upon-Trent. He became well known for his rose studies and floral arrangements in hanging baskets. It is thought he had no formal art education, learning his craft at Copeland. His rose and floral paintings are unique, usually signed T. Sadler or with the monogram TS. Examples of his work can be seen at the Spode Museum.

Salt, W.H., active 1871–1903

Artist gilder employed at Copeland. He is recorded in their Special Order reference books in 1873 as having worked on a Berrisford-shaped vase, which was painted by Lucien Besche (q.v.). He also gilded the dessert service exhibited at the London International Exhibition of 1871, which was painted by Charles Weaver (q.v.).

Salter, Edward, born 1860

Landscape and fish painter who worked for Royal Worcester, known for his landscape painting that shows distance and perspective, difficult to achieve on the ceramic surface. Harry Davis (q.v.) became his apprentice and his influence can be seen in Davis's work. Salter committed suicide and his death a great loss to the ceramic industry.

Bone china Copeland plaque painted and signed by T. Sadler

Saunders (Sanders), Henry, active c. 1870

Painter born in Stoke, Staffordshire. He was apprenticed to Leon Solon (q.v.) at Minton, specialising in pâte-sur-pâte decoration, but in 1877 joined Moore Bros, Longton, Staffordshire, where he signed or initialled his work. The family emigrated to America, where he painted for the Etruria Pottery, Trenton, New Jersey.

Schenck, Frederick Emil Eberhand, 1849–1908

Artist and modeller born in Scotland, the son of a lithographer, writer and professor of German. He worked for his father for two years and then started his formal art education at the Edinburgh School of Art. From 1872-1873 he was employed by Wedgwood, paid five shillings a day. Schenck studied at the Hanley School of Art in the evenings, winning the Armstrong Scholarship to the Government School of Design, South Kensington, London. He continued his studies at the Scottish Academy, where he attended life classes. From 1878-1886 he was employed at the George Jones, Crescent Pottery, Stoke-upon-Trent, executing fine pâte-sur-pâte work, which was exhibited at the Exposition Universelle, Paris in 1878. Although known and documented as a modeller, no doubt because of his later success in London, he is regarded in the Potteries as a superb pâte-sur-pâte decorator. He married in 1879 and lived at Bedford Street, Basford, Stoke, and taught modelling at the Hanley School of Art. He obtained commissions from the Brown-Westhead & Moore pottery. By 1888 the family had moved to London, where he worked on architectural sculpture and exhibited architectural panels. A vase in the Stoke-on-Trent City Art Gallery collection, signed F. Schenk sc., is a fine example of his work.

Scott, Arthur, born 1896

Flower painter apprenticed at Doulton, Burslem under Robert Allen (q.v.) and trained at the Stoke School of Art. Scott specialised in painting roses. He left the Potteries to teach at the Government School of Design, South Kensington,London. In 1919 he became Principal at the Watford School of Art, until 1948.

Sebright, Richard, 1865–1951

Fruit and flower painter employed at the Royal Worcester Porcelain Co. He is regarded as one of the finest fruit painters of all time and is remembered as a quiet, unassuming man and a confirmed bachelor. His work is usually signed and is easy to recognise, having a quality all its own. It is highly prized and widely collected. Sebright also exhibited watercolours at the Royal Academy.

Sedgley, Walter, active 1889–1929

Painter of flowers, especially roses, garden scenes and golden pheasants. He painted for the Royal Worcester Porcelain Co. and signed his work or initialled it as W. Sedgley, Seeley or J. Walters.

Sheerin, Eugene, 1855–1915

Landscape painter born at Drumbinnion, County Tyrone, Ireland. He was confined to a wheelchair so was unable to attend school, but was taught to write and draw by his mother. Sheerin first exhibited his drawing at the Annual Exhibition of Drawings in Belfast, where he was awarded a certificate of merit. By 1878 he was employed in the painting department at the Belleek Pottery, where he learnt to paint all subjects. 1881-1882 and 1884-1885 he and his brother went to the Dublin Metropolitan School of Art. His most noted work at for the Belleek Pottery is a service decorated with landscapes. He either signed or initialled his work.

Shelley, John, active 1869

Gilder born in Madeley, Shropshire, employed at Coalport from 1869 until it closed in 1926.

Sheriff, James, born 1825

Flower painter who was an apprentice at Minton around 1836. By 1851 he had moved to Worcester to the Kerr and Binns factory, specialising in floral subjects. His son James painted for the Worcester Royal Porcelain Co. and is noted for his floral and grass compositions.

Bone china Royal Worcester Cabinet plate c. 1903 painted and signed by R. Seebright

Sherwin, Henry, active 1800s

Designer, engraver and painter who worked for Wedgwood. Sherwin is named in the unidentified pattern book located in the print room collections at the Victoria & Albert Museum (accession number 8822, Press mark 93 C21, ends 7 June 1809). He contributed an article *The Art of Drawing* to the Potteries institute magazine of 1861.

Sherwin, Ishmael, active 1820s

Artist gilder at Flight and Barr, Worcester, designing patterns and gold and jewelled ornament.

Sherwin, John (?), active 1800s

Fruit and flower painter, the premier artist painter at the Spode works, Stoke-upon-Trent, Staffordshire. He first painted for Henry Daniel in his decorating establishment and it is thought that he stayed with Spode after Daniel left. He is named in The *Progress of Enamelling* by Henry Daniel (Stanza 14):

'Here's Sherwin, Hancock, Burgess and some more,
I could not enter in my verse before;
Great artists of fair Flora's flow'ery reign
From which the Factory receives great gain;
The first Pomonna in wreath'd flowers enclose,
From which the Prince of Wales order rose.'

There is one entry in the Spode pattern books recording him painting fruit and flowers. Some watercolour studies are included in the Bemrose Collection volumes, inscribed Sherwin. It is possible he was the John Sherwin who married in Burslem in 1803.

Shingler, Cyril, born 1902

Flower painter and designer born in Stoke-upon-Trent. He was educated at Newcastle-under-Lyme School and won a scholarship to Christ's College, London. On his return to the Potteries he worked for the North Staffordshire Railway Company, then at Doulton, Burslem. After some time in America he became the designer at the George Jones, Crescent Pottery, where he was known for his patience and for encouraging the young apprentices. In 1931 he went to the Grindley Pottery then spent some time at Doulton. During WWII he served in the Intelligence Co., then was at the Worcester Royal Porcelain Co. as a designer, until he was appointed curator of the Dyson Perrins Museum.

Shuck, Albert, 1880–1961

Fruit and flower painter at the Royal Worcester Porcelain Co who specialised in painting orchids. His work is often signed and is becoming recognised and collectable.

Detail Spode Comport the decoration attributed to Sherwin

Shufflebottam, Arthur, active 1908–15

Fruit and flower painter who worked in Bristol before joining the South Wales Pottery Co., known for painting fruit and flowers with free, wide brush strokes.

Shufflebottam, Roger A., born 1939

Painter and freelance artist born in Stoke-on-Trent, who studied under Percy Lloyd at the Stoke College of Art. He was trained at Minton under Arthur Dale Holland and some of his early work is signed with his mother's maiden name, R. Scott. In 1974 he joined the Caverswall factory, until 1982, when he became a freelance artist.

Sieffert, Louis Eugène, active *c.* 1880

Painter of figure subjects and an outside decorator who trained at the Sèvres manufactory. He came to the Potteries and was employed by the Brown-Westhead, Moore & Co. Much of the Coalport ware painted by him bears the retailer Daniell's backstamp. He painted in a fine stippled style and is especially known for his pâte-sur-pâte technique. Some of his work is initialled in monogram form.

Silk, active 1780

Landscape and figure painter who may have painted for Thomas Turner at the Salopian Works, and also for Flight and Barr, Worcester.He is thought to have run an outside decorating establishment, in London.

Simeon, Harry, active 1894-1935

Painter and designer, son of a monumental stonemason and modeller.He studied at the Huddersfield School of Art, where he won a scholarship to the Government School of Design, South Kensington, London. Simeon decorated Doulton's jugs with flowers and leaves and with designs using a leopard skin effect. They also had stylised animals, flowers, etc. in coloured glazes. He designed models for a series of Toby jugs, and also earthenware or stoneware plaques. His work is monogrammed HS.

Simeon (Simyan), Victor Etienne, 1826–1886

Sculptor modeller born at Saint-Gangoux-le-Royal, France.He exhibited at the Paris Salon between 1855 and 1861. Simeon founded an art pottery in England and received commissions from Minton, including the vase *Prometheus* shown at the Exposition Universelle, Paris of 1896 and the figures *Romeo and Juliet, David and Goliath* and *Perseus and Andromeda*, which were reproduced in Parian. He was an eccentric man, known to walk around Trentham and Oak Hill, near Stoke-upon-Trent, carrying his French horn, which he played only when he had found and climbed a suitable tree.

Simmance, Elise, active c. 1900

Paintress trained at the Lambeth School of Art. In 1873 she was employed at the Doulton Art Pottery, Lambeth. Her fine painting was rather over-shadowed by the work of the Barlow sisters (q.v.) A versatile artist whose work was exhibited at many of the International Exhibitions, she was described by John Sparkes (q.v.): 'Her work is not only designing with the stylus, but especially she excels in painting the pâte-sur-pâte patterns. There are examples of her work, which are so eminently graceful and well drawn, as to emulate the same qualities in the work of the Italian ornaments. She, too, has so many ideas to spare – more than she can work out by herself – that she keeps a staff of rising artists occupied in carrying out her instructions. An example of her work is partly painted, partly incised, and the main body of the ornament is carried out of the solid clay.' By the early 1900s she was experimenting in the Art Nouveau style and developing tube-line decoration.

Doulton Lambeth Stone ware jug designed and decorated by E. Simmons Courtesy of the M.O.H. Baker Collection

Simpson (family), active c. 1850

William Scarratt mentions a Mr Simpson as a Ridgway painter who had also been employed at Copeland, Stoke-upon-Trent. Members of the Simpson family of artists are shown in the Copeland archives 1845-1864, then again 1881-1902. It is possible that the early entries are those of the father and son. Lady Peel is shown as ordering a cream boat and cover. They painted small delicate groups of flowers and roses, but none are signed. Pattern numbers 7169, 7720, D1723, D 1873 are recorded as their work.

Simpson, Aaron, active c. 1860–1880

Artist gilder first employed at the Minton Art Studio in London. He was awarded a Co-operators medal at the Vienna Exhibition of 1873 for his fine Sèvres style of gilding. After the Minton Studio closed due to a fire in 1876 he was employed at Minton in Stoke-upon-Trent. In 1881 the family were living at Newcastle Road, Shelton. He stayed at Minton the whole of his working life.

Simpson, John, 1811–1884

Painter of figure subjects and landscapes and art teacher born in Derby, son of Mundy Simpson, a gilder and Japan painter. He trained at the Nottingham Road, Derby works but came to Stoke-upon-Trent in 1837 and worked as a painter of figure subjects at Minton until 1847. He moved to London to become head of the department of enamel painting on porcelain at the Government School of Design, South Kensington. He exhibited his work at the Royal Academy from 1831 to 1871. Simpson was known for his fine miniatures on enamel, and he obtained several commissions from Queen Victoria. Some of his work is preserved at Osborne House on the Isle of Wight and in the Victoria & Albert Museum.

Simpson, Percy, 1890–1956

Painter and art director born in Hanley, Staffordshire, the son of Samuel Thomas, a china painter.He started at Coalport in 1901 and may have been apprenticed to Arthur Perry (q.v.). He was an artist painter of all subjects, particularly snow studies, who signed his work. When Arthur Perry left Coalport, Percy then specialised in fish studies. He stayed with Coalport the whole of his working life, becoming Art Director.

Simpson, Richard, born 1833

Painter born in Hanley, Staffordshire, known to have been painting for Coalport during the 1860s, specialising in landscapes.

Simpson, Samuel, active c. 1870–1900

A painter and gilder at Minton who, in 1875 became Superintendent of the china decorating and gilding department.

Simpson, Thomas, active c. 1860

Flower painter, brother of Samuel (q.v.), who is first recorded as working for Mr Thomas Barlow of Longton at Market Street Works, Longton, Staffordshire. The report of the London International Exhibition of 1862 describes the Barlow exhibits: 'Cups and saucers are the needs of every household in all the parts of the civilised world; they are especially so in England. All our manufacturers produce them; but in the case at the Exhibition there was a collection of these objects only: they were the production of Mr Thomas Barlow of Longton, and manifested much taste and artistic skill, being highly creditable to the manufacturer and the artists in his employ: the designs, both shapes and decoration, were by Mr H.J. Kane, and the whole of the flower painting were by Mr Thomas Simpson. The subjects were by no means exclusively floral; they were frequently arabesque, sometimes had heraldic devices, and often were ornamented with raised gold.' Simpson is probably the same artist who specialised in fruit and flowers known to have been at the Minton Art Studio, London and also at their Stoke pottery. His work was exhibited at the Vienna Exhibition of 1873. After the Minton Art Studio closed it is thought that he joined Coalport in the early the 1890s, taking over from Walley (q.v.), painting floral groups and becoming the works manager.

Simpson, William, 1893–1917

Artist gilder of great skill, who worked with Harry Milward (q.v.) at Doulton, Burslem. He decorated most of the important pieces for their distinguished customers. In 1917 he left to work in Trenton, New Jersey, USA.

Simpson, William Page, born 1845

Painter of animals, birds and figures, born in London, son of John Simpson (q.v.). He worked for Minton, Stoke-upon-Trent, and may have received commissions from Queen Victoria. In the 1 October 1897 'Fancy Trade' supplement to *The Pottery Gazette and Glass Trade Review*, an article 'A landscape in tiles' describes an order received by Minton for work for a large butcher's shop in Belfast: 'The contract comprises two large friezes about thirty feet long by five foot deep consisting of nearly 1,500 tiles. For the manipulation of this extraordinary surface of tiles a special easel and stand had to be constructed and this was erected in a suite of rooms at the rear of the factory, where the artist W. P. Simpson has arranged, designed and executed one of the finest series of the cattle pieces that it has been our lot to see... The artist has depicted on each panel a group of antlered deer on rocky eminences which remind us of the best of Landseer's work... a pair of white ptarmigans are represented as sitting among the heather which warms the rocks into life and beauty...'. The 1901 census shows the family living at Yeovil Villa, Minton Place and his occupation is given as an artist decorator on tiles.

Sims, active 1795–1820

Flower painter and outside decorator who was apprenticed at the Derby Nottingham Road factory. He worked under William Duesbury II (q.v.) as a flower painter. He and his son William started their own studio in Pimlico, London c. 1805–31. Landscape painter Z. Boreman and flower painter James Turner were commissioned by them. Simms was especially known for painting large open roses.

Skeaping, John Rattenbury, 1901–1980

Painter and sculptor born in Essex, the son of the painter Kenneth Mathieson Skeaping. He studied first at Blackheath School of Art, then at Goldsmiths College and became a scholar at the Royal Academy Schools. He studied in Rome for three years but had returned to England by 1926. Skeaping married Barbara Hepworth, who influenced his work. He was commissioned by Wedgwood to create a series of animal subjects, which included a polar bear, bison, kangaroo and buffalo, and were produced in basalt and cream ware, then reproduced in the 1950s with a tan-grey glaze. In the 1950s he became Professor of Sculpture at the Royal Academy and a Royal Academician in 1959. He died in France.

Skellern, Victor, ARCA, FSIA, NRD, 1909–66

Designer and decorator born in Fenton, Staffordshire, who trained at Burslem and Hanley School of Art under Gordon Forsythe (q.v.). In 1923 he joined the Wedgwood design department, where he served his apprenticeship painting flower and fruit designs, working closely with Art Director John Goodwin (q.v.). He won a three-year scholarship to the Royal College of Art, where he studied stained-glass painting. In 1934 he returned to Wedgwood and succeeded John Goodwin as Art Director. Skellern developed new glazes and bodies for

Wedgwood tableware and introduced the controversial use of lithographs on Wedgwood Queen's Ware. He encouraged freelance artist/designers including Eric Ravilous, Laura Knight and Rex and Laura Whistler. He travelled to Europe and America lecturing about Wedgwood and helping to market the company's products. Batkin quotes him saying 'Decoration must be designed for the shape and must add something relevant to it' and 'there is no such thing as Traditional or Contemporary design, these are merely convenient labels. Design is either good or bad – if good it lasts, if bad it doesn't'.

In 1946 Wedgwood exhibited at the *Britain Can Make It* exhibition in London and their exhibits included sixteen of Skellern's designs. Now he and John Wedgwood went on official promotional trips to America, visiting the departmental stores that stocked their ware and assessing market trends. In 1962 Skellern designed six commemorative mugs, which were awarded a Design Council award. However, by now his health was failing; he retired in 1965 and died a year later.

Skinner, William, 1886–1916

Artist gilder apprenticed at the Davenport Pottery. In 1908 he went to Doulton, becoming one of their most talented artist gilders, doing work with Raby (q.v.), Churnock (q.v.), Dewsbury (q.v.) and other premier artists.

Skitt, Christopher, born 1852

Artist gilder born in Coalbrookdale, Shropshire. He was employed by Coalport, where he became known for his fine raised and jewelled work, particularly on vases of the 1889 period. In 1881 he was living at Park Street, Madeley,Shropshire.

Slater, Albert, born 1846

Flower painter born in Derby, son of Joseph (q.v.). He joined Minton under the guidance of Arnoux (q.v.), painting birds and flowers. He then moved to Messrs Pinders Bourne of Burslem as a pattern designer and foreman of the enameller paint shop. He was next employed at Messrs Minton & Hollins, the tile makers in Stoke-upon-Trent. In 1881 he was living at 15 Clive Street, Stoke-upon-Trent, described as artist at patent tile factory.

Slater, Eric W., 1902–1984

Painter and designer, son of Walter (q.v.),who trained at the Hanley and Burslem Schools of Art under Gordon Forsythe (q.v.).He worked first in the design department of the North Staffordshire Railway, but in 1919 went to the Wileman & Co. pottery, training with his father Walter. In 1925 the firm changed its name to Shelley and in 1929 became a limited company. By 1928 Eric had succeeded his father as Art Director, joining the Board of Directors of Shelley in 1946.

Eric was influenced by Art Deco and Cubism, which is seen in the shapes he designed and painted with floral and geometrical themes. In 1930 he designed the *Vogue* tea shape, made in bone china, which had the striking pattern *Sunray* and was displayed at the British Industries Fair in 1933.

From 1935 to 1939 he taught at the Burslem School of Art and became a member of the Joint Advisory Committee of Art in Stoke-upon-Trent. In 1946 he designed all the Shelley exhibits for their stand at the *Britain Can Make It* exhibition. By 1950 his designs featuring sgrafitto patterns of leaves or simple scroll motifs were shown at the Festival of Britain in 1951. He continued designing new shapes and patterns throughout his career, keeping pace with the changing market styles.

Minton and Hollins tile picture of *Winter* painted by A. Slater

Minton and Hollins tile picture of *Summer* painted by A. Slater

Slater, Frank, died 1939

Crest painter, son of George Joseph (q.v.), who was employed at Copeland, succeeding William Fenton (q.v.). He is shown in the Special Order reference books as painting on tiles. Frank served in WWI, where he was serious wounded.

Slate, Frederick, born 1869

Modeller, son of Albert (q.v.).In 1893 he went to the Belleek Pottery, Ireland, where it is thought he designed the vase that won the gold medal at the Exposition Universelle, Paris of 1900. The piece is urn shaped and the scrolled base supports three Irish Wolfhounds. It is decorated with flowers and three Irish harps. In 1967 a version of this vase was made to commemorate the Century of Canadian Confederation and is on display at the Manitoba Centennial Centre, Winnipeg.

Slater, George Joseph, 1836–1897

Flower painter and gilder born in Derby, second son of Joseph (q.v.). He was first employed as a pattern gilder at Minton, then moved to Doulton, Burslem, working with his brother John (q.v.),eventually becoming foreman of a small decorating department. He is thought to have been the artist of a ewer, now in Australia, described in the Sidney Museum of Arts and Sciences as 'a unique piece by George Slater, brother of John'. In 1891 he was described in the census as a potters' gilders foreman.

Slater, John, 1844–1914

Artist and potters designer born in Derby, son of Joseph (q.v.). He trained at the Stoke-upon-Trent Art School under Silas Price (q.v.) and became an apprentice at Minton under Leon Arnoux (q.v.). In 1868 he was awarded a one-year free scholarship to the Government School of Design, South Kensington, London. John won the first prize two years running at the Hanley Exhibition and received a mention for his work shown in the London International Exhibition of 1871. On his return from London, he succeeded his brother Albert as Art Director of Pinder Bourne & Co. and continued to work for the firm after it was bought out by Doulton.

He followed the policy set by the Doulton Lambeth Studio, training young artists from the local art school and giving them freedom to produce fresh designs. Slater ran the decorating department at Doulton, where he introduced lustre decoration. He also carried out research into the transfer painting of earthenware by photographic means and in 1889 he took out a patent for 'Improvements in decorating china and the like by means of which paintings and designs are printed on a photographic plate to obtain a negative and from the negative a gelatine printing surface produced, from which the design can then be printed on transfer paper in any of the colours commonly employed for china painting'.

Around 1884 Slater invented a process by which fine lace and other fabrics were used to form patterns on pottery, and in the late 1880s designed stained-glass patterns. In 1883 Henry Doulton sent him to France to study the ceramics in Sèvres and Limoges. Slater eventually persuaded Henry Doulton to allow research into the production of bone china at Burslem, which resulted in very successful products for the company. At the Exposition Universelle, Paris of 1889 his new style of flower painting, painted to perfection by Raby (q.v.) and other artists, was praised. Slater and Charles Nokes (q.v., who was to succeed him) researched flambé ware, which was to become one of Doulton's most successful products. In 1881 Slater lived at 208 Waterloo Road, Burslem, Stoke-upon-Trent, and he retired in 1914.

Slater, Joseph, 1814–1896

Crest painter, gilder and designer born in Derby and served his apprenticeship at Derby. After the factory closed, he went to work for the Hill Top Pottery under Samuel Alcock, but later joined Minton (1856-1875) as a foreman in the painting and majolica departments. He became head of the majolica department at Brown-Westhead Moore & Co. In 1881 he was living at Cauldon Place, Shelton, Stoke-on-Trent. Joseph had four sons who followed him into the ceramic industry.

Slater, Walter, 1865–1938

Painter and designer, eldest son of Albert (q.v.).He first trained at Minton but in 1885 became an apprentice at Doulton, Burslem. Charles Nokes (q.v.) was impressed with his artistic talent and praised him for the delicacy and fine composition of his painting. In 1905 he left to become a designer at Wileman & Co, The Foley Pottery, Fenton, later Shelley Potteries Ltd. Eventually he succeeded F.A. Rhead (q.v.) as Art Director. Walter designed oriental patterns and shapes for vases. His son Eric succeeded him. He died soon after his retirement in 1938.

Slater, William, 1784–1867

Artist, gilder and painter, father of Joseph (q.v.). He was born in South Normanton, Derby and served part of his apprenticeship at the Pinxton Pottery as a gilder and ornamental painter. He left because of a wage dispute and joined Derby. He was persuaded to join R. Robins and T.M. Randell in London, where he painted armorial and heraldic designs with raised and chased gold. By 1820 he had returned to Derby, becoming decorating manager. When the Derby works closed he moved to the Davenport

Pottery, where he remained until his death. He was noted for his painting of fruit and insects, and crests and heraldic devices. He had great ability when decorating with gold. He died in Burslem and was buried in Dalehall Church.

Slater, William (Junior), 1811–67

Gilder, son of William (q.v.) and apprentice at Derby. He moved in 1833 to Davenport as earthenware designer and manager, and stayed until his death.

Slater, William Henry, born 1835

Painter and designer, eldest son of Joseph (q.v.)and an apprentice at Derby. When it closed he was employed at Messrs Holmes coachbuilders. He then went to the Potteries, first to Samuel Alcock & Sons, where he painted a vase called *Peace and War*, which was designed by George Eyre (q.v.) and exhibited at the London International Exhibition in 1862. He then moved to Minton as a heraldic painter. He won prizes for his Limoges-style

Doulton Burslem bone china Ewer Reg no RA 3344 Shape no 604 painted and signed by William Slater

enamels on porcelain. His next employment was designer and manager of the decorating department at Messrs Harvey Adams & Co. of Longton, where he designed Chinese, Japanese and Persian influenced patterns for all forms of ware. He became decorating manager to Taylor Tunnicliffe and Co., Eastwood, Hanley, living at 48 Queen Anne Street, Shelton, Stoke-upon-Trent, and by 1881 he became decorating manager at the larger factory of RH & SL Plant in Longton.

Smith, Henry, born 1869

Painter employed at Minton. After A. Birks (q.v.) retired he became known for his fine pâte-sur-pâte decoration and was an assistant to Bradbury (q.v.). He may be brother to James William, who was born in Madeley, Shropshire.

Smith, Jessie, born 1819

Flower painter born in Stoke-on-Trent and apprenticed at Minton c. 1831. He became a specialist painter, known for his rose painting. His work was shown at the London International Exhibition of 1862, but by 1867 he had joined Copeland at the Spode factory. Scarett comments that 'dealers would wait patiently for this true artist's work'.

Smith, John Holmes, active c. 1820

Artist and bird painter born at Worcester and worked at Coalport. He left the ceramic industry to teach drawing and became a well-known topographical watercolour artist.

Smith, Joseph, born 1802

Bird painter born at All Saints, Worcester. He went to Minton around 1835, specialising in bird painting. In 1842 Ralph Sneyd of Keele Hall, Staffordshire commissioned a dessert service from Minton that Smith painted. He is shown in the 1881 census as artist, draper, independent (lay preacher) living at 24 Park Street, Stoke-on-Trent, Staffordshire.

Soare, Thomas, 1785–1885

Artist gilder,one of the earliest apprentices at Derby. Samuel Keys says he was the principal painter in gold, especially of arabesque patterns, and was foreman of the painters. Around 1810 Soare advertised in *The Derby Mercury*, citing his long association with the Derby factory and offering to undertake heraldic work, and to teach ladies to paint china in their own apartments on liberal terms. His address was given as Navigation Row, near St Mary's Bridge, Derby. In 1815 he was appointed Governor of the Poor in the parish of St Alkmund's. In 1819 he was again employed by Robert Bloor of the Derby factory as a traveller and clerk.

Solon, Albert Loius, 1887–1949

Painter, son of Louis (q.v.).He trained at the Minton Hollins tile factory, Stoke-upon-Trent, but in 1908 he emigrated to America and 1913 took over as Director of the Ariquipa Pottery from Frederick Hurten Rhead (q.v.) until the pottery closed in 1918. He then became a teacher at the California State University.

Solon, Camille Antoine, 1877–1960

Painter, son of Louis (q.v.), born in Stoke-upon-Trent. In 1901 he is described as a faience draughtsman, painting murals for Minton, but around 1914 joined his brother Albert (q.v.) at the Arequipa Pottery.

Solon, Gilbert Charles, 1879–1929

Painter, who worked with his father Louis (q.v.) at Minton and is shown in their wages book from 1905 to 1912.He then joined the Royal Worcester Porcelain Co. as General Manager until he retired in 1927.

Solon, Leon Victor Albert, 1872–1957

Painter of landscapes and portraits, designer and illustrator, son of Louis (q.v.) and grandson of Leon Arnoux (q.v.) who studied at the Hanley School of Art and at the Government School of Design, South Kensington, London, where he was awarded a Royal Exhibition. At Minton he executed slipware decoration and from 1896 he revived Minton's interest in art pottery. His pottery panels were exhibited at the Arts and Crafts Exhibitions of 1896, 1899 and 1903, interestingly entered under his name and not that of the company. They were highly praised, although some critics felt they were too pictorial for the medium for which they were designed. Leon became Chief Designer and Art Director at Minton 1900–09, taking inspiration from the work of Alphonse Mucha and from the Art Nouveau style. Haggar describes him as 'a versatile artist, inventive and fertile of ideas and a frequent exhibitor at the Royal Academy, he exercised considerable influence upon the trend of ceramic design at the turn of the century. Solon and John Wadsworth [q.v.] designed Secessionist ware with slip-trailed Art Noveau designs.'

From 1912-1925 he was a designer for the American Encaustic Tiling Company in Ohio, winning a gold medal for Applied Arts from the American Institute of Architects, and designing architectural ornament and colouring for the Rockefeller Centre in New York and the Museum of Fine Arts in Philadelphia. Leon became a bookbinder and illustrator and designed a poster for

The Studio magazine. He contributed to *The Parade* in 1897 and an edition of poetry, *Les trophées* by José-Maria de Heredia, in 1904. It is said he gained commissions from Queen Victoria. He died in Florida.

Solon, Louis Marc Emmanuel (Miles), 1835–1913

Painter, artist, designer and author born in Montauban, Tarn-et-Garonne, France and trained in Paris at a small private school of design, the Atelier of Lecoq de Boisbaudrannt. The students were allowed great freedom and taught to develop their talents by studying Greek vases and terracottas. Louis first trained as an illustrator and produced a small book of his etchings, which came to the notice of Lord Frederick Leighton (sometime President of the Royal Academy), who was studying art in Paris at the time and was art director at Sèvres. His influence assured Solon's appointment at Sèvres. M.V. Regnault, a world-famed chemist, was the Administrator at Sèvres and Solon learnt the pâte-sur-pâte technique of decoration. Eugene Rousseau, a Paris art dealer and designer, encouraged and commissioned his work, which was exhibited in the Union Centrale des Beaux-Arts Appliqués à l'Industrie in 1865. M. Regnault wrote a report for the exhibition and pointed out that Solon had created his own method of pâte-sur-pâte, which varied greatly from that of Sèvres. He commissioned a vase, which was exhibited with the Sèvres products at the London International Exhibition of 1867.

In 1870 Solon and his fellow artist V. Gallan left Paris as the Prussian Army advanced to the outskirts of the city. Louis knew Minton Art Director Leon Arnaux (q.v.), who gave him a studio and directed him to design pâte-sur-pâte, which was very popular and sold well. Louis trained Alboine Birks (q.v.), T. Mellor (q.v.), Frederick.H. Rhead (q.v.), H. Sanders (q.v.), C. Toft (q.v.) and Laurence Birks (q.v.) in the technique. One of his famous vases, *The Spartan Girls Wrestling before Lycurgas*, took seven months to complete and another was presented to Queen Victoria in her Jubilee year in 1887. He never repeated his designs; each one is unique. Solon first signed his work MILES when in France, but in England either with a monogram or the signature L. Solon.

Louis married Leon Arnaux's daughter Maria, they had eight sons and one daughter, and lived at No 1 The Villas, Stoke-upon-Trent, Staffordshire. Their daughter Marie went back to France, where she became headmistress of the Paris School of Art, specialising in copying many of the finest pictures in the Louvre.

Solon retired about 1903 but continued to design and decorate, also writing books on pottery, such as *A Brief account of pâte-sur-pâte* and *The Art of the Old English Potter.*

L. M. E. Solon

He collected many examples of salt-glaze porcelain, which he sold in 1912. After his death, his library was sold to the North Staffordshire Polytechnic, now part of North Staffordshire University.

Spangler, Jean Jacques, born 1755

Modeller and painter born in Switzerland, son of the director of the Zurich porcelain factory, who was apprenticed to Valentin Sonnenschein, a sculptor. In 1790, on the invitation of Vulliamy, a clock maker, he came to England to decorate clocks with marble and porcelain figures. When William Duesbury's agent Lygo persuaded Vulliamy to use Derby figures for his decoration, Spangler went to Derby on a three-year agreement, dated 13 September 1790, which shows he was paid £3 a week for the first month, but if the arrangement worked his wages were to be reduced to £2.10s. He was to model figures for Duesbury, some of which would be used by Vulliamy. Spangler was unreliable and temperamental; he only worked either when in the mood or when he needed money for good living. His terms of employment were nevertheless stated clearly: he was to work in his own house ten hours each day in summer and eight hours in winter. Spangler never conformed to the agreement, soon getting into debt, and although Duesbury lent him money he went on the run and was arrested and imprisoned in Ramsgate. Duesbury continued to employ him and get him out of trouble. Spangler never repented or changed his lifestyle and returned to London. His models were produced in Derby Biscuit and included *Two Virgins Awaking Cupid*, *Russian Shepherd Group* and *The French Seasons*, a set of four models made in different sizes. His style was romantic rather than classical. He disappeared, probably returning to France.

Sparkes (née Edwards), Catherine, born 1843

Artist, designer and painter trained at the Lambeth Art School 1861-1866 and at the Government School of Design, South Kensington, London 1862-1868, finishing her studies at the Royal Academy. Her work was exhibited at the 1862 International Exhibition London: the painting, from a scene from Milton's *Comus* on Dutch tiles, was ten feet long and two feet wide. After the exhibition Henry Doulton acquired if for his billiard room. At the Philadelphia Centennial Exhibition in 1876, her painting *The Pilgrim Fathers*, a thirty-six foot tile panel was shown. Catherine exhibited paintings at the Royal Academy from 1866 to1890 and also at the Dudley Art Gallery. Some of her wood drawings were used as book illustration. She married John Sparkes (q.v.) and together they created many innovative new designs.

Sparkes, John, active 1833–1907

Artist designer and art teacher who helped Canon Gregory to establish the Lambeth School ofArt,becoming headmaster in 1856.He believed art and industry must be a partnership and that students should fully understand the product for which they were designing. When he first broached the subject of establishing a small art studio in the Lambeth Pottery he was not successful, but the experimental ware he produced finally persuaded Henry Doulton, and in 1860 the Prince of Wales (the future Edward VII) laid the foundation stone for the Art Studio on part of the old Vauxhall Gardens. In *Royal Doulton 1815–1965*, Eyles writes: 'In 1873 Doulton said to Sparkes after a visit to an exhibition of English Art pottery in a fashionable West End china shop, "Is that the best the English potters can do,that wishy-washy stuff? Can't we make Lambeth the centre of a real art product? Have you any students? Can you send me a whole batch of them?"'.

Sparkes took up the challenge. He built up a formidable team of artists and modellers, including George Tinworth (q.v.) and Perceval Ball (q.v.), who had both won gold medals at the Royal Academy. He had the vision to encourage women artists, whose work became well known and is highly collected today. Sparkes truly believed that ceramics should have original decorative artwork. He lectured to the Society of Arts in 1874 and again in 1880, where he spoke of many of the artists at Doulton, describing their various styles and undoubted talents. He was appointed Headmaster of the Government School of Design, South Kensington, London around 1891, where he remained until he retired in 1901.

Sparks, Thomas, 1773–1848

An engraver, living in Hanley who supplied engravings for tableware for Ridgway, Spode, Stevenson's of Cobridge and Wedgwood.

Speight, George, 1809–1879

Painter of figure subjects and outside decorator born in Yorkshire and apprenticed at the Rockingham pottery. His father William was a pot painter and his grandfather Godfrey a potter. Speight was employed from 1826 at the Swinton Pottery (Rockingham) and became well known for painting figures, but also painted shells and flowers. He is shown to have painted the service for William IV with heraldic devices. He left for Shelton in the Potteries around the 1840s, employed by the Ridgeway Pottery, and exhibited at the first exhibition of the North Staffordshire Society of Artists in 1842. He returned to Swinton in 1857 as an independent decorator.

Stanesby, John, 1786–1864

Flower painter born in Derby and apprenticed at the Nottingham Road, Derby Pottery in 1800. He excelled in painting roses and worked fast, achieving the effect with sweeping lines of his brush. In about 1808 he moved to London, where he and his partner Beekler ran a stained-glass decorating business. They received commissions for windows in public buildings and held exhibitions of their work, visited by royalty, including Prince Leopold. Stansby also painted miniature portraits on ivory. By 1825 he had returned to Derby, working on small portraits, but in 1832 he was once again in London, where he was awarded a medal from the Society of Arts. He tried to introduce a process of relief engraving as a substitute for wood engraving, but this was not successful. Some of his work was exhibited at the Royal Academy. Stansby had three sons, Joshua, Alexander and Samuel, who inherited his talent exhibiting their paintings at the Royal Academy.

Stanley, Jack, 1905–1972

Painter and modeller who worked for the Worcester Royal Porcelain Co., 1919-1932. He studied flower painting under E. Philips and figures under W. Hawley. His paintings include portraits after Meissonier (q.v.) Frans Hals and Vermeer (q.v.), and he also painted Doris

Lindner's (q.v.) dog models. He trained as a modeller under F.M. Gertner (q.v.) and designed patterns for transfer printing.

Statham, William N., 1863–1940

Landscape painter born in Matlock, Derbyshire and apprenticed to Langraf (q.v.) at the Osmaston Road, Derby pottery. Although he is known to have signed his work and his name appears in the Derby pattern books, few examples of his work have been found. After leaving Derby he had a photographer's shop in Matlock, where he also sold Derby and other china. He was a churchwarden and designed a pulpit for the parish church and also designed the Matlock War memorial. Statham taught at Riber Castle and wrote a history of Matlock parish church.

Steel, Aaron, 1765–1849

Bird painter employed by Wedgwood in their decorating studio in Greek Street, London, who painted the famous Etruscan vases at Etruria around 1812.

Steele, Edwin, 1805–1871

Flower and fruit painter born at Burslem,son of Thomas (q.v.). He was apprenticed to Derby 1815-1820 and trained by his father. From 1828-1832 he was at the Rockingham factory at Swinton,Yorkshire. He must then have become a freelance artist as he is known to have painted for Coalport, Bristol, S. Alcock's Hill Top Pottery, Burslem, Minton and Davenport. Some of his work is signed.

Steele, Edwin (Junior), born 1840

Flower painter born in Hanley, son of Edwin (q.v.) and grandson of Thomas (q.v.). He spent a short time as a glass painter, but in 1878 set up a decorating business with John Bloor (q.v.).

By around 1880 Edwin was continuing the business on his own. In 1901 he was concentrating on painting in oils and watercolour and is described in the census as artist in oils.

Steele, Horatio, died 1874

Flower painter trained by his father Thomas (q.v.) at Derby, where he stayed until the factory closed in 1848. He did some of the floral decoration on a service for Queen Victoria, which was exhibited at the company's Bond Street, London showrooms during Christmas week in 1842.

Steele, Thomas c. 1772–1850

Fruit and flower painter apprenticed at Wedgwood, but by 1815 at Nottingham Road, Derby. Haslem comments: 'As a painter of fruit on china he had no superior if indeed he had any equal in his day'. His painting of fruit was said to have been better than that of flowers, showing light and shade of the fruits blending into each other. He achieved some of the effects by carefully dabbing on the colour with his finger. His work is noted for fresh, naturalistic painting. 1826-1830 Thomas painted for Rockingham, and then possibly Davenport 1828-1830. From 1832-1850 he was working at Minton, where he

Porcelain plaque signed Thomas Steele and dated 1824

and Samuel Keys (q.v.) shared a workbench. When told of Keys' death he packed his tools and left the bench, never to return. He died in Stoke-upon-Trent soon afterwards. Steele signed and sometimes dated his painting.

Steele, Thomas, born 1815

Landscape painter, son of Thomas (q.v.), apprenticed at Derby. He was employed at Coalport 1840-1845, where he specialised in Scottish scenery. He died young and his undoubted talent was lost.

Stephan, Pierre, active 1770

Modeller born in Switzerland who was at the Tournai factory around 1769. He went to England and was employed by the Chelsea Pottery, modelling the flowers seen on many of their elaborate vases. When William Duesbury bought the Chelsea pottery, Stephan moved to Derby on a three-year contract to Duesbury to model and repair china or porcelain ware. His wages were two and a half guineas a week.

A statuette of *Lord Howe* marked Derby and modelled by Stephan is in the British Museum. He stayed at Derby until 1795, when he joined the Wirkworth Pottery.

He became a freelance modeller doing work for Wedgwood, Derby and in 1819 for Coalport. He modelled many well-known people of the day, such as Pitt and Lord Rodney.

Stephan, Peter, born c. 1796

Artist modeller born in Staffordshire, the son of Pierre (q.v.),who was responsible for many fine Coalport vases, inkstands, dinner and dessert services and centrepieces. Wolliscroft Rhead records that he established a small pottery at Jackfield producing encaustic tiles and blue-printed ware, but no other evidence to date has emerged to support this view.

Stephans, William, 1756–1836

Painter born in Cornwall and thought to have been apprenticed first by Cooksworthy then transferred to Richard Champion. He became a skilful decorator at the Bristol Pottery, painting floral subjects. There is a theory that his mark was a number 2.

Stevens, Hamlet, born c. 1802

Painter born in Hanley, Staffordshire, who joined Coalport in the 1820s,staying with the pottery all his life until about 1880. He is known to have painted Sèvres flowers and Chelsea groups. He married a Coalport girl and their children William Henry and George, aged twenty and twenty-one in the 1851 census, became china painters.

Stinton, Harry, 1882–1968

Landscape painter, son of John (Junior, q.v.) trained by his father and studied at the Government School of Design, South Kensington, London. He was employed at the Royal Worcester Porcelain Co. to paint cattle, sheep, game birds and landscapes, becoming known for his scenes of Highland cattle on large and small pieces of porcelain. He was an excellent watercolour artist. He retired in 1963.

Stinton, Henry, active 1800s

Flower painter employed at Flight and Barr, Worcester. He painted floral groups 1819–40 and exhibited three floral studies at the Royal Academy *c.* 1830-1831.

Stinton, James, 1870–1961

Painter of birds, game, grouse and a watercolour artist,youngest son of John (Senior, q.v.), employed at Grainger Worcester and then the Worcester Royal Porcelain Co. He is well known for his paintings of pheasants and grouse and signed his work Jas. Stinton. He painted small watercolours, some as pictures and others that were used for birthday or Christmas cards.

Stinton, John (Senior), born 1828

Landscape painter born in Worcester and in 1881 living at Northfield Street, Claines, Worcester. He became the premier artist at Grainger Worcester Pottery. His landscapes always had small groups of delicately painted figures. He had five sons; three became known painters of porcelain. He is not known to have signed his work.

Stinton, John (Junior), 1854–1956

Painter of all subjects, eldest son of John (Senior) and in 1881 was living at East Street, Claines, Worcester.He first started work at Grainger Worcester, but in 1899 moved to the Worcester Royal Porcelain Co., where he stayed until he retired in 1938. John painted a variety of cattle subjects, also old castles – for example, Kenilworth and Ludlow. His work is highly collectable today. He had three children who continued the family tradition of fine ceramic painting: Arthur (1878–1970), who worked at Grainger Worcester until 1899 and then went on to decorate glass; Kate (1880–1955) and Harry (1883–1968) were also skilled painters.

Stinton, Walter, 1869–1950

Landscape painter, fourth son of John (Senior), trained at the Worcester School of Art, where he won three prizes. He was first employed as a landscape painter for Grainger Worcester and then joined the E. Locke pottery as an artist. When the pottery failed he joined 'Pump'

Worcester Royal Porcelain cabinet plate painted and signed by John Stinton Junior 1926

Thomas's hydraulic windmill firm in Droitwich. In 1896 he exhibited in the Royal Society of Arts exhibition in Birmingham. His work is usually signed.

Stoney, Charles Butler, active 1880s

Artist, freelance flower painter and designer. He painted flower studies in oils and his work was exhibited at the Royal Academy from 1889 to1893 and in the Arts and Crafts Exhibition of 1890. This same year he became Honorary Secretary of the Torquay Arts and Crafts Exhibition.

Street, George Edmund, 1824–1881

Architect, author and designer born in Woodford, Essex. He became one of the leading figures in the Arts and Crafts movement and is known in the ceramic field for designing tiles for Maw & Co. He became President of the Royal Institute of British Architects in 1881.

Sturgeon, Katie, active c. 1870

Artist and painter of figure subjects,who worked at the Minton Art Pottery Studio, London. By 1875 she was at the Doulton Lambeth Pottery, where she specialised in painting figure subjects on plaques and tiles until 1883. She was a fine watercolourist whose work was shown at the Royal Academy from 1890 to 1895 and the Royal Society of British Artists from 1881 to 1891. Her work was exhibited at the Walker Art Gallery, London, the Royal Institute of Painters in Watercolour and finally the Society of Women Artists. She signed her work at Doulton with the monogram KS.

Sutton, Frederick Nathaniel, active 1870s

Figure painter born at Worcester, son of a local architect and surveyor. He served his apprenticeship at Worcester and painted figure subjects and heads. By 1892 he was employed at Coalport, staying until 1898. Here he painted fine cameo heads often surrounded by rich jewelling and gilding. His work was exhibited at the World's Columbian Exposition, Chicago of 1893. Sutton was a prolific painter, known to have been associated with over one hundred designs at Coalport, many of which were gilded by Frank Lewis. Around 1904 he joined Doulton in Burslem, where he continued to produce fine miniatures after famous portrait artists. Much of his work is signed.

Swan, active 1880

Flower painter noted by Jewitt (q.v.) as working for Harvey Adams & Co, Longton. No other references have been found, and whether he is a member of the family below is not proven.

Swan (family), active from the 1850s

Floral painters at the Copeland Spode works, Stoke-upon-Trent. Their work is recorded there during 1858-1872 as Swan, Swan Senior, Swan Junior, Swan's boys and Swan & Co. It would seem that father and son worked together at Copeland throughout this time, painting delicate floral studies and small groups of flowers on the D pattern number series from Nos 1308 to 1720. One example has been found of Swan's work, a dessert plate with pattern number credited to Swan, but no signatures have been recorded. E. Swan went to the Belleek pottery in Ireland around 1860.

Swetman, active 1845–1851

Crest painters at Copeland, Stoke-upon-Trent. They are shown in the Special Order reference books as Swetman and T. Swetman, painting and gilding from pattern numbers 5613 to 8546 and also painting crests and badges for Regimental orders. One entry is of a special interest: pattern number 6554, a china pen tray, was ordered for Lord Calthorpe.

Swettenham, Louis, born 1860

Etcher and artist trained at Minton but in 1886 joined Doulton, where he became known for his fine and detailed etchings. He did fine work for Burgess & Leigh in the late 1880s, whether as an employee or freelance etcher is not known. He also travelled to London for the company and designed a plaque commemorating the death of Gladstone. He lived at Nettlebank, Smallthorne, near Tunstall, Staffordshire.

Tallandier, P., active c. 1890

Flower and figure painter. It is thought he may have been an apprentice at Sèvres in Paris and a descendant of a Sèvres flower painter. He was employed at Coalport from 1890 to 1894 designing floral studies, which were engraved and hand-coloured by women and painted with cupids and some figures. Around 1894 he went to the Osmaston Road, Derby pottery as an assistant to Desiré Leroy (q.v.), painting classical and romantic figures.

Tams, William Stevenson, born 1812

Potter's printer and engraver Copeland, born in Stoke-upon-Trent and married Jemima Wood (1828–88), daughter of a family of figure makers of Longton, Staffordshire. They had four children, three of whom were employed in the pottery industry. Arthur became a gilder and Ann and Elizabeth (Lizzie) paintresses. Ann married George Rooney, a warehouseman at Copeland, and they moved to work at Royal Crown Derby. Lizzie married Arthur Peach (q.v.), a pottery artist also employed for some time at Copeland. Tams believed in educating his family. He had a fine selection of books from which he read to his assembled children, keeping them happy with a supply of sweets, which he kept in the grandfather clock.

Taplin, Millicent, 1902–80

Artist paintress born in Hanley, educated at the local church school, from which she won a three-year scholarship to attend evening classes at the Stoke School of Art. Her first job was in a millinery shop but she soon found a job as a liner of cups and saucers at Greens in Fenton, moving on to Minton to train as a freehand paintress. By 1917 she joined Wedgwood and was chosen to work in Alfred and Louise Powell's studio. The relationship between the three developed into one of trust and respect; as the Powells were based in London they relied on Taplin to interpret their designs into saleable patterns. The designs were popular and the department grew under her control, so that by the 1930s she had established herself as a designer of merit.

In 1925 Wedgwood followed their success at the Exposition Universelle, Paris of that year by establishing a small handcraft studio. This was opened in 1928 with Millicent Taplin in charge assisted by Margery Hall and Mary Simpson, both of whom had trained at the Burslem School of Art. They decorated ware with Queensware enamels and lustres and used designs inspired by Rhodian and Persian wares. They also used Milicent's own designs, including *Buds and Bells* and *Sun Lit*. In 1932 Taplin married Joe Winfield and in 1935 started to teach part time at the local art schools. She was now a member of the Society of Industrial Artists and a member of the National Council of the Society during WWII. She was now teaching full time at the Stoke School of Art and one day at the Burslem School of Art, but remained a design consultant at Wedgwood. After the War she returned to Wedgwood, becoming more involved in over-glaze lithographic transfer design and in 1955 was appointed head of the Wedgwood school of freehand paintresses. In 1957 *Strawberry Hill*, a pattern designed by Taplin and Victor Skellern (q.v.) won the Design of the Year award from the Council of Industrial Design. She retired in 1962, having been at Wedgwood for thirty-four years.

Tasker, Robert, active c. 1797–1815

Artist gilder at Chamberlain Worcester Porcelain. He is listed in the factory records as Mr Tasker. He would therefore have been in charge of one of the gilding decorating departments,

Tatler, Elijah, 1832–76

Flower and bird painter, son of the flower painter Thomas (q.v.). Elijah was apprenticed at Minton *c.* 1831 then employed by Spode, but was at Coalport during the 1840s, painting birds and floral designs. Around 1848 he emigrated to America, where he worked as chief decorator for Charles Cartlidge & Co. of Brooklyn, New York. A doorplate he painted with a view of New York harbour was exhibited in the American Porcelain 1770–1920 Exhibition and in 1989 in the Metropolitan Museum of Art, New York. Tatler returned to England soon after 1850 and stayed until after the American Civil War, then went back to the United States, where Taylor & Davis at Trenton employed him as a decorator. By 1876 he had established his own decorating workshop in Trenton, New Jersey, which closed a couple of years after his death but was reopened by his son William, trading as W.H. Tatler Decorating Co.

Tatler, Thomas, 1797–1873

Flower painter, son of Joseph Tatler, a potter of Stoke-upon-Trent and shown in the Minton wages book from 1831 to 1838. He married Hannah Malkin in August 1818 and they lived at Oak Hill, Penkhull, Stoke-upon-Trent, close to Minton. He painted excellent fruit and floral studies that are often signed T. Tatler

Tatlow, Joseph, active c. 1800

Painter and gilder, apprentice at the Derby Nottingham Road pottery. He was employed at the Pinxton Pottery, working with William Billingsley (q.v.) and he is known for excellent arabesque gilding borders. It is more than possible that he became an outside decorator in one of the London establishments.

Tatlow, Thomas, active c. 1800

Artist, flower and shell painter, brother to Joseph (q.v.) and an apprentice at Osmaston Road, Derby pottery and later at Nottingham Road. He was an expert fisherman who painted fine oil paintings of fish subjects. Tatlow kept the pub The Seven Stars on the north side of St Mary's Bridge, Derby, which became a favourite haunt for his artist colleagues. The pub had the added advantage of a bowling green, and on the summerhouse wall was a view of Darley Grove, painted by William Corden (q.v.).

Tatton, Mabel, 1885–1973

Paintress who joined Wedgwood in 1907. She had already had experience working at both Minton. In 1914 she left to study at the Hornsea College, Middlesex but by 1920 had returned to Wedgwood to take over charge of the painting and enamelling departments from her sister Ethel. Mabel signed with a monogram some of her work, which was exhibited at the Exposition Universelle, Paris of 1925. She married a Mr Wilder and left the company around 1928.

Taylor, Harry, active 1897–1900

Fruit and flower painter at Doulton who painted in a unique, rich style often outlined or overlaid with gold, and was a pioneer in the field of photo-lithography.

Taylor, W. Howson, 1876–1935

Designer and potter who created *Ruskin Ware*. His father Edward Richard was for a time Headmaster of the Central School of Art, Birmingham and also a member of a potting family from Hanley, Staffordshire. He was a friend of William Morris and Edward Burne-Jones, believing and teaching their ideals. Taylor spent his childhood in and around kilns and potters' wheels making pottery, encouraged by his father and his sister Nellie. He was determined to become a successful art potter, deploring the mechanical methods of production that were becoming more and more mainstream in the potting industry of 1904. He was fascinated with the effect of different glazes on the simple, oriental-shaped pots he produced and became known for the lustre, flambé and soufflé high-fired glazes that characterise his work. He exhibited at the International Exhibition in St Louis, where his ability was recognised, followed two years later by exhibition in Milan and in 1908 in London. Taylor was influenced by the work of Chinese potters. He worked in an old malt house in Smethwick, using local clay. He was inspired by the principles of John Ruskin and was an avid supporter of the Arts and Crafts movement. From 1898–1935, fourteen different marks have been found on his wares, which with the Ruskin family's approval have became known as *Ruskin*. Taylor was a secretive man and all the recipes he created were never found after his death.

Taylor, William, born c. 1828

Flower painter active at the Worcester Pottery from 1845 to1870 and known for painting Australian floral and fern designs.

Theaker, Harry, RBA, A.R.C.A., born 1873

Painter of figure subjects, son of George (1835–1903),

who was headmaster of the Wedgwood Institute, 1869–02. Harry trained at the Wedgwood Institute, Burslem. He was a fine painter of classical subjects and was employed by the Doulton, before becoming an art teacher. Theaker succeeded Percival Gaskell as Principal of the Regent Street, Polytechnic School of Art, London. Two of his watercolours, *Corney Beach* and *Chiswick and The Thames at Mortlake*, were shown at the Century Exhibition in Hanley, Stoke-on-Trent in 1953.

Thompson, Albert, active 1850s–1903

Artist gilder first employed at Coalport, then Copeland. By the 1900s his eyesight was failing and he wore two pairs of spectacles, but was still capable of really fine, skilled work. He went to the pub every day for his tot of whisky and was a really popular character in the works.

Thorley, John, born 1860

Artist and portrait painter, son of Joseph and father of Joseph Palin (q.v.). He was an apprentice at the Ridgway factory under his father and became an engraver and designer until 1892, when he left the ceramic industry and became a successful artist.

Thorley, Joseph 1821–1883

Landscape painter employed at Minton whose work was shown at the Exposition Universelle, Paris 1867. A Mr J. Thorley is reported in the *Art Journal* of 1864 as inventing ceramic crayon drawings, which were shown at the South Staffordshire Industrial Exhibition by a Mr F.J. Emery. The ceramic crayons were, however, not approved, being judged only suitable for amateur painting classes. Whether this is the same painter is not known. He is recorded in the 1881 census as a landscape artist (painter) living at 8 King's Street, Stoke-upon-Trent with his son John (q.v.), also listed as a landscape artist.

Thorley, Joseph Palin, 1892–1987

Painter designer and art director born in Stoke-upon-Trent, son of John Thorley (q.v.), who trained at the Hanley School of Art. In 1906 he became an apprentice in the painting department at Wedgwood under James Hodgkiss (q.v.), also practising the art of pâte-sur-pâte decoration. He spent three days a week at the factory and three days at art school. After serving in WWI with the South Staffordshire Regiment he returned to Wedgwood for a short period, before joining the Simpson Pottery Co., Soho Works in Cobridge, Hanley, where he designed the *Victoria* shape. By 1920, Thorley was employed as designer and manager of the decorating department at the New Chelsea Porcelain Co. and four years later as Art Director for Charles Allerton & Sons, Longton, where he used his own backstamp, *Thorley Ware*.

The family then emigrated to America, where he became Art Director for the American China Corporation, also designing for Taylor Smith & Taylor and noted for designing the E shape for the Hall company in East Liverpool in the early 1940s.

He had now established a reputation as a fine designer and author, receiving an Honorary Doctorate from the University of West Virginia. By 1929 he was described as the internationally known Ceramist and Director of the University of Pittsburgh Ceramics Department. In 1939 Thorley moved to Williamsburg and set up a pottery, establishing a retail business selling to gift shops and department stores in Washington DC, New York and Boston, whilst still designing for the Colonial Williamsburg factory.

Till, Thomas, 1782–1858

Artist gilder of raised and chased work first employed at Derby but moved to Minton by 1830, becoming one of their principle gilders.

Tinworth, George, 1843–1913

Modeller born near Camberwell Gate, Lambeth, son of a London wheelwright. He initially worked for his father, whilst studying modelling in the evenings at the Lambeth School of Art. When his father died he was unable to continue the business and was offered thirty shillings a week to work at the Doulton Lambeth Pottery. He was one of the first artists from the Lambeth School of Art to be associated with Doulton's Art Studio. He began by touching up old moulds but soon progressed to sculpting medallions in terracotta and realistic heads. He entered the Royal Academy Schools in late 1864, where in 1867 he won a silver medal. He exhibited at the Academy in 1866. George came from a religious family and his work shows this influence. John Sparkes (q.v.) described his work: 'He prefers the clay soft from the thrower's wheel, so soft as to be too tender to handle. His delight is a spiral band or ornamental ribbon, sometimes deeply inter-digitated, or elaborately frilled. The ornament flies over the surface in wild luxuriance; bosses, belts, or bands or carve moulding keep this wild growth to its work, put it all in its place, and subject it to its use. No two pots are alike and, although he has done many thousands, all different, he will still produce them in endless variety out of the same materials. Of course no one could produce such ever-new combinations unless he had invention.'

Tinworth was known for his terracotta panel illustrations of Biblical scenes, although he did model humorous figures and mice. In 1883 an exhibition devoted to his work was held in London at the Conduit Gallery, organised by Henry Doulton and accompanied by a book *The Critical Essay on the Life and Works of George Tinworth*. It was visited by the Prince and Princess of Wales, who were most impressed, and the exhibition by popular request remained open longer than was first intended. On 21 October 1899 *The Pottery Gazette and Glass Trade Review* reported that the Bishop of Rochester unveiled and dedicated a reredos in the chapel of St Thomas Hospital to the late Sir Henry Doulton designed by George Tinworth and executed in terracotta. He stayed with Doulton until his death, marking his work with a GT monogram.

Tipping, Edward, active 1880s

Artist gilder trained at Worcester, who may then have then moved to Copeland. However, it is his work at Doulton that achieved high acclaim as he gilded many of their exhibition pieces.

Tittensor, Harry R.I., 1887–1942

Artist, figure painter and art teacher, son of Jarvis Tittensor, a potter, and Hannah Cliffe. He trained at the Burslem School of Art and was apprenticed to Doulton. He painted vases with classical, literary and genre subjects and assisted in the artistic development of Holbein and Titanian wares. He left Doulton in 1925 but continued to teach at local art schools, becoming Master in Charge from 1932 to 1934 at the Stoke School of Art and was known as a fine teacher who inspired his students to work hard and to achieve their potential. Tittensor was commissioned by the London North Eastern Railway to paint scenes that could be seen when travelling on their railway. These were engraved and two scenes were shown in each carriage of the trains. His work was exhibited at the Fine Art Society, London.

Toft, Albert, 1862–1949

Modeller born in Birmingham, eldest son of Charles (q.v.). He was an apprentice at Wedgwood and studied at the Hanley and Newcastle-under-Lyme Schools of Art. He then spent two years at the Royal College of Art studying under Professor Lanteri. Albert exhibited sculpture from 1885 to1893 at the Royal Academy and Suffolk Street Gallery, London. He designed Christmas cards and possibly did some book illustration. He established his studio in London, and became a well-known sculptor.

Toft, Alphonsus, 1796–1850

Engraver who lived at Tinkersclough, Shelton, Staffordshire. He had eleven children, the sons continuing the engraving establishment after his death.

Toft, Charles, 1833–1909

Modeller born in Hanley, Stoke-on-Trent, son of Alpohonsus (q.v.). He trained at the Stoke-upon-Trent Art School in the 1850s and at Minton under Solon (q.v.), working on inlaid wares. By 1853 the family had moved to Worcester, where he was employed by Kerr & Binns modelling figures and busts for their Parian ware range. Charles then moved to become one of the chief modellers at Elkingtons in Birmingham, also teaching at the Birmingham School of Art in the late 1860s. By 1877 he was chief modeller at Wedgwood. His vase *War and Peace* was exhibited at the Exposition Universelle, Paris of 1878. In 1889, Toft established his own small pottery, taking over the Swan Works, Stoke-on-Trent. He made rustic wares including earthenwares with lacy decoration in brown and white slip. In 1881 he was living at 171 Howard Place, Stoke-on-Trent with his wife, four children and a servant, described as an artist modeller potter.

Tomlinson, Reginald Robert, OBE, 1885–1978

Artist and art director trained at the Royal College of Art, studying etching under Sir Frank Short. He first found employment with Moore Bros, Longton but in 1913 he was appointed Art Director of the Crown Staffordshire Porcelain Company in Fenton, remaining until 1919. He is better known as an art teacher from 1925 to1951. He became Principal of the Cheltenham School of Art and Senior Inspector of Art to the London County Council. He was a member of the Royal Society of British Artists.

Tooth, George, active 1900s

Painter affectionately known as Georgie employed at the George Jones Crescent Pottery, Stoke-upon-Trent. He and Art Director Charles Birbeck (q.v.) were old school friends. Georgie was known for landscapes but was a painter capable of executing all subjects with equal skill.

Tooth, Henry, 1842–1918

Designer and art potter born in Newport Pagnall, Buckinghamshire and apprenticed to a butcher. He became a theatrical scenery painter in London in the 1860s and then went to live on the Isle of Wight, working as a domestic and ecclesiastical decorator and painting on stained glass. Christopher Dresser (q.v.) advised him to become an art potter, and Tooth went to T.G. Green & Co. to learn the intricacies of this craft. In 1879 he joined the Linthorpe Pottery as manager on Christopher Dresser's recommendation. He and H. Venables, manager of the clay department, successfully reorganised production and designed glaze effects. Meanwhile he worked as a freelance artist in Middlesbrough. In 1882 he left Linthorpe to start the Bretby Art Studio with William Ault but after five years William left to start his own business from 1887. Henry ran a successful business alone, trading as Henry Tooth & Co. Bretby Art Pottery, Woodville, near Burton-on-Trent, Derbyshire.

Townshend, Henry Charles, 1810–90

Modeller born in Taunton, Somerset who initially trained as a surgeon. In 1847 he helped design the *Hop Story* jug at Minton, commissioned by Henry Cole (q.v.) and another jug depicting coaching and rail travel. His Parian figures included the infant *Neptune*, which was shown at the Great Exhibition of 1851. He was a colleague of Sir Henry Cole and was involved with the Summerly Art Manufactures design and production.

Trowell, Edwin, born 1869

Landscape and flower painter, son of James, a railway engine fitter. He worked at the Osmaston Road, Derby 1882–92 and is named in the Derby pattern books with entries such as Pattern number 2584, Cambridge dessert plate, landscape centre by Trowell. He left the ceramic industry in 1892. His work can be seen at the Derby Museum.

Turner, Samuel, 1826–94

Flower painter apprenticed at Minton around 1836 who probably stayed there all his working life, as a Samuel Turner is still listed in the wages books as late as the early 1880s. In the 1881 census he is shown as a china decorator living at 50 Liverpool Road, Stoke-upon-Trent, Staffordshire.

Unwin, Ralph, active 1770–1812

Miniature landscape painter and enameller. In 1770 he joined the Chelsea decorating studios run by Wedgwood as a painter of landscapes on their Frog Service, and also on part of the Husk Service for Catherine II. He exhibited thirty-three works at the Royal Academy, many of which were miniatures.

Ushingham, S. Arthur, active 1900s

Artist, figure and portrait painter first at the Pinder Bourne Pottery and then joined Doulton, where he worked on figures and portrait heads. He taught at the local art school but after 1922 left to start a new career as a society portrait painter and became very successful.

Vidal, S. Jorl, active 1790

Flower painter who exhibited at the Royal Academy 1790–92, and lived in London at 1 Grosvenor Row, near the Bun House, Chelsea. He sent samples of his paintings to Mr Duesbury (q.v.) at Derby; although he had never painted china in Britain he claimed experience in the art and arranged to paint in 1795.

Vivien, N., active 1870s

Bird and butterfly painter at Minton. He painted a pair of vases dated 1878 that were decorated with scenes of exotic birds, cacti and butterflies. They were signed with the monogram NV and ordered by J.E. Caldwell and Co. china retailers of Philadelphia.

Voyez, Jean (John), c. 1740–91

Modeller and painter who served an apprenticeship as a watchmaker and enameller, qualifying in 1766 as a master craftsman. He came to London about 1767 to work for Philip Rundall, the jeweller, where he enamelled watches, vinaigrette bottles and chatelaines with a peacock tail decoration, which was exhibited at the Free Society of Arts. Vovez was working for the Adam Brothers when Wedgwood discovered him in 1768 and took him to the Brick House works, Burslem where he had his own studio. Although a brilliant craftsman he drank too much and was totally untrustworthy. He arrived at Etruria in July 1786 but by January 1769 had been found guilty of stealing moulds of clay from Wedgwood, for which he was sentenced to a whipping and three months imprisonment.

Although copies of Voyez's Wedgwood seals and cameos were being sold in Birmingham and Wedgwood could have taken legal action, they were advised the action would be unlikely to succeed. On his release in 1769 Voyez went to Humphrey Palmer, a rival manufacturer. Next he went into partnership with T. Hales, a potter in Cobridge, but in 1772 he started a business of his own and in 1773 issued a catalogue of cameos and intaglios, describing himself as a member of the Society of Arts. In 1791 he took his wife and child to London and disappeared. He may have done freelance work in London, even have joined the sculptor and glass medallion maker James Tassie (1725–1799), but it is more than likely he had to leave the country to escape his debtors.

Voysey, Charles Francis Annesley, 1857–1941

Architect and designer born at Hessle, near Kingston-upon-Hull, son of the clergyman Rev Charles Voysey who founded the Theistic Church but was defrocked because of his views on the church's teaching on Hellfire. Voysey was educated at Dulwich College, and then became articled to the architect J.P. Seddon. He became well known as a designer of wallpapers, textiles and tiles, his designs recognised for their freedom and sympathetic subject matter. Voysey designed tiles for Pilkingtons, Maw & Co. and Wedgwood. His work was exhibited at the Arts and Crafts Exhibitions of 1896 and 1903 and at the Glasgow Exhibition of 1901. In 1915 he became chief designer to the Liquor Control Board. He joined the Art Workers' Guild in 1884, and became Master in 1924. In 1936 Voysey became one of the first Royal Designers for Industry, and the Royal Institute of British Architects awarded him a gold medal in 1940.

Tile design c. 1899 by C. Voysey

Vyse, Charles, 1887–1927

Engraver apprenticed to Heath & Baddaley of Burslem, Staffordshire, one of the leading engraving businesses in North Staffordshire. He had the ability to create a copper plate of great detail from the designer's pattern, and was responsible for many of Doulton's fine engravings.

Vyse, Charles H., born 1856

Painter engraver, son of Charles Vyse, a licensed victualler. His monogram CV has been found with the backstamp of W.P. & G. Phillips on Minton pieces.

Vyse, Charles H., ARCA, RBS, active 1900s

Sculptor and modeller trained at the Hanley Art School 1894–1905, where he was awarded a gold medal and a National Scholarship to the Royal School of Art. He modelled the figure *Darling* for Doulton.

Wadsworth, John William, 1879–1955

Art Director, designer and watercolour artist born in Macclesfield, son of a cabinetmaker. He was apprenticed to the local silk mill and trained at the local art school and at the Stockport Art School, where his designs for patterns on silk won him prizes both locally and in national competitions. He was awarded a scholarship to the Royal School of Art in 1898, from where he won a travelling scholarship to France. His designs were influenced by the work of Walter Crane and W.R. Lethaby. An ornamental metalwork foundry first employed him but he soon found his true métier in ceramics. After joining Minton c. 1900 he became assistant art director to Leon Solon (q.v.) and they designed the Secessionist Ware range about 1902. Wadsworth succeeded Solon as Art Director in 1909 until 1914. In 1915 he became Art Director at the Worcester Royal Porcelain Co. and when the company hit financial problems in 1930 the receiver put him in charge. He was commissioned by Maddock, who were makers of graniteware, to design especially for the American market. In 1930 he returned to Stoke-on-Trent, setting up a business as a consultant designer. In 1935 he was appointed Art Director at Minton. He designed *Haddon Hall* tableware and in 1952 the *Queen's Vase*, the gift of the Potters' Federation on the occasion of Her Majesty's Coronation.

Wale, John Porter, 1860–1920

Flower, and animal painter born in Worcester, the son of a cordwainer. He studied at the Worcester School of Art and was employed at Royal Worcester from 1874 to 1877. He moved to the Osmaston Road, Derby pottery, lodging with Mr and Mrs Moffat at 4 Oxford Street, Litchurch, Derby. He became known for painting flowers, cottages, gardens and small animals. Wale continued his art studies at the Derby School of Art in the evenings. There are many entries under his name in the Derby pattern books: for example, 'pattern number 2218, Cambridge dessert plate, turckini flowers in enamels, gossamer in white gold by Wale'. He became head of the painting room at Osmaston Road until 1919. He exhibited at the Royal Watercolourists Society and was a member of the Derby Sketching Club.

Walklett, Frederick Thomas, born 1863

Flower painter trained at the Wedgwood Institute, Burslem who won the silver medal for flower painting in 1889. He was employed at Doulton and was an artist able to paint flowers and landscapes with equal ability. He signed his work.

vase, factory unknown, painted and initialed by Fred Walklate

Wall, Peter, ARCA, DDesARCA, MSIA, born 1926

Artist, designer and art director, he studied at the Burslem School of Art, then at the Wimbledon Art School. In 1951 his designs won a silver medal at the Festival of Britain. In 1952 he was appointed to the Wedgwood Art Department, becoming Deputy Art Director in 1954 and then Design Manager. He stayed with the company for sixteen years designing nursery ware and is known for the patterns *Hathaway Rose*, *Woodbury* and *Penhurst*. In 1968 he left the ceramics industry to become Head of the School of Ceramics at Birmingham Polytechnic. He retired in 1988.

Wallace, Robert, active 1864–1900

Artist gilder apprenticed at Copeland on 7 January 1864. His fine jewelling on pieces of the *Midsummer Nights Dream* service, painted by Samuel Alcock (q.v.), was exhibited at the Exposition Universelle, Paris of 1889. Wallace spent all his working life at Copeland, becoming Decorating Manager in the 1900s. At the celebrations of 150 years' trading at the Spode works, he was presented with a gift. In his speech he spoke of his training at the local art school and how he had studied art from Mr Ronald Copeland's library, for which he was most grateful. He said that nothing was produced easily and quickly but 1930 had been a good year, as by then the relationship between men and management was better. He congratulated Mr Hewitt on the modernisation of the factory. Wallace helped many of the artists and gilders, encouraging them to study at the local art schools.

Wareham, Joseph, 1783–1874

Flower, fruit and bird painter born in Stoke-on-Trent, and apprenticed at the New Hall Works, Longton, Staffordshire. He then worked at the Don Pottery, Yorkshire and was also employed by the London retailer Mortlock. Wareham returned to Stoke, joining Minton c. 1846-1849, becoming one of their principal artists.

It is said he moved his family and possessions from London by canal boat, landing at Ebbens Wharf, Stoke-on-Trent. He painted flowers, fruit and birds in both Dresden and Sèvres style on Minton's finest dessert services. Wareham was a fine singer, often singing as he worked. He boasted he had decorated for all the crowned heads of Europe. So far no signed pieces have been found. He had a son Joseph, who was also a china painter.

Watson, William, active c. 1830

Artist gilder, at the Derby factory. He worked in gold, drawing small figures or landscapes. Some of his work was unconventional and achieved by using the end of his paint brush. He worked for a short time at a pottery in Burton-on-Trent and from there went to the Potteries. He was a strange character, preferring to eat his lunch in a tree. He met an untimely end, being found dead in a ditch.

Watt, Linnie, active c. 1880

Figure paintress who studied at the Lambeth School of Art from 1874 and worked at the Doulton Lambeth Studio 1875-1890, specialising in rustic scenes and figures. John Sparkes (q.v.) described her work: 'Miss Linnie Watt had a distinguished gift for conveying the impression of a picturesque scene with rustic figures in excellent colour and with artistic breadth of effect, quite admirable in its truth. Her works will speak for themselves to every artist who sees them…'. Watt's work was exhibited at the Paris Exposition Universelle in 1878 and the Philadelphia Exhibition of 1876. She was a fine artist and her work was chosen for exhibition at the Royal Academy from 1877 to 1901, Dudley Art Gallery, Dowdeswell Gallery, Glasgow Institute of Fine Art, Manchester City Art Gallery, Royal Society of

British Artists (1875-1889), Society of Women Artists and the Walker Art Gallery, Liverpool. In London in 1908 she had her own exhibition at the Dore Gallery. Linnie was awarded the Silver Medal of H.H. the Crown Prince of Germany for her painting on a plaque called *Gathering Spring Flowers*. She signed her work with either her signature L.Watt or a monogram.

Weaver, Charles, born 1862

Animal and bird painter born in Worcester the son of James (q.v.). He finished his apprenticeship at Copeland in 1886. Arthur Perry (q.v.) said he never achieved the same artistic skill as his famous father, but was a versatile artist; Charles painted birds and Japanese subjects after the style of his father. However, his painting of cattle and landscapes shows his own artistic skill. He retired early due to ill health.

Weaver, James, died 1877

Bird painter at Copeland. He is shown in their Special Order books 1869-1877 as painting grasses, insects and later bird studies. His work was shown on the Copeland's exhibits at the Great Exhibition of 1851. It is thought he was at Copeland before going to the Worcester Royal Porcelain Co. c. 1853 and then returning to the Potteries. He was one of the premier artists of this time, painting for the London International Exhibitions of 1871 and 1872. His bird paintings influenced by both the Chinese and Japanese are distinctive, true to nature and have the appearance of being in flight. Often his designs have flies and grasses to show birds in their natural habitat, and are jewelled and superbly gilded. Unfortunately very few of the entries in the Copeland Special Order reference books show pattern numbers, but they record that the artist gilders Owen and Salt gilded his work. Jewitt recorded: 'Weaver, now dead (but worthily succeeded by his son), whose birds are equal to those of any other painter.'

Webber, Henry, 1754–1826

Sculptor and modeller, the son of a Swiss sculptor, who studied at the Royal Academy School, London, winning both silver and gold medals for his work. He was a pupil of J. Bacon the elder and exhibited at the Royal Academy from 1773 to 1779. In 1784 Sir Joshua Reynolds and Sir William Chambers recommended his work and talent

Bone china Copeland Belinda shaped dessert service plate portraying a different bird attributed to Charles Weaver

to Josiah Wedgwood, and he was given a seven-year agreement with the pottery. In 1785 he was appointed head of the ornamental department on a salary of £252 a year. In 1787 he accompanied John Flaxman and John, Wedgwood's eldest son, on a visit to Rome, acting in the dual capacity of John's guardian and scout for new sculptors needed for Wedgwood's basalt and Jaspar ware. They sought out artists and commissioned them to create new designs. He modelled many figures, for example, *Apollo and Daphne*, used to decorate Wedgwood bough pots. Although described as a modeller, examples of his work show great talent and perhaps the term sculptor is more appropriate. Webber left in 1795, for London, where he worked on the monument to David Garrick in Westminster Abbey, He died on 7 August 1826 at 11 Cross Street, Bedford Square, London. Josiah Wedgwood was one of the executers of his will.

Webster, Eric, active c. 1900

Painter trained at Doulton under Herbert Betteley, known for painting all subjects. He was of importance as one of the first artists to paint Royal Doulton figures, giving them life and character. In 1925 he became head of the animal painting shop, where he helped to train many young artists. He painted the first championship dog model *Lucky Star of Ware*.

Webster, Moses, 1792–1870

Flower painter born at Becket Well Lane, Derby, son of Robert and Elizabeth (née Bentley). He was apprenticed as a flower painter at Derby and was at Worcester 1814-1816, where he had some instruction from Thomas Baxter's School of Art. Mr Binns said of him that 'his roses had a dashed and faded appearance but that his groups were tastefully arranged'. He then joined Thomas Martin Randall from 1819 to 1822 at the Randell & Robins outside decorating establishment in London, painting on white Sèvres ware. In 1818 some of his work was exhibited in London. Webster returned to Derby and in 1825 was painting the John Trotter Service. The dessert plates were designed with five dark panels of chrome green and a central floral decoration. He ended his working career with Robins & Randall and his work there is often seen on Nantgarw pieces. His landscape painting on Grainger Ware at Worcester was superb, usually drawn in pencil and depicting gentlemen's country estates, and many lithographed. In 1825 Webster became a drawing master, taking over the position on John Keys death, teaching both flower and landscape drawing.

An advertisement in *The Derby Mercury* of 13 July 1825 reported that his work could be seen at the *Mercury* and *Reporter* offices and at Mr Moseley's Corn market. He will always be remembered for his superb floral painting on china, although he last painted on china thirty years before he died, preferring to paint with watercolour and to teach. He was a premier artist whose unique painting skills were sought by both outside decorating establishments and leading potteries. When at Derby a colleague wrote:

'When Moses composes
His posies of roses
Of sweeter he can't them compose
No flower else that grows,
Can compare with the rose;
If you doubt it, consult your nose'

Wells, Luke (Senior), active 1850s

Animal painter employed at Kerr & Binns, Worcester, known especially for painting dogs.

Wells, Luke (Junior), active 1860s

Painter of animals and figures employed at Worcester from 1860 to 1880. His style of painting was influenced by the work of Watteau (q.v.).

Whalley, active 1880s–1900s

Flower painter at Copeland, one of the premier artists of this period He painted mainly on prestige dessert services, and tea wares. His floral studies used a combination of wild flowers and grasses, but he also painted roses and designed hanging baskets of flowers, which became popular. His work was gilded by the finest gilders, and is usually seen on the1/over series of pattern numbers from 1/5943. The latest entry is a tea service of a rose pattern number R 2056, painted in 1904.

Wheeldon, William, born 1789

Flower painter at Derby, who went to Mansfield in January 1801 to join his uncle William Billingsley in his enamelling business. He returned to Derby and was apprenticed to Duesbury (q.v.) and Kean. He continued to work there until 1823 when he left to run a retail business in Bridge Street, Derby. Later his business interests included publican malster, corn and flour dealer. Wheeldon was a friend of Haslem (q.v.) and knew many of the Derby artists. He was often seen at the Lamb Inn in St Alkmund's churchyard and loved to tell of his time at Derby and of the talents of his uncle.

Whittacker, George (Senior), active c. 1860–1880

Painter,and gilder at Minton who specialising in cupids, figures and cloisonné decoration. His work with Albert Wright (q.v.) was shown at the Vienna Exhibition of

1873 and at other exhibitions. There is a Whittacker (no initial), who may have been his son, in the Minton pattern books of September 1887, shown as painting a centre to pattern number G 6211.

Whitaker, John, 1804–1874

Modeller, and figure maker, the son of William and grandson of Richard, also a modeller. He was apprenticed in 1818 at the Nottingham Road, Derby pottery. In 1830 he succeeded S. Keys (Junior, q.v.) as foreman of the figure modellers and became superintendent of the department from 1842 to 1848. A prolific modeller who, when the Nottingham Road factory closed, went to Minton. During the later years of his life he worked on models similar to those of Derby.

Whitaker, John (the younger), 1813–1871

Painter and designer, the second son of John and Anne Whitaker. He was taught to paint at Derby under Moses Webster (q.v.) but went to London, eventually settling in Manchester, where he became a designer of fabrics.

White, George, 1885–1912

Figure and portrait painter, who trained at the South Kensington and Lambeth Art Schools and became chief painter of figure subjects at Doulton. His portraits conveyed the spirit and personality of his subjects. His work was influenced by D.G. Rossetti, Millais and Watteau (q.v.). Some of the subjects he painted on vases included *Romeo and Juliet*, *Cupid and Psyche*, *Sleeping Beauty* and *Feeding the Swans*. He also painted portraits on china of the Doulton family, including Sir Henry and his brother James. He may have undertaken freelance commissions as his painting has been found on unmarked vases.

Wilcox, Ralph, active 1820s

Painter, who served his apprenticeship at the Philip Christian Pottery, Shaw Road, Liverpool and painted for Worcester and Wedgwood.

Wilcox, Sarah, active 1820s

The daughter of Thomas Frye of Bow, a paintress of great talent. She and her husband Ralph painted part of Wedgwood's Queen Catherine Service. He painted some of the borders and she painted landscapes.

Wilkes, Charles, 1864–1957

Modeller, born in West Park, Stoke-on-Trent, son of Charles, a pottery manager in Fenton, who trained at the Burslem School of Art. He joined Burgess & Leigh, eventually becoming Head Modeller. His designs kept pace with the changing fashions and art movements throughout the whole of his long life. He and Frederick Rhead (q.v.) set up a small pottery producing ornamental wares and wall masks, but it failed.

Williams, Frederick Edward, active 1880s

Painter and possibly designer born in Worcester but by 1891 employed at Royal Crown Derby. He was a prolific artist and there are many entries under his name in the Derby pattern books.

Williams, Joseph, active c. 1840–1870

Animal and landscape painter employed at the Kerr and Binns, Worcester factory. He copied the work of masters such as Turner (q.v.) and Myles Birket Foster (q.v.) onto the ceramic surface, which have been said to be as good as the originals. Some of his work is signed J. Williams.

Willems, Joseph, 1715–1766

Modeller, born in Brussels but living in London in 1748, his name is in the Chelsea rate books. The Chelsea Pottery employed him to model figures 1749–1766. He exhibited terracotta models at the Society of Arts 1760–1766. He left England in 1766 to take up a position at the Academy in Tournai, but his style continued to influence many of the Chelsea and Derby productions. He is known for his landscape painting but was capable of painting all subjects with equal skill.

Wilson, Samuel Seabridge, 1852–1909

Fish, and game painter, born in Dresden, Stoke-on-Trent, who became the premier painter at Doulton from 1880 to 1909. He created designs of all subjects but notably animals, fish and game in their natural surroundings. His designs and paintings were very popular in America. Wilson painted the *Diana Vase* decorated with red grouse and ptarmigan for the World's Columbian Exposition, Chicago of 1893. In 1894 Princess Louise, Queen Victoria's daughter, ordered a service, which she presented to her mother to celebrate her Diamond Jubilee. In 1881 the family were living at 50 Price Street, Burslem, Staffordshire and he is described as an artist on pottery.

Wilson, Scottie, 1889–1972

Landscape artist and designer, born in Glasgow who had little formal education. He began to draw birds, flowers, trees and streams with salvaged gold nibs from fountain pens using closely hatched black lines and with coloured crayons. He designed plates for the Royal Worcester Factory and tapestries for the Aubusson factory; also a mural for a bank in Zurich. In 1930 he went to Canada and opened a junk shop in Toronto.

Winkle, Arthur, active 1900s

Landscape and bird painter, a talented artist: signed examples of landscape and birds of prey painting have been found on Cauldon China, and he also painted birds and flowers for the Crown Staffordshire Pottery around 1903.

Winkle, Kathie, born 1932

Designer, and paintress, born in Penkhull, Stoke-upon-Trent, she had little formal art training. After she left school she was employed by Shorter & Co. as a paintress.

Bone china Cauldon small vase painted and signed by A. Winkle

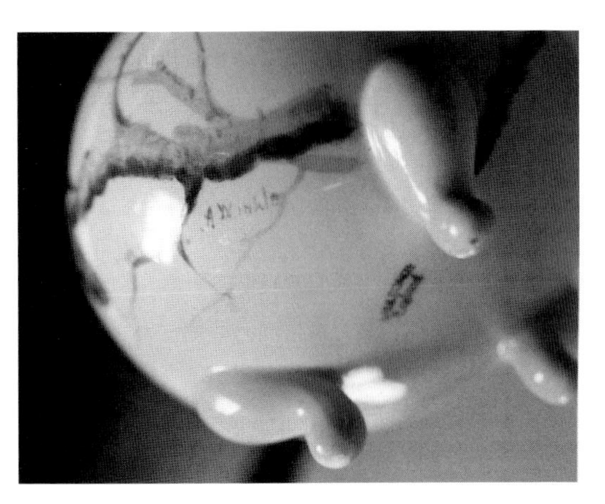

In 1950 she went to James Broadhurst & Sons, who made earthenware for the lower end of the market and had gained a reputation for low-cost ware with bright patterns that was delivered on time. Kathie worked on printed and hand-coloured patterns and started to design for the company in 1958.Her designs were successful and by 1964 the patterns *Mandalay* and *Lagoon* were issued with the backstamp *A Kathie Winkle Design*. In 1969 she designed the Riviera shape and Kofti teapot, which were modelled by Stan Edge. By the 1970s Broadhursts had introduced a studio range of ware called Sandstone for which Kathie designed a range of patterns: *Snowden, Moorland, Hillside, Morning Glory and Country Lane.*

She then moved into quality control for the company until 1992, when she retired.

Wise, William, 1845–1889

Artist,and designer, born in Hanover Square, London, and trained as a painter on a national scholarship at the Government School of Design, South Kensington, London. He worked in the studio of F.W. Moody and was involved in the decorative panels at the South Kensington Museum. Wise was employed by Minton 1871-1775, first at their art pottery in London then in Stoke-on-Trent, where he was influenced by Leon Arnoux (q.v.). He worked on the designs for the Minton tiles for the Victoria and Albert lecture theatre staircase. By 1877 he was a freelance designer, and in 1878 his work was exhibited at the Exposition Universelle, Paris. Wise's sources for design included Birket Foster (q.v.) and Walter Crane (q.v.).He designed tiles with animal and farm scenes, also a series depicting village life. He taught drawing in the evening, possibly at Stoke School of Art.

Wise married twice and had eight children. In 1881 the family were living at 28 Wilson Street, Stoke-on-Trent and in the census he is described as an artist in pottery. Some Minton tiles previously thought to have been designed by him are in fact the work of L.T. Swetnam (q.v.) who succeeded him.

Withers, Edward, active 1770s

Flower painter first employed at the Chelsea pottery, then at Derby 1770-1780. He was one of the first of the formal flower painters, painting floral studies with great accuracy. When there was no work for him at Derby, he left for Staffordshire, thence to Birmingham, where he painted Japan patterns, and from there to London. In 1789 he returned to Derby. According to Haslem, he was often in trouble with the management and is known to have headed a list of painters opposed to the employment of women. It is thought he formed the 'Loyal Club', whose members gave support and help to fellow painters and work people in need.

Edward Withers was a sociable and convivial character and became President of the Derby Painters Club, whose members held their meetings in a pub, and drank from the Rodney jug that he had painted. The jug was made to commemorate Admiral Rodney's victory in 1782 and was sold for £117.12s.

Withers' flower painting, particularly of roses, was simple when compared to that of Billingsley (q.v.) or Moses (q.v.), but the flower remained conventional and this very simplicity created an old-world charm, which characterised all his work. He died a pauper, but his fellow workers and friends paid for his funeral and burial.

Wood, Edwin, 1898–1938

Flower painter trained at Crown Derby. He was next employed at Wedgwood but in 1927 went to Doulton. He painted small groups of flowers in the Chelsea style and signed his work.

Wood, Enoch, 1759–1840

Modeller and pottery manufacturer, who trained with William Caddick of Liverpool, but was apprenticed to Humphrey Palmer of Hanley, Staffordshire. He was a modeller of great talent, who became a partner with Ralph Wood II, making earthenware, coloured bodies, seals and ciphers. He modelled many famous people, for example, Handel, and many classical groups and figure subjects. Some of his work is signed.

Wood, Isaac, 1792–1832

Modeller,who came from Burslem in Staffordshire, to Nantgarw to work for William Billlingsley (q.v.). He was the chief modeller, creating shapes for all types of ware with great skill. Wood went with Billingsley to Swansea and returned with him to Nantgarw. He became works manger at the Bevington Pottery, Swansea 1817–1821, where he designed a ram impressed with the factory mark and the incised initials 'IW', which is now in the Victoria & Albert Museum collection. His last post was works manager at the Cambrian pottery.

Woodhouse, William, active 1850s

Heraldic and crest painter at Minton, thought to have been their premier heraldic artist at this time.

Woodings, Norman, born 1902

Flower, fruit and bird painter apprenticed in 1916 under R. Allen (q.v.) at Doulton, where he stayed until 1967. He is remembered for the new styles and colours which he painted on Doulton figures, but also painted seascapes.

Woodman, Walter Stanley, ARCA, NRD, active 1930s

Artist painter trained at the Macclesfield School of Art in Derbyshire, where he later taught, and at the Royal College of Art, London. Woodman joined Minton and became their Art Director, reviving old styles of majolica glazes. He did not respond to the styles of the 1920s and when Reginald Haggar (q.v.) was appointed he left and joined Grindleys. In 1935 he joined Doulton as a designer and worked in modern as well as traditional styles.

Worrall, James (Jimmy), active c. 1900

Flower painter apprenticed at Copeland, where he became known for fine rose studies on all types and shapes of ware, mainly on the R pattern number series, from R 1000 to R 3000. He signed his work J. Worrall, but his signature is often difficult to find, hidden in, for example, the leaf of a rose. Much of his work was done for American china retail houses, such as Tiffany's of New York. When the fashion for highly painted, rich services ceased there was no work for him at Copeland and he joined a lithograph firm. A roma-shape, two-handled, oval centrepiece can be seen in the Spode Museum, a fine example of his artistic ability.

Copeland Stone China vase painted by J. Worrall

Worrall, William, active 1880s

Painter apprenticed at Minton from 1870 to 1876. He decorated some Minton pieces with pâte-sur-pâte decoration.

Wright, Albert H., active 1870–1906

Bird, fish and game painter, son of Arthur (q.v.), apprenticed at Minton and probably attended Stoke School of Art. A fine painter, who executed all subjects with equal skill, and signed his work.

There are many examples of his work to be found in the Minton pattern books, especially on the G pattern number range. In 1892 he was living within walking distance of the Pottery at 26 Penkhull Terrace, Stoke-upon-Trent.

Wright, Albert L., born 1845

Designer and etcher, first at the Pinder Bourne pottery and then at Doulton, where he studied under George Holdcroft (q.v.).He is described as a potters' decorator born in Hanley and in 1881 was living at Jenkins Street, Burslem.

Wright, Arthur, 1813–1887

Potters manager, colour maker and chemist born in Derby. He came to the Potteries in 1841 as a colour maker and pottery chemist at the Minton and Hollins Encaustic Tile Works, becoming Superintendent. He was the founder of the London Road Baptist Chapel, Stoke-upon-Trent and became the Librarian of the Stoke Athenaeum c. 1846. He had nine children and in 1881 the family were living at 12 Bath Street, Stoke-on-Trent.

Wright, Charles Newbold, 1866–1954

Artist gilder,and painter of flower and figure subjects, born in Derby, son of an engine smith, and educated at the Derby Grammar School. He was an apprentice at the Royal Crown Derby Porcelain works until 1887, when he went to Wedgwood. Wright became an expert in raised paste work with gold decoration and also painted for Minton and Doulton. He became chief designer for Bishop & Stonier Ltd, Hanley until 1912. From then until his retirement in 1915 he worked for F. Wilkle & Co., Fenton.

Bodley China plate painted with a Chinese duck and signed by A. Wright

He then became a farmer in Rudyard and Leigh and was one of the first to introduce Friesian Cattle to this country. But 1922 he sold his farms and returned to the pottery industry, working for Malings of Newcastle-upon-Tyne and later for Keelings of Longport, Stoke-upon-Trent. As an artist and designer he did not conform to any of the prevailing artistic fashions, having a style all his own. Wright painted landscapes and portraits in watercolour and oils. He was a versatile artist with the ability to work in many mediums. He died aged 88 at his home in Newlyn, Grindley Lane, Blythe Bridge, and Staffordshire.

Wright, Samuel, active 1850s

Inventor of the encaustic tile process, which was not for him a commercial success, but he sold the technique to Herbert Minton, who was able to exploit it. Minton also bought for £5,000 the experiments done on tile production at Copeland by Spencer Garrett. Herbert Minton employed talented artists, designers and painters on tile designs that reflected the changing fashions of the day, keeping the Minton name at the forefront of the ceramic industry.

Yale, William (Billy), born 1843

Landscape painter born in Newport, Shropshire. He trained at one of the local art schools, where he won many gold medals. Whether he served an apprenticeship at Copeland is not known, but he was employed there c. 1869–83. He is first shown as painting china vases with swallows in landscape for the London International Exhibition of 1872. In this early part of his artistic career he painted marine views and winter scenes. These paintings are much finer than the later style he adopted of painting saggar ware plaques for the Exposition Universelle, Paris of 1889. He did pattern number 1/5945 with painted views, and also eggshell cups and saucers with two views on the cup and three on the saucer. But most of his work seen today is on plaques. Yale left Copeland to set up his own studio at 82 Liverpool Road, Stoke-upon-Trent, where he displayed his paintings and his gold medals in the window. He advertised in *The Staffordshire Sentinel* around 1893 under General Trade as a Tile and Slab Decorator.

A Descriptive Account of The Potteries, published about 1895, states that 'Mr Yale acquires the pottery in its rough undecorated state from the best of the manufacturers, painting it with his own hand and submitting it to the final processes of firing and fixing in kilns attached to the premises'. Yale was a portly gentleman who in 1881 was living at Birch Villa, James Street, Stoke-on-Trent with his wife, two children and mother- and father-in-law. The large rectangular painting *The Nearest Way in Summertime*, from a sketch by T. Cresswick and R. Ansdall, shows the quality of Yale's work.

Copeland Saggar Ware plaque.
Detail of centre decoration by W. Yale

Bone China Copeland, one of a series of plates decorated with Continental views by William Yale

Yates, John, died 1821

Gilder and painter apprenticed at Derby, becoming a fine gilder and decorator of figures. His obituary in *The Derby Mercury* recorded: 'On the 10th instant, Mr John Yates of the Seven Stars, King Street, in this town. He was a worthy unassuming character and one of the artists attached to the Porcelain manufactory of this place, where he exercised his profession for upwards of half a century.'

Yeomans, Charles, 1871–1955

Landscape painter at Doulton trained under John Slater (q.v.). He became skilled at both under- and on-glaze painting of landscapes, fruit and flowers. He retired in 1936 but in November 1949 he was asked to paint again and was one of four artists presented to Her Royal Highness, Princess Elizabeth when she toured the factory. He continued to serve the company until 1951.

Young, William Weston, 1766–1847

Artist, painter, surveyor and book illustrator born in Bristol and moved to Neath in the late 1700s. He was originally a corn merchant and owned coalmines. He became known in the locality as a skilled watercolourist, painting all subjects but especially natural history. By 1803 he was painting landscapes on Swansea and Nantgarw ware for his friend Mr Dillyn. He was also illustrating Dillyn's work on natural history, *The British Conserva*, which included a description of recent shells and a catalogue of the rare plants found in the neighbourhood of Dover. From 1811–13 he worked as an estate surveyor producing the map *Merthyr Mawr Place*. In 1835 he published his *Guide to the of Glyn Neath*. By now he had learnt the art of ceramic painting and had a muffle kiln in his home. He painted natural birds at Swansea, copied from *Curtis's Botanical Magazine* and was an expert painter of butterflies, birds, insects and shells. Some pieces may be found with his signature, either 'Young pinxit' or 'Young f.', but they are rare. Young become one of the owners of the Nantgarw china works and a Fellow of the Linnaean Society.

ARTISTS AND ROYAL ACADEMICIANS WHOSE WORK WAS USED AS SOURCE MATERIAL BY THE POTTERY INDUSTRY

In the mid-seventeenth century, there were three main areas of production of porcelain in Europe: French and German manufactories, subsidised by their ruling houses; and privately owned, large and small potteries throughout Britain. This new ceramic material replaced the silver settings of dinner and dessert services and the highly decorative and ornate centrepieces that had dominated dining room tables. Manufactories generally followed the Chinese style of decoration, adapted to European tastes, but as travel became easier and the Grand Tour fashionable in the late seventeenth and eighteenth centuries, new influences affected demand and shapes and designs changed. Potters used two main sources for new ideas– books about art and design and the works of artists. Turners, of Lane End, Staffordshire, for example, had a vast library, including four volumes of *Hamilton's Antiquities* and eighteen volumes of the *Repertory of Art*. Josiah Wedgwood, for instance, had a very successful association with modeller John Flaxman and painter George Stubbs. Leading European manufactories used the work of artists such as Jean-Antoine Watteau and François Boucher. The ways in which these inspirations had been realised in ceramic design became evident, and the good and bad points of the results discussed, when examples were displayed at the Great Exhibition of All Nations in the Crystal Palace in Hyde Park in 1851. This section records the biographies of those fine artists and illustrators whose work was the inspiration for the creation of art on the ceramic surface and their association with British potters.

Allingham (née Paterson), Helen, 1848–1926

Artist and book illustrator born in Burton-on-Trent. She trained at the Royal Academy Schools, eventually becoming known for her watercolours of rural landscapes and interiors. She moved in artistic circles, counting Myles Birket Foster (q.v.) and, particularly, Kate Greenaway (q.v.) amongst her friends. She contributed illustrations to many popular journals, including in 1868 *Once a Week*, in 1870 *London Society* and *Cassell's Magazine*. In 1871 she illustrated the children's book *The Fairies and Dawn to Daylight* and in 1903 *Happy England* included many reproductions of her paintings.

Alma-Tadema, Lourens (Lawrence), Sir, OM, RA, 1836–1912

Victorian classical artist born at Dronryp, Netherlands and in 1852 studied at the Antwerp Academy. He came to London in 1869. Although the intelligentsia disliked his classically inspired work, it was very popular with the Victorian nouveaux riches. By 1873 he had been accepted as an Associate Member of the Royal Academy and in 1879 was made a full member, and he exhibited fifty-seven paintings of historical subjects. His second wife, Laura Teresa, daughter of G.N. Epps, a pupil of Sir Lawrence, was also a talented artist; they lived at 17 Regents Park, St Johns Wood and were known for their hospitality and their popularity with other artists. In 1882 Alma-Tadema had a one-man exhibition at the

Courtesy of the Spode-Copeland China Collection Trelissick Cornwall

Grosvenor Gallery, London. He was prolific, producing complex classical scenes, then later figures or groups of figures in more simple settings by the sea or with flowers, using Mediterranean colours, a style copied by many artists. In 1889 he was knighted and received the Order of Merit in 1905. One of his paintings was copied by the Copeland artist Harry Lea (q.v.) and is exhibited at the Spode–Copeland China Collection, Trelissick, Cornwall.

Ansdell, Richard, RA, 1815–1885

Sporting and animal artist and book illustrator born in Liverpool and educated at the Blue Coats School and the Liverpool Academy. He travelled to Spain in 1857 and his 'Spanish' paintings became very popular. Andsell executed many pictures with his friend Thomas Creswell (q.v.), who painted the landscapes around his animals. He contributed to *The Illustrated Times*, *Once a Week* and *Rhymes and Roundelays*, and also to the Etching Club's publications. He became an Associate of the Royal Academy in 1861 and a full member in 1870. By 1871 he and his wife Maria and their large family had moved to Lytham House, Kensington. He was a popular figure, well known for his generosity. His work was used as source material by such ceramic artists as William Yale (q.v.) at Copeland. He exhibited at the Royal Academy 1840–85.

Barlow, Francis A., active 1680

Painter, illustrator and engraver noted for sporting subjects. Some of his illustrations to a 1687 edition of Aesop's *Fables* were used by Josiah Wedgwood I on his early Queen's Ware transfer printed plates.

Barrett, George, RA, c. 1730–1784

Landscape artist born in Dublin, the son of a clothier. He was apprenticed to a stay maker, but took instruction in drawing at Robert Lucius West's Academy in Dublin and was employed by a colour printer. Edmund Burke advised Barrett to study the Irish countryside and specialise in landscape painting. He entered a competition sponsored by the Royal Dublin Society and won £50. Barrett gained the patronage of Lord Powerscourt and came to London in about 1761. Although earning a large salary, he was constantly in financial difficulties. Josiah Wedgwood I used some of his fine landscapes on the famous Frog Service. In later life he was appointed master painter to the Chelsea Hospital.

Bewick, Thomas, 1753–1828

Engraver and book illustrator born at Cherryburn House, Ovingham, Northumberland, the son of a colliery manager. He became an apprentice to Ralph Beilby in Newcastle-upon-Tyne and started his career cutting woodblocks for local printers. He soon developed his own techniques and is credited with founding the English School of Wood Engraving. His engravings for A *General History of Quadrupeds*, 1790, *British Birds, Land Birds*, 1797 and *Water Birds*, 1804 were used as source material by Coalport, Swansea, Ridgway and Minton. Bewick drew small landscapes, houses and animals with great accuracy, paintings ideally suited for pottery design.

Blake, William, 1757–1827

Engraver, painter, poet and printer born at 28 Broad Street, London, son of a hosier. He became an apprentice to the engraver James Basire after an early training at the William Parr Drawing School. In 1779 he went to the Royal Academy School and first exhibited there in 1780. Blake started illustrating books such as the 1796 edition of *Original Stories from Real Life* by Mary Wollstonecraft, and was described as contentedly poor, a gentle genius, whose work was not appreciated in his time. The Victorian art world recognised his poetic works rather than his artistic ability and it was not until the late 1800s that illustrated texts were recognised as a legitimate book form. Blake was introduced to Josiah Wedgwood I by John Flaxman (q.v.) and engraved copper plates for Wedgwood, used in the Queens Ware Catalogue of 1817.

Bone, Henry, RA, 1755–1834

Artist, outside decorator and miniaturist born in Truro, Cornwall, son of a cabinetmaker. He was apprenticed first to Cookworthy at Plymouth and in 1772 to Champion at Bristol. Bone moved to Plymouth, where he started to paint miniatures and excelled at painting figure subjects. Then in London he became an enameller of watches and trinkets, only occasionally painting a miniature in watercolour. In 1780 he exhibited a portrait of his wife at the Royal Academy and between 1781 and 1834 exhibited two hundred and forty-two miniatures. Bone was appointed enamel painter to the Prince of Wales in 1800 and to the King in 1809, also gaining commission from the Duke of Bedford. He became an Associate of the Royal Academy in 1801 and a full member in 1811. His Elizabethan-style enamel portraits of celebrities of the time were very popular. When living in Bristol and in London he bought undecorated ware from the New Hall pottery, which he then decorated.

Boucher, François, 1703–1770

Artist born in Paris, son of a painter who also designed upholstery. He was apprenticed to the artist François Lemoyne, who painted the Salon d'Hercules at the Palace of Versailles. When seventeen, Boucher went to work for an engraver called Cars, creating book designs and trade plates. After he gained the patronage of the Baron de Thiers, he spent three years in Rome.

In 1733 he returned to France and married Maria Jeanne Buseau, and the next year was elected to the Academy. He became a favourite of Madame de Pompadour, who commissioned him to design stage settings for her private theatre in Versailles. Boucher had a great influence on the decorative arts of France and by 1740 was painting landscapes inspired by the Far East, many of which became copper engravings. In 1743 he was employed by the Paris opera designing costumes and scenery for the Ballet Indes Galantes. Examples of his work on Sèvres porcelain may be seen in the Wallace Collection at Manchester House, London. His work was used by many Minton artists, who took a small cameo from a large original and painted it on china. Minton pattern books show designs named after Boucher.

By 1748 Boucher had moved to the more fashionable address on the Rue Richelieu, had a studio in the King's library and had become a wealthy man. His designs were in great demand, not only by the Gobelins tapestry factory but also by 1749 by the Sèvres and Vincennes porcelain manufactories. Four years later Boucher had an apartment and studio in the Louvre and had been awarded a large pension. In 1754 his style of painting shepherds and shepherdesses in a pastoral setting found universal appeal with pottery art directors and artists. For example, Dr Bernard Watney read a paper to the English Ceramic Circle at the Victoria & Albert Museum in April 1987 that outlined the influence of Boucher in both ceramic and enamel decoration.

Browne, Hablot Knight (Phiz), 1815–1882

Painter, Illustrator and etcher born in London. He was apprenticed to the line engraver William Finden and attended life classes at the St Martin's Lane Academy. In 1834 he and a fellow apprentice Robert Young started an illustrator's workshop, producing etchings and watercolours. He first signed himself 'Nemo' then later when working with Charles Dickens 'Phiz' (a depicter of physiognomies). In 1836 Browne went to Yorkshire to research the idiosyncrasies of schoolmasters. Copeland used his '*Going to the Derby*' illustration on one of their jugs, which carried the Phiz signature.

Burne-Jones, Sir Edward Coley, RA, 1833–1890

Artist, designer, book illustrator, caricaturist and writer born in Birmingham and educated at King Edward's School, Birmingham. He attended evening classes at the Birmingham School of Art then went up to Oxford. By 1853 he had become a friend of William Morris and John Ruskin. He studied nature, painting the countryside around Oxford. It is thought that he took drawing lessons from Dante Gabriel Rossetti around 1856. In 1861 he helped to form Morris, Marshall, Faulkner and Co., a fine art workshop for which he was the principal artist and designer, John Ruskin, then Slade Professor at Oxford, devoted a whole lecture to his friend's work and talents. In 1885 Burne-Jones was elected President of the Birmingham Society of Art. His work was widely known and appreciated and was used by Minton as tile decoration.

Buss, Robert, active 1841

Artist, book illustrator and journalist who came to Staffordshire in the 1840s to paint scenes of Tittensor and Newcastle-under-Lyme. His large oil *The Mock Mayor of Newcastle* and the paintings and sketches made for it form part of the Newcastle-under-Lyme Museum art collection. After Robert Seymour, the first illustrator of Dickens's *Pickwick Papers*, shot himself, Buss completed the work. He lectured on Art and for a short time edited *The Fine Art Almanac.*

Corot, Jean-Baptiste-Camille, 1796–1875

French landscape artist born in Paris, son of wealthy parents. He studied under Jean Victor Bertin, a neoclassical painter, and at the Louvre, but soon developed his own style that proved very popular. In 1825 he explored Rome and Venice. Corot spent spring and summer sketching and painting outside and in the winter retired to his Paris studio to finish his work. His output was prolific and his paintings sold well. In 1855 he exhibited at the Paris Exhibition, where he won a first class medal. In 1862 he visited England and his paintings were used as source material by the many of the pottery artists.

Crane, Walter, RWS, 1845–1915

Designer, book illustrator, writer and lecturer, born in Liverpool, second son of Thomas Crane, a portrait painter. He served his apprenticeship with wood carver W.J. Linton in London and studied at the Heatherley's Art School. Crane was introduced to the Wedgwood family by Mr and Mrs Wilbraham and in 1866 was commissioned to paint four pairs of vases, which he returned to the factory for firing on 30 January 30 1869. Later the same year he painted two single vases and three trays in monochrome. However, Wedgwood did not think that these designs would appeal to the market, even though his coloured paintings were being commissioned and some were shown in the Paris Exhibition of 1867. In 1870 he designed the '*Grape Vine Holder*', a centrepiece for real fruit, at the suggestion of Mrs Wilbraham, which was produced. He was asked to design and etch a border for a Henry ii-style chess table made for the 1871 London International Exhibition. Crane then travelled to Italy, Greece, Bohemia and the United States. Around 1874 he designed picture tiles for Maw & Co. Ltd. His work was exhibited at the Arts and Crafts Exhibitions of 1888 and 1889 and in 1890 his panel '*Seed Time*' won praise. Crane became known as a designer, book illustrator and writer and was the first President of the Art Workers' Guild in 1884, and a leading figure in the Arts and Crafts movement. In 1888 he was elected President of the Arts and Crafts Exhibition Society, which was formed to encourage and promote the work of designers and craftsmen. By 1898 he was the Principal of the Royal School of Art, introducing a range of applied art, craft and design subjects. He became Art Superintendent of the London Decorating Co., which specialised in encaustic tiles. Crane's designs were commissioned by Minton around 1870, Wedgwood from 1867 to 1877 and Pilkinton from 1905 to 1908. He signed his work with his monogram, a C enclosing a crane. He is well known for his illustrations for children's books, and also designed furniture and wallpaper.

Creswick, Thomas, RA, 1811–1869

Landscape painter born in Sheffield and trained in Birmingham with Joseph Vincent Barber, but by 1828 had moved to London. He was first noticed for his Welsh and Irish views, but his North of England landscapes are regarded as his best work. He exhibited at the Royal Academy from 1828 to 1870, became an Associate member in 1842 and a full member in 1851. He was a founder member of the Etching Club, contributing many plates for publication. Creswick painted his pictures on location, despite the weather, then took them back to his studio to be finished. He loved painting summer scenes, water in brooks and lakes, forded by quaint carts, and pretty bridges, and some pottery artists copied his work.

Daniell, Thomas, RA, 1749–1840

Landscape painter and aquatint engraver of landscapes born at Kingston-on-Thames, son of an innkeeper. He was apprenticed to a heraldic painter for coachbuilders. In 1773 he was admitted to the Royal Academy Schools, where in 1774 he exhibited flower paintings and in 1784 landscapes. The following year he went to India with his nephew William, recording not only the buildings, but also the life and religious art of the people. He published *Oriental Scenery, A Picturesque Voyage to India and Views of Calcutta*. He became an Associate of the Royal Academy in 1796, a full member in 1797 and a Fellow of the Royal Society and of the Asiatic Society. His work was a source of new inspiration for pottery designers of his time and continued to be used into the nineteenth century.

Daniell, William, RA, 1769–1837

Landscape painter, aquatint engraver and topographer. When only sixteen years old he started to accompany his uncle Thomas (q.v.) on many journeys to India and is also well known for his work *Voyage Around Great Britain*, published from 1814 to 1825, which contains many of his best watercolours. He became an Associate of the Royal Academy in 1807 and a full member in1822.

A View of the Long Walk Windsor in the Royal Collection is regarded as one of his best paintings.

Edwards, George, 1694–1773

Artist, author and drawing instructor born at West Ham in Essex and as a young man lived with Mr. John Dodd in Fenchurch Street, London. His interest in rare birds began in 1716 when he travelled to Holland, Norway and the Scilly Isles. In 1722 he started to collect and draw birds and his *A Natural History of Uncommon Birds* was published in 1743. In the preface he wrote: 'I have made the drawings of these birds directly from nature, and have, for variety's sake, given them as many different attitudes and turns as I could invent.' He explains: 'Great part of the birds were living when I drew them; others were in cases well preserved and dry, and some were kept in spirits.' In 1733 he became Library Keeper to the Royal College of Physicians and in 1750 was awarded the gold medal of Royal Society of London for his new discoveries in art and nature.

The Chelsea figure of a ptarmigan was modelled from his drawing of the white partridge. Many of the bird designs on the Mecklenburg Service, first made by the Chelsea pottery and later copied by Copeland, are taken from his book.

Duncan, Edward, 1803–1882

Marine and coastal artist and illustrator born in London and trained under Robert Havell & Sons, aquatint engravers. He became a member of the New Water Colour Society in 1834 but resigned and joined the Old Watercolour Society in 1847. For the next few years he toured the country, meeting William Taylor Copeland and staying at his home for six months painting pictures of racing and hunting. As a thank you to his host he gave him a series of rural scenes, which, when engraved, were used to decorate Copeland earthenware. The pattern was first registered in September 1850. Richard Pirie Copeland had more engravings made from the original paintings by George Hemmings in the 1900s, which were used for designs on bone-china ware.

Edwards, Lionel Dalhousie Robertson, RI, 1878–1966

Artist born in Clifton, Gloucestershire, son of a doctor. He studied under A. Cope and Frank Calderon at the School of Animal Painting, Kensington, London, specialising in sporting subjects. The retail firm of Sloane & Smith Ltd of 27 Brompton Road, Knightsbridge SW3 commissioned Edwards to paint twenty-four sketches of hunting scenes and commissioned Copeland to manufacture the ware. Arthur Perry (q.v.) was asked to do the artwork for the engravings from the original sketches, which was approved by Edwards. On 22 October 1922, the first consignment of Lionel Edwards' hunting scenes on earthenware left the Spode works. The series was a commercial success and four years later Sloane & Smith issued a booklet telling the story of production and how the Copeland modellers cut twigs from oak trees to model the handles. A tea service for twelve cost twenty guineas, plaques were ten guineas, and muffin dishes thirty shillings. In the 1920s Edwards worked for *Punch* magazine and lived in Salisbury, Wiltshire.

Etty, William, RA, 1787–1849

Artist born in York, son of a miller. He was apprenticed to a letter-writer printer in Hull, and in 1807 was admitted as a student to the Royal Academy Schools, his tuition financed by an uncle who lived in London. His first known success, *Combat*, was painted in 1825. He exhibited one hundred and thirty-eight paintings at the Royal Academy and seventy-eight at the British Institution from 1811, mostly mythological subjects. In later life, suffering from ill health and poor patronage, he painted nude studies, which were very popular and often the inspiration for ceramic artists, such as Robert Frederick Abraham (q.v.), Art Director at Copeland. His determination and influence led to the foundation of the York School of Art, which encouraged and trained many good artists.

Birket Foster, Myles, 1825–1899

Watercolour artist, engraver and book Illustrator born at North Shields near Tynemouth into a Quaker family. He attended the Quaker schools at Tottenham and Hitchin, and was first apprenticed to a Mr. Stone, then to Ebenezer Landells. By the age of twenty-one he was illustrating books and contributing to *The London Illustrated News* and *Punch*. He started his own business in London in 1846 and married Ann Spence. By 1858 he refused commissions for illustrations and applied to join the Society of Water Colour Painters. His application was refused, but accepted the next year. By 1859 he was concentrating solely on painting. He is known as a pastoral painter and his detailed landscapes with pretty cottages provided source material for artists at Minton and Copeland, his influence seen on many of the dessert services of the late 1880s. His most famous works were the vignettes to Longfellow's poem *Evangeline* in 1850 and illustrations for Gray's *Elegy*, Milton's *Paradise Lost* and Tennyson's *Hyperion*.

Fragonard, Jean-Honoré, 1732–1806

Artist and engraver born in Grasse and studied in Paris under Boucher (q.v.) and Chardin. In 1752 he won the Prix de Rome and is known for his light-hearted paint-

W.T. Copeland Bone china plate the centre scene of Venice attributed source Birkett Forster

W.T.Copeland primrose-shape bone china dessert plate the centre decoration after Fragonard. Artist unknown

ings in romantic settings with a pastoral theme, such as *Girl on a Swing* now exhibited in the Wallace Collection, Manchester House, London. He was a fine artist and engraver, and his paintings are colourful and technically brilliant. He gained the patronage of Madame Du Barry, but the French Revolution ruined his career as his paintings were no longer fashionable. Ceramic artists in the Potteries often used parts of his paintings as source material.

Fuseli, Johann Heinrich (Henry), RA, 1741–1825

Artist born in Zurich, second son of a portrait and landscape artist who did not want him to follow in his footsteps, insisting upon an academic, not artistic, career. Fuseli was sent to Caroline College, Zurich, where he attained a Master of Arts degree and entered holy orders. It was not until 1767 that he met Sir Joshua Reynolds in London, who encouraged him to paint. He went to study in Italy and slowly achieved recognition for his work, being elected Professor of Painting at the Royal Academy and delivering his first lectures in 1801. For the last twenty years of his life he combined the roles of Keeper and Professor at the Royal Academy. His work was bold and energetic and professionals engraved many of his paintings. Fuseli did some lithograph design, such as the successful *A woman sitting by a window*. Alternately sarcastic and kind, he was popular with his students and greatly respected. He died at Putney Heath and was buried in St Paul's Cathedral.

Gould, John, 1804–1881

A natural history artist and ornithologist especially interested in humming birds. His work *Birds of the World*, published in six volumes, became the primary source for bird designs on Coalport china and was used by John Randall (q.v.) their premier bird painter.

Greenaway, Catherine (Kate), RI, 1846–1901

Artist, designer and book Illustrator born in London, daughter of John Greenaway, a master wood engraver, who trained at the Islington, London school Heatherleys, and at the Slade School of Art. She first worked for Edmund Evans, a printer and publisher. John Ruskin admired her work and influenced her style of design. She illustrated children's books, and specialised in drawing little girls in frilly dresses and ribbons and boys in frilled shirts and pantaloons. Her work was popular and adapted by Wedgwood for designs on plates and nursery tiles. Kate exhibited 1868–91 at the Royal Academy, the Suffolk Street Gallery and the New Water Colour Society and died in the house designed for her by Norman Shaw in Frognal, Hampstead, London.

Oil Painting of King Cole owned by William Taylor Copeland

Herring, John Frederick (Senior), 1795–1865

Artist who became famous for his paintings of horses. The family lived in York but moved to London where they ran a fringe and upholstery shop in Newgate Street. He was not encouraged to paint, and when nineteen left home and took the stagecoach to Doncaster. Here he became a coachman, driving between Wakefield and Lincoln and York and London, but at the same time painting inn signs and decorating coaches. After two years on the road, which he said ruined his health, giving him bronchitis and asthma, he met Alderman William Copeland, who was travelling to London by coach and recognised an old school friend. Realising that not only was he in debt, but ill, he gave him a cottage on his estate. Herring painted many of the winning horses from the Copeland stud. In 1931 these sketches became the source material for a series of patterns called '*The Hunt*', produced first in earthenware and later in china. This became one of Copeland's best-selling patterns. Herring slowly regained his health and became noticed by the local gentry, who gave him commissions to paint their hunters and racehorses. He became a very popular artist, never short of work, and returned to London, where he gained commissions from Queen Victoria. He contributed illustrations to *The London Illustrated News*, *The Illustrated Times* and *Sporting Life* and exhibited work from 1818 at the Royal Academy, The British Institution and the Suffolk Street Gallery. He was commissioned to paint the St Leger winners at Doncaster.

Howitt, Samuel, 1756–1822

Sporting artist, etcher, aquatint engraver and illustrator who lived and worked in London. He was a drawing

Above: Wedgwood Bowl decorated with *The Dancing Hours* originally designed by Flaxmen in 1779, this bowl c. 1960

Left: Detail of honey suckle pattern, William Morris, arts and crafts designer, courtesy of Wightwick Manor, Wolverhampton

Below: Wightwick manor Bedroom, William Morris, arts and crafts designer, courtesy of Wightwick Manor, Wolverhampton

master in Ealing and exhibited at the Incorporated Society of Artists, contributing drawings and etchings to *The British Sportsman*.

His illustrations were used in T. Williamson's *Oriental Field Sports* in 1805 and became the source of many blue-and-white printed designs on Spode and Ralph & James Clewes ware.

Houghton (née Bolton), Elizabeth Ellen, active c. 1800

Book illustrator, cousin of Walter Crane (q.v.). She studied at the Warrington School of Art and Minton used her drawings on a series of tiles that depicted the days of the week.

Huysum, Jan van, 1682–1749

Floral and landscape artist born in Amsterdam, eldest son of the painter Justus. He studied with his father and became famous for his still-life paintings of flowers. Jan was the first Dutch painter to use a light background to his floral studies. Many ceramic painters copied his work; a fine example is a tray in the Spode–Copeland China Collection at Trelissick, Cornwall.

Jewitt, Llewellyn Frederick William, 1816–86

Engraver and author born at Kimberworth, Yorkshire and educated by his father. He became a wood carver and went to London to work for F.W. Fairholt as an engraver. In 1849 he worked carving the blocks for *The Pictorial Times*, *The Illustrated London News* and *Punch*. He became chief librarian of the Plymouth public library and curator of the museum there. In 1853 he moved to Derby as Curator of the Museum and Vice President of the Archaeological Society. He was one of the founders of *The Daily Telegraph* newspaper, which he edited until 1869. His son married the daughter of W.H. Goss of the Falcon factory, Stoke-upon-Trent. His *The Ceramic Art of Great Britain*, published in 1878, is a standard text on the Staffordshire ceramic industry.

Kauffman, Maria Anna Katharina (Angelika), RA, 1741–1807

Artist born at Chur, Switzerland, daughter of a painter, who travelled widely and was an accomplished musician. She became a favourite of the young Queen Victoria, who commissioned her to decorate a room in Frogmore House with floral studies; it is still called the Flower Room. Kauffman had an unhappy liaison with the Count de Horn's valet, who posed as his master. They entered into a secret marriage but when the deception was discovered he was paid 300 guineas to disappear. She was a founder member and exhibitor at the Royal Academy from 1768 to 1797 and a friend of Joshua Reynolds She etched plates, mainly classical, after old masters, and pottery artists and designers used many of her works as source material. In 1876, Daniels, the London china showroom, commissioned a dessert service from Minton specifying they use her designs.

Landseer, Sir Edwin Henry, RA, 1802–1873

Artist and animal painter born in London, son of John Landseer, engraver writer and antiquarian. Edwin was the youngest son and first taught by his father. In 1815 at the age of sixteen he was awarded the Silver Medal from the Society of Arts for his drawing of a hunter. He studied under B.R. Haydon, who later ran an art school and encouraged his pupils to study anatomy. Landseer and his brothers went to the school run by Sir Charles Bell, one of the greatest anatomists of his day, and then to the

Spode Tray painted with flowers after Van Huysum, Courtesy of the Spode-Copeland collection Trelissick Cornwall

A Random shot by Landseer copied by F W Furnival and painted in a friends visitors book c. 1900

Royal Academy School. His talent was soon recognised and he gained commissions from notable patrons, such as the Duke of Bedford. He was elected to the Royal Academy in 1831 and Knighted in 1850. His paintings of animals are well known, as are his sculptures of the lions in Trafalgar Square, London. Ceramic artists, especially those at Minton, copied many of his paintings. Minton produced two services for Queen Victoria painted by Henry Mitchell (q.v.) after Landseer. He is buried in St Paul's Cathedral, London.

Marks, Henry Stacey, RA, RWS, HRCA, HFRPE, 1829–1898

Historical painter, designer and book illustrator born in London and trained at Leigh's School, Newman Street, and the Royal Academy Schools. He became a regular exhibitor from 1853 to 1893 at the Royal Academy, British Institution, Suffolk Street Gallery, Grosvenor Gallery and Old Water Colour Society and was a member of the Junior Etching Club. Marks was elected Associate of the Royal Academy in 1871 and a full member in 1878, and a member of the Royal Water Colour Society in 1883. He was a prolific illustrator of books and magazines, including *Punch*, *Passages from Modern Poets* and *The Graphic*. In 1894 he wrote a two-volume autobiography, *Pen and Pencil Sketches*, which shows the range of his designs, including costumes and embroidery, and discusses the artists of the day. He was commissioned through Minton's Art Pottery Studio in London to design their business card, mural plaques and a series of tiles depicting the seven ages of man. In 1877 he spoke at the Burslem School of Art Annual General Meeting, exhorting the students always to do their best and to strive for the highest excellence they could attain. Marks collaborated with other artists to design the frieze of figures around the Royal Albert Hall, London. When Minton was commissioned by the Duke of Westminster for important decorative work for Eaton Hall in Cheshire

The Cavalier painted by Messionier. The original is in the Wallace collection. It was used by F Micklewright and painted on a Paragon china plaque

(now demolished) the large horizontal fireplace frieze with figures in medieval costume representing the signs of the zodiac was designed by Marks. His best artistic works are his bird studies and his stained-glass windows.

Marny, Paul, 1829–1914

French artist whose landscape and marine paintings were used by Minton as a source for some of their designs, painted by John Evans (q.v.). Marny exhibited landscapes at the Royal Academy from 1866 to 1890.

Messionier, Jean-Louis-Ernest, 1815–1891

Artist, sculptor and illustrator born in Lyons, France. He had no formal art education and specialised in small genre scenes. His work shows fine detail and accuracy, which is especially noticeable in his military paintings. In 1861 he became President of the Académie des Beaux-Arts and in 1889 was elected President of the Jury for the Paris Exposition Universelle, and was the first artist to be awarded the Légion d'honneur. Some of his paintings were copied by F. Micklewright (q.v.) on Paragon China, including the then popular *The Musketeer*. The original painting is now exhibited at the Wallace Collection, Manchester House, London.

Morland, George, 1763–1804

Artist, engraver and crayon draughtsman born in London, son of Henry Robert Morland (1712–97), a painter and engraver. George was his eldest and favourite child and when he was only ten years old he exhibited at the Royal Academy. He was taught mainly by his father, under a very strict regime, painting not for the love of art but for the rewards it could bring. In the evenings he escaped to join the friends in the nearest taproom, sketching to pay his bill. He became more at home with oslers and prize fighters than respectable society. At the age of nineteen he rebelled when a picture dealer who first befriended him exploited his talents. He got into debt and left London for Margate, Kent. His next patron was a lady from Margate who found him employment painting miniatures, and took him to France. Yet again he lead a life of debauchery. Eventually in July 1786 he married Anne Ward, sister of James Ward, RA, but the marriage was not a success and he went to live with his brother-in-law in High Street, Marylebone, returning to his old haunts. However, his work was eagerly sought after; possibly his lifestyle provided experiences that are shown in his paintings. Morland painted English rural life, concentrating on small sentimental subjects, but after the 1790s he began to paint landscapes and marine scenes. He became famous for his pictures of stable and farm animals. A Spode artist copied his painting *Winter* onto a tray that is exhibited in the Spode–Copeland China Collection, Trelissick, Cornwall. Unable to pay his debts, he was sent to prison and on his release continued his old ways, selling his sketches for drink. He died of a fever, destitute, but was buried by his old friends in St James Chapel Cemetery, Hampstead, London.

Morin, François

French artist who may have painted at the Sèvres Porcelain factory. The Minton ship vases, commissioned by Thomas Goode of Mayfair, London, are painted with marine landscapes attributed to Morin. The Minton archives hold a series of framed watercolours thought to be his work. His style is very distinctive and after careful study may be found on other well-known factory products. It has been suggested that he is the same François Morin known to have been a chemist and naturalist, who succeeded in experiments to make porcelain.

Moyr Smith, John, 1839–1912

Artist, book illustrator and freelance designer. He trained as an architect, first under Alfred Darbyshire and later with Sir Gilbert Smith. In the 1870s he designed for the Minton Art Studio in London, creating innovative and popular designs, for example, '*Rustic scenes*', twenty-four scenes from Shakespeare, designs taken from Tennyson's *Idylls of the King* and Thompson's *Seasons*. Sir Walter Scott's novel *Waverley* was the inspiration of a series of twelve tiles.

He also painted classical figures with musical instruments, which were used to decorate flasks and tiles. His designs were clear and linear, similar to those of Walter Crane (q.v.). For Burmantoft he designed relief-moulded tiles and panels named '*Deerstalking*', '*The Tennis Player*', '*Skating*' and '*Dancing*'. Although he initialled his designs, the marks are difficult to find, often hidden within the picture. He also designed art furniture for Collinson and Lock and published *Ornamental Interiors* in 1887.He was editor of the magazine *Decoration* 1880–89 and contributed illustrations in *Punch* 1872–78. He exhibited at the Royal Academy, elsewhere in London, and in Birmingham and Glasgow.

Spode large platter centre after a painting of *Winter* by George Morland, courtesy of the Spode-Copeland Collection, Trelissick, Cornwall

Brass Gilded Jardiniere by H Greaves New Street Birmingham The tiles of the Four Seasons made by Minton and designed by Moyr Smith

Poynter, Sir Edward John, 1836–1919

Artist, President of the Royal Academy 1896, Director of the Tate Gallery 1881–94. He designed tile panels illustrating months and seasons, which were painted by some of the women students at the National Art Training School, under the direction of the chief paintress Miss Black, who was afterwards employed by Minton. These tiles, which were held in a wooden framework, lined the walls of the Victoria & Albert Museum. They were commissioned from Minton, and it is thought that their success enabled the company to secure a five-year lease on a plot of land close to the Albert Hall, where they built their Art Pottery, which became a showcase for ceramic art in London.

Pugin, Augustus Welby Northmore, 1812–1852

Designer, architect and writer born in London, a pioneer of the Gothic Revival style. He was the son of Auguste Charles Pugin, a French émigré who found employment in the office of architect John Nash, who asked him to research Gothic ornament. Pugin inherited his father's love of the Gothic style. He trained at the Royal Academy School then lived for some time in Wales painting the scenery around Carmarthen. He painted scenery for Mr Mastermann of the Wind Street Theatre, Swansea and he turned the top floor of his father's house into a theatre, where he designed sets. His interest in and contribution to the pottery industry began when he met Herbert Minton and they discovered a medieval tile factory at King's Lynn in Norfolk. Pugin began to design tiles with a medieval theme, manufactured by Minton, which proved a commercial success, ideal for Victorian fireplaces. Cheadle Roman Catholic church in Staffordshire has some of the finest examples of Pugin's work. He also designed the Shamrock and Gothic tea ware patterns for Minton.

Pugin's work was popular, resulting in more important commissions. The Earl of Shrewsbury commissioned designs for his fine house Alton Towers, providing him with the necessary funds and allowing him free artistic license. He converted to Catholicism and spent the rest of his short life designing churches to the glory of God.

Sandby, Paul, RA, 1730–1809

Watercolour artist, etcher and aquatint engraver of landscapes, architectural views and some portraits. He was born in Nottingham and went to London with his elder brother Thomas, an architect. He studied for two years in the draughtsman's room at the Tower of London and from 1747 to 1752 was engaged by the Duke of Cumberland to survey the north and western parts of the Highlands of Scotland. He learnt the art of etching in Edinburgh and became a fine watercolour artist, painting landscapes, portraits and caricatures. By 1768 he was drawing master to the Royal Military College, Woolwich

Model of the Madonna designed by Pugin for the Birmingham Exhibition of 1849, inscribed

and one of the founder members of the Royal Academy. In 1771 he was employed by Sir Watkins William Wynn to paint at Wynstay and to travel North Wales painting pictures that became part of the Wynstay collection. At the Wynstay Theatre he painted scenery of Llangollen Bridge, a garden and a castle. Sandby taught George III's children drawing and many of his paintings are of Windsor and Eton. Wedgwood copied his work *The Gate of Coverham Abbey* onto a trial plate for the Frog Service. His engravings for *The Virtuosi's Museum* of 1776 were a source of Derby designs. His work was also used by the Caughley pottery.

Stubbs, George, ARA, 1724–1806

Animal painter born in Liverpool, the son of a currier and leather dresser, who encouraged his son's talent but died when George was only fifteen years old. In 1744 Stubbs had moved to Leeds and set up as a portrait painter. In 1766 he illustrated his book *The Anatomy of the Horse* with his own engraved plates. Mathew Boulton introduced George to Josiah Wedgwood I, who produced models from Stubbs' paintings, including *The Frightened Horse* and *The Fall of Phaeton*, which were made into cameos on Jasper and proved very popular. Examples of Stubbs' painting on creamware plaques are in the Lady Lever Art Gallery, Port Sunlight. He painted a portrait of Josiah Wedgwood on an earthenware biscuit plaque in enamel colours. George exhibited from1761 to 1806 in various exhibitions, including fifty-three paintings at the Royal Academy.

Street, George Edmund, 1824–1881

Architect, writer and designer, one of the leading figures of the Arts and Crafts movement. For a short time around 1856 William Morris employed Street, but he is known in the ceramic field for designing tiles produced by Maw & Co. In 1881 he became President of the Royal Institute of British Architects.

Teniers, David (the Younger), 1610–1690

Artist, born in Antwerp, son of David Teniers the Elder (1582–1649). He was trained by his father, a landscape and rustic painter who was influenced by the work of Rubens and Brouwer. Teniers was known for his paintings of peasant life, depicting humorous figures in everyday situations. In 1644 he was appointed Dean of the Guild of Saint Luke, but in 1650 he moved to Antwerp and was active in founding the Antwerp Academy of Fine Arts. In 1651 he became court painter to Archduke Leopold William, who named him Director of his picture gallery at Brussels. Teniers' paintings were used to decorate vases and jardinières that were popular in the reign of Louis XV. Josiah Spode II used his paintings on a garniture of vases, now exhibited at the Spode–Copeland China Collection, Trelissick, Cornwall.

Turner, Joseph Mallord William, RA, 1775–1851

Landscape artist born in London, the son of a Covent Garden hairdresser and wig maker, who trained at the Royal Academy School in 1789 and became a pupil of Thomas Malton. He exhibited his first watercolour at the Royal Academy when only fifteen years of age. From 1791 to 1798 he went on sketching tours throughout England and Wales and by 1799 was elected an Associate of the Royal Academy, and in 1802 a full member. His topographical views became very popular. Turner travelled widely throughout his life, to Switzerland, France and Italy. His ability to paint not only in watercolours but also in oils earned him acclaim in his lifetime. He was elected Professor of Perspective at the Royal Academy in 1811. Slowly Turner began to paint more pictures in oils and to try to represent changing light. In 1815 he exhibited *Crossing the Brook*, a view of the river Tamer that divides Devon and Cornwall. His work from *The Rivers of France* series of c. 1837, a re-issue of *Annual Tours*, 1833–35 in three volumes, was devoted to the scenery of the rivers Loire and Seine. Paintings from this work were chosen by the Copeland to decorate a dessert service, painted by Daniel Lucas Junior (q.v.), which was exhibited at the London International Exhibition in 1862. Also exhibited were vases with a rose du Barry ground decorated with Turner's painting of the rebuilding of Carthage and Caligula's palace. Turner also explored Yorkshire, and in the 1920s Arthur Perry (q.v.) at Copeland used his painting of Scarborough to decorate a bone china tray, which is exhibited at the Spode Museum, Stoke-upon-Trent.

Courtesy of the Spode Museum Trust

Vermeer, Johannes (Jan), 1632–1675

Genre artist born in his father's market tavern in Delft, Holland. He was a painter of interior genre subjects who was greatly influenced by the life around him. He was a quiet man, often in debt to the local tradesmen, whom he paid with his paintings. His talent was not truly recognised until after his death. Pottery ceramic artists have used his paintings as source material.

Vernet, Claude-Joseph, 1714–1789

Landscape and marine artist born in Avignon, and studied in Rome under the marine artist Bernando Fergioni. Vernet returned to France in 1766 and was commissioned by Louis XV to paint a set of twenty-six French seaports, but only sixteen were finished. He was known as one of the foremost landscape and marine painters of his day. Wedgwood decorated a creamware bowl sourced from Vernet's *A Collection of Figures and Conversations*, published in 1771. Minton's well-known painter Antonin Bouillemier (q.v.) also used his work as source material.

Wale, Samuel, died 1786

Book illustrator, engraver and landscape painter apprenticed to a silver engraver in London, who became a pupil of Francis Hayman. He was a founder member of the Royal Academy, where he exhibited fourteen paintings. Writing to his brother John in London around 1765 about designs for creamware vases, Josiah Wedgwood said: 'Mr Saml. Wale (Little Court, Castle Street near Newport Street) is the principal person that designs for us, of great merit, shd, you see him wd. sketch you a pattern or two…

Have this day received drawings from Mr Wale among which is Harvest Home.'

Wallis, George, FSA, 1811–1891

Artist, art educationalist and writer born in Wolverhampton and educated at the local grammar school. He became an established artist of genre and portrait subjects in both watercolours and oils, and was patronised by the Earl of Wilton.

George was appointed one of the first headmasters of the Government School of Design, South Kensington, London and was associated with the Spitalfields and Manchester Art Schools. In 1846 he organised the First Exhibition of Art Manufacturers in England, and lectured on the principles of decorative art. In 1851 he became a Deputy Commissioner for the Great Exhibition, representing England and Ireland. He was also involved in the London International Exhibition of 1862, and the Paris Expositions of 1855 and 1867. By 1852 he had become Headmaster of the Birmingham School of Art. He was appointed Art Superintendent of the district for the next five years. His influence on art and design in manufacture was of paramount importance to the ceramic industry at the time. Wallis was one of the pioneers of Free Libraries and was in 1860 appointed Keeper of the Art Collections at the South Kensington Museum, London, until 1891.

Watteau, Jean-Antoine, 1684–1721

Landscape artist born in Valenciennes, son of a plumber. He studied under M.J.A. Gerin, a friend of his father, who encouraged him to visit churches and art galleries, interesting him in genre painting. But in 1702 he ran away to Paris and worked as a scene painter for M.C. Gillot at the Paris Opera House. Five years later he became an assistant to M.C. Audran, decorative artist and keeper of the Luxembourg Gardens. Watteau painted scenes of the Gardens, which provided settings for his *fêtes galantes* paintings depicting courtiers in pastoral settings. He was also at this time painting tavern scenes and military life in the Flemish style and his Chinese designs were especially popular. In 1717 his *L'Embarquement pour l'île de Cythère* won him membership of the French Academy. During the French Revolution his paintings became unpopular but by the end of the nineteenth century they were again appreciated. Watteau's work was influenced by that of Boucher (q.v.) and Fragonard (q.v.). Many small vignettes of his *fêtes galantes* can be seen on English porcelain as they appealed to many ceramic artists and greatly enhanced British design.

Wright of Derby, Joseph, ARA, 1734–1797

Portrait and landscape painter born in Derby, son of an attorney, who studied in London under Hudson and Reynolds. He returned to Derby, where his work became fashionable, and then travelled to Italy for two years, studying the works of old masters, which he copied with skill. He returned to Bath in 1775 and two years later to Derby. It is thought he supplied William Duesbury II with drawings and advice. Wright was a great friend of Zachariah Borman (q.v.) the Derby landscape painter. Although trained as a portrait painter, he is remembered for his landscapes and his paintings of scientific subjects, and for his dramatic use of light and shade. His work was exhibited at the Royal Academy and the Society of Arts from 1765–1794 and in 1781 he was elected Associate of the Royal Academy. A number of his works are in the collection of the Derby Museum and Art Gallery.

Sculptors and Royal Academicians whose work was widely known throughout this period and used by the ceramic industry

The ceramics industry has always needed the skills of those capable of creating new shapes for domestic wares. But it was the invention in about 1842 of the new body that resembled marble and is known as Parian, or statuary porcelain, which provided the medium in which well-known sculptures could be reduced and faithfully copied. The London Art Union first commissioned Minton and Copeland to produce small statuettes or groups of well-known sculptures, which were then offered as prizes to its members. As more British art unions were founded, they too commissioned pieces. The name of the sculptor of the original can often be found on the back of a piece, sometimes with that of the relevant Art Union. By allowing their work to be copied by the master potters, sculptors brought their art into the lives and homes of many Victorians who would not have been able to see the originals, contributing to art education.

Abbott, George, 1803–1883

Sculptor born in London, who exhibited the group *Alexander the Great Crossing Granicus* at the Great Exhibition of 1851. Copeland commissioned two busts from him, one of the Prince Consort and the other of the Duke of Wellington, which they reproduced in Parian. Abbott modelled a seated figure of the Duke of Wellington c. 1852, which was used by Samuel Alcock & Co., Burslem, Staffordshire. From 1829 to 1867 he exhibited twenty-six sculptures at the Royal Academy, eleven at the British Institution and twelve at the Suffolk Street Gallery exhibition. In 1881 he was living at 27 Lupus Street, St George, Hanover Square, London.

Acheson, Anne C., 1882–1962

Sculptor and freelance modeller born in Portadown, Northern Ireland and trained at the Victoria College, Belfast. She studied at the Royal College of Art under Professor Lanteri and exhibited her work at the Royal Academy and the Paris Salons of 1914 and 1922. Acheson was awarded an OBE for her work on plaster of paris and surgical wound dressings and in 1938 won the Gleichen Memorial award. Her first commissions for the Royal Worcester Pottery in 1931 were a popular figure of a girl, *Tangles*, and Irish subjects in 1931. From 1936 to 1937 she designed three more models, *Child with a Butterfly*, *Mermaid* and *Queen in the Parlour.*

Avoine, Maxime, active 1880s

Sculptor born in Paris, France. Around 1875 he was living in London, and then the family moved to the Potteries, where he found employment at Minton. It is said he was paid the high hourly rate of eighteen pence; he lived at 238 Cauldon Road, Shelton, Stoke-upon-Trent. He left Minton to establish an independent studio, which was still flourishing in 1906 and is known to have gained commissions for buildings in London.

Bacon, John, RA, 1740–1799

Sculptor born in Southwark, son of a cloth maker. At the age of fifteen he was apprenticed to Crispe, a china manufacturer at Lambeth who also had a shop in Bow churchyard. He started as a sculptor by experimenting on artificial stone at Coades Artificial Stone Works, Pedlers Lane, Lambeth, becoming manager there for a short time. In 1769 he attended the Royal Academy Schools, working with marble. Bacon invented a machine for transferring designs in plaster to marble. In 1770 he was elected an Associate of the Royal Academy. He is said to have modelled for Bow, Chelsea and Wedgwood. William Duesbury of Derby used his model *Four Seasons*. His sculpture of *William Pitt* was in Westminster Abbey. He was buried at Whitfield's Chapel, known as the Tabernacle, Tottenham Court Road, London.

Barye, Antoine Louis, 1796–1875

Sculptor who worked in bronze. Minton chose his statuette of ballet dancer *Fanny Elssler* (1810–84), which is in Osborne House on the Isle of Wight, to manufacture in Parian.

Beattie, William, active 1829–1864

Sculptor born in Edinburgh, Scotland and exhibited at the Royal Academy 1829–64 and the British Institution

1834–48. He modelled the well-known bronze statue of *Nelson,* which is at Windsor Castle. His commissioned work, reduced and made in Parian, and gave the buying public the opportunity to have a small replica of the original. He became principal modeller for Wedgwood c. 1850–64, living at Boothen Ville, Penkhull, Stoke-upon-Trent. His models included *The Finding of Moses, The Flute Player* and *Abraham offering up his son Isaac.* His statuettes personifying America, Ireland and Scotland were made in Carrara ware and in majolica around 1857. Other sculptures used were *Joseph before Pharaoh,* which was derived from Benjamin E. Spence's sculpture model, *Joseph interpreting Pharaoh's Dream.* His work for the Minton pottery, *Love Restraining Wrath,* was shown at the Great Exhibition of 1851. He also modelled *The Good Race* and *David's Triumph and Reward* for Minton.

Copeland also produced models from his sculptures, for example, *Burns and Highland Mary,* which was purchased by Queen Victoria at the Dublin Exhibition. The comport he modelled from designs suggested by Madame Temple of Regent Street, Brighton, a well known china dealer, was superb, the female supports representing *Joyfulness, Gratitude and Abundance.* It was shown at the 1862 London International Exhibition. Beattie also created sculptures for the potteries of James Duke and Brown-Westhead & Moore. After 1864 it is thought he went to live in London but still received commissions from the Staffordshire potters.

Bell, John, c. 1812–1895

Sculptor born at Hopton, Suffolk and trained at the Royal Academy Schools in 1829. He exhibited a religious group at the Royal Academy in 1832, and in 1833 won a silver medal from the Society of Arts, but his best-known work in London is the Crimea monument of the Brigade of Guards at the junction of Pall Mall and Waterloo Place. Many of his sculptures were used by Minton and produced in Parian in association with Summary's Art Manufactures, such as the 1847 *Una and the Lion.* Minton exhibited the Parian figure *Clorinda* at the Great Exhibition of 1851 that was originally sculpted by Bell. In 1845 he designed a hall table for

W.T. Copeland, comport sculpt. William Beattie from designs by Madame Temple of Brighton. The figures represent joyfulness, gratitude and abundance. The comport was exhibited at the International Exhibition of 1862

Dorothea, sculpt, John Bell, 1850, reproduced by Minton

Parian Group, *Paul & Virginia*, reproduced by W.T. Copeland after the sculpture by Charles Cumberworth, date unknown

the Coalbrookdale Pottery with life-sized deerhounds supporting the table and decorated with emblems of the chase. The Summerley Art Manufactures commissioned two pieces from him produced by Wedgwood – *The Bonfire Spill* and *The Dolphin Salt.*

Bell, Robert Anning, 1863–1933

Painter, sculptor and decorator of stained glass and ceramics. He became head of Liverpool School of Architecture, where he met Harold Rathbone, who established the Della Robbia pottery in Birkenhead in 1893 and commissioned some of his work. He designed picture tiles for Minton but was better known for his book illustrations and as a lithographer of figure subjects. He exhibited at the Royal Academy from 1885 and the Royal Society of Arts 1880–93. From 1918 to 1924 he was Professor of Design at the Royal College of Art. Bell's designs and forward thinking greatly influenced ceramic design in his day.

Brodie, William, 1815–1881

Sculptor, son of a shipmaster at Banff, who studied at the Mechanics Institute in Aberdeen whilst apprenticed as a plumber. In 1847 he went to Edinburgh to study at the Trustees' School of Design, learning the art of modelling. In Rome under Laurence Macdonald he modelled *Corinna the Lyric Muse,* which was reproduced by Copeland in Parian four years later. He exhibited a group *Little Nell and her Grandfather* at the Great Exhibition of 1851. Brodie exhibited at the Royal Academy and the Royal Scottish Academy, becoming a full member in 1859 and secretary in 1876.

Calder, Marshall William, 1813–1894

Sculptor born and trained in Edinburgh and at the Royal Academy School, London, where he studied under Chantrey and Bailey. In 1835 he went to Rome, returning to London in 1839. His work is of interest because of his great support and involvement with the Art Union movement who commissioned many pieces. He won a premium for his sculpture A *Dancing Girl Reposing.* Many of his sculptures were commissioned by all the major potteries. Calder exhibited at the Royal Academy from 1835 to 1891, becoming an Associate in 1844 and a full member in 1852. He lent his sculpture *Ophelia* to the Fine Art Treasures Exhibition held in Manchester in 1857. His other fine sculptures *Sabrina* (loaned by G. Moore), *Paul and Virginia* (loaned by the Earl of Ellesmere) and *Little Red Ridinghood* and *The Broken Pitcher* (loaned by F. Bennoch) were also exhibited there. In 1871 he became a Chevalier of the Légion d' Honneur.

Cumberworth, Charles, 1811–1852

Sculptor born in Verdun, son of an English officer and a French mother. His artistic talent was recognised by his parents, who sent him aged eighteen to train under Pradier (1792–1852) at L'école des Beaux-Arts He won a travelling scholarship from the Paris Academy, which was withdrawn when it was realised he did not have French nationality and therefore did not qualify. He exhibited his work at the Salon from 1832 to 1843. In 1846 he sent his sculpture of *Paul and Virginia* to the Royal Academy in London but it arrived to late for the exhibition. This fine sculpture became one of the most popular ones ever produced in Parian by many potteries, including Copeland. They produced his figures *The Indian Fruit Girl* and *The Water Carrier*, which they exhibited at the Great Exhibition of 1851. Cumberworth was well known for his fine sculptures of famous people and subjects taken from romantic literature. He obtained commissions from the Orléanist royal family.

D'Orsay, Count Alfred Guillaume Gabriel, 1801–1852

Sculptor who exhibited seventeen paintings on scriptural subjects at the Royal Academy from 1843 to 1848 and three at the Suffolk Street Gallery. Minton produced his statuette of *Jenny Lind* in Parian. He was a friend of Lady Blessington of Russborough, Co, Wicklow and attended her fashionable London salon, where he received many important commissions.

Durham, Joseph, ARA, FSA, 1814–1877

Sculptor born in London apprenticed to F.J. Francis, who first exhibited at the Royal Academy in 1835. He exhibited one hundred and twenty-six sculptures at the Royal Academy from 1835 to 1878. His statue of Prince Albert, completed in 1863, was then in the Royal Horticultural Society Gardens, Brompton, London. Minton, Copeland and Worcester executed many of his works in Parian. One of the well-known Copeland models is *Go to Sleep;* the original was commissioned by F. Bennoch and exhibited at the Royal Academy in 1862. This Parian figure of a child with a dog was selected by the Art Union of London as a prize in 1863, 1864 and 1865.

Falconet, Etienne-Maurice, 1716–1791

Sculptor and Director of the modelling department at Sèvres from 1757 to 1765. He left and went to Russia. He modelled *The Cupid* in 1758 and the companion *Psyche* in 1759; both became very popular and were adapted and produced by many Staffordshire potteries. His models *Venus at Toilette* and *Venus at Bath*, originally Sèvres biscuit models, were especially chosen by Minton to be reproduced in Parian ware.

Flaxman, John, RA, 1755–1826

Artist and sculptor born in York, second son of John Flaxman (1726–95), a plaster cast maker and modeller who ran a small business at New Street, Covent Garden, London. As a small child, although suffering from ill health, Flaxman began to show great promise in drawing and modelling. He studied with the local clergyman, who taught him to read Latin and Greek. At the age of eleven he won a premium from the Society of Arts and in 1769 was one of the first students to enroll in the newly founded Royal Academy School. He exhibited at the Free Society of Artists in 1767and 1769 and in 1770 won a silver medal for models exhibited at the Royal Academy.

Asia sculpt, J Durham, reproduced in Parian by W.T. Copeland for the Art Union of London 1873

Above: *Ino and the Infant Bacchus* Sculpt, J. H. Foley, 1840, reproduced in Parian by W.T. Copeland for the Great Exhibition in 1851

Left: Hiram Powers sculpture, *The Greek Slave*, reproduced by W.T. Copeland & Sons in Parian

John Flaxman Senior was supplying casts to Wedgwood as early as 1770 and the work of father and son has been difficult to accredit accurately. However, Josiah Wedgwood had noticed John Junior as early as 1771 and in January 1775, when Wedgwood needed a portrait modeler, Thomas Bentley (partner and great friend of Wedgwood) commissioned Flaxman to model vases and bas-reliefs. Four months later Josiah suggested to Bentley that Flaxman should be asked to model figures. His work for Wedgwood was varied and extensive but he specialised in portrait medallions and classical relief subjects for ornamenting vases and tablets (plaques). Among his most famous works for Wedgwood are *Dancing Hours* (c. 1775) and *The Apotheosis of Homer*, modelled in 1778 after an engraving of a bell krater featured in a work by Hugues d'Hancarville in the collection of Sir William Hamilton. Flaxman and Wedgwood had a harmonious association: as the sculptor, Flaxman was perfectly happy to adapt his designs to the needs of the manufacturer. Flaxman was a man of great skill with a prolific output. He designed for Wedgwood a set of Jasper chessmen, with pawns modelled as warriors, and King and Queen reputedly based on the famous theatre players David Kemble and Sarah Siddons. The original *trompe-l'oeil* drawings for the set still survive In the Wedgwood Museum Trust Archives. Flaxman also designed for the silversmiths Rundall, Ridge and Rundall, who were patronised by the Prince Regent.

In 1772 Flaxman married Ann Denman and they rented a small house in Wardour Street, London. In 1787 they went to Rome, partially subsidised by Josiah Wedgwood. Flaxman supervised the Wedgwood 'Roman School' of artists and produced models from the antique. From Rome he sent drawings depicting archaeological discoveries and the current fashionable designs. When Flaxman returned to London in 1795 he lived at Buckingham Street, Fitzroy Square, and remained there for the rest of his life. He then devoted his time and talents to ornamental sculpture and provided the memorial tablet to Josiah Wedgwood I in St Peter and Vincula, the parish church of Stoke-upon-Trent. He was elected an Associate of the Royal Academy in 1797, becoming a full member in 1800, and in 1810 Professor of Sculpture to the Royal Academy. After his death, his sister-in-law and his adopted daughter founded the Flaxman Gallery at University College, London.

Foley, John Henry, RA, 1818–1874

Artist sculptor born in Dublin, second son of a grocer. In 1831 he went to the Art Schools of the Royal Dublin Society, where he won the major medal for modelling

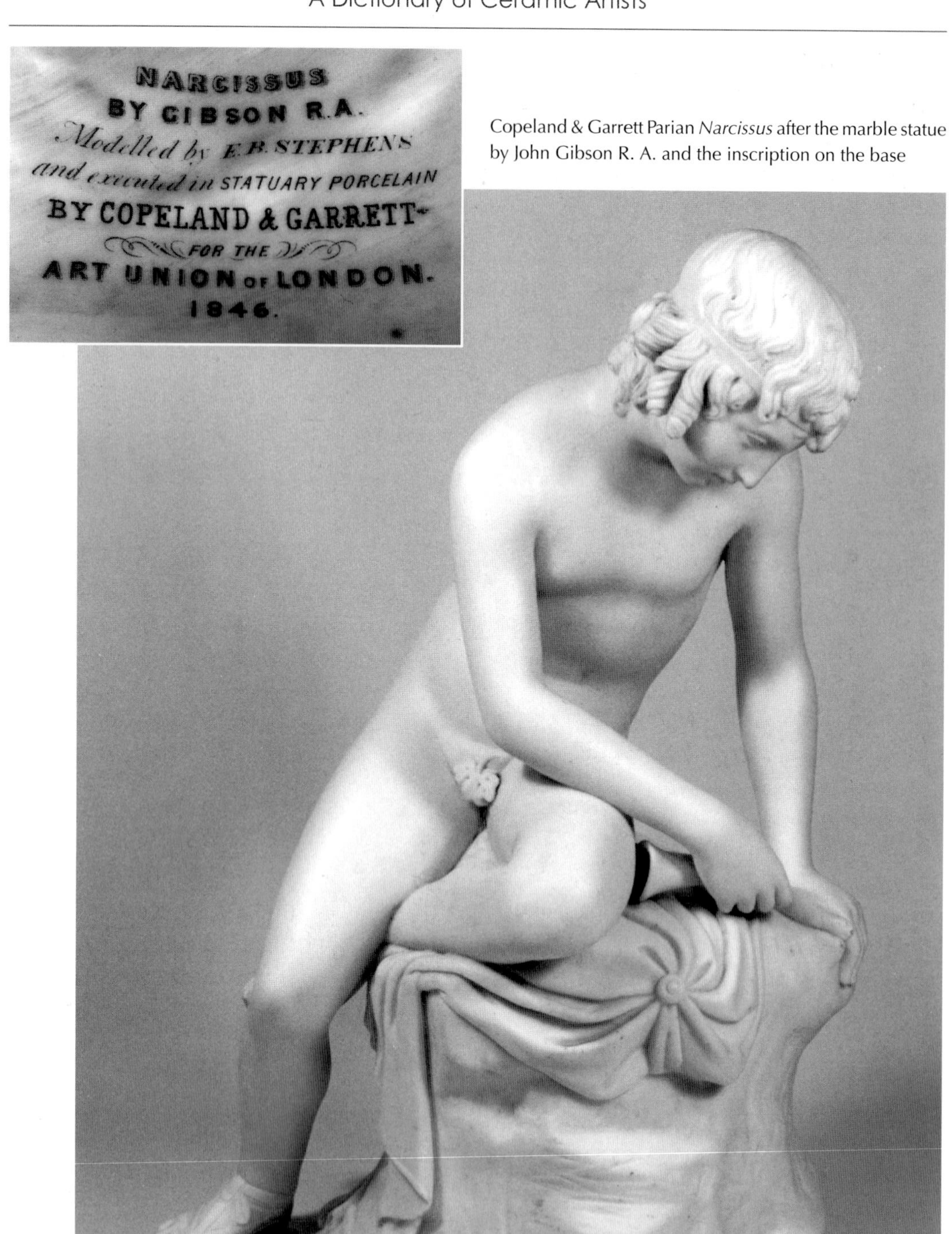

Copeland & Garrett Parian *Narcissus* after the marble statue by John Gibson R. A. and the inscription on the base

and drawing. He joined his brother Edward Arlington, an accomplished sculptor, in London and became a pupil at the Royal Academy School, where he won a silver medal. In 1847 he married Mary Ann Gray at St Pancras, London. Foley designed silver work but Copeland used his sculptors to reproduce in Parian: for example, *Ion and the Infant Bacchus, Innocence* and *Egeria*. In 1849 he was elected an Associate of the Royal Academy and in 1858 a full member. He died at his home The Priory, Hampstead, London, leaving most of his estate to the Artists Benevolent Fund and his casts to the school of the Royal Dublin Society. He is buried in the crypt of St Paul's Cathedral.

Fuller, Charles Francis, 1830–1875

Sculptor born in England and trained as a soldier. He then trained under Hiram Powers (who was famous for his *Greek Slave* sculpture, which was reproduced in Parian by Copeland). He travelled to Florence, Italy, where he established a reputation as a fine sculptor. *Nydia* and *The Peri and her Child* were used by Minton.

Hale, Owen, born 1837

Sculptor and watercolourist born in Birmingham, who worked in London in the late 1880s. Hale is known for his portrait busts and his work in terracotta. His statue *Riverside* was reproduced by Copeland as a Parian statue in about 1881. He designed many models for Copeland, usually depicting a mother and child.
He exhibited at the Royal Academy.

Gibson, John, RA, 1790–1866

Sculptor born at Gaffing, near Conwy, son of a gardener. He was apprenticed to a cabinetmaker in Liverpool, but soon transferred to a wood carver, ending his apprenticeship with Samuel Francis, a sculptor who worked in marble. In 1817 he went to London, then travelled to Italy, becoming a student under Canova. In 1827 he exhibited *Psyche borne by Zephyrs* at the Royal Academy. His friends pleaded with him to return to England but he loved Italy and lived in Rome for over forty-eight years, visiting England regularly. When he died he left all his working models and unfinished work and money to the Royal Academy.

Jerichau, Jens-Adolph, 1816–1883

Danish sculptor trained at the Thorwalden's studio of Copenhagen and became President of the Royal Academy of Copenhagen. Minton's reproduced his marble group *The Bathers*, which was shown at the 1862 London International Exhibition and became one of their most popular Parian groups.

Malempre, Louis Auguste, 1820–1888

Sculptor who is known to have worked with William Theed (q.v.). Many of his fine sculptures were chosen by the Ceramic and Crystal Palace Art Union to be reproduced by Copeland in Parian and given as prizes. He exhibited at the Royal Academy.

Marochetti, Baron Carlo, RA, 1805–1867

Italian sculptor and modeller born in Turin of French parents. The family moved to Paris, where his father was an advocate. He was educated at the Lycée Napoleon, but when seventeen went to study in Rome. The political situation in France forced him to come to London around 1849 and in 1851 he was living at 34 Onslow Square, St Mary, Kensington with his wife Camille and his daughter Jeanne. Queen Victoria noticed his work and he was employed on public works. He designed large vases and cisterns in the Renaissance style, which were decorated with majolica glazes. His work was included in the 1851 Great Exhibition. He sculpted busts and figures of members of the British royal family, some of which were produced in Parian by Minton. He exhibited thirty-five sculptures at the Royal Academy from 1851 to 1867 and designed the Scutari monument to commemorate the Crimean War. Marochetti died suddenly at Passy near Paris.

Owen Hale Sculpt, *Queen Victoria* commissioned for the Diamond Jubilee

Meli, Giovanni, born 1815

Sculptor, modeller and potter born in Palmero, Sicily. In the 1840s he accepted and invitation from Samuel Alcock of the Hill Top Pottery, Burslem to come to England. The relationship was not a happy one and from 1840 to 1850 he became an independent modeller for Copeland, producing *Sir James Duke and Nephew*, and may have obtained commissions from Minton. Meli established a workshop in Glebe Street, near the Stoke Town Hall, Stoke-upon-Trent, modelling figures that were reproduced in Parian. In 1851 he was living at Liverpool Road, Stoke-upon-Trent with his wife Jane and three children. He was one of the original members of the Stokeville Building Society, which built a group of Italianate houses, The Villas, in Stoke-upon-Trent. He never lived there and sold his plot in 1853. In 1865 Meli sold his business to the Robinson and Leadbeater pottery. His religious and literary figures, varying from two to twenty-five inches high, and butter tubs, dessert ware and vases, were all exhibited at the London International Exhibition of 1862. The family returned to Italy, where Meli hoped to establish a pottery producing terracotta ware, but he could not find suitable clays. He left for America and set up a factory in Chicago.

Monti, Raphael, 1818–1881

Sculptor born in Iseo, Ticino and trained by his father Gaetano Monti of Ravenna and at the Imperial Academy, Milan, where he was awarded a gold medal for the group *Alexander Taming Bucephalus*. In 1838 he went to Vienna but returned to Milan in 1842. Monti came to England in 1846 but went back to Italy and became a chief officer of the Popular Party. The political situation caused him to flee and return to England in 1848. From 1853 to 1860 he exhibited at the Royal Academy. His figures and groups were often reproduced in Parian by well-known potteries; for example, Wedgwood made a bust of Thomas Henry Huxley. Monti became known for his marble sculptures of veiled vestals. He recognised the market trend for small Parian sculptures, and his most famous, the mythological Greek *Veiled Bride* was reproduced by Copeland in 1861 for the Crystal Palace Art Union. Other well-known sculptures include *The Sleep of Sorrow* and *The Dream of Joy*, made for the Ceramic and Crystal Palace Art Union, and *Morning* and the companion piece *Night*, exhibited at the London International Exhibition in 1862 and again in Vienna in 1873. Monti also designed silverware for C.F. Hancock.

A *Giovanni Meli* Parain Figure commissioned by S Alcock of Burslem

The Bride, modelled by Rafaelle Monti, courtesy of the Spode Copeland China Collection Trelissick Cornwall

Above left: Left: *Boy with Rabbit,* Parian figure by W. T. Copeland. Right: original marble figure, sculptor unknown

Above right: W. C. Marshall Sculpt, *Ophelia*, commisioned by the Crystal Palace Art Union from W. T. Copeland

Below: Parain Group Cavaliers pets after the painting by Edwin Landseer, height 5″, impressed mark COPELAND on base

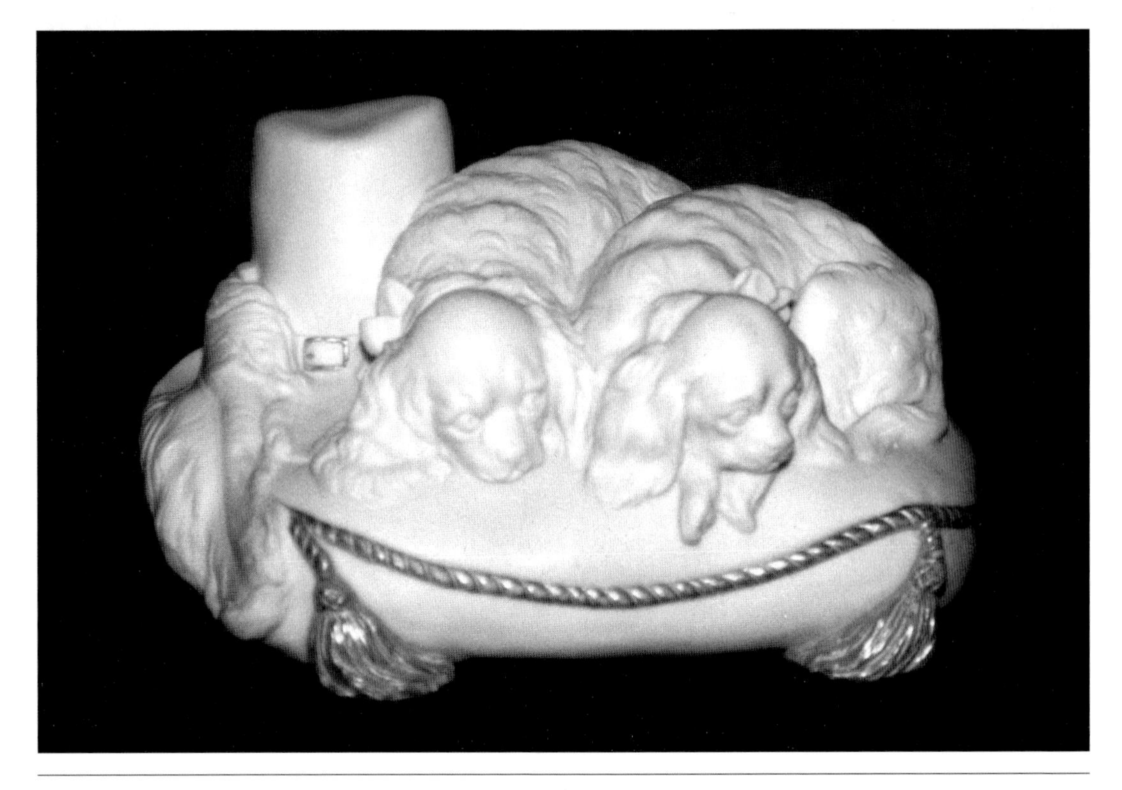

Rossi, John Charles, RA, 1762–1839

Sculptor born in Nottingham, son of an Italian doctor. In 1781 he went to the Royal Academy School for three years, where he won a gold medal for the group *Venus Conducting Helen to Paris*. In 1785 he won a three-year travelling scholarship to Rome but by 1788 he had joined Derby, producing for them models of *Venus and Mars, The New Diana, Venus and Cupid* and *Aesculapius and Hygeia*. By 1789 he was working for the clock maker Vulliamy, and then went to Coade of Lambeth, working on terracotta. His work was popular and in 1797 he was appointed sculptor to the Prince of Wales. He exhibited at the Royal Academy from 1782 to 1834 and the British Institute from 1806 to 1834.

Roubillac, Louis-François, 1695–1762

Sculptor born in Lyons who became sculptor to the Elector of Saxony but returned to Paris to work with Nicolas Coustou. Around 1732 he came to England, where his work became very popular. In 1752 he and a group of artists travelled to Italy. Although it has been debated which of the potteries adapted his work, there is little doubt he did work for the Chelsea Pottery. Nicholas Sprigmont was a friend of the family and in 1744 became godfather to Roubillac's daughter. His influence can be found in later Derby ware. It is thought the Wedgwood basalt figure of Hogarth's dog *Trump* is modelled after his original sculpture.

Steell, Sir John, 1804–1891

Sculptor born in Aberdeen, son of a carver and gilder. The family moved to Edinburgh, where he was apprenticed to a wood carver and studied at the Trustees' Academy. After he had completed his apprenticeship Steell decided to become a sculptor and went to Rome to study. His work became recognised and in 1829 he became a member of the Royal Scottish Academy. Although encouraged by his influential friends to leave Scotland and come to England, he declined. He is best known for his statue of *Sir Walter Scott* in Princess Street, Edinburgh. He exhibited at the Scottish Academy from 1827 to 1880 and at the Royal Academy from 1837 to 1876. He was a prolific sculptor of great talent whose achievements were recognised in his lifetime. In 1838 was appointed sculptor to Queen Victoria, and he was knighted in 1876.

Theed, William (the Elder), 1764–1817

Painter and sculptor born in London, son of a wigmaker in Wych Street. He trained at the Royal Academy Schools, becoming a portrait and classical subject painter, and exhibited at the Royal Academy from 1789 to 1805.

The Four Seasons Sculpt, W Theed, reproduced by W.T. Copeland

Theed studied in Rome for about four to five years, then returned to London, where he began to model for Wedgwood. In 1799 Josiah Wedgwood I sent him a letter offering him employment for three years, and by 1801 he was working at Wedgwood, Etruria, near Stoke-upon-Trent on a freelance basis. In 1803 he advertised as a drawing master in Newcastle-under-Lyme, saying he could teach in either French or Italian. His son William was born in Trentham, a pretty village near to Newcastle, a year later. In 1804 Theed left Wedgwood and went to silversmiths Rundall and Bridge, where he designed gold and silver. However, he continued to complete Wedgwood commissions and in 1811 modelled a portrait of Thomas Bryley. He was elected a Royal Academician in 1813. His best-known work is the group *Hercules Capturing the Thracian Horses* that is on a pediment at the Royal Mews, London.

Theed, William (the Younger), 1804–1891

Sculptor born in Trentham, Staffordshire, son of William Theed (q.v.). He was trained at the Royal Academy Schools, London and for five years in the studio of sculptor Edward Hodges Bailey. In 1820 he won the prestigious Society of Arts silver Isis medal for a figure of *Hercules*. In 1826 William went to study in Rome under the sculptors Thorwaldsen, Wyatt and John Gibson (q.v.). He was back in London in the 1830s, then in Rome with his family between 1842–48. When Prince Albert was looking for marble sculptures for Osborne House on the Isle of Wight in 1848, John Gibson sent him as a representative. Theed exhibited at the Royal Academy from 1824 to 1855. Many of his fine works have been used by major potteries reproduced in Parian: particularly by Copeland and Brown-Westhead & Moore.

Westmacott, James Sherwood, 1823–1900

Sculptor from the famous Westmacott family of sculptors. He exhibited at the Royal Academy from 1846 to 1885 and won the gold medal of Dresden in 1845 for a figure of *Victory*. Copeland used many of his sculptures, including a bust of *Robert Peel* and the group *Christ and Mary*, originally exhibited in 1854 at the Royal Academy. He lived in London.

Wyon, Edward William, 1811–1885

Sculptor and modeller, son of Thomas Wyon, chief engraver of the Seals to George III and George IV. In 1829 Wyvon joined the Royal Academy Schools on the recommendation of E.H. Bailey. Two years later he exhibited a bust of *General Maitland* at the Royal Academy and from 1831 to 1876 he exhibited another ninety-four sculptures. In 1851 Wyon exhibited a tazza that he had modelled from a Greek design for the Art Union of London at the Great Exhibition. Minton and Wedgwood reproduced his busts of famous figures in Parian, In 1853 Wedgwood reproduced *Wellington* and in 1866 *Palmerston*.

The Net Mender sculpt, E.W. Wyon, reproduced by W.T. Copeland for the Art Union of London 1873

Outside Decoraters and Retailers Specialist decorating establishments who employed many of the artists and painters

Outside decorating establishments have played an important part in the history of ceramic art. Many were founded in the mid-1700s to provide new markets with oriental-style designs. They bought white ware from various potteries to decorate, often on a commission basis, and they sourced and trained their own decorators.

As the market expanded, china warehouses, whose owners were called 'Chinamen', eventually incorporated large retail establishments, such as Thomas Goode and A.B. Daniell. They commissioned special wares from potteries and designed their own backstamps, which became trademarks. Their clientele included the royalty of many countries and members of the aristocracy, who bought large services finely painted, gilded and decorated with their armorial arms and crests. Eventually the major potteries opened their own showrooms in fashionable parts of London. However, it was not until the1860s that both retailers and potteries appreciated the commercial value of a painter's signature on their wares. Originally this was recorded only in pattern and costing books purely for factory records, but slowly customers wanted to know who had painted the magnificent services they had just acquired.

After the financial and prestigious success of the Great Exhibition of 1851, exhibitions became one of the retailers' and potteries' major promotional outlets. They were staged in London, Dublin, Vienna and Paris, and later in America, Australia and New Zealand.

Retail establishments were now catering for the growing wealthy middle class, which was also starting to commission specially designed dessert services and ornamental ware. Retailers would even arrange for the pottery artist to go to a customer's country estate to paint the local landscape, or into an orangey to paint the new, exotic plants brought into the country from other parts of the world. Many painters were employed on a freelance basis, but some were employed in the Potteries. By the middle of the century, most potteries had their own decorating department and the need for outside establishments slowly faded.

The many decorating establishments that existed in Georgian Britain have not been exhaustively researched and explored, but those that played an important part in the development of ceramic design and decoration in the Potteries are described here.

Absolon, William, 1751–1815

Painter, independent decorator and enameller. He was a member of the Absolon family of china and glass dealers in Yarmouth in the early nineteenth century. William set up his decorating business *The Oven* on the Denes. He decorated cream earthenware obtained from Wedgwood, Shorthose, Leeds and Davenport with crests, flowers and monograms. The painting and decoration was naïve and directed at the souvenir trade. In 1808 he and his daughter bought a shop at the corner of Market Street, Yarmouth. Some extant pieces, although marked Wedgwood or Turner and other known potteries, also have the mark 'Absolon Yarm O' (the final letter is Greek for 'th'). Not all the pieces he painted are signed or marked by him. Some had an impressed arrow, which may be the pottery of Shorthose of Hanley, Staffordshire. One of his favorite decorations was the Yarmouth coach taken from the print *Yarmouth Coach* published by D. Boulter of Great Yarmouth, engraved by J. Thompson of Norwich. In 1792 a halfpenny decorated with a three-masted ship and the coat of arms of Yarmouth was issued with the inscription 'Payable at the Glass Warehouses of W Absolon'.

Allen, Robert, 1744–1835

Outside decorator trained at the Lowestoft porcelain manufactory and eventually in 1802 became manager of the works. By 1803–04 he is thought to have had a shop in Crown Street, Lowestoft, where he had a decorating kiln to fire ware from Rockingham and other factories then sold in his shop, He also stocked some Chinese porcelain. His business flourished for the next thirty years. His signature 'Allen Lowestoft' has been found. Some of his ware was made especially for the tourist trade, inscribed 'A Present from Lowestoft' and bearing the initials R.A.

For the Encouragement of British Manufacturers Artists and Dealers and for Receiving General Property for Sale on Commission Established Text 1st 1817

Aynsley, John, 1752–1829

Engraver, painter and probably outside decorator, the founder of the Aynsley factory. He was apprenticed to Thomas Jeffrys, a well-known engraver, and by 1775 had established a pottery. When he married in 1777 he was described as a painter, possibly on china, and by Liverpool printer John Sadler as an enameller. Family documents reveal that he left his home in Harley Towers, Northumberland and became one of the original partners of the first Fenton Colliery in 1790, and that it was his love of porcelain that then led him to become a master potter. From 1788 to 1791 he ran a decorating business in Lane End, Longton. *The Staffordshire Mercury* of 1828 describes him as one of the first manufacturers of porcelain and as a lustrer. He made beer and cider mugs, decorating them with coloured and black printed patterns. He had two sons and twelve daughters; he was succeeded by his eldest son James and then by his grandson John, who continued to manufacture porcelain of a high standard with fine decoration. By 1856 grandson John had become a well-known figure in the Potteries, elected Mayor of Longton four times and died in 1907.

Barlow, Charles, c. 1883–1920s

Outside decorator at Hanley, Staffordshire. He decorated white ware from many of the local factories using two-coloured gold and fine hand-painting. His backstamp has been found.

Battam, Thomas Esq., and Thomas Battam & Sons

Outside decorators and enamellers. Thomas Battam (Senior, 1786–1861) founded the firm. He married Louisa (née Harrison) at Finsbury, London in January 1809 and two of their children, Thomas and Frederick, were to become well-known artists and designers, while John (born 1813) ran the business with his father. After Thomas Battam (Senior) died John and Frederick were partners in the company; John took over the day-to-day running and Frederick continued to decorate pieces. In 1871 John was described as a china decorator employing three men, three apprentices and two women, but by 1881 he is described as a china decorator master employing four men, two boys and one woman.

The Battam family of decorators traded from two addresses: Gough Street and Johnson's Court, London and were known for their Etruscan and Grecian designs on terracotta ware. Haslem (q.v.) lists the firm of Battam decorators as one of the best in the 1810 to 1830 period when most potters did not have decorating departments on their factory sites and were totally reliant on outside decorating establishments. In the early 1800s Battam created patterns and designs that were popular in fashionable circles and they are known to have decorated ware for many of the Staffordshire potteries in their London establishment.

The company is shown in the *London Commercial Directories* of 1846 as operating from 2 Gough Square, London. They exhibited vases in the Etruscan style at the 1851

Great Exhibition and were described in the illustrated catalogue as 'Mr Battam of Johnson's Court, Fleet Street, Enameller of Porcelain and Glass'. The 1862 London International Exhibition catalogue lists them as 'Messrs Battam & Son of 2 Gough Square, Fleet Street' and the accompanying article states: 'It cannot fail to interest our readers to know in the very heart of the city of London close to its densest and darkest thoroughfare, there is a manufactory in which many beautiful works of Art are designed, modelled, painted and produced.' In 1860 The Ceramic and Crystal Palace Art Union, founded by Thomas and Frederick Battam, commissioned the company to supply Greco-Roman-style vases, which were then given as prizes in the annual draw.

Battam also produced drawing-room ornaments from French models, buying some of the undecorated ware from Blanchard & Co. Frederick and John retired some time between 1881 and 1891; it seems that neither Thomas nor John had children and that Frederick's son was not interested in the family firm. As by now most factories had their own in-house decorating departments, the business closed.

Baxter, Thomas, born 1760

Outside decorator. He was first employed as a painter and gilder at Worcester, and it is thought his decorating establishment at 1 Goldsmith Street, Gough Square, Clerkenwell, London was probably started in 1797. He decorated tea wares supplied by Chamberlains of Worcester and later blanks from John Rose of Coalport, Shropshire. Some were signed and dated after 1799, but it is not possible to tell whether all those found of this date are his work or that of his talented son. However, it is thought that the business closed around 1814 when his son Thomas (q.v.) returned to Worcester.

Boulton, Matthew, 1728–1809

Designer and inventor born in Birmingham and continued his father's silver inlaying business. He and Josiah Wedgwood believed art should be applied to industrial manufacture and designed their ware to this end. Boulton built Wedgwood a lathe with an eccentric movement that created geometrical, diced and incised fluted decoration. He also mounted Wedgwood ornamental pieces in well-designed surrounds. He was associated with James Watt, manufacturer of steam engines.

Bow Manufactory

Bow wares were advertised in Derby and London newspapers during 1753 to 1757. The warehouse and showroom was at St James Street, Cornhill, London and the goods displayed were displayed there on the terrace. Bow advertised useful ware with the real price marked on each piece, saying that artists from Dresden painted many of their Japanese designs. Many dealers at this time preferred to buy undecorated white ware, which they could then decorate specifically.

Bradley & Co., or Bradley & Co. of Pall Mall, London, or J. Bradley & Co.

Retailers and outside decorators who bought Worcester and Swansea pottery blanks, which they backstamped with the company name. They employed some of the best painters of the day. An 1885 *Pottery Gazette* article noted that the brothers fired their ware at Pall Mall and that they had brought china painting back into fashion by teaching it to members of the aristocracy. The Bradleys came from Staffordshire and both had artistic talent. One brother is known to have painted on ivory and the other was probably a canvas artist. A superb landscape painting on an undated Derby plaque is known and is signed J. Bradley (q.v.).

Broadfoot, William, active c. 1800

Painter and Chinaman, an apprentice painter at Dr Wall's Pottery, Worcester in 1765 and may have become the manager of the Flight & Barr factory retail shop in High Street, Worcester. By 1820 the *Worcester Directory* lists 'Broadfoot and Ballenger, Glass and China Warehouse, 1 The Cross, Worcester'.

Brown(e), William, c. 1770

Painter and outside decorator apprenticed at Chelsea. He set up business in Coppice Row, Cold Bath Fields, London. In September 1765 the *St James Chronicle* reported that this building had caught fire and in 1774 the premises were sold by auction. Brown went into partnership with William Hay of Bow, near Stratford, London, but this was dissolved in 1775. He wanted to start a pottery factory in Dublin and is known to have asked the Earl of Derby for help, but whether or not he achieved his ambition is not known.

Callowhill & Co., active 1870–1880

Outside decorating business in Worcester run by the brothers James and William Scott Callowhill (q.v.). They bought white undecorated ware from the Staffordshire potteries, especially tea wares.

Chamberlain, Richard

Enameller, gilder and outside decorator who ran a decorating shop with a retailing outlet for Worcester. He also worked for Turner of Caughley enamelling and gilding their products, which he sold in his shop.

Chamberlain, Robert, 1737–1798

Painter and outside decorator who was possibly the first apprentice at the Worcester Porcelain Co. in the 1750s. He became head of the decorating department and left c.1786 to start his own decorating establishment at Diglis, Worcester. Robert and his son Humphrey (1762–1841) bought blanks from the Cauldon factory; some were decorated by Thomas Turner of the Caughley Works and sent to their London warehouse; others were sold in the Chamberlains' shop at 33 High Street, Worcester.

Coningsby, Norris, born c. 1804

Freelance landscape painter and outside decorator. He was an apprentice at the Grainger Worcester factory around 1826. He married Mary Grainger, daughter of Joseph Grainger. Coningsby worked on a freelance basis and by 1835 had an outside decorating business and a china shop at 55 Tything, Worcester, which is shown in Bentley's local guide c.1840–41 under china gilders and enamellers. He had other interests and is shown in the 1851 Lascelles & Co. Directory as a manufacturer of burnished gold china tea and breakfast sets. However, it is unlikely that he actually made the ware. Painted marks have been found of 'C Norris Worcester' and 'Norris Worcester'.

Cooper, Samuel, active 1860

Independent painter of china operating from 62, Caroline Street, Longton, Staffordshire.

Daniells of London

In 1810 Alfred Daniell (1785–1855) owned a small china shop in Baker Street, London. He had two sons, Alfred Bainbridge (1812–88) and Richard Percival (1819–1913). From 1825 to 1828 the firm is shown in the *London Gazette* as a china retailer, styled 'Chinaman', trading in Wigmore Street with an unknown partner. How long this partnership lasted is not known. However, by 1837 Alfred had established a glass and china retail warehouse at 129 New Bond Street, London. This was very successful and about 1840 was granted a Royal Warrant to trade as 'Chinamen with Special Appointment to Her Majesty'. The business expanded and is shown as trading from two establishments, one at 18 Wigmore Street and the other at 129 New Bond Street, a fashionable part of London.

On the death of their father, the brothers Alfred and Richard took over the family business. In 1858 they were trading as A.B. & R.P. Daniell China and Glass Dealers, having been awarded the Royal Warrant allowing them to trade 'By Special Appointment to Her Majesty'. As often happens in families, the brothers felt it necessary to trade independently and split the business. Alfred took the Wigmore Street establishment and his brother New Bond Street. Both were very successful, commissioning wares from well-known potteries in Stoke-upon-Trent, such as Minton, Copeland and Doulton, from Worcester, Crown Derby, and also Limoges in France. The brothers had different marketing ideas, Alfred expanding the Wigmore Street business to cover numbers 42, 44 and 46 by selling antiques and china, while Richard sold fine china combined with an interior decorating business. In 1879 Alfred handed the business over to his son Henry Spencer Daniell who, the family remember, said that in the early 1900s the antique business was suffering from china dealer auction rings, which he felt made honest trade impossible, so he sold the antique part to his cousin, George Agnew of Agnew's of Bond Street, London.

Unfortunately few family and trading records have survived, making it difficult to trace the Daniell businesses and record the various Daniell backstamps. Throughout their many years of trading, Daniells ordered china and earthenware from many potteries, often choosing standard productions of fine patterns and shapes with care to reflect changing market trends. They also bought white ware, which they passed to outside decorators. Daniells sold specially designed and commissioned ware, dessert, tea and coffee services, and vast dinner services to the wealthy at home and especially in America. They gained an important commission from the Mountbatten family villa overlooking Hyde Park in Park Lane, London, the designs for which were influenced by the work of William Morris and the Arts and Crafts movement. The family remembers another large order from Pierpoint Morgan, who owned a sumptuous house *Manresa* at Roehampton.

Henry Spencer Daniell was a great collector of snuff-boxes, a hobby he had in common with the Marquess of Hereford and his son Richard Wallace. He was commissioned to buy many antiques for the family. During WWII the collection was moved to a disused mine in Wales for safety. All the walls, floors and rooms had been charted to ensure the collection could be reassembled correctly, and after the War the collection was returned to its original home at Manchester Square, London, where it has now become the Wallace Collection. Family stories reveal that by 1910 the family business had closed. Henry walked in to the shop one morning and announced, without any warning, that he would no longer trade, paid his staff and closed the doors forever.

Davenport & Co.

Owned and operated a showroom and warehouse at 82 Fleet Street, London. A bill headed 'Davenport & Co.' shows that in 1840 they had an outlet at 36 Canning

BY SPECIAL APPOINTMENT TO H.M. THE KING

A. B. DANIELL & SONS

Old Oak Rooms Oak Panelling

SPECIALISTS IN INTERIOR DECORATION

42, 44, 46, WIGMORE STREET, W.

Left: Advert for Daniells
Below: Daniells Stand

Street, Liverpool, a warehouse at 221 Schusselbuden, Lubeck and an outlet in Hamburg at 4 Grosse Johannes Strasse.

Day Lewis, F., 1845–1910

Designer and author born in London but educated and trained in Germany and France. He acquired experience in many craft workshops and specialised in stained glass designs. In 1870 he established his own business, producing designs for pottery, textiles, wallpaper, stained glass and embroidery. In 1899 he designed exclusively for the Pilkington Pottery. Lewis Day was a founder member of the Art Workers' Guild (1884) and the Arts and Crafts Exhibition Society (1888). He wrote articles for the *Art Journal* and *The Studio Year Book*.

Derby manufactory

Held auction sales throughout the country that were well advertised. The sale by auction of 9 and 10 February 1773 at the Royal Academy, Pall Mall, London included twenty-three items of Derby and Chelsea ware. Derby opened a warehouse at 1 Bedford Street, Covent Garden, London, advertising over two hundred items for sale.

Dillwyn, Lewis Llewellyn, born 1814

The son of Lewis Weston Dillwyn (q.v.), who entered his father's factory in 1831 and by 1836 was in sole charge. He tried to introduce Etruscan ware, which was designed by his wife (the daughter of De la Beche, a noted geologist) who had travelled widely with her father and was influenced by Greek art. Mrs Dillwyn had her own room at the pottery, but the venture was unsuccessful, although some examples do survive.

Dillwyn, Lewis Weston, born 1778

Naturalist and potter interested in the secrets of porcelain manufacture and with the artistic ability to produce exquisite decorations. In 1802 his father leased the Cambrian pottery at Swansea for him, where he employed many of the finest ceramic painters of the day; he even tried to persuade Bramheld of the Rockingham factory to join him at Swansea. In 1814, believing that William Billingsley and S. Walker knew how to produce fine porcelain, he engaged W. W. Young, a painter of butterflies, and T. Pardoe a floral artist, as decorators.

Dixon, William, born 1770

Outside decorator and landscape painter at the Herculaneum pottery, Liverpool from1810 to 1820. He painted allegorical decorations: one on a new oval-shape teapot is known, as is a portrait of the factory manager William Smith on a bough pot. Dixon married Elizabeth Whittle in 1797 and they lived at 5 Northumberland Street, Liverpool. He was described as an enameller.

Doe & Rogers, active 1840s

The history of this decorating business is difficult to establish accurately. E. Doe and G. Rogers were painters of great skill and the Chamberlain factory in Worcester, where it is thought they served their apprenticeships, employed both at some time. In 1805 they set up a decorating business at 25 Clerkenwell Close, London but it closed in 1807. In 1808 George Rogers was employed as a traveller for Chamberlain's Worcester factory while E. Doe continued to paint, exhibiting at the Royal Academy from 1832 to 1846. Sometime in the 1820s they returned to the Worcester area and again went into partnership in a decorating business. This continued to flourish until George Rogers' death in 1835, and it was then run by George's widow and son and E. Doe. In 1841 a Doe and Rogers decorating business is shown in the Worcester Directories operating from High Street, Worcester. The partners exhibited at the Great Exhibition of 1851 and E. Doe also sent some exhibits under his own name from the same address. Whether Doe had a son who worked with them is not proven; the only clue is a 'Doe J.' shown in the Chamberlain records. There is a jug marked Doe and Rogers in the Worcester Porcelain Museum.

Donovan, James and Son, Dublin, trading 1770s–1829

Outside decorators working from Poolpeg Street, Dublin. They bought white ware from English and continental potteries, which they marked with 'DONOVAN' or 'Donovan Dublin'. The trade directory shows James Donovan & Son China and Glass Merchants at Georges Quay, Dublin. The names of the painters who decorated their ware are so far not known.

Duesbury & Co.

Manufacturers of Derby and Chelsea porcelain who in June 1773 opened a showroom at 8 Bedford Street, Covent Garden, London selling a variety of useful and ornamental articles and an assortment of biscuit groups and single figures.

Duesbury, William, 1725–1786

Artist, outside decorator and master potter born at Cannock in Staffordshire, son of a tanner. He first worked as an outside decorator from 1751 to 1753. It is thought he may have had a financial interest in the James Giles decorating establishment, and may have been by 1755 in partnership with Mr. Littler at the Longton Hall Porcelain factory. A partnership agreement between Duesbury, Andrew Planche and John Heath describes him as an enameller. A deed found by Jewitt shows that J. Heath put up the money for making china wares. However, Littler had already failed twice in this venture and Duesbury is thought to have traded some of the Longton Hall productions from Derby. In 1770 he bought the Chelsea Porcelain factory. The designs on some of his wares were taken from his library of books, including Middiman's *Select Views of Great Britian*, Milton's *Views in Ireland* and Farrington's *Views of the Lakes etc in Cumberland and Westmorland*.

Elkington and Co., The Silver Wares, founded 1830s

The company was established by George Richard Elkington and his cousin Henry. They made silver mounts for pottery articles such as cake stands and sugar and fruit bowls, which were shown at all the major exhibitions. They employed Christopher Dresser (q.v.) and Pierre-Emil Jeannest (q.v.) as designers. The Company had many retail outlets throughout the world and bought goods from Wedgwood and Copeland. Their invention of EPNS (electro-plated nickel silver) catered for the middle and lower end of the market. All their wares were well marked and show a high standard of decorative art.

Faugeron, active 1870

Painter and freelance artist. His work was exhibited on a pair of Coalport vases in the London International Exhibition of 1873. It was bought by Sir Richard Wallace and possibly specially commissioned by the London retailer Daniell (q.v.).

Giles, John (James), 1718–1780

Painter, outside decorator and enameller, son of James, a china painter. Giles was apprenticed to jeweller John Arthur at St Martins-in-the-Fields and then came to Worcester, but by 1756 had taken over a decorating shop with a kiln in Kentish Town, London. He bought black printed wares, which he painted with enamel colours, and also decorated white ware from Worcester and Bow. He then moved to 82 Berwick Street, Soho, where he stayed for thirteen years, persuading many well-known ceramic and also amateur painters to come to London. As part of his business arrangement with the Worcester factory, James hired a showroom in the art museum in Cockspur Street, where he showed a great variety of Worcester, Derby and Liverpool wares that he had decorated, and also Chinese porcelain.

By 1771 the Worcester connection ceased and Giles then leased a large property, again in Cockspur Street, near to Trafalgar Square, renting the warehouse on a twenty-one year lease at £110 per annum and taking John Higgins as his partner. Unfortunately Higgins died and Giles hit severe financial problems. He is recorded in Mortimer's Directory of 1763 as 'James Giles China and Enamel Painter Berwick Street Soho.This ingenious artist copies Patterns of any china with the utmost likeness, both with respect to the design and the colours, either in the European or Chinese taste. He has brought the enamel colours to great perfection and thereby rendered them extremely useful to the curious artists in that branch.' He bought copper plates from Thomas Turner of Worcester and sold Worcester and Derby wares on fifteen per cent commission; it is thought he may have gained the Royal commission to decorate the Mecklenburg Service made by Chelsea.

Giles worked for several London dealers, such as Charles Vere, and had many well-known customers, including Lord Palmerston, Richard Sheridan and the Duke of Richmond. Although an excellent designer and painter, he was not a successful businessman so was fortunate when William Duesbury of the Derby China works lent him money and eventually bought his business. He died in August 1789 and was buried in the family vault in Paddington old churchyard. Giles's activities are difficult to trace accurately but his undoubted ability as a painter, decorator and designer set a standard that influenced ceramic design into the next century, and his attributed pieces are avidly collected.

Goode, Thomas, of Mayfair, London, founded 1827

In 1826 Thomas Goode (1793–1870) married Sophia Vickery, daughter of a Chinaman in Regent Street, London and by 1827 he had established a business selling fine china and glass at Mill Street, Hanover Square, London. This was an ideal location near to Mayfair. His fine decorative china with new and exciting designs and patterns appealed to the aristocracy, who became his customers. By 1844 he had expanded and moved to 19 South Audley Street, Mayfair. In 1851 he and his family was still living on the premises.

William James Goode (q.v.) was not only a fine businessman but also an accomplished artist and painter. He regularly visited Minton and Copeland and often altered their designs and brought some of his own that they then produced. In 1856 he was married to Millicent Fores at St Georges, Hanover Square and the next year his father Thomas made him a partner in the business. By 1871 William and Millicent were living at 18 South Audley Street, next door to the showroom, and he was described as a china dealer.

By 1876 the South Audley Street business had grown into twelve spacious showrooms exhibiting the finest glass and china, and was patronised by royalty from home and abroad. Now William and his family of five girls and four boys had moved to Hampstead to a large house with sixteen bedrooms and a musician's gallery. William was an avid collector of antiquities, jewels, snuffs boxes and early Chinese and Viennese porcelain; some of the rare pieces in his collection he had copied by Minton. The Paris Exposition of 1878 was a great success for the Minton–Goode combination. William James had helped to design some of the exhibits, and his company bought the whole of the Minton display, which they then exhibited at the South Audley Street Galleries 1–10 April. The exhibition attracted many members of royalty who ordered large quantities from the company. The Goode and Minton families were not only business associates but also family friends. William and Millicent named two of their boys after members of the Minton family. They were trained by their father to continue the family firm and travelled widely learning the business. Minton Goode concentrated on the administrative part of the business leaving Herbert to follow in his father's footsteps, showing the same aptitude for design. When William died he left the business to Herbert and Minton, and his personal fortune to the other twelve children.

The Paris Exposition of 1889 proved very successful for the Goode business. Although they had their own display, they were so impressed with the Copeland exhibits that they bought them all. After WWI the pattern of trading changed forever. The aristocracy and minor royal houses of Europe had been decimated and their estates sold. Goode adapted to the changes. In 1918 they became a limited company and were joined by younger brother Ernest, who was to prove just as able as his brothers and the company continued to prosper. They used their backstamp on the ware, sometimes alone and at other times alongside the maker's backstamp. The company, no longer a family business, continues to trade from South Audley Street, London.

Howell & James (& Co.)

Retailers of home furnishings who held annual china painting exhibitions. The first one in 1876 was rather disappointing but they later became events of the London Season, providing an opportunity for anyone with talent to display their work. Originally they were dominated by the work of those training at the Lambeth School of Art and often on Doulton ware. However, many other artists, both amateur and professional, showed their work. The prizes awarded were eagerly sought after. Labels of 'Howell and James Art-Pottery Exhibition' may still be

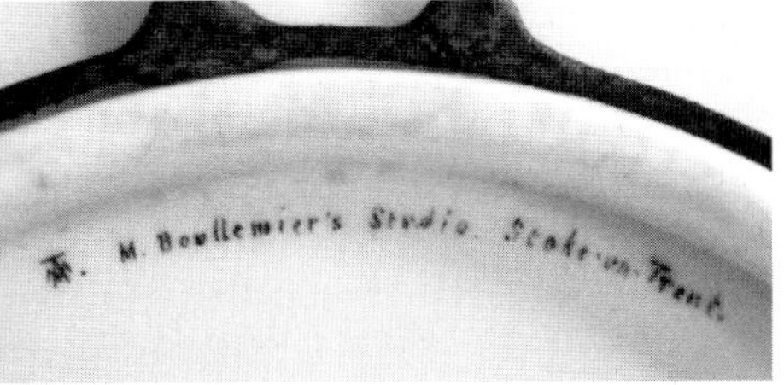

Above and Left: Boullimiers studio photo of detail and photo of studio mark detail, *Sailor Girl* Minton bone china small plaque, private collection

Above: Copeland Advertisement Coaster typical of the late Victorian Era

Left: Copeland crest designs, sample from pattern book, courtesy of the Spode Museum Trust Stoke on Trent

Below Left: W T Copeland's Show Museum at Stoke on Trent

Below Right: Copeland Modernistic Dog produced in the 1930s in Velamore Glaze

found on some pieces collected today. They include the artist's name, the title of the work, the price and whether the artist was professional or amateur.

Lewis, Charles, active 1840

Painter, gilder and china figure maker, originally a grocer but had a small decorating business operating from Slack Lane, Hanley, Staffordshire. In 1845 he was made bankrupt and had to sell his moulds, enamels and stock (such was the fate of many small potteries, and original moulds, designs and enamels were continually circulating throughout the pottery industry).

Liberty & Co.

Oriental Warehouse and Retail Shop, Regent Street, London, founded 1875

Sir Arthur Lasenby Liberty (1843–1917) was employed, aged eighteen, at Messrs Farmer & Rogers. He was fascinated with the Japanese exhibits at the London International Exhibition of 1862 and began to study Oriental art. In 1875 he opened his first shop at 218a Regent Street, London, with one assistant and one porter. It was an instant success, selling Oriental art and Japanese blue-and-white porcelain and artifacts. The business was patronised by such artists as Rossetti, Whistler, and Burne Jones (q.v.). Liberty pioneered art pottery and the innovative art designs of his day, and commissioned ware from Moorcroft, Aller Vale Art pottery, Della Robbia pottery, the Ruskin pottery and Doulton.

When James McIntyre & Co. ceased art pottery production, Liberty went into partnership with William Moorcroft, their designer. Many of the wide range of wares Liberty sold bear the backstamp Liberty & Co or Liberty instead of or in addition to that of the actual maker. He was the first dealer to introduce new Celtic designs, selling Cymric silver and garden furniture; by 1908 Liberty's 'Barum' Ware is illustrated in their Yuletide gifts catalogue. The name Liberty's became synonymous with good contemporary design.

Minton's Studio, South Kensington, London

The Studio, designed by Gilbert R. Redgrave, was built on land owned by the Commissioners of the Great Exhibition and rented to Colin Minton Campbell for a ground rent of £136.13s.4d for seven years. It was situated between the Royal Albert Hall and the Horticultural Gardens and it consisted of a number of small studios, workshops and firing kilns. The first superintendent was William Coleman (q.v.). The *Art Journal* of 1872 states that between twenty and twenty-five women, all of good social standing, were employed. Many had attended the Central Art School in Lambeth; some of their teachers were young male artists who had been trained at the Minton factory, Stoke-upon-Trent. Minton sent biscuit ware of chargers, tiles, plaques, vases and flasks to the Studio to be decorated and then fired. It became well known for innovative designs and decorations. By special agreement the engine house chimney at the Royal Albert Hall was used as a smoke vent from the firing kilns. Although the location was ideal and the finished ware was highly priced, the Studio failed to cover its expenses. Coleman was not an ideal manager and after John Eyre joined him spent more time on his own pursuits. Mathew Elden replaced Coleman but he was an eccentric, certainly not blessed with managerial skills. In 1875 a fire devastated the Studio and all its records. Although Minton would have rebuilt the Studio, the authorities at South Kensington refused to give their permission.

Artists associated with the Studio include Thomas Allen (q.v.), Hannah Barlow (q.v.), Lucien Besche (q.v.), Helen Cordelia, Rebecca Coleman and William Stephan Coleman.

Mist, J., 82 Fleet Street, London

J. Mist was a well-known London selling agent who went into partnership with William Abbott, trading as Abbott and Mist. The printed bill head in Bevis Hillier's book *Master Potters of the Industrial Revolution: the Turners of Lane End* claims that they were potters to His Royal Highness, the Prince of Wales, stocking china and glass. It was thought Abbott retired around 1811 aged 68 but the partnership agreement shows the date as 1809. James Underhill Mist continued to operate the retail business. Some of the ware sold is impressed with the trading name; eventually the Davenport factory took over the business.

Mongenot, Joseph, 1769–1814

Modeller, engraver and designer born in Switzerland, son of an officer in the French army. In 1788 he escaped from France and worked on a freelance basis in London, moving to Birmingham before joining the William Adams factory at Tunstall, Staffordshire. His work in the classical style was used in their bas-relief patterns.

Mortlock's Old Pottery Galleries, operating 1746–1930

John Mortlock established the firm in 1746, which became one of the foremost influential china warehouses in London and was operated by succeeding members of the family. In 1777 John and William Mortlock traded from the Staffordshire Warehouse at 250 Oxford Street, London. As the business expanded they sold Rockingham ware and also purchased much of the white ware from the Nantgarw Pottery, which was decorated by fine painters, such as Randall (q.v.) and Webster (q.v.) and sent to Robins & Randall of Spa Fields, London for firing. Two years later Mortlock were decorating and selling most of the output from the Coalbrookdale China Company and traded under that name.

In 1812 John Mortlock took over the firm and by 1835 had taken Simon Sturges into a partnership that lasted until 1840, after which time John traded alone. In 1872 John William, who was possibly the most controversial member of the family, took over. He became heavily involved with the organisation of the Great Exhibition of 1851. As a member of the Jury of the Ceramic Court he visited various Potteries to see their exhibits. As his firm had their own exhibits at the Exhibition and they had also ordered exhibits from the leading Potteries, including Minton, his choice as a Juror was said to be inappropriate. When the medallist was published and Minton was awarded the premier medal, Copeland lodged complaints, but the decision held.

In 1877 the business traded as Mortlock's Old Pottery Galleries. In the 1880s Mortlock had a decorating studio at 31–32 Orchard Street, London, where they employed many of the painters who had been previously employed at the Minton Art Studio. Their showrooms were at 466, 468 and 470 Oxford Street, London and at 2b Granville Place, Portman Square, London. The company prospered and influenced design and decoration from the 1770s into the twentieth century.

Ring & Carter, 7 Bath Street, Bristol

Manufactures and dealers of all kinds of earthenware. Their manufactory was at Temple Banks, Bristol. They either impressed the ware or used a backstamp.

Sadler & Green

John Sadler (1720–89) was the son of Adam Sadler (1682–1765), one of the Duke of Marlborough's soldiers in the Low Countries. After Adam left the army he lodged with a printer and learnt the business. John was trained by his father and rented a house from him in Harrington Street, Liverpool for five shillings a year. He started his own business as a transfer printer around 1756. He and Guy Green, who had also been an apprentice under his father, became partners and may have produced some earthenware. John applied for a patent for printing on pottery in August 1756. It is said he and Green were able to print more than twelve hundred tiles in six hours. Richard Abbey, who was to start a pottery at Toxteth Park, 'later known as the Herculaneum Pottery, the largest in Liverpool', Jeremiah Evans and Thomas Billinge were apprentices with the firm. Josiah Wedgwood used Sadler & Green to decorate many of his wares, such as those with scenes from Aesop's *Fables*. After John retired in 1770 Guy Green continued the business into the 1790s. Adam Sadler died in 1788 aged eighty-three and John in 1789 aged sixty-nine.

Sayer, Robert, 1725–1794

Print and map dealer trading from the Golden Buck, 53 Fleet Street, London, who after twenty-four years of dealing on his own, in 1775 took J. Bennett as a partner until 1784. After this he again traded alone. Sayer published *The Ladies Amusement* 1758–62, described thus on the title page: 'Extremely useful to the PORCELAINE and other manufacturers depending on design'. In it are illustrations by Pillement (q.v.), Hancock (q.v.) and others. Wedgwood, Bow, Chelsea and Worcester potteries adapted some of these designs and Sadler & Green printed them. The book shows contributions by C.K Herrick of superb butterflies; C. Fenn of butterflies and fruit; J. June and P. Benazsch of birds; Elliott of horses; and James Roberts of all animals, single flower studies and flower sprays. This book is the work of many fine artists. As ceramic design continues to be researched, more pieces will be found that were decorated from this source.

Seeman, Abraham

Painter and colour maker. An advertisement in the *Birmingham Gazette* of 23 September 1751 shows him as: 'Enamel painter at Mrs Weston's in Freeman Street, Birmingham, makes and sells all sorts of enamel colours, especially the ROSE colours, likewise all sorts for china painters.' He also enamelled on copper.

Sharpus, Messrs R. & E.

Retailers of 13 Cockspur Street, London. Around 1801 their trade card read: 'Coalbrookdale China and Art Glass manufacturer'. In 1806 they stocked all varieties of Coalport pottery, which was very popular. Their stock was large, varying from garden furniture to chimney ornaments. Although Coalport was their main selling product, they also stocked items from other well-known potteries.

Smith, William, active 1800s

Painter and outside decorator, one of William Duesbury's (q.v.) first apprentices. When he left the works he set up an enameling business in St Alkmund's Churchyard, Derby, where he had a kiln. He moved to two other premises, first Spring Gardens, London Road and finally to Robin Hood Yard, Iron Gate. Smith may have been apprenticed to his father, a colour maker who created *Smiths Blue*, a favourite Derby colour.

Sparks, George, 1804–1874

Outside decorator and painter of good quality porcelains, based at Worcester. He was a talented painter and was probably trained at one of the Worcester potteries. In 1834 he set up his own establishment, specialising in heraldic and crest decoration. He designed a unique backstamp for his Worcester and Coalport ware and gained a Royal appointment to Queen Adelaide, Queen Consort of William IV; pieces can be found bearing this mark. George Sparks had a warehouse at Broad Street, Worcester, where he sold a range of products, such as lamps, lustres and Bohemian vases and was proud to advertise that he sold Coalport pieces at the same price that they could be bought from the factory. He was an agent for Minton's waxed flowers and had many aristocratic customers, including the Duchess of Kent. The pieces of porcelain that bear his backstamp are well painted and of a fine quality. He supplied the armed services with arms and crests, for which he charged sixpence each; boarding houses, hotels and schools were quoted a special discount price for similar products.

Temple, Charles M., 1857–1940

Painter, designer and outside decorator working for Maw & Co of Ironbridge designing and painting tiles. Around 1890 he adapted designs from a church reredos by Weatherstone for tiles commissioned by the Shrewsbury ear, nose and throat hospital. They represented Faith, Hope and Charity. His output was prodigious and his designs gained the company exhibition success in Chicago in 1893. His work was also exhibited in the Arts and Crafts Exhibition of 1893. Charles designed portrait tiles and invented a process of photographic transfer. In 1906 he left Maws to establish his own decorating studio, but continued to use their blanks. He signed his work 'C.M. Temple'.

Temple, Madame, Regent Street, London

Madame Temple was a retailer and designer who is especially remembered for the service she designed in 1862 for Copeland. It was made of Parian and bone china and had seven centrepieces supported with figures, which were sculpted by James Beattie (q.v.). The dessert plates, with pierced borders, were decorated with flowers and chased gold. She displayed the service at her large, fashionable showroom in Regent Street, and it was then exhibited at the London International Exhibition of 1862. The Temple establishment continued to commission wares from Copeland into the early twentieth century.

Wedgwood Decorating Studio, Chelsea

In 1768 Messrs Wedgwood and Bentley established a decorating studio behind their large showroom at 1 Great Newport Street, Chelsea, London, where they installed a special muffle kiln. It was essential that they had the facility to paint armorial crests on the premises for their wealthy customers. Wedgwood searched for suitably skilled painters and succeeded in luring David Rhodes from Yorkshire. Rhodes had been employed in the firm of Rhodes and Robinson in Leeds, which bought large quantities of earthenware from Wedgwood. David Rhodes joined Wedgwood in Chelsea and even-

Wedgwood Showroom London

tually became manager of the decorating department, answerable to Bentley. He not only painted but also prepared colours and was privy to many secret recipes. His association with Wedgwood lasted for over ten years. Rhodes may have had a partner, William Hopkins Craft, a talented painter of landscapes, portraits and fine encaustic vases, but in 1771 he left Wedgwood to become an independent decorator.

The famous Frog Service was decorated in this studio and when finished was displayed in the Wedgwood showroom at 12 Greek Street, Soho, London. The studio premises also had living accommodation, which was used by Bentley and his wife. However, the premises were soon too small for their trade and the business was transferred to 2 Little Cheyne Row, Chelsea. By the mid-1770s it is thought that thirty-three painters and paintresses were employed at Chelsea. The decorating studio closed in 1774 and the painters were transferred to Portland House, Greek Street, London.

Whitaker and Cocker, active 1830s

Painter, gilders and outside decorators. John Whitaker was an apprentice gilder and border painter at the Derby factory until 1826. He married Anne, sister of John Stanesby, and became George Cocker's partner at his Friar Gate, Derby decorating business. They made small figures, which Whitaker gilded and decorated. By 1853 he was at Minton, but only for a brief period as he was now receiving commissions from many of the Staffordshire potteries, including John Mountford (q.v.).

Below: Copeland Bone china Fish service paintd by H. Lea commissioned by Phillips of London c. 1895

Right: Back stamp showing Brown Westhead Moore & Co. were commissioned by Tiffany's of New York

Right: Slip Decorators, showing Harry Barnard

Below: Jasper Decorators, showing Bert Bentley

Bibliography

Elizabeth Adams and David Redstone, *Bow Porcelain,* 1981, Faber and Faber

Louise Ade Boger, *The Dictionary of World Pottery and Porcelain,* 1971, A & C Black Ltd

John Allwood, *The Great Exhibitions,* 1977, Studio Vista

M Althorpe-Guyton with J Stevens, *A Happy Eye a school of art in Norwich 1845-1982,* Jarrold & Sons Ltd

Ruth Irwin Weidler, American Ceramic Circle, *The Callowhills, Anglo-American Artists, an introduction,*

Isabelle Anscombe and Charlotte Gere, *Arts and Crafts in Britain and America,* 1978, Academy Editions

Frank Ashworth, *John Aynsley, 1823-1907,* Post Graduate Research Diploma, Southampton Institute

Paul Atterbury, *Moorcroft 1897-1993,* revised edition, Richard Dennis & Hugh Edwards

Paul Atterbury, Editor, *The Parian Phenomenon,* 1989, Richard Dennis

Paul Atterbury & Maureen Batkin, *Dictionary of Minton,* 1990, Antique Collectors Club

John C Austin, *J Palin Thorley 1892-1987 Potter and Designer part 1,* 2005, Ceramics in America

J. & B. Austwick, *The Decorated Tile and Illustrated History of English Tile-making and Design,* 1980, Pitman House

Diane Baker, *Potworks, The Industrial Architecture of the Potteries,* 1991, The Royal Commission of Public Buildings

David Barker, *William Greatbatch A Staffordshire Potter,* 1991, Jonathan Horne

Franklin A Barrett & Arthur L Thorpe, *Derby Porcelain,* 1971, Faber & Faber Ltd

Brian Bates, 'William Hackwood; His life Ancestry and Descendants', *ARS Ceramica,* 2001, No 17, The Wedgwood Society of New York

Maureen Batkin, *Wedgwood Ceramics 1846-1959 a new appraisal,* 1982, Richard Dennis

Oliver Becket, *J. F. Herring & Sons,* 1981, J A Allen & Co

John Bedford, *Chelsea and Derby Porcelain Collectors Pieces,* 1967, Cassell and Co.

Quentin Bell, *The Schools of Design,* 1963, Routledge & Kegan Paul

Geoffrey Bemrose, *19th Century English Pottery and Porcelain,* 1952, Faber and Faber

Victoria Bergeson, *The Encyclopedia of British Art Pottery 1870-1920,* 1991, Barrie & Jenkins

Michael Berthoud F.R.I.C.S., F.S.V.A., *H & R Daniel 1822-1846,* 1980, Micawber Publications

J.F. Blacker, *19th Century English Ceramic Art,* 1912, The Copp, Clark Co.

Gaye Blake Roberts, *Proceedings of the Wedgwood Society of London,* 1995, No 15, 'Wedgwood's London Decorating Studio'

Steve Bond, *James Holland The Forgotten Artist,* Churnet Valley Books

Cheryl Buckley, *Potters and Paintresses,* The Womans Press

Bernard Bumpus, *Pâte-sur-Pâte the Art of Ceramic Relief Decoration 1849-1992,* 1992, Barrie and Jenkins

Elizabeth Cameron, *Encyclopedia of Pottery and Porcelain Nineteenth and Twentieth Centuries,* 1986, Faber and Faber

Andrew Casey, *20th Century Ceramic Designers in Britain,* 2001, Antique Collectors Club

Miguel de Cervantes Saavedra, *The Ingenious Hidalgo Don Quixote, de la Mancha,* part 1, Chapter XVII

Chambers Biographical Dictionary, edited by Magnus Magnussen, 1990

Robert Cluett, *George Jones Ceramics 1861-1951,* 1998, Shiffer Publishing Company

George Coke, *In Search of James Giles,* 1983, Micawber Publications

Fifty years of Public work of Sir Henry Cole K.C.B., Two vols, 1884, George Bell and Sons

Alwyn Cox & Angela Cox, *Rockingham Pottery & Porcelain 1745-1845*, 1983, Faber & Faber

Alwyn Cox and Angela Cox, *Rockingham 1745-1842,* 2001, Antique Collectors Club

A.J. Cross, *Pilkington's Royal Lancastrian Pottery and Tiles,* 1980, Richard Dennis

John and Margaret Cushion, *A Collectors History of British Porcelain,* 1992, Antique Collectors Club

Richard K Degenhardt, *Belleek The Complete Collectors Guide and Illustrated Reference,* 1993, Second edition, Wallace – Homestead Book Company

Derby Porcelain International Society Newsletter

Gerald Pendred, *Newsletter,* No 40, 1997, 'Michael Kean and Colonel St Leger'

Gaye Blake Roberts, *Newsletter,* No 48, June 2001, 'Review of the Derby International Porcelain Society Journal'

Una Des Fontaines, *The Proceedings of the Wedgwood Society of London,* No 5, Fairyland Lustre, 'The Work of Daisy Makeig-Jones 1881-1945'

Arthur A. Eaglestone & T.W. Lockett, *The Rockingham Pottery,* 1973, David and Charles

English Ceramic Circle

Reginald Haggar, *Transactions*, vol 2, 1975-76, 'Thomas Allen and Silas Rice'

Brig-General Sir Gilbert Mellor, *Transactions*, vol 2, Bristol Delftware

F Severne Mackenna, *Transactions,* vol 4, part 1, 'William Stephans Bristol China Decorator'

Aubrey J Toppin, *Transactions,* vol 4, 'William Hopkins Craft'

Reginald Haggar, *Transactions,* vol 8, part 2, 'Miles Mason'

Jonathan Gray Jewitt, *Transactions,* vol 17, part 2, Trade tokens: Their connections between the 17th and 19th centuries

Rosalind Pulver, *Transactions,* 14 vol 3 Thomas Tatler. Flower Painter, Transaction 1, 1933, page 31

A. J. Toppin, Contributions to the History of Porcelain Making in London

Transaction 2 page 53 *Thomas Hughes. First Enameller of English China, of Clerkenwell*

Oliver Fairclough, vol 16 part 2, 'The London China Trade 1800-1830 Factories Retailers and Decorators supplying a luxury market'

Dr H Bellamy Gardner, *English Porcelain Circle Transactions,* No III, The Chelsea Birds

Gordon Elliott, *The Design Process in British Ceramic Manufacture 1750-1850,* Staffordshire University Press

Desmond Eyles, *Royal Doulton 1815-1965,* 1983, Faber & Faber

Desmond Eyles, *The Doulton Burslem Wares,* 1980, Barrie & Jenkins and Royal Doulton

John Fineran, The *Index of Derbyshire China Painters, Modellers & Gilders connected by Birth, Education, employment or Domicile,* 2000, published by the author

Stanley W. Fisher, *The Decoration of English Porcelain,* 1954, Derek Verschoyle

Frank Freeth, *Absolon of Yarmouth,* The Connoissuer

Alice Cooney Frelinghuysen, *American Porcelain 1770-1920,* 1989, The Metropolitan Museum of Art

Sharon Gater, *Proceedings of the Wedgwood Society of London,* No 11, 1982, Alfred and Louise Powell an Introduction

Sharon Gater, 42nd Wedgwood International Seminar held at Pasadena U.S.A, *Harold Barnard-Pioneer Potter and Philosopher*

Peter S. Goodfellow, *The Vine Pottery, Birks, Rawlins and Company, influences from Minton and Spode/Copeland on Lawrence Arthur Birks and his sculptor/modeller relatives*, unpublished

Graham and Oxley Antiques Ltd catalogue to the Summer Exhibition, 1981, *English Porcelain Painters of the 18th century*

Algernon Graves F.S.A., *A Dictionary of Artists who have exhibited in the Principal London Exhibitions from 1760-1893*, third edition, Kingsmead Reprints

John Greene, *Brightening the Long Days, Hospital Tile Pictures*, 1987, Architectural Ceramic Society

Nigel Griffin, *Research on William Henry Goss*, 2001

Leonard Griffin, *Clarice Cliff, The Art of Bizarre*, 2001, Pavilion Books

Geoffrey A. Godden, *Coalport and Coalbrookdale Porcelains*, 1970, Herbert Jenkins

Geoffrey A Godden, *The Illustrated Guide to Masons Patent Ironstone China*, 1971, Barrie & Jenkins

Geoffry A Godden, *Ridgway Porcelains*, 1972, Antique Collectors Club

Geoffrey A Godden, *Chamberlain-Worcester Porcelain*, 1982, Barrie & Jenkins

Geoffrey A Godden, *Minton Pottery & Porcelain of the First Period*, 1968, Herbert Jenkins

Geoffrey A Godden, *Staffordshire Porcelain*, 1983, Granada Publishing

Geoffrey A Godden, *Encyclopedia of British Porcelain Manufacturers*, 1988, Barrie & Jenkins

Peter Goodfellow, *The Vine Pottery Birks Rawlings & Co*, 2007, Antique Collectors Club

Eva Adelaide Goss, *Fragments from the Life and Work of W.G. Goss*, 1907, Hill and Ainsworth

Graham II, John Meredith and Wedgwood Hensleigh Cecil, *Wedgwood Catalogue*, 1948, The Brooklyn Institute of Arts and Sciences (from the Brooklyn Museum Exhibition)

Rupert Gunnis, *Dictionary of British Sculptors 1660-1851*, The Abbey Library

Reginald Haggar, *A Century of Art Education in the Potteries*, 1953

Reginald Haggar, *Art in Staffordshire 1800-1914*, unpublished work, City Art Gallery and Museum, Stoke on Trent Ceramic archives

Reginald Haggar, *The Proceedings of the Wedgwood Society of London*, No 6, 'Thomas Allen'

Reginald Haggar, *The Proceedings of the Wedgwood Society of London*, No 9, 1975, 'William Theed and Wedgwood'

Rodney Hampson, *Pottery References in the Staffordshire Advertiser 1795-1865*, 2000, The Northern Ceramic Society

Haslem John, *The Old Derby China Factory*, 1878, Bell and Sons

David Hill, *In Turner's Footsteps*, 1984, John Murray

Bevis Hillier, *The Master Potters of the Industrial Revolution, The Turners of Lane End*, 1965, Cory, Adams & Mackay

Bevis Hillier, *Pottery and Porcelain 1700-1914*, 1968, Weidenfield and Nicholson

David Holgate, *Newhall*, 1971, Barrie and Jenkins

Simon Houfe, *The Dictionary of 19th Century British Book Illustrators*, 1996, revised edition, Antique Collectors Club

Therle Hughes, *Pottery and Porcelain Figures*, 1883, Country Life Books

Frank Hurlbutt, *Old Derby Porcelain and It's Artist Workmen*, 1928, second impression, T Werner Laurie

Llewellyn Jewitt, *The Ceramic Art of Great Britain*, 1985, New Edition, New Orchards Editions

Carol A Jones, *A History of Nottingham School of Design*, 1993, Nottingham Trent University

Joan Jones, *Minton the First Two Hundred Years of Design and Production*, 1993, Swan Hill Press

Ray Jones, *Porcelain in Worcester 1851-1951, an Illustrated Social History*, 1993, Parkbarn

A.E. Jimmy Jones & Sir Leslie Joseph, *Swansea Porcelain Shapes and Decorations*, 1988, D. Brown & Sons

J Johnson & A Greetzner, *A Dictionary of British Artists 1880-1940*, An Antique Collectors Club Research project

Paul Joyner, *Artists in Wales 1740-1851*, 1997, The National Library of Wales

S Keates, *Gazetteer & Directory of the Potteries and Newcastle under Lyme*, 1892

Keele; The Spode Museum Trust archives held at Keele University Staffordshire

Ref 109 List of showroom Stock 1895

Ref 110 Summary of private stock

Ref 137 Spode 160 Celebration report

John Keys, *Sketches of Old Derby and Neighbourhood,* 1895, Bemrose & Sons

D&E Lloyd-Thomas, *The Old Torquay Potteries,* 1978, Stockwell

Terence A. Locket, *Collecting Victorian Tiles,* 1979, Antique Collectors Club

Terence A. Lockett and Geoffrey A. Godden, *Davenport,* 1989, Barrie and Jenkins

Malcolm Haslam, *The Martin Brothers Potters,* 1978, Richard Dennis

Ian Mackenzie, *British Prints Dictionary and Price Guide,* 1998, Antique Collectors Club Reprint

David Manchip, *Artists and Craftsmen of the 19th Century Derby China Factory,* 2004, Landmark Publishing

Julie McKeown, *Burleigh the Story of a Pottery,* 2003, Richard Dennis

Wolf Mankowitz & Reginald G Haggar, *The Concise Encyclopedia of English Pottery and Porcelain,* 1968, Second Edition, Andre Deutsch

Michael Messenger, *Coalport,* 1995, Antique Collectors Club

Lynn Miller, *ARS Ceramica,* No 17, 2001, The Wedgwood Society of New York, 'William Hackwood; A Lifetime of work for Wedgwood'

Minton Tiles 1835-1935, Exhibition Catalogue, Stoke on Trent City Museum and Art Gallery

Peter and Linda Murray, *Dictionary of Art and Artists,* Thames & Hudson

Derek H Chitty, *Northern Ceramic Society Newsletter,* No 197, 'Harry Tittensor RA 1887-1942'

Harry F Blackburn, *Northern Ceramic Society Newsletter,* No 122, A Head of his Time

Peter Goodfellow, *Northern Ceramic Society Newsletter,* No 119, 'The Reuter influence at the Vine Pottery, Stoke'

Richard Ormond, *Sir Edwin Landseer,* 1981, Thames and Hudson

T. H. Peake, *William Brownfield and Son(s),* 1995, T. H. Peake

Keith Poole, *The Art of the Torquay and South Devon Potteries,* 1996, The Torquay Pottery and Collectors Society

Rina Prentice, *A Celebration of the Sea,* 1994, The Decorative Arts Collection of the National Maritime Museum

E. Stanley Price, *John Sadler a Liverpool Pottery Printer,* 1948, published by the Author

Martin Pulver, a paper read at the Linnean Society on 15th November, 1986, *A Nineteenth Century Newspapers Description of the Potteries trade*

John Randall, *The Clay Industries including the Fictile and Ceramic Arts on the Banks of the River Severn,* 1877, Shropshire County Library Publication, Madeley, Salop

Philip M. Rayner, *Thomas Goode of London 1827-1977,* Published to celebrate the 150th Anniversary of the Company

Richard and Samuel Redgrave, *A Century of British Painters,* 1981, Second edition, Phaidon Press

Samuel Redgrave, *A Dictionary of Artists of the English School,* 1970, Samuel Redgrave Kingsmead Reprints

Alan B. Reed, *Collectors Encyclopedia of Pickard China,* 1995, Collector Books, USA

Gaye Blake Roberts, *The Green Frog Service,* 1995, Cacklegoose Press in association with The State Hermitage, St Petersburg

Gaye Blake Roberts, *Proceedings of the Wedgwood Society of London,* No 12, 'The Wedgwood School in Rome'

Robin Reilly, *Wedgwood The New Illustrated Dictionary,* 1995, Antique Collectors Club

Robin Reilly & George Savage, *The Dictionary of Wedgwood,* 1980, Antique Collector's Club

Frederick Rhead, *New Hall China,* The Connoisseur

J.R. Riggott, unpublished research into the Cauldon China Factory, Stoke upon Trent, Staffordshire

Clifton Roberts, *The Connnoisseur,* 'Salopian China part II'

Henry Sandon, *Flight and Barr Worcester Porcelain 1783-1840,* 1978, The Antique Collectors Club

Henry and John Sandon, *Grainger's Worcester Porcelain,* 1989, Barrie and Jenkins

David John & Henry Sandon, *The Sandon Guide to Royal Worcester Figures,* 1987, Alderman Press

George Savage, *Seventeenth and Eighteenth French Porcelain,* 1960, Barrie and Rockliff

William Scarrett, *Old times in the Potteries,* 1969, County History reprint

Marc Louis Solon, *A Brief Account of Pâte sur Pâte,* 1985, Minton

Robert Speake, Editor, *The Old Road to Endon,* 1974, The University Keele

Judy Spours, *Art Deco Tableware,* 1988, Ward Lock

Alan Smith, *The Illustrated Guide to Liverpool Herculaneum Pottery,* 1970, Barrie & Jenkins

Staffordshire Advertiser Nov 6th 1869, W. F. Rhodes

Staffordshire Advertiser Feb 11th 1871, Henry Lark Pratt

Staffordshire Advertiser Feb23rd 1867, Thomas Allen Henry Mitchell and E Rischgitz, painting for 1867 Paris Exhibition

Norman Stretton, *The Proceedings of the Wedgwood Society of London,* No 10, 1979, Scenes from Vernet on a Wedgwood Bowl

Roy Strong, *The Collectors Encyclopedia Victoriana to Art Deco,* 1974, Studio Editions

Denis Stuart, Editor, *People of the Potteries,* 1985

Jane Turner, *The Dictionary of Art,* 1996, 24 vols, Macmillian Ltd

William Turner, *Swansea Pottery and Nantgarw Porcelain and Artists,* 1907, The Collector

John Twitchett, original unpublished research on ceramic artists

John Twitchett, *Derby Porcelain,* 1980, Barrie & Jenkins

John Twitchett, *Derby Porcelain; An Illustrated Guide,* 2002, Antique Collectors Club

John Twitchett & Betty Bailey, *Royal Crown Derby,* 1976, Barrie & Jenkins

Glynn Vivian Art Gallery, *Swansea and Nantgarw Porcelain from the Clyne Castle Collection,* 1971, second edition

E. J. D. Warrilow, *A Sociological History of the City of Stoke on Trent*

Wenger's Collection of Pottery, Etruria, Stoke on Trent England. Historical notes on Ceramic Artists of various periods, 1914

Widar Halén, *Christopher Dresser A Pioneer of Modern Design,* 1993, Phaidon Press

Vega Wilkinson, *Turner Copeland and Arthur Perry,* April 1989, The Antique Collector

Vega Wilkinson, *Minton's Landseer Dessert Services,* October 1986, The Antique Dealer and Collectors Guide

Vega Wilkinson, *Spode-Copeland-Spode: The Works and Its People 1770-1970* 2002, The Antique Collectors Club

Vega Wilkinson, Copeland family archives research, Trelissick, Cornwall, unpublished

Vega Wilkinson, Minton Archives research, unpublished

Wilstead John.O & Bernard Morris, *Thomas Baxter the Swansea Years 1816-1819, A study of the Artist's Ceramic and Topographical work at Swansea with a survey of his life and background,* Gomer Press

Peter Woodger, *James Hadley & Sons Artist Potters Worcester,* 2003, published by author

Christopher Wood, *Dictionary of British Art vol IV Victorian Painters,* 1995, Antique Collectors Club

G Woolliscroft Rhead and Frederick Alfred, *Staffordshire Pots and Potters,* 1977, E.P Publishing

George Woolliscroft Rhead, *British Pottery Marks,* 1910, The Pottery Gazette

Hilary Young, *English Porcelain 1745-95,* 1999, V&A Publications

Magazines and other journals

Antique Dealer and Collector

John Sandon, vol 45, No 9, April 1992, *Designer of Influence*

Aantique Collector

Sue Snodin, August 1982, *Susie Cooper's Designs*

Gaye Blake Roberts, October 1980, *Curator of the Wedgwood Museum suggests that her hobbies and private collecting provide one of the best insights into the wide ranging interests of Josiah Wedgwood*

Chris Watkins, October 1981, *A late 19th century earthenware Shelley Intarsio a little known and exciting find*

Antique Collecting

Henry Sandon, January 1978, *Royal Worcester Porcelain Painters 1862-1962*

Audrey Wildish, April 1981, *George Rogers Gilder and Decorator*

Rosemary and Martin Pulver, June 1983, vol 18, No 2, *Rare and Unusual Spode and Copeland Ceramic Pieces*

Moira Thunder, September 1984, vol 19, No 4, *William Wise- A late 19th Century Ceramic Painter*

Neil Fletcher, October 1984, vol 19, No 5, *Sixty Glorious Years the work of Susie Cooper O.B.E.*

Diane Taylor, April 1987, vol 21, No 11, *Design of the Times Keith Murray Designer in Glass, Ceramics & Silver*

Richard Charlton-Jones, 1987, vol 21, No 11, *The Sincerest Form of Flattery George Morland & his Imitators*

Yvonne Jones, November 1988, vol 23, No 6, *The Wolverhampton Style Products of the Old Hall Japan Works*

Maureen Batkin, March 1898, vol 23, No 10, *20th Century Cotswold Furniture painted by Alfred and Louise Powell*

Lars Tharp, November 1989, vol 24, No 6, *William Moorcroft Master Potter of the 20th Century*

John Sandon, February 1990, vol 24, No 9, *Gold … everywhere the glint of Gold*

John Sandon, February 1991, vol 25, No 8, *The Awakening of Worcester porcelain*

Roger Edmunsen, February 1994, *Thomas Martin Randall's Decoration on Porcelain*

Lars Tharp, April 95, *The Rise of the Victorian Tile*

Michael Messenger, October 1995, *Bird painting at Rose's, Coalport*

Andrew Casey, November 1995, *Dynamic Designer a tribute to Susie Cooper OBE, RDI*

Andrew Casey, March 2001, *Tube-Lined Variations*

Antique Dealer & Collectors Guide

W. D. John and G. T. Coombes, December 1873, *Gallic Elegance from Staffordshire*

B. G. Burrough, January 1974, *C.R.Ashbee, His Guild and School of Handicraft*

L.B.Powell, January 1974, *Chinese Influence on Ruskin Pottery*

John Ferlay, February 1974, *Auctions Market Favourites*

A. J. Cross, September 1974 *Pilkington's Royal Lancastrian Pottery 1904-1957*

Margaret Foden, October 1973, *Marine Scenes on Porcelain*

Desmond Harrison, November 1973, *Royal Worcester Figures of Children*

Roger Pinkham, December 1975, *William De Morgan Tile Maker par Excellence*

Margaret Foden, August 1976, *Bird Painting on Porcelain*

Art Journal

Art Journal, 1858, F. H. Hulme

Art Journal, 1859, The Royal Picture

Art Journal, 1871, Report of Hanley Art School

Art Journal, 1872, Report of Stoke School of Art

Art Journal, 1877, Burslem School of Art

Art Journal, 1881, Sir Henry Cole obituary

Pottery Gazette

Pottery Gazette, 1877, page 97, Thomas Dean

Pottery Gazette, 1897, page 104, Aaron Green obituary

Pottery Gazette, Oct 1st 1897, Green Supplement, *A Landscape of Tiles,* page 1278

Pottery Gazette, Stoke, School of Art, page 615, Ellis Roberts

Pottery Gazette, June 1899, page 697, Ref G, Leason obituary, May 1911, page 559

Pottery Gazette, 1899, Willow Refridegeration Co.

Pottery Gazette, 1900, page 555, Anton Boulimer's obituary

Pottery Gazette, 1900, page 205, Louis Bilton

Pottery Gazette, 1906, page 212, Mussill obituary

Pottery Gazette, 1906, John Brook obituary

Pottery Gazette, Sept.1908, article on Minton tiles

Pottery Gazette, 1908, George Woolliscroft Rhead obituary

Pottery Gazette, Feb 1909, Samuel Seabright Wilson obituary

Pottery Gazette, May 1911, Louis Jahn obituary

Pottery Gazette, 1935, Thomas Hassall obituary